Beethoven in German Politics, 1870–1989

David B. Dennis

Beethoven in German Politics 1870–1989

Yale University Press

New Haven & London

Published with assistance from the Louis Stern Memorial Fund.

Designed by James J. Johnson and set in Trump Mediaeval type by Tseng Information Systems, Inc., Durham, North Carolina.
Printed in the United States of America by BookCrafters, Inc., Chelsea, Michigan.

Library of Congress Cataloging-in-Publication Data

Dennis, David B.
Beethoven in German politics, 1870–1989 / David B. Dennis.
p. cm.
Includes bibliographical references and index.
ISBN 0-300-06399-7 (cloth : alk. paper)

1. Beethoven, Ludwig van, 1770–1827—Influence. 2. Beethoven, Ludwig van, 1770–1827—Appreciation—German. 3. Music and state—Germany. 4. Music—Political aspects—Germany. I. Title.
ML410.B4D34 1996
780'.92—dc20 95-20936

A catalogue record for this book is available from the British Library.

The paper in this book meets the guidelines for permanence and durability of the Committee on Production Guidelines for Book Longevity of the Council on Library Resources.

10 9 8 7 6 5 4 3 2

With words of Beethoven, I dedicate this book to Claudia Bruce Dennis:

> Sie war mir eine so gute, liebenswürdige Mutter.
> Sie war meine beste Freundin.
> O wer war glücklicher als ich, da ich noch den süßen Namen
> 'Mutter' aussprechen konnte und er wurde gehört?

Your Beethoven is not my Beethoven.

—GUSTAV MAHLER

Contents

Acknowledgments ix

CHAPTER ONE Beethoven in German Political Culture 1

CHAPTER TWO The Second Reich 32

CHAPTER THREE The Weimar Era 86

CHAPTER FOUR The Third Reich 142

CHAPTER FIVE Germany Divided, and Reunified 175

Notes 205

Index 245

Acknowledgments

Good scholarship is produced by reading, thinking, and writing about things that move one deeply. I hope that my own work proves this to be true. In this book I bring together much that I love. My love of music, especially Beethoven's, derives from ever-growing curiosity about creative genius. My love of European culture stems from a wonderful year my family spent in Munich when my brother and I were boys. My love of history came with a good education in a fine—and fun—university town. My love of life and applying myself to it is a gift from my mother, father, and brother. Every line that follows is an expression of these and other profound influences. Most rewarding when studying something one loves, one meets people, deals with institutions, and visits places that resonate with one's soul. If nothing more, work on this book has pleasantly confirmed this methodological assumption.

This project began with a conversation my father and I had on a summer day in Munich. Sitting on the steps of the Feldherrenhalle I expressed my desire to live a life of the mind, so he asked me what I really liked to think about. Upon hearing my response, he took me to the Staatsbibliothek and helped me draw up a bibliography of literature on the image of Beethoven in German culture. Since then he has counseled me at every stage of writing this book. For being my academic adviser as well as a great Pop, I thank him with all my heart.

Back in Madison, my apprehension of German culture and politics was strengthened by courses and seminars at the University of Wisconsin under George L. Mosse. For his generous advice on this project I am deeply thankful.

Pursuing this subject remained a pipe dream until I studied with Robert Wohl at the University of California at Los Angeles. Indeed, when I started my graduate studies, I might have settled on a more traditional topic. But Professor Wohl's seminars on the intellectual and cultural history of modern Europe equipped me to confront this cross-disciplinary challenge. I am most grateful to him for advising me through all my work at U.C.L.A., and beyond.

For assurance that this study be of interest to music scholars, I turned to Robert Winter of the Department of Music at U.C.L.A. His contagious enthusiasm convinced me that a cultural historian could contribute to Beethoven scholarship. I would also like to thank Eugen Weber, Saul Friedländer, David Sabean, Peter Reill, Maynard Solomon, Peter Wapnewski, and Albrecht Dümling for their invaluable guidance.

At U.C.L.A. Giuseppe Casale, Mark Kleinman, Peter Pozefsky, Norman Wilson, Ellen Healy, and Alan Baer provided excellent intellectual company. Still, no matter how bright we students thought ourselves, none would have gone far without the help of Barbara Bernstein.

I am indebted to the Department of History at U.C.L.A. for financial support throughout my graduate studies, to the Friedrich-Ebert-Stiftung for a fellowship that helped me start my research between 1988 and 1989, to the Deutscher Akademischer Austauschdienst for a scholarship for language study in 1988 and a *Direktstipendium* that allowed me to complete my archival work from 1989 through 1990, and to Loyola University Chicago Research Services for help obtaining illustrations.

The study and research made possible by this funding took place at many institutions in Germany and the United States. For their services I thank the administrators and staffs of the Staatsbibliothek Preußischer Kulturbesitz, Berlin; the Beethovenhaus in Bonn, especially Sieghard Brandenburg; the Staatliches Institut für Musikforschung, Preußischer Kulturbesitz, Berlin, particularly Jutta March; the Deutsche Staatsbibliothek, Berlin; the various libraries of the Freie Universität Berlin, principally that of the Institut für Musikwissenschaft; the various libraries of the Technische Universität Berlin; the Hochschule der Künste, Berlin; the Akademie der Künste, Berlin; the Amerika Gedenkbibliothek, Berlin; the music library of Sender Freies Berlin; the Center for Beethoven Studies in San Jose, California, especially the curator of its Beethoven Bibliography Database, Patricia Elliot; the U.C.L.A. library system, especially the Music Library; the Newberry Library in Chicago; the Goethe-Institutes in Munich, Berlin, and Chicago; and the Cudahy and Lewis Libraries of Loyola University Chicago. For enhancing my knowledge and experience of music, I am also obliged to the administrators, staffs, and artists of the Los Angeles Philharmonic Orchestra, the Japan America Symphony of

Los Angeles, the Chicago Chamber Musicians, and the Chicago String Quartet.

For warm encouragement I thank all of my colleagues at the Department of History at Loyola University Chicago, above all Joseph Gagliano, who has expressed belief in me and my work ever since I arrived, Robert Bucholz, who has offered astute comments on my manuscript and shared knowledge about music to which all should aspire, and Zouhair Ghazzal, who has been a most stimulating officemate. I also appreciate the support of my colleagues at Albion College in Michigan, particularly John Hall and Geoffrey Cocks.

To Harry Haskell of Yale University Press I am beholden for guiding this manuscript (and its author) through the daunting procedures of publication. For her insightful copy-editing I thank Vivian Wheeler. For cheerfully tending to the subsequent stages of production I commend Margaret Otzel. I also extend my gratitude to Elizabeth Iwano, who carefully edited this manuscript twice.

For assistance in gathering and processing illustrations for this book I give thanks to my brother, John Dennis at Time Warner Interactive in Burbank; Mark Knoll of Early Bird Publishing, Berlin; Susan Sink at the Loyola University Center for Instructional Design; Friederike Grigat and Friedhelm Loesti at the Beethovenhaus, Bonn; Daniel Barenboim and his assistant at the Chicago Symphony Orchestra, Megan Quigley; Günter Brosche of the Österreichische Nationalbibliothek; Jocelyn Clapp at Bettmann Archives; Raphaele Hernandez and Eike Kässens at Deutsche Grammophon; Vilna Joven at Sony Classical; Hans-Georg Knopp and Angela Greiner of the Goethe-Institut Chicago; and the staffs of the Cudahy and Lewis Libraries at Loyola University Chicago.

For favors and kindnesses innumerable, I am grateful to a host of friends and colleagues on both sides of the Atlantic, among them Robert Bast, Giuseppe and Annalisa Casale, George Freeman, Mark Gingerich, Joseph and Molly Iwano, Dietrich Kalkum, Peter Kreek and his family, Leon and Tatjana Mangasarian, David Alan Miller and Andrea Oser, John and Kelly Rock, John and Carol Schmidt, Jon Smoller, and the rest of the Madison gang.

Frustrated by a practically illegible score, one of Beethoven's copyists wrote in the margin, "God help me." Seeing this, the composer responded with a note of his own, "Man, help thyself." The above list proves that I, like the poor copyist, could not have completed this project alone. And most unlike the composer, I have had at my side throughout this scholarly adventure a companion the likes of which he could only dream. Amy Kikue Iwano blesses me with all that Beethoven considered the main sources of true joy. With the lucky ones I sing:

> Wem der grosse Wurf gelungen,
> Eines Freundes Freund zu sein,
> Wer ein holdes Weib errungen,
> Mische seinen Jubel ein!

Recognizing how much the care and compassion of others means to my work elevates my respect for one who created such beautiful music despite such terrible loneliness. *Stürzt nieder, Millionen!*

1

Beethoven in German Political Culture

"Eusebius," I said very calmly, "do you, too, dare to praise Beethoven? Like a lion he would have reared himself before all of you and asked, 'Who are you that you dare be so presumptuous?' I do not mean you, Eusebius, you are a good soul, but does a great man *have* to have thousands of dwarfs in his train?"

ROBERT SCHUMANN

At dawn on Sunday, 12 November 1989, the border patrol of the German Democratic Republic (GDR) began dismantling the Berlin Wall in the midst of the field that had once been Potsdamer Platz. After guards punctured the Iron Curtain, jubilant crowds of East German citizens exercised their new right to travel and passed into West Berlin. For most, the mecca of this pilgrimage was West Berlin's main shopping strip along the Kurfürstendamm; but the destination of some East Germans that morning was a place for reflecting rather than consuming: the gilded Berlin Philharmonie. All East German citizens were invited to attend a concert there by the Berlin Philharmonic Orchestra. Led by the conductor and pianist Daniel Barenboim, the legendary orchestra would commemorate the transition (*Wende*) that had occurred in German politics over the past few days by performing the music of Ludwig van Beethoven.

Many had traveled all night to be at Potsdamer Platz early enough to obtain tickets, presumably believing there was no more appropriate way to celebrate the reunion of the German people than to enjoy the music to be played that day: Beethoven's First Piano Concerto, op. 15, and the Seventh Symphony, op. 92. Audience members agreed that these compositions—commonly considered among the most cheerful of the composer's works—corresponded perfectly with the jubilant occasion. Some felt the *Wende* would have been best marked by a performance of Beethoven's Ninth Symphony, op. 125, with its chorus announcing that all mankind would someday become brothers. After all, that weekend Germans seemed to have done exactly that. But most listeners acknowledged that the festive tones of Beethoven's Seventh Symphony harmonized with the feelings of the day.[1]

In the winter of 1989—after five more weeks of peaceful revolution in the GDR—Germans were offered another musical ceremony marking the transition. Organized by Justus Frantz and Leonard Bernstein, the Berlin Celebration Concerts realized the hope that a performance of Beethoven's Ninth Symphony would punctuate the latest developments in German politics. On the night of 23 December 1989, an orchestra made up of musicians from the major combatant nations of the Second World War gathered in the Philharmonie to play the "Ninth" for an exultant crowd. Huge video screens erected under the bombed-out skeleton of the Kaiser Wilhelm Gedächtniskirche enabled thousands of Berliners to enjoy a broadcast of the concert. Many joined with the chorus, singing Beethoven's *Ode to Joy* as an "Ode to Freedom" with tears streaming down their cheeks. On Christmas morning the scene was repeated in East Berlin, where another Berlin Celebration performance of the Ninth Symphony was broadcast worldwide from the renovated Schauspielhaus.

That "classical" or "art" music was a significant, even central, element of the ceremonial events leading to the reunification of Germany comes as no surprise to observers of German political culture. Scholarship on the development of a "German Identity" consistently reveals the pivotal place of the fine arts in the developing symbolism of the nation.[2] The nineteenth-century consolidation of the German state coincided with a general transformation of European political behavior into a "new politics" that incorporated an aesthetic appeal designed to attract the increasingly large numbers of persons involved in political choice.[3] The disparate political and regional groups consolidated under the abstract notion of a German nation found common ground in mutual linguistic, literary, visual, and musical dispositions. Activists who wished to strengthen political ties emphasized the conceptions of beauty shared by these peoples. This phenomenon had repercussions throughout German political life; even those who resisted state aggrandizement had to compete with the secular religion of nationalism by incorporating decorative features into their discourse and ritual. Consequently, German politics and fine art penetrated each other; literature, painting, sculpture, architecture, and music all came to be seen as symbolic of political attitudes.[4]

The aestheticization of politics in the nineteenth century was not a uniquely German phenomenon, as the origins of this tendency lay in the cultural politics of the French Revolution.[5] But in German lands, notions of a grand nation-state were very tightly correlated with the arts. Ceremonies, dramas, festivals, and parades dedicated to the memory of Germany's cultural heroes were vital components of national propaganda by the Wilhelmine era.[6] In these extravaganzas, each mode of artistic communication was integrated to form *Gesamtkunstwerke* proclaiming the intellectual heritage shared by Germans everywhere. And when nationalism expressed itself in the form of parades, concerts, and *Singspiele,* rhythmic and melodic impetus came from music by the German masters.[7]

Of all the arts, classical music was the most significant source of cultural and, arguably, political pride among nineteenth-century Germans.[8] Unlike countries that chose popular works to inspire nationalist fervor—in France, the *Marseillaise;* in the United States, the *Star-Spangled Banner*—Germans have regularly selected works of art music as their anthems: the moving melody accompanying the oft-misunderstood words of the *Deutschlandlied* was appropriated from the second movement of Haydn's Quartet in D Major, op. 76, no. 3 (*Kaiser*); and the anthem of the former East German state was composed by Hanns Eisler, a student of Arnold Schoenberg.[9] Moreover, national anthems were not the only works infused with patriotic meaning as German nationalism evolved: based on the prodigious advancement of German music since Bach, leading to the apparent supplanting of "Italian fashion" as the leading form of the art, Germans discovered in compositions of high-classical style the artistic treasure they required as a cornerstone of common cultural pride.[10]

It is not astonishing, then, that the political eruptions of 1989 were synchronized with works of the German masters. Nevertheless, it is intriguing that the music of a single composer dominated the symbolic tapestry of the transition. Why was the music of Beethoven played on these occasions? Why did the audiences at these performances consider the music of Beethoven so appropriate? The recognition of a longstanding tradition and complex history of linking Beethoven's works to developments in modern German politics makes their symbolic use during the reunification process more comprehensible. German political leaders have consistently associated Beethoven with ideologies they promote and actions they undertake.[11] In support of this, ideologues have formulated legends of Beethoven as a "political man" and interpretations of his music as "political works" for use in disseminating dogma to the German public.

Concentrating on the nineteenth century, scholars have thus far highlighted references to Beethoven in the rhetoric of early German

Fig. 1. Border guards open the Berlin Wall at Potsdamer Platz on 12 November 1989. Soon after, many East Germans attended a concert of Beethoven's music played in their honor at the nearby Berlin Philharmonie. (Photo: Reuters/Bettmann)

nationalism, best described in this statement by the composer Robert Schumann: "When the German speaks of symphonies, he means Beethoven; the two names are for him one and indivisible—his joy, his pride. As Italy has its Naples, France its Revolution, England its Navy, etc., so the Germans have their Beethoven symphonies. The German forgets in his Beethoven that he has no school of painting; with Beethoven he imagines that he has reversed the fortunes of the battles that he lost to Napoleon; he even dares to place him on the same level with Shakespeare."[12] The evocations of Beethoven in nineteenth-century German political culture—particularly those before unification in 1870—enhance our understanding of the early development of a German identity based on cultural, in large part musical, nationalism. But attention restricted to the earliest Beethoven references in political discourse has hindered comprehensive study of how his music and life have been denoted as symbolic of the German condition *throughout* the modern history of the state.

The process by which Beethoven's music and life were assimilated into German political culture did begin during his lifetime; prior to the consolidation of the German state, lasting connections were drawn between him and numerous ideologies. But it was in 1870 that a confluence of events—the defeat of France, the founding of the Second Reich, and the one-hundredth anniversary of Beethoven's birth—inspired apotheoses of the composer that galvanized the symbolic connection between his works and German politics. Parades and performances celebrating his birthday and military conquest launched the tradition that led to the 1989 Berlin Celebrations. Ceremonial use of him and his music in late-nineteenth-century and twentieth-century political contexts indicate the ongoing significance of Beethoven in German national culture: the commemoration of the Kaiser Wilhelm Gedächtniskirche was marked with a performance of Beethoven's *Coriolan* Overture, op. 62; the short-lived Republic of Bavaria was heralded by a concert of his *Leonore* and *Egmont* overtures, op. 72, no. 2 and op. 84; Adolf Hitler's birthdays were announced with broadcasts of Beethoven symphonies; and the opening of the Bundestag of the Federal Republic of Germany was graced with a performance of Beethoven's *Weihe des Hauses,* op. 124. On the strength of these examples and more, I have undertaken to chronicle the custom among German politicians of evoking Beethoven and his music, one that has lasted into our time and will surely continue.

This does not mean that I scrutinize evocations of Beethoven as a symbol of national unity alone. Throughout modern German history, he has been used to signify not just one German Identity, but many points of view about what that national identity should be. Since his lifetime—especially after 1870—every major interest in Germany claimed this composer and his music to be symbolic of its particular vision of the German future. In the words of an observer of a single but intense phase of Beethoven politicization during the Weimar period, "every political party, every confession counted him as one of their own; all of them fought tooth and nail to demonstrate that he belonged exclusively to their circle."[13] This observation holds true for the entire history of Beethoven evocations in German politics. In view of the ongoing competition over the composer's "legacy," a comprehensive study of the reception of Beethoven in German political circles must treat its relocations in manifold efforts to propagandize a *variety* of potential German identities.

This book traces the reception given the life and work of Beethoven by all the major German political groups from the *Gründerjahre* through the East German Revolution of 1989. I examine how political leaders—and their "expert" accomplices[14]—have associated Beethoven's music with specific opinions, thereby transforming art and artist into powerful symbols of multiple ideologies. Perceived in literal terms by way of dogma, Beethoven's works have been transformed into inspirational elements of party liturgies across the ideological spectrum. Analysis of scholarly works, newspaper articles, political speeches, school textbooks, concert programs, radio transmissions, feature films, commercial advertisements, and television broadcasts shows that German propagandists project their often extreme views onto Beethoven's music, hoping to persuade others to interpret it similarly. Thereby the "meaning of Beethoven" has oscillated through two centuries of political turmoil and change. By tracing this process I hope to evaluate the history of the reception of Beethoven's music in political cliques more thoroughly than has been done to date, and to show that historians may employ music-related sources to study the political development of a nation.[15]

The History of Beethoven Reception

It must be clear from the outset that this book is not a biography of Beethoven nor is it a monograph on his music. My topics are meanings drawn from or attached to Beethoven's compositions once performed, and references to his life made principally after his death. The history of Beethoven reception in German political circles indicates how the most intangible of art forms is associated with sociopolitical development: not necessarily as a direct result of a composer's intentions, but more often via the responses of audiences. Analysis of performance reviews, scholarly works, policy directives, and other records of opinions formulated by politically active audience members prove that it is mainly upon its reception and subsequent employ by a public that music is imbued with "extramusical meaning." By explaining conceivable but unverifiable messages in musical works, music commentaries often signify, more than anything else, the ideas and concerns of those who formulate them.[16]

In tracing the "effective history" (*Wirkungsgeschichte*) of Beethoven's oeuvre within German politics, I defend the notion that the composer did not usually create music as a means of proclaiming dogma. Yet, while upholding this "purist" conception of his works, I investigate the fact that Beethoven's music has functioned significantly in the symbolism of German politics. Party leaders, public officials, music authorities, and the people at large have perceived it in literal terms and ultimately rendered it an inspirational element in the culture of many political groupings, especially when it is performed during ceremonial events. My approach is cultural-historical, not musicological. Because I am not dedicated to determining the extent to which music expresses personal or societal values, I do not introduce a new way of relating musical styles, structures, and passages to their specific social contexts. Rather than music history, I offer a history of music criticism and policy—a contribution to the "social history of musical life," distinct from what Theodor Adorno termed the "sociology of music" itself.[17]

Beethoven's biographer Maynard Solomon summarized the notions most fundamental to this method: "The meanings of a completed work of art are in constant flux: 'A work of art, once created, is a structure that has become entirely separated from its creator, that has started to live its own life. Its value is now utterly independent of its originator's intentions.'"[18] It is a "philosopher's truism," he noted, "that the true meanings of music are not translatable into language," but warnings have never discouraged people from "putting forth unprovable speculations as to the 'meaning' of one or another of Beethoven's masterpieces."[19] Solomon further granted that images used to "translate" his compositions "may tell us as much about the free associations of their authors as about Beethoven and his music."[20]

In his major work on *Nineteenth-Century Music,* Carl Dahlhaus addressed how the "myth of Beethoven"—distinct from the man and the music—constituted an "overpowering" agent in the musical life of nineteenth-century Europe. Dahlhaus insisted that the mythical figure cannot be conveniently "equated with the persona behind his works." But he allowed that legends have had a powerful effect on how listeners—expert and nonexpert—apprehend Beethoven's music: "It would be narrow-minded to call the myth-making process that began during Beethoven's own lifetime . . . a mere falsification of history, as though it could be refuted by documents. . . . This image can neither be supported nor undercut by empirical biography, where myth simply does not belong. . . . Still, this should not blind us to the fact that pseudobiography is meant, not to explain 'the way it really was,' but rather to function as a language of cryptograms expressing insight into Beethoven's music. And the anecdotes that mask this insight must not be measured by the standards of biography."[21] Here Dahlhaus sanctioned investigation into the influence "pseudobiographies" have on public perceptions of Beethoven. While he restricted his own study to the question of how Beethoven mythology affected the European music tradition, others have tried to relate details of Beethoven reception to issues outside music and its critical sphere.

A brief survey of this scholarship will demonstrate the value of studying the reception history of this composer, and—though not the primary aim of most of these works—it will help us to locate Beethoven's place in German political culture before unification. Alessandra Comini's *Changing Image of Beethoven* explored Beethoven's reception in the visual arts. Comini suspected that a nineteenth-century "mythmaking conspiracy of the arts and sciences cumulatively combined the musical authority of Liszt, Wagner, and Berlioz with fertile speculations of phrenology and psychology to produce a remarkable extramusical imago of Beethoven." Inquiring into this conspiracy, Comini—an art historian—detected that images of Beethoven's physical appearance in sculpture, painting, and printmaking constituted "autobiographies" (or, perhaps better, self-reflections) of the artists who formulated them. Acting on the hunch (shared by scholars of Beethoven reception) that much is to be learned from the extramusical images of Beethoven about the men and women who created them, Comini worked to "clarify signs of the cultural obsessions and aspirations of successive historical epochs" she found in various depictions of the composer.[22] Concentrating on stylistic analyses of portraits, Comini provided valuable insights into Beethoven iconography and the artists who contrived it.

In *Beethoven in France* Leo Schrade contended that when studying the "meaning" of Beethoven upheld by the French, "the purely materialistic method of approach proves to be completely inadequate" because "man's understanding, baffled by the mysterious forces [of music], sublimates them to ideas and imageries that his mind can grasp"; thus, " 'Beethoven in France' is, in essence, an idea, with manifold variations, to be sure, but persistently an idea."[23] Just as I report major disagreements among German political groups over the idea of Beethoven, Schrade announced French reception as a "struggle over the possession of a great man." According to him, "one presses images of one's own national life into his artistic work, regardless of whether they fit or not; one links artistic forms to the past and present sentiments of the nation, just to be able to say: 'Our Beethoven!' This image of Beethoven has nothing to do with Beethoven, but only with one's own experience."[24] Recognizing this, he asserted that "to follow the routes the idea of Beethoven cut out for itself is to penetrate into all the various channels of intellectual life, of life itself as conceived by the French mind."[25] Because he concentrated on French ideas about Beethoven, however, Schrade disregarded manifestations of this conflict in the political cultures of his homeland.

Peter Schnaus's *E. T. A. Hoffmann als Beethoven-Rezensent der Allgemeinen musikalischen Zeitung* demonstrated that the eccentric author and composer initated a Romantic style of music interpretation. Moreover, Hoffmann was one of the first to say anything positive about Beethoven's products, countering stodgy colleagues who judged many as "unplayable disappointments." However, in salvaging Beethoven's compositions from the academic scrap heap, Hoffmann initiated an individualistic method of explicating them which, in turn, opened the way to their politicization. While his early articles conformed to the "classical" norms of music analysis, concentrating on technical detail and thematic structure, Hoffmann gradually developed a style of "poetic interpretation." No longer listening to compositions just to identify their technical merits, he sought inspiration for creations of his own, thus transforming his reviews into veritable poems.[26]

Hoffmann found Beethoven particularly inspirational. "Beethoven's music," he wrote, "sets in motion the lever of fear, of horror, of terror, of grief, and awakens that endless longing which is the essence of Romanticism. He is consequently a purely Romantic composer." Hoffmann's most famous review included a précis of Beethoven's Fifth Symphony, op. 67, and here he let his poetic imagination fly free. To Hoffmann this music described—among other things—an "ever-mounting climax into the spirit kingdom of the infinite," the "premonition of tragedy," a "friendly form" that "draws near and lightens the gruesome night," a "pure spirit voice," a "terrible phantom," "lightning," "the wonderful spirit world," "dazzling sunlight," and "nameless premonitory longing."[27] Though Hoffmann was now and then in the employ of the Prussian state, none of his fanciful projections directly associated Beethoven with politics. Innocent of politicizing Beethoven, Hoffmann did nonetheless propose that listeners personally interact with his music, rather than be passively entertained by it. By promoting the idea that music speaks to the soul of the individual—who must find the particular meaning it holds for him or her alone—Hoffmann inadvertently opened a Pandora's box of sentimental interpretations that followed his, including those which drew Beethoven into the political culture of modern Germany.

Arnold Schmitz's *Das Romantische Beethovenbild* demonstrated that myths formulated by Beethoven's Romantic worshippers have colored most interpretations of him. Freed by Hoffmann of traditional constraints on aesthetic criticism, Romantics accentuated those characteristics of Beethoven which most appealed to their poetic and philosophical tastes. Schmitz contended that "the true Beethoven is not represented in the Romantic portrait" that resulted; instead, it describes "the typical Romantic artist." "Painted with colors which stem from the palette of Romantic philosophy"—Rousseau's natural good, the magical idealism of Novalis, Schelling's world-poetry—this image does not correspond to historical reality: all of this is merely "mirrored in the Romantic conception of Beethoven and projected upon Beethoven's historical form."[28] In Schmitz's view, most Romantics molded their depictions in ways which gave the impression that Beethoven was one of four basic character types: child of nature, enchanted sorcerer, martyred saint, or Promethean revolutionary.

Schmitz found all of these themes in the portrayal of Beethoven by Romantic *Wunderkind* Bettina Brentano. Though likely fraudulent, letters which Brentano claimed Beethoven wrote to her have long influenced the way he has been perceived, especially in a political sense. One of the most celebrated legends about Beethoven's political sentiments, the Teplitz Incident, first appeared in her fabrications. According to Brentano, while on a walk with Goethe at the resort town of Teplitz in 1812, Beethoven passed by a royal party without bowing or making any other sign of respect; he then chastized Goethe for conforming. The conception created by this story, that Beethoven was highly critical of aristocratic society, was compounded by her broadcasting the composer's complaints about giving piano lessons to aristocratic patrons.[29] These vignettes, authentic or not, strengthened Beethoven's reputation as a rebel without giving equal emphasis to his more conservative characteristics.[30]

In *Revolution im Konzertsaal* Ulrich Schmitt strove to better determine why early listeners—Romantic and otherwise—associated Beethoven's best-known music with myriad innovations of their era. Schmitt's close reading of reviews of Beethoven's Third, Fifth, and Ninth symphonies written before the Revolution of 1848–49 reveals that the discourse used to describe them was the same as that employed to relate breakthroughs in areas such as the visual arts, food, industry, transportation, and politics. According to Schmitt, Beethoven's contemporaries responded to his music in much the same way that they reacted to panoramic exhibitions, restaurant dining, steam engines, train travel, and social upheaval.[31]

Unlike compositions of the "classical" norm, Schmitt held, many of Beethoven's were not easily apprehended as sets of clearly announced themes developed in predictable fashions. And it was precisely the more impulsive works—those Beethoven himself said were of a new style—that piqued contemporary audiences. Those whom Schmitt termed conservatives rejected Beethoven's most inventive works, just as many shunned technological innovations; like people who argued that looking out of the window of a train could have debilitating psychological effects, traditionalists resisted the "rush" (*Reizflut*) of Beethoven's compositions. On the other hand, "modern" listeners, perhaps more comfortable with the effects of the Industrial Revolution, also associated Beethoven's music with these changes—but in a positive way. Such listeners found the rush of this music exciting and full of promise, just as they welcomed their first experiences of locomotive power, optical illusion, and bouillon cubes.[32]

According to Schmitt, this initial correlation of Beethoven's oeuvre—posited by both supporters and detractors—with the general dynamism of the Industrial Revolution led listeners to subsequently link him with political ideology. Contrary to musicologists who have tried to show that Beethoven's most eminent works were considered radical because they contained passages and forms borrowed from French revolutionary song, Schmitt insisted that such details were not pertinent to Germans who first deemed that music "progressive":

> Beethoven did—and this is undeniable—surely make use of a French vocabulary, but to the ears of the German listener, this vocabulary had no revolutionary significance. . . . Anyone who

> searches the masses of reception examples for indications to the contrary will be disappointed. . . . Not a single listener was capable of developing a chain of associations according to the following model: Beethoven cited French Revolutionary music ∠ this had something to do with the French Revolution ∠ this reminds one of Liberty, Equality, Fraternity ∠ consequently, Beethoven's music also sounds revolutionary ∠ therefore he infused his music with political significance that should exhort and arouse us. There are no historical indications of such a chain reaction.[33]

Nevertheless, both conservative and progressive listeners of the early nineteenth century did hear some of Beethoven's music as "revolutionary." By 1849 the opinion that works such as Beethoven's Third, Fifth, and Ninth symphonies communicated "French" values of Liberty, Equality, and Fraternity was loudly professed in the pages of the *Neue Zeitschrift für Musik,* and within political discourse in general.[34] Even before revolution spread to Germany, newspapers warned public authorities that they should not consider Beethoven concerts mere distractions; they were opportunities for thousands to hear "a music which would best resonate with fire and social collapse."[35] Government officials were encouraged to limit performances of Beethoven's music because "one can only pour so much water into a glass before it overflows."[36] Gustav Adolf Kietz reported that in such "excitable times" the Ninth Symphony had an "intoxicating effect" on audience members.[37] When disturbances broke out in German streets, Theodore Uhlig wrote that the "socialist consciousness" Beethoven expressed in his work had "reached its goal" with the 1849 rebellions.[38] Amid fighting in Dresden, Richard Wagner reported, a revolutionary guard shouted down from a barricade that "joy's beautiful divine sparks (*schöner Götterfunken*) had made a blaze," implying that flames emerging from the burning opera house represented the achievement of hopes Beethoven had recorded in the Ninth Symphony.[39] Like the Dresden opera house, the Revolution of 1848–49 went up in smoke; but these comments indicate that by the time of the uprisings, Beethoven and his music had become important elements in the culture of revolution in Germany.

The reason for this, said Schmitt, is not to be discerned by seeking passages that communicate radical dogma. One must simply recognize that the Industrial Revolution changed how people perceived the world, reducing their interest in details—of the natural world, for instance—and enhancing their taste for panoramic overviews and experiences of speed. Anything that offered such thrills was deemed "revolutionary."[40] According to early listeners, what fascinated and terrified them was the energy, velocity, and breadth of Beethoven's works when—and Schmitt underscores this point—taken as a whole.[41] It was not individual tones or phrases that inspired early-nineteenth-century listeners to link some of Beethoven's music with social and political upheaval, but the sheer multiplicity of themes that passed, as well as the churning rhythms in which they did so—their *élan terrible,* as contemporaries put it.[42]

The importance of Schmitt's arguments within the historiography of Beethoven reception lies in the credence they lend to the argument that audience members project ideas onto his music acting on an emotional response to its vigor, rather than precise comprehension of its structure. It is this impulsive "psychology of perception," more than specific intentions of the composer, that explains the Beethoven myths identified by the scholars above. By building "a bridge between Beethoven and railways, between loudness and speed, between the modern experience of hearing and technical progress" as a means of understanding why he became the *Komponist von Freiheit, Gleichheit, und Brüderlichkeit,*[43] Schmitt went far in explaining why, by the mid-nineteenth century, this composer was featured in German political culture.

Still, this explanatory bridge does not quite span the gap that prevents apprehension of Beethoven's music as an ubiquitous factor in German politics, one evoked by representatives of every ideological stance. By concentrating on reviews by "progressives," Schmitt omitted references to Beethoven by the increasingly significant right wing of German politicians. Although he discussed conservatives who snubbed Beethoven because the élan terrible of his works disturbed them, Schmitt did not point out that the same quality of his music that appealed to the left also attracted activists on the opposite end of the political spectrum, who connected him with militarism, authoritarianism, and ultimately racism. Elan being something that all political groups want to inspire in their followers, Beethoven's thrilled politicians of every ideological persuasion. As Robert Schumann noted, many contemporaries considered Beethoven not merely an exhilarating artist, but an exhilarating *German* artist: his works had "taught" the whole nation "greatness of purpose and pride in the Fatherland";[44] particularly his symphonies had "spiritually won back for the Germans those battles which Napoleon had taken from them."[45] While Schmitt's lack of attention to these themes is perhaps negligible in coverage of *Vormärz* material—where nationalist, conservative, and liberal ideologies commingled—it becomes crucial when he stretches his purview beyond 1849. He ended his book by cataloguing just nine "voices" meant to signify the uses of music "as a weapon in political conflicts" through the remainder of modern German history. Among these is a pair of right-wing evocations, namely statements by Richard Wagner and Hans von Bülow. But it is startling that Schmitt did not mention the "Nazi Beethoven" fabricated by Hitler's henchmen.

Mention of Wagner, however, is obviously appropriate, since no man had more impact on the politicization of Beethoven. Klaus Kropfinger's *Wagner und Beethoven* probed the ongoing glorification of Beethoven by the Bayreuth master, including the mutable associations Wagner made between his hero and political ideology. Throughout his life Wagner formulated perceptions of his fellow composer that influenced all succeeding Beethoven reception. Indeed, prior to Wagner's efforts to popularize it, Beethoven's music, especially that of the late period, was not well known to general music audiences. It was largely through Wagner's writings, concerts, and promotional efforts that Beethoven's Ninth Symphony became familiar to the European public.[46] Not surprisingly, he popularized Beethoven's music in strict accordance with his comprehension of it.

Wagner's knowledge and love of Beethoven's music started very early; as a fifteen-year-old, he heard Beethoven's Seventh Symphony at the Leipzig Gewandhaus and experienced a vision of the composer very similar to that of E. T. A. Hoffmann, Bettina Brentano, and other elder Romantics: "The effect on me was indescribable . . . I soon conceived an image of him in my mind as a sublime and unique supernatural being, with whom none could compare. This image was associated in my brain with that of Shakespeare; in ecstatic dreams I met both of them, saw and spoke to them, and on awakening found myself bathed in tears."[47] In 1840 Wagner wrote a short story for the *Gazette Musicale* in Paris which expressed his great love of Beethoven. *A Pilgrimage to Beethoven* portrayed a young man, much like Wagner himself, who journeys to visit the master in Vienna; along the way, the hero is regularly thwarted by a rich Englishman who has the same plan. In the end, the youth meets Beethoven and proposes a great aesthetic project: to fulfill the enterprise his hero supposedly initiated in the choral conclusion to the Ninth Symphony—completely integrating music and words. Of course, Wagner's fictional Beethoven encourages the youngster to pursue this course.[48]

Primarily, Wagner's *Pilgrimage* emphasized Beethoven's aesthetic achievements; by spreading the idea that his great predecessor had explained the "meaning" of the last movement of the Ninth Symphony to him—or someone like him—he legitimized his own theories about the relationship between music and word.[49] But Wagner also integrated his political predilections into this yarn. Some have argued, weakly, that the uncomplimentary depiction of the Englishman was an expression of Wagner's hatred for the French, who were rejecting his music.[50] Clearer is Wagner's intimation that Beethoven was uneasy with the superficial lifestyle of the European bourgeoisie; his story depicts Beethoven as a wild *Naturkind*—disorderly and asocial. Thus did Wagner, in his earliest published discussion of Beethoven, continue the Romantic tradition of portraying him as a rebellious type.

During the next few years, Wagner nurtured a revolutionary political outlook to accompany his operatic theory; by 1846, he was actively promoting dissent in the principality of Saxony, and using Beethoven's music to communicate his ideas. Between 1846 and 1849, Wagner produced a series of Sunday concerts featuring Beethoven symphonies. Before each of these concerts he published anonymous articles in the Dresden newspapers asserting that this music symbolized, among other things, the possibilities for political renewal in Germany. In an essay based on these tracts, entitled "The Revolution," Wagner prepared his audience to understand Beethoven's music in the ideological terms he preferred. In them, according to Kropfinger, the development of the Ninth Symphony is "transposed into the idiom of revolution"; "the abstract joy" of the finale "becomes a concrete social goal, understandable as a program for 'human happiness.'"[51]

Thus did Wagner enhance the notion of Beethoven's music as that of a rebel, correlating it with his evolving theories of art and revolution.[52] But neither his politics nor his interpretation of Beethoven remained consistent. While his enmity for the French grew, Wagner subscribed to the Germanic ideology emerging in his homeland. By the time of the Franco-Prussian War, he was a staunch German imperialist and included reference to Beethoven in his propagandistic writings. In December of 1870, Wagner took it upon himself to commemorate Beethoven's centennial birthday with an article representing him as a warrior in the national cause. From the moment of conception, Wagner intended that the article explain the relationship he perceived between Beethoven's music and the war. This goal is clearly indicated in the notes he sketched before writing the essay: "At St. Jakob 2,000 corpses defeated the 40,000 feared Armagnacs—a case of an idea proving all-conquering; war is, so to speak, a dance performed with the most dreadful of powers, like a Beethoven finale in which he unleashes all the demons in a magnificent dance."[53]

For the most part, the finished article, "Beethoven," consisted of theoretical self-promotion; in the first two-thirds, Wagner outlined Beethoven's aesthetic principles, implying, naturally, that they were the same as his own. But in the last pages he brought Beethoven down from the clouds of Romantic and utopian eulogy to link him directly to the *Realpolitik* of 1870. Omitting any reference to his precursor as "revolutionary,"[54] Wagner here established the aggressive Germanic interpretation of Beethoven that would henceforth dominate reception of his music on the right wing of German politics. Writing "whilst German forces [were] victoriously penetrating to the center of French civilization," Wagner argued that German music had led the way to national greatness. "Ridicule us who may, whilst we attribute this great significance to German music; we shall swerve as little as the German people swerved when, with well-calculated doubt as to its solidity and solidarity, its enemies ventured to insult it." And for Wagner, the greatest hero of the victory over France—both military and cultural—was Beethoven. Somehow it was he who had spurred the attack on Paris. "Nothing can more inspiringly stand beside the triumphs of . . . bravery in this wonderful year 1870 than the memory of our great *Beethoven,* who just a hundred years ago was born to the German people. There, at the high seat of 'insolent fashion,' whither our weapons are now penetrating, *his* genius has already begun the noblest conquest. . . . Let us then celebrate the great pathfinder in the wilderness of degenerate paradise!"[55]

Wagner's conception of Beethoven was mutable: he first embellished the revolutionary interpretation, then initiated what can be called the blood and iron version. As he would himself become the object of dispute among members of the German political community, his characterizations of Beethoven have fueled debate even until today. However, the version Wagner formulated in the violent year of 1870 would reign supreme in German culture for the rest of the nineteenth century and, as wielded by ideologues of the right and extreme right, continue to affect Beethoven reception into our own century.

By surveying the existing literature on the reception of Beethoven, then, we can gather much information about how he and his music were politicized up to the consolidation of the German nation. But to date no one has comprehensively treated ideas or myths about Beethoven as they evolved in conjunction with subsequent German political history. In a paper on the historiography of Beethoven reception given at the Academy of Science and Literature in Mainz in 1970, musicologist Hans Heinrich Eggebrecht outlined many promising approaches to this field. Among the tropes (*Begriffsfelder*) of reception that he deemed worthy of study was the utility (*Benutzbarkeit*) of Beethoven myths in the contexts of "ideology, politics, economy, apologetics, revolution, nationalism, internationalism, socialism, militarism, war, defeat, etc."[56] Eggebrecht did not himself follow through on this suggestion.

The only conscious effort to treat Eggebrecht's trope of political utility appeared in a 1986 anthology of essays on *Beethoven und die Nachwelt* (Beethoven and posterity); in it, Heribert Schröder documented exploitation of the Beethoven *Mythos* by the cultural politicians of the Third Reich.[57] Schröder's bibliographical essay is a useful reference for work on the National Socialist image of Beethoven. His inspection of Beethoven reception in the context of twentieth-century German politics is unique in that it broke the nineteenth-century boundary restricting prior work in the field. Yet by focusing exclusively on the Nazis' utilization of Beethoven, Schröder dispensed a mistaken notion that the composer was politicized mainly by twentieth-century activists on the right. By not comparing the Nazi Beethoven to appropriation of his legacy by other important political groups, Schröder provided another unidimensional view of the aggressive struggle that went on among many parties to claim this composer as "theirs."

To investigate thoroughly the incorporation of art works into German political cultures, we need to take a wide, comparative look at how this procedure was carried out by groups at every point of the political compass. Effective mass politics in the modern age has been in large part a cultural enterprise; politicians have consistently incorporated existing cultural images, phrases, or symbols into their propaganda in order to sway a susceptible public. This practice has been required of present-day politicians, who must gain the support of increasingly large numbers of people: to communicate with vast audiences, they utilize commonly known terminology and imagery. By employing cultural symbols, politicians have done more than transmit views on particular issues—they have surrounded themselves with inspirational auras. The struggle that has taken place over the right to use Beethoven and his music as a propaganda instrument is a profound—though by no means lone—example of this cultural-historical process.

To be sure, Beethoven was not the only great master, of music or any other media, invoked for such purposes. The habit of referring to masters and masterpieces as symbols of ideology is, after all, a prevalent one. In the German context, pamphleteers have long tried to demonstrate that the giants of *Kultur* have, or would have, supported their particular platforms: Dürer,[58] Goethe,[59] and Schiller[60] have all been exploited in comparable ways by politicians bent on inspiring awe in the competitive German political field. Steven E. Aschheim's study of *The Nietzsche Legacy in Germany, 1890–1990* plainly shows how that philosopher is appropriated and manipulated by politicians. Like mine, Aschheim's findings corroborate the suppositions of reception theory: "Nietzscheanism was effective as a public force only when it was structured by mediating systems and ideologies." All the versions he discussed "in some way nationalized or socialized the Nietzschean thematic, placing it at the service of other goals."[61] Nor is Beethoven the only composer politicized in this fashion. Historians have long noted the significance of Richard Wagner's biography, writings, and music in late-nineteenth-century and twentieth-century German political culture, culminating in the pathological reception they were given by Hitler and his followers.[62] But few artists—and no composers—have been so consistently employed as Beethoven for so many, often mutually exclusive, political purposes.[63]

Why Beethoven?

What is it about the biography, character, and art of this particular creator that has incessantly motivated German activists to invoke them in efforts to develop a political following? How is it that individuals with unrelated, even contradictory, political views have found facets of Beethoven's life story or music that make them feel, or wish, that he was a fellow traveler? Everyone who uses Beethoven in political rhetoric has singular reasons based on personal and ideological considerations. As the Gustav Mahler epigraph at the beginning of this book implies, each visualizes his or her own Beethoven on the basis of personal background and the particular conditions under which his works have been experienced. When I undertook this study, I expected that the politicization of Beethoven had been a very abstruse procedure, requiring close reading between the lines of sophisticated music analysis to discern subtle political insinuation. Instead, I discovered blatant, sometimes humorous, even embarrassing claims about Beethoven's relation to modern political developments.

Within this cacophony of voices, one generalization seems to hold true: in the minds of German politicians, the sound of Beethoven's music is inextricably entwined with his biography. If we recognize that the initial impetus to contemplate the "idea of Beethoven" usually comes from the music itself, it is nevertheless apparent that very few of his activist listeners interest themselves in the technical details of his compositions. Most sources in this context refer to his works not as inspirational in and of themselves, but as triggers of thoughts about the life led by their creator. In the majority of political interpretations, Beethoven the man, not his music, is the focus.[64] To some extent, this tendency results from the abstract nature of music itself. Faced with the problem of trying to explain its supposed significance to a mass audience, spokespersons, speechwriters, journalists, even music scholars tend to discuss the biography of the composer simply because it is more easily conveyed. Nevertheless, their concentration on the life of Beethoven seems to have deeper causes.

In efforts to use him to impress and motivate the German populace, the emphasis is inevitably on Beethoven as a man who overcame tremendous personal adversity. The most exploitable aspect of the Beethoven story for politicians is that of his struggle to create. Unlike Mozart, whose works seem—at least according to popular myth—to have flowed effortlessly from his mind (a legend that earned him the love and respect of German listeners, but not the status of "role model" or "educator" of the nation), the most appealing aspect of Beethoven's music for political interpreters is the painful and diligent effort that went into it. Overtly manifested in the tortured handwriting of his sketchbooks, it is his suffering that earned Beethoven his prominent place in the political culture of Germany. Expressed in many examples, his distressful deliverance was nowhere more dramatically presented than in a sculpture erected by imperial authorities in the Tiergarten of Berlin. In its depiction of three music masters, Haydn's image is associated with dancing maidens, Mozart's with a young woman strewing flowers, and Beethoven's with a titanic figure breaking free from a boulder. The condition of Beethoven's life that most challenged his willful nature was his deafness; the miracle of music created by an artist unable to hear provides a keystone for picturing Beethoven as a man of monumental will. Depending on the individual interpreter, several other aspects of Beethoven's life heighten his value as a multifaceted model: his suffering at the hands of his father, his unrequited quest for the companionship of a woman friend, his economic distress and—of obvious fascination to politicians and their operatives—his varied reactions to the accelerated political developments of his day.

It is of central significance to my approach that few propagandists undertake exacting analysis of Beethoven's music to justify their opinions about its "content"; frankly, most interpreters in this context—"experts" included—are incapable of doing so. Given the enormous discrepancies among competing assertions about the political content of various works, and the even broader gap between the historical context of these compositions and the largely anomalous claims made for them, there is no possibility of coming up with a singular rationale about why particular works inspired manifold interpretations. They simply varied with the many political currents in modern German history and the eddies within each. Ulrich Schmitt's explanation of why the music generated controversy before 1870 applies throughout the history of Beethoven reception in political circles. Little about the "psychology of perception" operating among the audiences discussed below differs from that of the listeners who first encountered Beethoven's works. Persistent quotes of enthusiasm regarding his élan terrible only prove that it is this initial impact that forges political links of various strengths.

Surely for this reason what some term Beethoven's "heroic" works—the Third, Fifth, and Ninth symphonies, the *Egmont* Overture, the overtures to his opera *Fidelio*[65]—are highlighted in political culture.[66] While no composition is immune to the process of politicization, far less is said in music propaganda about the other symphonies, the Violin Concerto, the Violin Romances, or the chamber music. Not even the more subdued movements of those works deemed heroic, or for that matter the gentler aspects of Beethoven's personality, get much attention. Little about the *sanfter* Beethoven appears in the following pages. Indeed, some might exclaim that those heroic works are precisely the compositions Beethoven conceived as doctrinal pronouncements in music, so they were destined to have a place in political culture. But again, the multiplicity of political "spins" put on each suggests that if the composer did want to send unambiguous messages through them, he failed. Efforts to isolate "Marxist" intentions behind the heroic works *might* help us learn more about Beethoven himself, but they reveal little about his place in German politics.[67] In this context, the lasting importance of whatever ideological program Beethoven might have executed in his compositions lies in the pro-

Fig. 2. The Beethoven aspect of a monument to music masters erected in the Berlin Tiergarten in 1904. (Photo: Mark Knoll)

found desire it sparked among his listeners to associate themselves with this music and, above all, with the man who created it.

Before we analyze how successive cultural politicians approached him and his music, therefore, it is vital that we review the phases of Beethoven's political evolution: therein lies the matter from which most myths of the composer as a political man emerged. To familiarize readers with this material, I close this introduction by reviewing those signs of Beethoven's political attitudes and activities—including but not concentrating on efforts he made to communicate literal opinions through music—that are most often cited in political contexts. Though constantly reorganized and reinterpreted according to the social, economic, and personal views of subsequent mediators, the following constitute the basic data from which the majority of political interpretations are formed. It is tempting to argue—as some of the above authors imply—that a political "mythmaking conspiracy" projected meanings onto Beethoven's life and works with absolutely no regard for the biographical record. This is not quite the case. No matter how far-fetched, most politicized versions of Beethoven's life have some basis in truth, albeit often tenuous. Instead of projection, the procedure I trace is the one that Steven Aschheim termed "selective scavenging and reinterpretation."[68] With few exceptions, propagandists choose those aspects of this protean figure most useful in inspiring others to follow a preferred course, and shut out all indications that the composer might have considered other options.

Reflections of a Political Man

Writing his *Reflections of a Nonpolitical Man* in the midst of the First World War, Thomas Mann cited some of E. T. A. Hoffmann's "Extremely Random Thoughts." "What artist has ever troubled himself with the political events of the day anyway? He lived only for his art, and advanced through life serving it alone. But a dark and unhappy age has seized men with its iron fist, and the pain squeezes from them sounds that were formerly alien to them." Mann quoted Hoffmann to communicate how in defense of his nation an artist such as himself had been forced to utter sounds that previously had been foreign to him. Pressed to write a series of essays on the politics of his day, Mann justified prosecution of the war as a way of protecting German "culture" against Western "civilization." However, Mann admitted that despite their apparent patriotism his reflections were "the detailed product of an ambivalence, the presentation of an inner-personal discord and conflict."[69]

These statements also aptly describe the situation Ludwig van Beethoven faced. Although an artist working in a presumably nonpolitical medium, Beethoven was gripped by ominous, difficult times that raised his concern for politics. As Sieghard Brandenburg attested in his study of the composer caught "between revolution and restoration," Beethoven was born into a time of great political and social upheaval that affected his life in many ways. His outlook was formed by the enlightened climate of Bonn, and he followed political developments in Vienna, his chosen home, critically. Though never to determine policy in political cabinets or on battlefields, he was a "political man."[70] Alive as the ancien régime was passing, Beethoven—the political man—was regularly shaken by the disruptions of his age. Amateurish at best, Beethoven's attitudes about government and society underwent drastic transformations, so that he often gave an impression of disorientation. As Maynard Solomon put it, the composer's paradoxical outlook combined—at various times—"Caesaristic formulations along with lofty humanistic statements, apparent support of Napoleon during the Consulate along with glorification of the monarchs assembled at the Congress of Vienna, and condemnation of the restoration of hereditary monarchy under the French imperium along with . . . admiration of a constitutional monarchy on British lines."[71]

Furthermore, Beethoven did react to political developments through his art.[72] But as in his verbal statements, any indications of political alignment his compositions might contain—the most obvious being dedications—varied with the composer's shifting ideological stance. A few well-known examples demonstrate this inconsistency. In the year following the outbreak of the French Revolution he wrote a pair of cantatas to honor enlightened monarchs. Later, he dedicated his Third Symphony, op. 55, to the revolutionary hero Napoleon. But when Bonaparte crowned himself emperor, Beethoven altered this inscription and composed a series of works meant to inspire resistance against French revolutionary forces. Thereafter, perhaps in response to the oppressive atmosphere of Metternich's Austria, Beethoven composed his great Ninth Symphony with its finale based on Schiller's humanistic "Ode to Joy." With characteristic ambiguity, Beethoven dedicated this symphony—in which so many listeners construe "progressive" meanings—to another monarch: the king of Prussia.

When we study the history of reception given Beethoven in German political circles, therefore, it is crucial to take into account the discordant nature of his opinions concerning the issues of his day. The fact that his political thought was so erratic has greatly influenced interpretations of the composer and his music. Because of his diversity of opinion, people of every political persuasion have discerned justification for claiming him and his compositions to be representative of their ideals, no matter how anachronistic or extreme. Those seeking to correlate his worldview with their own have found it easy to select particular incidents, utterances, writings, and compositions—without acknowledging the evanescence of his attitudes—and present them as evidence that he would have wholeheartedly shared their convictions. Unlike artists who were more constant in their political views (or expressed none), Beethoven's mutability rendered him vulnerable to subsequent misinterpretation and misuse by propagandists for many ideological positions. Although fraught with contradictions, Beethoven's political biography can be divided into four broad stages: his youth under an enlightened despot from 1770 to 1792; his period of "revolutionary fever" from 1792 to 1804; his experience of the Napoleonic wars from 1804 to 1815; and his discomfort under Metternich's regime from 1816 to 1827.

From 1770, the year of his birth, until he left to pursue his career in Vienna in 1792, Beethoven lived in Bonn along the Rhine River. During much of this period, Bonn was happily governed by a relative of the most famous enlightened despot of the late eighteenth century; Maximilian Franz, the elector of Cologne, ruled his principality from 1784 to 1801 largely according to the ideals set forth by his brother, the Hapsburg emperor Joseph II. In contrast to less open-minded despots governing German principalities, Maximilian spurned court etiquette and refinements, preferring the homes of the emerging bourgeoisie to palaces. In addition, he improved conditions for his subjects by reforming the financial and educational systems of the Rhineland.[73] The son of a singer at this court, Beethoven very early became aware of the possibilites of enlightened absolutism and, once he obtained a position as court musician, he enjoyed—at least secondhand—the advantages of a despotic system that functioned well. Within this atmosphere, Beethoven developed opinions about the desirability of a benevolent sovereign that colored his political thinking for the rest of his life.[74] Beethoven tried to communicate his youthful confidence in aristocratic redeemers via two cantatas: one for the funeral of the emperor Joseph, another for his successor, Leopold. The former was composed to a text that included the sentiment, "Joseph came with the strength of the gods" and destroyed a "raging monster," fanaticism; the latter included the line, "Peoples, weep no more; he is as great as Joseph."

However, there were inconsistencies in this ideological foundation. In the conducive atmosphere prepared by Maximilian's reforms, progressive thought fermented in Bonn during Beethoven's youth. Under the influence of his music instructor, Christian Neefe, and other mentors such as Johann Peter Eichoff and Franz Ries—all members of a secret, anticlerical Order of the *Illuminati*—Beethoven was exposed to the ideas of Voltaire, Rousseau, and German exponents of the *Aufklärung*, especially Immanuel Kant.[75] Moreover, Beethoven heard critical views of the old regime espoused by Eulogius Schneider, a notorious freethinker who taught at the university in Bonn. Schneider's radicalism was such that even the tolerant Maximilian Franz finally expelled him. In France he took part in revolutionary governments until arrest ultimately led to the guillotine on 1 April 1794. That Beethoven was aware of Schneider's teachings seems certain: he briefly enrolled at the university during the professor's tenure, and he subscribed to a publication of the rebel's poems, including one rejoicing at the storming of the Bastille.[76] Through Schneider and others of his ilk, then, Beethoven learned the ideals of democratic thought popular in France and crossing into the Rhineland.

Still, there is little evidence that Beethoven was more than superficially concerned with the actual events of the French Revolution. While France exploded, he concentrated on his work as a musician at the court and did not become personally involved with the struggle. His lack of engagement in the revolutionary cause is evident in the story of his trip to Vienna in 1792. By that time various German princes had launched their campaign against the new French republic; but as he prepared for his move, Beethoven seems to have been barely aware of the war. Traveling from Bonn to the Austrian capital, he was forced to avoid Hessian troops on their way to aid the French king; yet in his recollection of the trip, he exhibited no interest in the violent affairs going on around him—only worry about his own wellbeing. Beethoven was apparently buffered from the turbulence of the French Revolution by a combination of his art and a youthful complacency under an enlightened despot.[77]

It was not until he moved to Vienna that the young man exhibited symptoms of what he later called revolutionary fever.[78] There, between the years 1792 and 1804, a number of Beethoven's actions and statements show that he had paid attention to Schneider and his kind. Perhaps most indicative of his rebellious attitude was the way he interacted with the Viennese nobility. Beethoven's impudence toward his patrons was—and remains—infamous; the virtuoso pianist was infuriated by any intimation that he was inferior to the aristocrats for whom he played.[79] Other signs relate to his friendships with noted revolutionary enthusiasts such as Joseph von Sonnenfels, Gottfried von Swieten, Johann Friedrich Reichardt, Rodolphe Kreutzer, and especially Jean Baptiste Bernadotte—a French general who served as Napoleon's ambassador to Vienna and maddened Austrians by brazenly flying the *tricolore* from his new embassy.[80] Arguably an unfair case of guilt by association, it can nevertheless be assumed that Beethoven shared many opinions with this circle.[81] In 1793 he described his ethos as follows: "To do good whenever one can, to love liberty above all else, never to deny the truth, even though it be before the throne."[82] Another trace of the revolutionary malady appeared in 1801, when Beethoven wrote that he dreamed of establishing a "store of arts" (*Magazin der Künste*) for which all artists would work and from which all connoisseurs could purchase their products. From this warehouse, art would not be sold for the profit of dealers, publishers, or even the artists themselves, but for the benefit of the poor.[83]

Perhaps intended for this proposed *Magazin,* in 1792 the young composer borrowed a song text from a poem by G. C. Pfeffel that included lines such as "Who is a free man? He from whom neither birth nor title, peasant smock nor uniform, hides his brother man; who, enclosed within himself, can set at naught the venal favour of great and small alike—he is a free man."[84] It was during this period too—in 1793—that Beethoven professed his ambition to set to music Friedrich Schiller's *An die Freude.*[85] Controversy over the political connotations of Schiller's ode has marked the reception of the poet as well as of Beethoven since their lifetimes. Today's consensus is that Schiller did not first entitle this work an "Ode to Freedom," as has been contended; nevertheless, German rebels appropriated the poem during the French revolutionary era for use as the text of a political *Lied,* sung—with the word *Freiheit* replacing *Freude*—to the tune of the *Marseillaise.*[86] Whether Beethoven conceived of the poem as the arcadian reverie Schiller presumably intended or as the political symbol contemporaries made of it is a controversy that may never be resolved. Solomon holds, however, that the composer's interest in the poem may be taken as an "emblem of the idealism of Beethoven's youth, when he was enflamed by what he called the 'fever of the Revolution.'"[87]

The same might be said for another composition begun during this period: his Third Symphony. As will become clear below, the "meaning" of the *Eroica* Symphony is an issue of contention, owing mainly to Beethoven's revisions of its dedication. Conceived as a "symphonic apotheosis" of Napoleon, some abstract concept of heroism, or none of the above,[88] this work did mark a shift—in the composer's words—to a "new style" of composition. Here Beethoven mastered and modified the sonata form in ways that fully realized its epic potential: the Homeric proportions, valiant themes, and gallant rhythms of this symphony shocked, bewildered, and emboldened its first listeners. Whether this had been the aim of the composer or not, in the minds of many both work and creator became associated with the *élan—vital* and *terrible*—of the times. Also conceived and largely worked out at the pitch of revolutionary excitement in Europe was Beethoven's only opera, first entitled *Leonore,* then *Fidelio,* op. 72. With its drama around a French story of wrongful incarceration and its haunting "Prisoners Chorus" (*O Welche Lust*), *Fidelio* and its overtures have compelled associations with principles of political liberty. But the famous trumpet call announcing salvation at the hands of an aristocratic redeemer complicates reception of this "rescue opera" as a piece of revolutionary propaganda.

For the paradoxical worldview Beethoven brought to Vienna ensured that revolutionary fever did not completely dominate his political outlook. Even during this second period, each expression of quasi-leftist ideology was balanced by statements and actions proving that he had not wholly freed himself of the habits and values of aristocratic society. In 1794, when asked about the possibility of social uprising in Austria, Beethoven observed that the Viennese would never revolt as the French had: as long as they had their "beer and sausages," he felt, they would never become angry enough to fight the system.[89] Beethoven also made it clear that in spite of his reputation as a rebel, he would probably never have manned a barricade; in a letter of 1798 to one of the members of the Schuppanizigh Quartet, Beethoven let slip a joke that has been used ever since to associate him with authoritarian principles. Writing to Baron Nikolaus von Zmeskall, Beethoven quipped that "power is the morality of those who excel others" and announced that "it is also mine."[90] Another remark made during this period reveals that he was fully capable of using his might in a despotic way: in 1801, Beethoven admitted that he used his friends as "instruments" and that he did not consider any friendship worthy of him unless it served some purpose.[91]

Such quotations are no proof that Beethoven was reactionary, but other evidence from the revolutionary period suggests that he had not lost his respect for the ancien régime: musical manifestations of what Solomon terms the tension Beethoven felt "between obedience and rebellion" are songs written while Austrian forces were being mounted to fight Napoleon.[92] In 1796 Beethoven composed an *Abschiedsgesang an Wiens Bürger* (Farewell to Vienna's citizens), WoO 121, to such verses as: "Friends! Wish our noble journey all success; Follow us, beauties, not with looks of distress, but confident of victory and fame which we will boldly win and when returning claim."[93] Later, in 1797, as the emperor Franz called out the *Landsturm*, Beethoven composed other "battle songs": the *Kriegslied der Österreicher* (Austrian war song), WoO 122, opened with the lines, "We are a great German Volk, mighty and just; you doubt it, Frenchmen? You don't know us very well," and concluded with the exhortations, "Austrian man, woman, and child, know your own worth; never, Frenchmen, will we be conquered or even charmed by you!"

In order to support himself as a musician not employed at court, Beethoven had to maintain good relations with the wellborn benefactors of the Viennese art world; he worked to make himself a welcome guest in the homes of Vienna's nobility. In spite of occasional outbursts in front of blue-blooded patrons, he did become comfortable with their lifestyle, even to the point of assuming aristocratic characteristics of the worst kind—his treatment of servants was notoriously bad, his willingness to mix with commoners notably limited.[94] Perhaps because of his experiences at the Bonn court and in Viennese palaces, Beethoven felt himself a deserving member of the noble class. This belief was partly founded on an exalted view of the artist's status in society and a liberal conviction that men should be judged on the basis of ability rather than birth—in this sense, Beethoven's "noble pretense" was of an enlightened sort.[95] Nonetheless, it is evident that he had no desire to see erosion of class differences or leveling of the aristocratic milieu. The best-known example of Beethoven's desire to maintain the status that the "van" in his name afforded him is the anger he demonstrated when a noble court of law, learning that this Flemish predicate was not a sign of nobility, moved the case for guardianship of his nephew Karl into a court for commoners. Beethoven then wrote in a conversation book that "burghers should be seperated from higher persons, and I have fallen among them."[96]

Though contradictions in Beethoven's political views were present throughout his bout with revolutionary fever, a profound change in attitude seems to have occurred with the invasion of German lands by Napoleon and the ensuing Wars of Liberation. The most significant sign of impatience with the Corsican was, of course, Beethoven's rededication of the Third Symphony upon learning that Napoleon had proclaimed himself emperor in May of 1804.[97] But other experiences between 1804 and 1816 also led Beethoven to question the "French" ideas he had learned during his youth. Twice he underwent the trials of a city under siege. In 1805, while Napoleon fought his way through northern Italy and over the Alps to Vienna, Beethoven worked furiously to complete his opera; after he finished *Leonore,* however, his hopes for a theatrical success were dashed. The first productions were financial and critical disasters, partly because of the conditions of their performance, during the occupation of Vienna by French troops. In addition to professional misfortunes, Beethoven suffered physically because of Napoleon's invasions: his hearing condition required him to lie in the basement of his brother's apartment clasping pillows over his head to protect his ears from the noise of shelling. Although they alone do not explain his turning against France, these personal agonies certainly contributed to Beethoven's ultimate desire to see the French army driven back.

By the time of Napoleon's final defeat at Waterloo, the composer had climbed aboard the patriotic bandwagon of powers united to defend the old regime. In 1806 he fled from Grätz Castle, the summer home of Prince Lichnowsky, after refusing to perform in the presence of French officers.[98] In 1809 he reportedly confronted a French officer, saying: "If I, as general, knew as much about strategy as I, the composer, know of counterpoint, I'd give you something to do!"[99] In the same year he produced incidental music for Goethe's tragedy *Egmont,* its theme of national liberation one with which he and other Germans could easily identify.[100] Finally, he participated very enthusiastically in festivities celebrating gradual victory over France.

To these galas Beethoven owed his longest and most intense moments in the limelight, based not so much on his now most-respected works as on a series of compositions that capitalized on the patriotic spirit of the time: *Wellingtons Sieg* (Wellington's victory), op. 91, was written to mark the 1813 defeat of French forces at the Battle of Victoria; *Germania,* WoO 94, was a contribution to a Singspiel meant to celebrate the arrival of allied armies in Paris in the spring of 1814;[101] *Der glorreiche Augenblick* (The glorious moment), op. 136, and *Chor auf die verbündeten Fürsten* (Chorus to the united princes), WoO 95, were produced in anticipation of the revelry expected when the Congress of Vienna convened in the fall of 1814;[102] *Es ist vollbracht* (It is achieved), WoO 97, was composed in 1815 for another Singspiel celebrating the defeat of Napoleon.[103] After the premiere of *Wellingtons Sieg*, Beethoven wrote a letter to the *Wiener Zeitung* thanking all who had participated, stating that "we were all filled with nothing but the pure love of country and of joyful sacrifice of our powers for those who sacrificed so much for us," and expressing his gratitude for "the opportunity, long and ardently desired . . . to lay a work of magnitude upon the altar of the Fatherland."[104] Thus, when German principalities rose against Napoleon, Beethoven rode the wave of patriotism intent on liberating his homeland and conserving the order to which he was accustomed.

Even this conservative phase did not determine a final and stable political outlook for Beethoven. As was the case with many German and Austrian patriots, he was disappointed with the political system erected upon the repulsion of the French forces. Though he had committed himself to the defense of monarchical rule, he undoubtedly expected Napoleon's successor to govern according to the principles established by the exemplary patriarch Joseph II. The system of government he and other anti-Napoleonic patriots inherited was very different; after 1816, central Europe was administered repressively by Clemens von Metternich and his secret police. Beethoven's political views shifted again: between 1816 and his death in 1827, the composer reverted to his progressive views in response to the new oppression. Heedless of spies and informers, he railed loudly against the "paralytic regime," comparing it negatively with his memory of the Josephinian idyll and his impressions of the English constitutional system.[105]

It was in this atmosphere, on 7 May 1824, that the Ninth Symphony—its emotional panorama culminating as a heroic tenor and a military band march, or rather run, toward the realization of brotherhood and joy (and freedom?)—received its premiere. The language of contemporary reviewers gives us the best sense of the riotous impact this "colossal" work had under these circumstances: the "bizarre character," "the firestorm roaring upward," the "grotesque leaps," "the fullness, the newness, the richness of ideas . . . the flight into fantasy leading into incomprehensible regions," "the abundance of tones expanding before us, the youthful power [and] the eternal fire of his creations astounded; so stood before us the image of a Vulcan of the soul," "it carries the stamp of the gigantic, the monstrous, its forceful tempos rushing listeners from one sensation to another as in a storm."[106]

Beethoven's aide, Anton Schindler, believed authorities would have suppressed the work had they foreseen the spell it could cast: after five ovations from the first audience, the police commissioner was moved to shout, "Silence!"[107] During this period, only two things kept the composer from being arrested and interrogated along with some of his associates: his reputation as a great artist and the assumption that he was mad.[108] Insane or not, it is clear that throughout his life Beethoven was confused about politics. Surviving all the disruption that occurred in German and Austrian lands around the turn of the nineteenth century—enlightened reform, revolutionary struggle, military invasion, national liberation, and reactionary dictatorship—the composer followed an uneven path of political development.

By analyzing the various versions of Beethoven as a political man formulated through the past two centuries, we will see that few were founded on gross falsehoods. Even this cursory review of his political biography reveals that Beethoven did make statements and take actions which, if lifted from their historical context, could be construed as evidence that he would have agreed with many modern political ideologies, from the democratic to the autocratic. It has not been necessary for propagandists on the left or right to fabricate evidence that the composer held views consistent with their own; they could simply select single aspects of Beethoven's multifaceted worldview and insinuate that they represent his opinions as a whole. In this way Beethoven has been designated a precursor of every major political orientation in modern German history.

Beethoven was a political man. Beethoven was a supporter of enlightened despotism; Beethoven was a revolutionary idealist. Beethoven was an admirer of Napoleon; Beethoven was an enemy of Napoleon. Beethoven was a composer of revolutionary music; Beethoven was a composer of patriotic military music. Beethoven was all of these things, but not any one of them. The history of the evocation of this composer and his music in German political culture is the recounting of how partisans have ignored the complexity of the real man and tried to force "their" Beethoven onto the rest of Germany and the world.

2

The Second Reich

If I heard this music often, I would always be very brave.
OTTO VON BISMARCK

Folk songs, Beethoven, and drinking songs rang out in the twilight, which was thereby easily warmed so that a comfortable drowsiness filled his brain.
HEINRICH MANN
Der Untertan

"O Freunde, nicht diese Töne!"
HERMANN HESSE
1914

On the one-hundredth anniversary of Beethoven's birth—amid the 1870 struggle against the France of Napoleon III—the city of Dresden presented a Festspiel entitled *Das Erwachen der Künste* (The awakening of the arts). Produced two weeks prior to the formation of the German Empire and six weeks before the capitulation of France, this apotheosis closely associated the composer with the war raging at the time. As the Dresdner Festspiel began, the curtain rose to reveal the nine muses being awakened by strains of Beethoven's music; terrified by the war thundering below, they hesitated to return to earth and join the German people celebrating the composer's birthday. Aroused by Beethoven's works, nonetheless, the muses descended from their cloudy aerie to watch the German armies defeat their enemy. Moved by the German victory over France—and Beethoven's compositions—Polyhymnia knelt onto the battleground to recite the following verse:

> Out of laurels I found on the battlefield
> I wind this wreath for Beethoven.
> Because he also participated
> In this year's fateful events.
>
> In his seldom understood heart existed,
> Along with the drive to create,
> Above all joys, above all pains,
> The love of his Fatherland.[1]

Through this imagery, the first act of *Das Erwachen der Künste* declared that Beethoven's music had stirred Germans to conquer the French; the second honored him for thus contributing to the war effort. Before two altars dedicated to Freedom and Beauty, a festive parade marched onto the scene. Led by citizens tossing flowers and wreaths, the *Festzug* included a chorus singing Beethoven's works. Behind the singers came banners heralding each of the arts; the greatest names in German cultural history—portrayed by "astoundingly accurate" imitators—followed each flag. Upon reaching the temple, the chorus performed Beethoven's *Ruinen von Athen,* op. 113. Immediately thereafter peals of thunder sounded and the muses reappeared. Struck by lightning, the two altars shot flames while a third focus of worship ascended between them: a bust of Beethoven crowned with the laurel wreath formed by Polyhymnia. Illuminated by flame, the bust rose into the air surrounded by the banners and torches of the worshippers. The curtain descended as the muses sank before Beethoven's image "in ecstasy" and the faithful sang *Germania! Germania!*[2]

Farther to the west, an anonymous "Citizen of Bonn" wrote an equally fantastic birthday tribute to the composer as political hero in 1870. Later published by a Leipzig press, the play, *Ludwig van Beethoven: Ein dramatisches Charakterbild* (Ludwig van Beethoven: a dramatic portrait of his character), depicted the young composer in 1792, still in the service of Maximilian Franz, the elector of Cologne. Rather than concentrating on Beethoven's life as a court musician, the Bonn playwright crafted a political intrigue, the outcome of which designated the composer a true patriot. In search of traitors, a court official intrigues to implicate young Beethoven in the activities of a noted sympathizer to the French Revolution, Eulogius Schneider. To do so, the official monitors Schneider's attempt at convincing the composer to write music for an ode "On the Bastille." "Every civil war," declares the character based on Schneider, "requires its battle song. . . . I have written a song, a spirited song, that will carry hearts away. Beethoven should set music to this song . . . it will be, in a word, the *Marseillaise* of the German people." Upon listening to Schneider's poem, Beethoven agrees to the project, but not without stating that "the individual words mean nothing to me, I just grasp the tone and tempo of the totality, and provide color." Having overheard this conversation, the court official has proof of Beethoven's revolutionary undertaking; when French troops threaten Bonn he discloses the plot, and the cocky young musician is arrested along with Schneider.

Thrown into a dungeon, Beethoven suffers over his loss of freedom (no doubt, in the mind of this playwright, the basis for his sensitive treatment of prisoners in *Fidelio*). However, when Schneider visits him with a plan to escape and flee to Paris, the composer refuses and then rebukes the revolutionary: "Your freedom is nothing more than war and destruction, because to make you and your kind free [one] must shatter the existing world and kill the other half of mankind. Yes, your freedom is a bloodbath, it can only come after a torrent of blood. . . . What I am striving for is to be free in my art, to be able to express the contents of my soul in it, to be master of the laws and form of art—nothing more." Toward Schneider's plans to flee to Paris, Beethoven is equally contemptuous: "I admire Frenchmen in France, but I hate Frenchmen in Germany—and Germans in France." Finally he admits, "I cannot be a revolutionary: it just doesn't fit my personality. . . . So leave me to my fate. I will struggle with it as long as I can. If I fail, so be it—I will die, but not on foreign soil, not in the throes of battle, not at the blade of a guillotine—because, Sir, I say to you, he who forsakes his Fatherland, he who betrays his Fatherland, is going to get it sooner or later."

In this play Beethoven does not meet his end in the Bonn dungeon, for he is saved by the current object of his passion, Leonore von Breuning (model for the opera character of the same name?). Leonore convinces the elector that Beethoven took the "Bastille" commission as a creative endeavor, responding—as he had said—only to the rhythm of the verse, not to its political content. Thus, at the moment of Beethoven's despair—as he moans that "Schneider was right; now I know, they are tyrants, despots, executioners"—Leonore bursts into his cell with the words, "But no, Ludwig, I bring you neither tyrants nor despots, but freedom! . . . My love, here is the order of the elector to free the young Beethoven immediately!"

With this denouement, the anonymous playwright ended his court intrigue, one that so carefully—and fictitiously—vouched for the nationalistic, counterrevolutionary, and Francophobic credentials of his fellow "citizen of Bonn." But this did not end his celebration of Beethoven as national hero. To this drama was appended an epilogue wherein a character representing the "Genius of the Century" recites a poetic homage to Beethoven, with accompanying music from the Piano Sonata in F Minor, op. 57 (*Appassionata*), the finale from *Fidelio,* the Sixth Symphony, op. 68, and other works. Among the verses extolling the composer's achievements, "Genius" recited:

> Hail Germany, you are honoring your great son!
> Hail the Rhine River, you saw him born!
> And hail the city, whose vine-covered feet harbored his youth!

To the tones of the second movement of Beethoven's Third Symphony:

> The people rage—nations arise
> Out of bondage and chains,
> To overthrow courageously
> Despots and great powers.
> And strong hearts are crowned with victory,
> Above all the singer who gave the call to battle.

To conclude, the playwright recommended a performance of the choral movement of the Ninth Symphony, offering the following stage directions: "During the singing, a statue of Beethoven should rise from the floor. 'Genius' rushes to it and upon his signal members of the chorus adorn the pedestal with laurel and oak wreaths. Bengalese flames light the statue. The curtain falls."[3]

Beethoven's hundredth birthday was celebrated in Kassel in less dramatic but equally patriotic fashion. A three-day festival featuring his *Egmont* Overture and Ninth Symphony was preceded by a "prologue" that likewise celebrated the composer not just for creating beautiful music, but for somehow having initiated the German triumph. Event organizer Wilhelm Koffka contributed a poem expressing this notion:

> In this moment, when our Germany
> Raises itself over all other lands,
> Should we not honor a man
> Who achieved in art that which
> Heroes of war and rulers of state
> Only now carry forth:
> He led his Fatherland to victory![4]

Simultaneously, the music journal *Signale* reported that the "most original" celebration of Beethoven's 1870 birthday took place in Sarcelles, France. There officers and soldiers of the army surrounding Paris arranged their own glorification of the composer in a small concert hall. Instead of a large bust,[5] over the stage they hung a banner displaying Beethoven's name and titles of his works. Beneath it, musicians of the Second Prussian Garde-Regiment performed the *Egmont* Overture. Before this rendition, a speech by the officer in charge commemorated the "immortal genius of Beethoven" in terms meant to impart to the military audience the "mood of the day, and their duty."[6]

Festivals, parades, plays, and speeches such as these conveyed comparable themes throughout Germany in the heady days of military triumph and unification. The December 1870 and January 1871 issues of *Signale* and *Neue Zeitschrift für Musik* reported Beethoven celebrations tinged with nationalistic symbolism in Berlin, Bremen, Schwerin, Lübeck, Thorn, Karlsruhe, Laibach, Barmen, Brünn, Leipzig, and Munich.[7] Even events not directly associated with Beethoven's birthday linked him and his music with the ongoing military and political action of the *Gründerzeit.* At a benefit for the War Aid Association (*Kriegshilfeverein*) in Pössenek, Thüringen, commentary correlated Beethoven's music with the battle going on—listening to it, audience members were expected to feel the urge to donate money for care of the wounded.[8] After the conclusion of the war, occasions such as a "Celebration of the German Victory!" in Barmen continued the common practice of programming Beethoven's music along with renditions of *Wacht am Rhein,* the most popular song in Germany during the war.[9] Thereafter, such celebrations of major artistic figures—Beethoven prominent among them—were at the heart of the political culture of the new nation.[10] Once celebrated for "leading the Fatherland to victory," Beethoven was evoked throughout the existence of the Second Reich as a cultural symbol of German national prowess.[11] Designated by Richard Wagner an integral part of the emerging nationalist symbolism, Beethoven's music became ubiquitous in the political pageantry designed to give Germans a sense of national identity.

Beethoven in Bismarck's Germany

Connections drawn between Beethoven and Otto von Bismarck were early components of the new national propaganda. The founder of modern Germany was not a committed concertgoer; Bismarck explained his reluctance to attend concerts and operas by saying that the memory or "residue" of the compositions kept him awake at night.[12] However, Bismarck was fond of Beethoven's chamber music. An audaciously Romantic student in Göttingen, Bismarck often implored his friend Alexander Keyserling to play Beethoven's piano sonatas for him.[13] Evidence of his continued affection for these compositions exists mainly in records of Bismarck's amorous adventures. When in 1846 Bismarck romanced Johanna von Puttkamer, his future wife, their activities were often enhanced by music; on one occasion, Robert von Keudell, an accomplished pianist, played Beethoven's *Appassionata* Sonata for the couple. In his memoirs Keudell recalled noticing tears in Bismarck's eyes during the last movement.[14] Later, when separated from Johanna, Bismarck reminisced about their relationship and described his loneliness by using Beethoven's music as a metaphor: "I feel as one does when looking at the leaves turning yellow on a beautiful September day: healthy and cheerful, yet somewhat melancholic—somewhat homesick, longing for the woods, the lake, the meadow, for you and the children—everything as if mixed with sunset and Beethoven's symphonies."[15] Bismarck also associated Beethoven's music with another romance: his 1862 tryst with the Russian Princess Orlow at Biarritz. Herself a pianist, the princess played Bismarck's favorite pieces for him each day. Later he fondly remembered standing at an open window listening to her play "the C Major and the A-flat Major," by which he meant Beethoven's Sonata no. 21, op. 53 (*Waldstein*), and Sonata no. 31, op. 110.[16]

Two other references to Beethoven in Bismarck's biography became vital features of the Iron Chancellor's legend. The first was a remark that if he "listened often to music" such as the first movement of the *Appassionata* Sonata, "he would always be very brave." Like the statements above, Keudell reported that Bismarck made this one in wholly unofficial, private circumstances—it was a "comic twist," insisted Keudell, since the chancellor "never required musical inspiration to be brave."[17] Another widely publicized episode resulted from the Bismarck family tradition of arranging music performances on Frau Bismarck's birthday. As a gift for the year 1866, Keudell had Beethoven's Fifth Symphony performed in the concert hall of the chancellor's ministry. In his memoirs Keudell noted that Bismarck enjoyed the music performed on that occasion, but he did not describe a more momentous response.[18] As will be seen below, this seemingly innocuous event—in which Bismarck played only an indirect role—subsequently gained great symbolic significance because this birthday concert occurred on 11 April 1866, one month before Prussia declared war against Austria.

These anecdotes show that Bismarck and his family enjoyed and admired Beethoven's music, but none indicates that the chancellor interpreted it in political terms; all were personal references to the composer made in situations that had little to do with politics. Within German political culture, nevertheless, these episodes were transformed into legends implying that Bismarck considered Beethoven's art a source of strength for his political achievements; in this way, the music of Beethoven itself was increasingly related to German political and military affairs. Bismarck's statement that Beethoven's music made him feel brave has been repeated countless times in patriotic German literature, usually as part of arguments that the compositions motivated the chancellor to undertake martial endeavors.[19] Moreover, ongoing embellishments to the story of Frau Bismarck's birthday insinuated a direct connection between Beethoven's music and Bismarck's policies; ever since the defeat of Austria at Königgratz, biographers of Bismarck have enhanced this story in ways that impart to Beethoven's music the power of inspiring military deeds.

An 1885 novel by Oscar Meding and Gregor Samarow initiated the steady process of rewriting this story. Their work of historical fiction, *Um Zepter und Kronen* (About scepters and crowns), alleged that the performance of Beethoven's symphony arranged by Keudell spurred Bismarck to go into his office and sign the declaration of war on Austria, saying, "Even to be defeated in such a way would be beautiful."[20] Successive versions of this story purported that Bismarck himself had requested the performance of the Fifth Symphony just before giving mobilization orders. By the time of the First World War, conservative newspapers such as *Der Tag* rendered the story along the following lines: "As Bismarck decided to march in the Bohemian campaign, he had his orchestra come to his house and play Beethoven's Symphony of Fate for him alone."[21] In all such versions, the circumstances and chronology of the event were manipulated in ways suggesting that Bismarck sought and found a source of courage for military action in Beethoven's music. By 1898 this myth was so common that Robert von Keudell felt it necessary to clarify the issue; in a letter of that year, he insisted that the music he performed for the Bismarcks "had absolutely nothing to do with politics."[22] Nonetheless, popular literature about the first chancellor continually repeated modified versions of the story—enough to indelibly etch the association of Beethoven with Bismarck and bellicosity in German culture.[23]

Bismarck's supposed love for the stirring music of Beethoven accentuated the legendary strength of the Iron Chancellor. But it was not just with reference to Bismarck that Beethoven was integrated into the cultural politics of united Germany: his music was commonly played at ceremonies organized by the cultural authorities of the Reich. A performance of the *Weihe des Hauses* inaugurated the Berlin Philharmonic in 1884 and the second movement of his Third Symphony was used for many state funerals. Demonstrating the polish of its cultural tastes, the imperial family even purchased Beethoveniana: between 1875 and 1898, the Prussian Royal Foundation (*Königlicher Kulturbesitz*) acquired an extensive collection of Beethoven scores and letters.[24]

Meanwhile, the Prussian state designated the Rhenish house in which Beethoven was born a national landmark.[25] Since monuments of this sort were "statements of national self-consciousness," it was "on behalf of Germany" that Bonn was proclaimed the birthplace and nurturer of Beethoven.[26] Moreover, the German school system included the composer in the pantheon of national heroes: "Youth had to follow role models—mainly terribly inaccurate misinterpretations—which made it clear that Luther and Bismarck, Frederick the Great and Moltke, Goethe and Richard Wagner, Bach and Beethoven alone could be German. To be a hero meant to be German, to be German meant to be a hero."[27]

It was hardly necessary to develop a fresh interpretation for use in the cultural politics of the new nation; as the empire associated itself with Beethoven, patriotic interpretations of his music formulated during the Franco-Prussian War were merely repeated. Above all, myths of Beethoven as Germanic hero concocted by Richard Wagner perfectly suited the needs of imperial ideologues. Members of the Wagnerian circle proved effective promulgators of his ideas about Beethoven in the service of Bismarck's Reich. The conductor Hans von Bülow, once-close associate of Wagner, played an important role in popularizing Beethoven's music during the eighteen seventies and eighties. Noted for marathon performances of the Ninth Symphony twice in one evening, Bülow often supplemented his concerts with speeches explaining the music in Wagnerian terms.[28] Bülow repeatedly celebrated the "symphonist" (*Symphoniker*) as an "awakener of the Volk" (*Volkserwecker*);[29] thus did the conductor "render the Ninth Symphony a living possession of the nation," as contemporaries noted, at the same time that he perpetuated Wagner's association of Beethoven with nationalistic ideology. According to one of his admirers, Bülow led the "true victory march of Beethoven through the world" which commenced "with the assumption of worldwide stature by the newly unified Germany."[30] Even after his wife, Cosima, had been seduced by the Meister, Bülow endorsed Wagner's music theories—including those about Beethoven—so readily that, on his death, obituaries stated that "with Bülow the German Volk has lost Beethoven and Wagner a second time."[31]

Another important purveyor of the Wagnerian Beethoven interpretation was Hans von Wolzogen, longtime editor of the *Bayreuther Blätter.* Worshipful of Wagner, Wolzogen was quick to second his master's wartime Beethoven invocation. Already in early 1871, Wolzogen agreed enthusiastically that the anniversary of Beethoven's birth should be celebrated as a national event. "Our nation can be proud that this man, a national hero and more, was a German—that he *had to be* German—which is why this Volk is justified, even obliged, to arrange a secular high mass (*Hochfest*) for this great master." Beethoven, Wolzogen continued, was one of the most scintillating examples of those German artists who undertook to free themselves from "chains of fashion"; a genuine, energetic, truth-loving German, he struggled his whole life against the "Latin specter." It was in this spirit, Wolzogen was certain, that Richard Wagner penned his 1870 *Jubiläumsschrift:* much more than a publication of music criticism, that essay was a "catechism" of artistic consciousness—particularly its conclusion, which offered a new perspective on the latest historical developments, interpreting battles of the Franco-Prussian War as "Germanic world deeds" comparable to Beethoven's own. The greatest representatives of fashion, the "disgusting enemy of honorable effort," were the French, whose supremacy Germans had to destroy on the aesthetic battlefield. And Beethoven was the savior: through him the German spirit rose wielding "the fine arts"—along with bloody swords—as "weapons" against insolent fashion, countering "the hex put on us by Latins in their witches' kitchen" (*die Hekate der romanischen Hexenküche*). Beethoven's was "a Germanic deed, a Germanic art, a Germanic effort toward a Germanic goal." True, because his achievements transcended the narrow boundaries of nationality, the composer had become "more than a German," but he achieved this "as a German." For this reason, Wolzogen agreed with Wagner that the most fitting celebration of Beethoven was the "victory of German valor" in the war against France.[32]

Throughout his career, Wolzogen endlessly reminded readers that Wagner had provided the definitive interpretation of Beethoven. In his 1897 survey of the *Großmeister deutscher Musik* (Great masters of German music), Wolzogen again deferred to his personal hero: "We cannot discuss Beethoven without lapsing into the tone of our master, without constantly . . . returning to the pronouncements of the great successor and inheritor of his spirit." Wagner had created in his *Festschrift* for Beethoven's one-hundredth birthday something wonderful "as the new German Empire arose in place of the French revolutionary state and trod on the pinnacle of so-called civilization." By linking these events, Wagner had "made the essence of Beethoven and his art comprehensible to us."[33] Wolzogen not only championed notions about Beethoven that Wagner had placed on the record, but added ideas that even his master had hesitated to publicize. In 1906—"one hundred years after the end of the first German Reich and thirty-six years after 1870"—he revealed that Wagner had trimmed some seven hundred words from the final section of his "Beethoven" article. "How should we celebrate our Beethoven?" Wagner had asked in the conclusion of his original draft. Of course, the Bayreuth maestro had supplied an answer:

> History comes to our aid, placing the hundredth birthday of this great composer in the same year as the victorious emergence of the German Volk after several hundred years of disgrace. Celebrate both of these events so that the festival for one is worthy of the other. Celebrate his birth in a way that is worthy of this rebirth. Complement that which Beethoven was with that which is signified by the victories of German armies. If you sense the power of the German deed in the energy of a heart filled with Beethoven's music, you will grasp the significance of both. On the one hand, deeds; on the other, works of art. Let the deeds of our victory lead to construction of a true and genuine German Empire; let the works of the great Beethoven lead to achievement of the most honorable deeds of the German spirit.[34]

By republishing Wagner's discarded conclusion, Wolzogen further involved Beethoven with past and future belligerent actions against France.

In response to these one-sided interpretations of Beethoven's music as a symbol of restless nationalism, alternative views did arise. Opponents of Bismarck's system were also respectful of Beethoven's art and occasionally included references to it in their rhetoric. On 10 March 1841 in the concert hall of Bremen, the young Friedrich Engels attended a concert of his "favorite pieces of music": Beethoven's Third and Fifth symphonies. The next day he wrote to his sister, Marie, about the experience, especially the performance of the Fifth Symphony: "Last night's was such a concert! If you don't know this splendid piece, you have never heard anything like it in your life. The desperate inner strife in the first movement, the elegiac melancholy [and] soft plaintiveness of love in the Adagio, and the powerful, youthful celebration of freedom by the trombones in the third and fourth movements!"[35]

Highly personal, even sensual, Engels' enthusiastic interpretation of the Fifth Symphony echoed the Romantic mode of music criticism prevailing in 1841; he cannot be accused of having deliberately politicized Beethoven's music in this letter, since only its last line had even the vaguest political connotation. But Engels' interest in Beethoven did not dwindle as he became a principal in the socialist movement. In his "Notes on Germany" of 1873, Engels suggested that while Beethoven's works constituted the culmination of musical expression, most remarkable was that their creation had coincided with the "greatest foreign humiliation": occupation of German lands by Napoleon's forces. Beethoven's life was therefore an encouraging model for all citizens of oppressive systems.[36] The fact that Engels was enamored of Beethoven's music, though on very vague political terms, would provide his Social Democratic movement with justification for making it a centerpiece of its cultural-political program.

In the early phases of German socialism, however, only theorists such as Engels perceived Beethoven's suitability as a symbol of radical ideals; activists in the field did not. Led by Ferdinand Lassalle, the German workers' movement recognized the importance of "cultural politics" (*Kulturpolitik*) on the political battleground. Lassalle's speeches and rallies were replete with references to art, literature, and music. Moreover, inspirational song was a significant part of the events Lassalle orchestrated, as he requested that an anthem, the *Bundeslied des Vereins,* be composed for his rallies.[37] Nonetheless, Beethoven's music was not an important component of the cultural program of the early socialist movement. Rank-and-file participants in workers' choirs were responsible for the selection of music performed at rallies and while they did incorporate some "bourgeois" songs—borrowing from the *Liedertafeln* of middle-class choirs—they generally performed popular tunes that originated in their own class, not high-cultural works.[38] Use of Beethoven compositions as anthems for the workers' struggle became common later. In the meantime, during the Bismarck era, one had to look outside the grass-roots culture of the socialist movement for an alternative to the Wagnerian version of the Beethoven myth. Until the turn of the century, it was primarily in the work of the intellectual elite that biting criticism of Wagner's interpretation appeared—for instance, in the writings of Friedrich W. Nietzsche.

As a student, Nietzsche found Beethoven's music "too difficult." Although himself a pianist and aspiring composer, he felt that such sophisticated music was too complex for popular consumption and therefore did not fit into his concept of a new theater on the Greek model.[39] Though Nietzsche gradually learned to appreciate the composer, he felt his comprehension of the man did not increase correspondingly. In 1864 the philosopher wrote a poem on the theme of

Beethoven's death that expressed this dilemma. Calling Beethoven an "eternal traveler of the heavens" whose blood "overflowed its earthly scepter," Nietzsche imagined a fleeting confrontation with the composer:

> I look upon you mutely,
> Wishing to ask your eyes,
> Why, you miraculous man,
> Does my pulse beat stormily
> When you pass through the forest of my soul,
> So fiery and yet so cold,
> So distinct and yet so undefined,
> Like church bells sounding in the night?
> I am unable to grasp or even see you,
> Though I sense you striding past, going away.

Despite his entreaties, Nietzsche's dreamy, Romantic vision of Beethoven did not offer guidance on how one might touch souls so profoundly.

> You wink—and your motion initiates
> Glowing waves, sultry like a thunderstorm.
> You wave—and fresh, mild air
> Flutters about me in light play.
> You thunder—and lightning strikes.
> I stare, unmoved,
> As you move heavenward, clad in white robes,
> And observe the ages spreading forth before me,
> Endlessly, timelessly.[40]

Early reservations notwithstanding, Nietzsche's love for and comprehension of Beethoven deepened throughout his life. In philosophical allusions to Beethoven, he described the composer as having lived a Dionysian mode of existence.[41] Especially overwhelmed by Beethoven's depiction of the "starry canopy" (*Sternendom*) in its fourth movement,[42] Nietzsche suggested in *Human, All-Too-Human* that one could use the Ninth Symphony to comprehend the philosophy of Dionysus. He made this explicit in *The Birth of Tragedy:* "Transform Beethoven's 'Hymn of Joy' into a painting, let your imagination conceive the multitudes bowing to the dust, awestruck—then you will approach the Dionysian. Now the slave is a free man, now all the rigid hostile barriers that necessity, caprice, or 'insolent fashion' have fixed between man and man are broken."[43] Elsewhere, Nietzsche characterized Beethoven as having himself been an *Übermensch.*[44]

Like much of his thought, Nietzsche's view of Beethoven was closely connected to his opinion of Wagner. When he read the 1870 essay linking Beethoven and the Franco-Prussian War, Nietzsche agreed with his mentor's belligerent insinuations. In his "Preface to Richard Wagner" for *The Birth of Tragedy,* Nietzsche complimented Wagner's *Festschrift* on Beethoven—composed "amid the terrors and sublimities of the war that had just broken out"—as "splendid."[45] But when Nietzsche and Wagner grew apart, their opinions of Beethoven also differed; indeed, one might trace their break by following the divergence of their Beethoven interpretations. Nietzsche first compared Wagner with Beethoven positively: like Bach and Beethoven, Wagner had "a German music in mind, free from the Latin yoke."[46] But once Nietzsche turned "contra Wagner," he considered any comparison of the Bayreuth master with Beethoven "blasphemous."[47]

Apart from these personal and aesthetic references to Beethoven—more important to study of his philosophy than to this analysis of his contribution to German political culture—Nietzsche made regular allusions to the composer as symbolizing ideas with which he combated Germanic jingoism.[48] In this context, the philosopher insisted that Beethoven was influenced more by French than by German cultural traditions: Beethoven's "morality," Nietzsche held, had been "that of Rousseau."[49] In Nietzsche's opinion, Beethoven was a Romantic, but not a German one; he was the "first great Romantic in the sense of the French notion of Romanticism."[50] In opposition to the popular German notion that Beethoven would have wholeheartedly supported Bismarck's rule, Nietzsche reiterated the argument that the composer had been a revolutionary. "Mozart's music," he felt, "contained the Rococo," whereas Beethoven's music represented "the air of France, the gushing enthusiasm out of which the revolution had emerged."[51] Without the occurrence of the French Revolution, Nietzsche said, "Beethoven would be unimaginable."[52] By making such statements, the philosopher revived pre-Bismarck notions of Beethoven as revolutionary and reestablished a line of interpretation that would be replenished as opposition to the Second Reich grew. Nietzsche's depictions of the composer as Francophile also constituted a rare contradiction of claims to his "legacy" by aggressive German nationalists. Such observations fueled an explosive debate about Beethoven's national identity that would later detonate between German and French patriots.

But Nietzsche himself was less interested in the role Beethoven's music could play in competition between nations than in cooperation among them; he often referred to the composer in expressing his hopes for a "European" future. Here Nietzsche's efforts to use Beethoven in the fight against exclusive nationalism—of any variety—are most apparent. Despite occasional patriotic outbursts, Nietzsche held, Beethoven had not really been a German, but a model for the "European of the Future"; the composer was among those who "only in their weaker moments . . . fell into the narrow-mindedness of the *Vaterländer.*"[53] Beethoven's was the last "European" achievement of German music.[54] Perhaps angered by the interpretation given Beethoven by Germanic ideologues, Nietzsche did what he could to liberate the composer from their imperial control. He argued that the music was not reflective of nationalist ideology and associated Beethoven with ideals of neutral cosmopolitanism. Still, Nietzsche's efforts to this end were frustrated within his own lifetime: just as the socialist interpretation remained the province of an isolated few, Nietzsche's erudite views had little initial effect on public perceptions. Even though critical thinkers such as Nietzsche and Engels renewed a Beethoven image contrary to the nationalist mainstream, they did not disrupt the dominant tendency of reception in the Second Reich—which was to associate Beethoven's music with the belligerence of *Realpolitik.*

The ongoing connection of Beethoven with the Iron Chancellor found its most dramatic representation at the very end of the Bismarck era. On 28 March 1892, exactly two years after Bismarck was dismissed by the new emperor and three days prior to the birthday of the former "pilot" of the German nation, Hans von Bülow led the Berlin Philharmonic Orchestra in a performance of Beethoven's Third Symphony. As soon as the work was over, Bülow voiced an explanation of the composition, as was his habit. But there was little discussion of music in this speech; instead, Bülow reiterated the most common association between Beethoven's music and the politics of the day. Regretting the dismissal of Bismarck, Bülow considered it his duty to impress his audience with the greatness of the former chancellor. To this end, he equated policies of blood and iron—as he put it, "infantry, cavalry, and artillery"—with the music of the *Eroica.*[55]

Retelling the story of the composition and rededication of the Third Symphony, Bülow insisted that the work had never had a true dedicatee, because Napoleon failed to meet Beethoven's standards. Since that time, no one had sufficiently lived up to the heroic ideals Beethoven had in mind to warrant rededicating the work. In 1892, though, Bülow felt this void could be filled at last: considering that an event "even more significant than the anniversary of the victory at Sedan"—Bismarck's birthday—was approaching, the victor of that battle could be made the new dedicatee. The ideal hero represented in Beethoven's Third Symphony had finally been manifested in real life —in the person of Otto von Bismarck! Therefore, Bülow announced, he was rededicating the work to "the brother of Beethoven, to the Beethoven of German politics, to Prince Bismarck!" and asked the crowd to honor the former chancellor with a *"Hoch!"*[56]

To his surprise, the Berlin audience disapproved Bülow's motion. Loyal subjects of the new emperor reacted against the stunt, rising in "loud protest." Shocked, the conductor coughed into his handkerchief, turned red, and left the podium.[57] But Bülow was not daunted by this adverse response. In the city of Hamburg, to which he traveled after resigning his post in Berlin, Bülow had special handouts printed for his next performance—on Bismarck's birthday. His supplement to the regular program reproduced a melody from the Finale of Beethoven's Third Symphony; to these bars, however, Bülow added a text: "Bulwark of the Volk, hail to you, O hero. The new German world is realizing your prophecy. Henceforth, every enemy must go about armed to the teeth even in his inner heart, since you united us." At the bottom of this flier the conductor stamped his imprimatur: "The copyist Hans von Bülow guarantees the authenticity of these corrections."[58] Thus did Bülow take to extremes his effort to politicize Beethoven's music, suggesting anachronistically that the composer himself had dedicated the *Eroica* to Bismarck.

It was also in Hamburg that Bülow read press commentary on his actions in Berlin. Critics accused him of having transformed Beethoven's music into an "ugly political song."[59] Political cartoons chastised his "treasonous" behavior: one depicted a worn-out Bülow superimposed on the score of the symphony while Bismarck applauded in the background, alone;[60] another portrayed Bülow as Papageno from Mozart's *Die Zauberflöte,* his lips sealed by a large lock to keep him from telling tall tales.[61] All that Bülow said about the debacle was that he thought the people of Berlin would have agreed with his estimation of Bismarck and would have supported this way of honoring him.[62] Undaunted, he continued to associate Beethoven with the former chancellor, as in Augsburg, where he thanked the audience for allowing him to conduct the "Bismarck Symphony" for them.[63] That audience members in Berlin did not welcome Bülow's gross politicization of the *Eroica* does not mean they did not consider Beethoven's music representative of Bismarck or his political methods; by 1892, Ger-

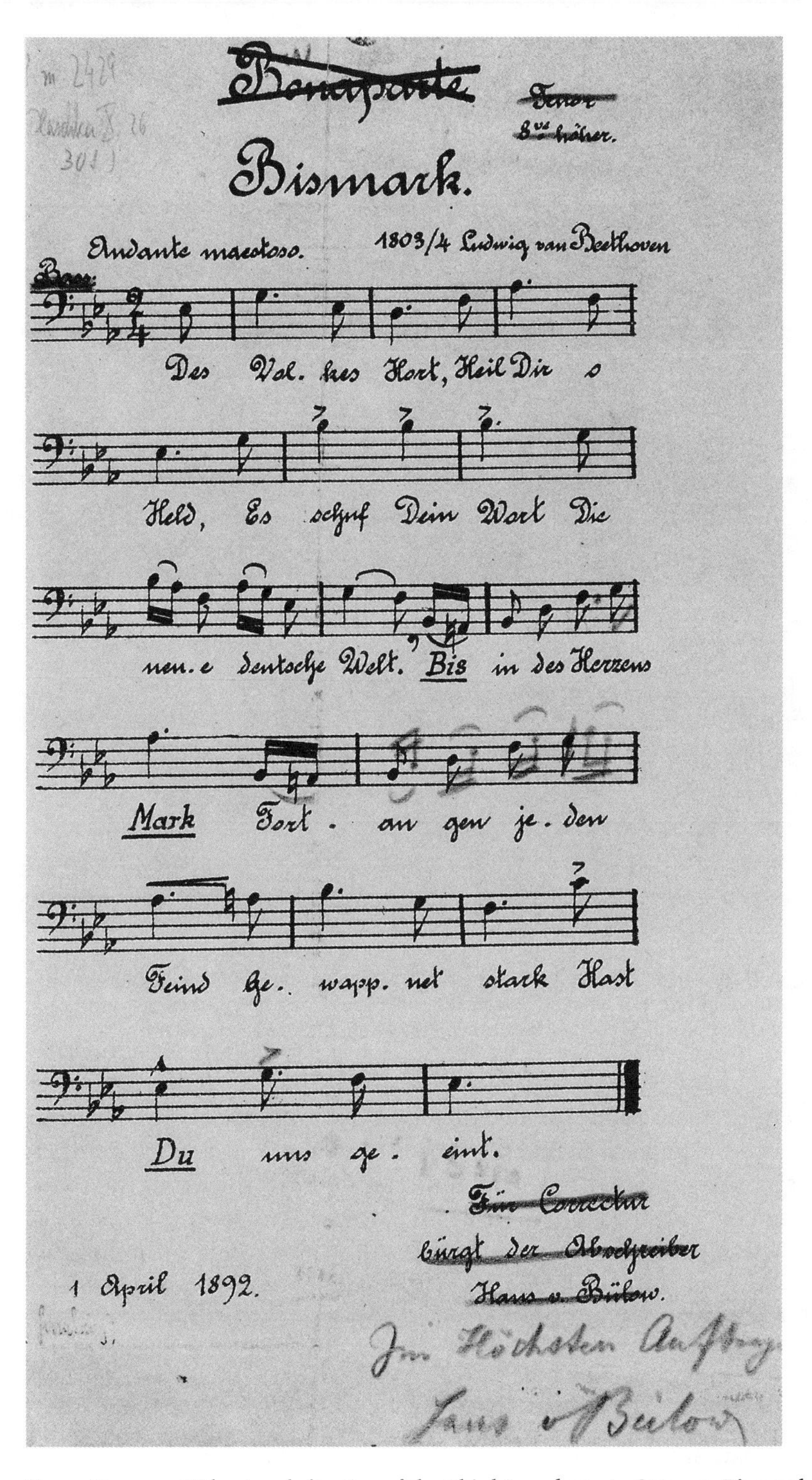

Fig. 3. Hans von Bülow's rededication of the Third Symphony to Otto von Bismarck. (Mus. Hs. 2429 from the music collection of the Österreichische Nationalbibliothek)

Fig. 4. Hans von Bülow applauded for rededicating Beethoven's *Eroica* Symphony—by Otto von Bismarck alone. (*Neue Berliner Musikzeitung* [1892], courtesy of the Staatliches Institut für Musikforschung, Preußischer Kulturbesitz, Berlin)

man audiences were accustomed to the symbolic connection. Most likely, their reaction was an expression of loyalty to the new emperor, who had dismissed Bismarck, rather than shock at anyone's linking Beethoven's music with blood and iron politics. Although the crowd disagreed with the linkage made by Bülow at that particular moment, his speech shows that a myth of Beethoven infused with exclusive nationalism thrived throughout the Bismarck era, despite the efforts of more cosmopolitan thinkers such as Nietzsche.

Beethoven in Wilhelmine Germany

That nationalistic ideas about Beethoven survived Bismarck's passing was apparent five years later, when on 21 March 1897 the streets of Berlin filled with German princes and armies marching in memorial tribute to Wilhelm I. Led by his grandson, the nation honored the first modern German emperor on what would have been his hundredth birthday. In the grandest style of fin-de-siècle aristocratic culture, every form of artistic expression was included in the pageant, especially music. Magnificent parades wound through the center of the city, with bands playing military tunes—particularly the old emperor's favorite, *Wacht am Rhein.*[64] A ceremony backed by the devotional music of Bach and Handel consecrated the Gedächtniskirche in memory of Kaiser Wilhelm. At ceremonial banquets that night, toasts were raised and songs were sung—the emperor's personal anthem, *Heil dir im Siegerkranz,* chief among them. The next day, after another impressive parade, Wilhelm II dedicated a tremendous monument to Wilhelm I in the Tiergarten, and in the evening a "gala production" at the Royal Opera House constituted the climax of the festivities. Just as on the hundredth anniversary of Beethoven's own birth, the theatrical tribute performed on this night directly associated him with the nineteenth-century political achievements of the German nation: a rendition of his *Coriolan* Overture served as prelude to yet another "symbolic representation of the German wars of liberation and unity."[65] Even after the crowning of the new emperor and the dismissal of Bismarck, then, Beethoven remained an important part of Wilhelmine political culture. Perhaps the favorite musical symbol of Germanism at the court of Wilhelm II was the work of Richard Wagner,[66] but the above-described symbolic representation and others like it show that Beethoven and his music remained widely associated with German patriotism. His compositions had become national symbols equal to those of swords and shields, high-held flags, calls of *Heil,* and the German Oak.[67]

Under Wilhelm II's rule, in fact, Beethoven's music was performed so often that many complained of its being overplayed in the concert halls of Germany. One critic grumbled that, as a result, young Germans were no longer becoming musicians: they were becoming "Beethovenians" who knew little of the rest of the repertoire. Even the music of Mozart, Hermann Freiherr von der Pfordten felt, was missing from contemporary programs. "Play Beethoven," he encouraged, "but not only Beethoven."[68] The Freiherr was not alone in protesting that all of German music society had become a "Beethoven cult"; reacting to a "Beethoven-cycle," in which the Berlin Philharmonic performed his works six nights in a row, progressive listeners—so-called music futurists—groaned against "Beethoven without end."[69]

That imperial cultural politics under Wilhelm II continued to emphasize Beethoven's music is evident in a number of examples. Numerous Beethoven festivals took place not only in the *Beethoven-Stadt* Bonn,[70] but in places such as the Wartburg Castle in Eisenach —the site of many nationalist rituals.[71] In June of 1904 a monument to the "German Masters"—Haydn, Mozart, and Beethoven—was dedicated in the Berlin Tiergarten. On it the pedestal under Haydn was decorated with a relief of dancing maidens, while Mozart's niche was embellished with a young woman strewing flowers. In contrast, Beethoven was depicted over a relief showing a titanic figure breaking free from a boulder.[72] Funded by the Prussian state, this sculptural homage to the musical legacy of the national community singled out Beethoven as a source of inner strength and willpower. Efforts to popularize his music, with the rest of the classical repertoire, were also an important part of Wilhelmine cultural policy: a series of People's Concerts (*Volkskonzerte*) at which major ensembles such as the Berlin Philharmonic and the Blüthner Orchestra performed free of charge was initiated by 1912.[73] It was at these concerts, where the general public could enjoy serious music, that some found overplay of Beethoven's compositions most irritating.[74]

Articles arguing that he represented values predominant in the empire also vouch for the continued importance of Beethoven as a political symbol in the Wilhelmine era. The *Neue Preußische Kreuz-Zeitung*, a powerful journalistic supporter of the imperial system, referred to the composer when defending Wilhelmine culture against a growing sense of pessimism on the part of some critics. A 1912 editorial in that journal insisted that the German populace had never esteemed Beethoven's music more; admitting that "to understand Beethoven the way a musician understands him is possible for only a small number of persons," the editor had "often discovered sincere joy over his music" in people he would not have considered capable of appreciating it.[75] He took this discovery—made at one of the People's Concerts—as a signal that the cultural prowess of the nation continued unabated. Other patriots associated Beethoven with the military strength of the nation as well. On the occasion of a 1905 Schiller Festival at which Beethoven's Ninth Symphony was performed, *Deutsche Wehr* (an army publication) republished parts of Wagner's "Report on the Performance of Beethoven's Ninth Symphony in the Year 1846 in Dresden," highlighting his delineation of the first movement: "In opposition to a violent enemy, we recognize an honorable sense of defiance, a manly energy of resistance, which

Fig. 5. Monument to music masters, Berlin Tiergarten, 1904, detail. (Photo: Mark Knoll)

builds until, by the middle of the movement, it is in open battle with the opponent. In this struggle, we believe ourselves to witness two powerful wrestlers who both leave the battle having proven their invincibility."[76] Clearly, Wagner's description of Beethoven's music in terms of violence, defiance, manly energy, resistance, battle, struggle, and invincibility was appropriate for the soldierly readership of the *Deutsche Wehr*.

The conservative *Deutsch-Soziale-Blätter* likewise endorsed a militaristic interpretation of this artist. Its review of his biography on the eightieth anniversary of Beethoven's death in 1907 did not begin by telling of the composer's youth in idyllic Bonn; like many in the era of Germany's quest for a place in the sun, this commemoration linked the anniversary of Beethoven's death to the centennial of the Napoleonic Wars. "Now, when we must so often think about the violent world-historical events that occurred one hundred years ago, when we remember the terrible defeats which Bonaparte prepared for the German peoples near Jena, near Enlau, and on many other bloody battlefields, now memory also recalls the words that Ludwig van Beethoven called out: 'It is a shame that I do not understand the art of war as I understand the art of music, for then I would defeat him.' What a statement! It could only have come from the mouth of a truly mighty man, who fully and without delusion comprehended his superiority. He and Napoleon—he, however, the victor."[77]

Among those who upheld the Wagnerian association of Beethoven with nationalistic ideology, Houston Stewart Chamberlain did so most vociferously. In a series of letters to Wilhelm II, Bayreuth's spokesman encouraged the kaiser to pursue his brand of *Weltpolitik* as a means of spreading German culture throughout the world. Chamberlain rationalized this policy by supplying the emperor with a list of the famous innovators who had emerged from the German race. Referring to Goethe's poetry, Chamberlain argued that "only Germany could have engendered this phenomenon." He wondered whether Kant could have been "anything other than German": though he "sprouted from Scottish blood, he had to be born in Germany in order to express his thoughts—which no form of translation can relate in English." Considering the achievements of these men, Chamberlain decided, the "highest thoughts that man's spirit is capable of can find adequate expression only in the German language."

The example that Chamberlain developed most completely in support of his argument was Beethoven. His personality and art, Chamberlain felt, best certified assumptions about the holy destiny of the German race: "Beethoven is one of the greatest powers, one of the most unmediated godlike manifestations that ever emerged from our race." In him stands before us "genius personified; the pure poetic genius; the poetry of the holy Magi torn away from all temporality, from all contingency of language and moment; pure expression; the language of the future; the language of a higher race, which lives still unborn in our wombs. Here the presence of God flames more brightly than in the bush on Sinai, and it is here—if anywhere—that we can distinguish a voice which may be His. And I ask: where could this voice sound, if not in the breast of a German?"[78]

In other writings, Chamberlain consistently presented Beethoven as a genius responsible for the nineteenth-century renaissance of the German race and culture—the process he hoped the new emperor would advance. According to Chamberlain, the history of the German peoples consisted of an ongoing fight against anarchy; the worst periods of disorder had been overcome, but the struggle still had to be waged against "Jewish socialism." Through political, religious, and especially cultural rebirth, the German race had to surmount "Jewry, Rome, democracy, free thought, foreigners, the cult of erudition, scientific madness, and pornography."[79] In his most famous work, *Die Grundlagen des neunzehnten Jahrhunderts* (The foundations of the nineteenth century), Chamberlain presented Beethoven as spearheading the cultural aspect of this battle. "The perfection of a new artistic language by Beethoven is without question one of the most consequential deeds in the area of art since the days of Homer" (also a German hero, in Chamberlain's mind); his music provided Germans with a "new means of expression, and therefore new power."[80]

It was not only in artistic terms that Chamberlain described Beethoven's contribution to the new German age. In "The Battle," the third part of his treatise, Chamberlain announced that in waging war against anarchy the heroes of order had to ignore moral issues. Great men, he argued, rarely have time to think of justice—for the most part each fights for his goals ruthlessly, without considering the rights of others. That, said Chamberlain, is a condition of life: "moral thought must not influence our judgment" in the war against chaos; "the more ruthlessly an authority expresses itself, the more viable it proves itself." To clarify his point, Chamberlain cited a jest by Beethoven, but interpreted it with deadly seriousness. "Beethoven once said, 'Power is the morality of persons who distinguish themselves from others.' Power was also the morality of the ages of the first wild fermentation [of races]. . . . These proceedings continue today, since we are in every respect still living in a transitional time." Beethoven's words, Chamberlain implied, provided German politicians with justification for applying *Staatsräson* in the battle for national, and racial, supremacy. So did his music: whoever does not recognize the "unity of impulse" in the fact that Bismarck, "the statesman of blood and iron," had to have Beethoven's sonatas played for him at the decisive moments of his life, will "never understand anything about the essence of Germans and cannot accurately judge their role in the past and the present of world history."[81]

Like Chamberlain, other German nationalists who initially championed the new kaiser later concluded that Wilhelm II was not going to fulfill world-political ambitions or overcome the debilitating effects of modern industry and technology. Such pessimists formulated a "politics of cultural despair" to express their disgust with modern German culture, and to overcome the deficiencies they perceived within it.[82] Also like Chamberlain, volkish ideologues wove references to Beethoven into their complaints about national decline. The *Neue Preußische Kreuz-Zeitung* ran the article cited above, defending the status of Wilhelmine culture on the basis of popular familiarity with Beethoven, in response to a volkish critic who complained that no one in modern "proletarian society" understood Beethoven's works any more. This cynic held that the only worthy music enjoyed by the modern Volk consisted of "a few chorales and a pair of folksongs"; otherwise, modern Germans merely "tapped" (as from a beer keg) music out of "operettas, military bands, dance halls, garden parties, and phonographs." "Who, therefore, 'posesses' Beethoven?" he asked. "In relation to the overall population of Germany, very few understand music as anything more than mere entertainment; very few—whether through talent, inherited capacity, or education—stand in any other relation to music." Modernism—in the form of popular music—was eating away at the cultural inheritance of the German Volk, depriving it of its opportunity to "possess" Beethoven. A stronger Germanic culture, argued this pessimist, would ensure that every man, woman, and child be aware and appreciative of this composer's creations.[83]

Another component of turn-of-the-century volkish thought was the pseudoscience of racial anthropology, put to use for nationalistic purposes. As in Chamberlain's statements, references to Beethoven appeared early in the development of racist theories. Racial anthropologist and anti-Semite Ludwig Woltmann claimed that practically every European cultural leader since the Renaissance had been of Germanic background. In his *Die Germanen und die Renaissance von Italien* (Germans and the Italian Renaissance), Woltmann tried to prove that all the great creators of the Italian Renaissance were Nordic. After studying descriptions, portraits, and paintings for racial features, he concluded that Palestrina was a racial *Mischling*, Botticelli was blond with blue eyes, Cimabue's real name was "Walther," Bellini had "German facial features," and Leonardo da Vinci was "the purest offspring of the Nordic race."[84] He elsewhere identified the "Germans in France": Napoleon, Mazarin, Sieyès, Lafayette, Saint-Just, Robespierre, Marat, Descartes, Montaigne, Pascal, Condorcet, Voltaire, Rousseau, Molière, Corneille, Hugo, Balzac, Zola, David, Ingres, Delacroix, Courbet, Rodin, and Berlioz, among many others. The German origins of each, claimed Woltmann, could be "scientifically proven."[85]

When staking his claim to Beethoven, however, Woltmann drew biting criticism: the journal of the League in Defense against Anti-Semitism countered his inclusion of Beethoven in the Nordic ranks by pointing out that the composer "was small and ugly, his skull was wide, his hair was black and brittle, and the coloring of face and eyes was dark." Said the defense league, "It seems to us" that if racial mixing "doesn't reduce the German race down further than to the level of Beethoven and Goethe, there is no particular danger to be feared." The attribution by racists (*Rassengläubigen*) of "all excellence to German background and all mediocrity to foreign influence," the league concluded, is scientific proof of nothing but the "mediocrity of their own thinking."[86] Thus commenced controversy over the composer's race that would continue on the margins of Beethoven reception history into the Hitler era.

While using Beethoven to transmit pessimistic and racist views, volkish critics of Wilhelmine culture also assigned him a more positive function. In one of the seminal books of volkish thought, *Rembrandt als Erzieher* (Rembrandt as educator), Julius Langbehn sought cultural instead of political solutions to the troubles of the fin-de-siècle. He chose to counter the decline of German society by heralding cultural heroes who would inspire moderns to regenerate their country.[87] As the title of his work implies, Langbehn suggested Rembrandt van Rijn as the primary role model for Germans to imitate. Though Dutch, Rembrandt was a medium, Langbehn asserted, through which the spirit of ancient German heroes would be transferred to contemporaries; from his art issued the "essence of German heroism." By applying themselves to life in the mystical ways that Rembrandt had applied himself to his creations, Langbehn felt that Germans could cure themselves of modern malaises. But while explaining the role Rembrandt played in German culture, both during his lifetime and at the end of the nineteenth century, Langbehn found it necessary to refer to other manifestations of Nordic spirituality. To clarify his abstract notions about the North German artist's mission, Langbehn often compared Rembrandt to others he considered worthy—chiefly Beethoven. Throughout his erratic arguments Langbehn consistently paired this composer with the painter, intimating that Beethoven's art was the musical manifestation of the Germanic themes he discerned in Rembrandt's images.

Introducing Rembrandt as "the model for today," Langbehn noted that until the end of the nineteenth century, not scholars but artists represented the "pinnacles of German *Bildung*": Walther von der Vogelweide and Albrecht Dürer, Shakespeare and Rembrandt, Goethe and Beethoven were the epitomes of German cultural eminence. Langbehn then singled out Beethoven as sharing the characteristics he attributed to Rembrandt. While delineating the "soul and character" Rembrandt captured in his self-portraits, Langbehn noted that both Rembrandt and Beethoven had the appearance of being "absolutely mad"; this apparent insanity, the volkish critic held, confirmed their creative natures. Describing Rembrandt as an "educator" for German artists, Langbehn contended that, if transposed into musical terms, Rembrandt's works would be painted in the same *tempi* as Beethoven's compositions. "What is more German than an adagio by Beethoven? Here we recognize our souls. Rembrandt's images are suspended in adagio; to the extent that they approach musical sensibility . . . it is a North German music and a North German melancholy that lives in his pictures. . . . A bitterness resolved into harmony fills them—like the works of Beethoven." Both artists, Langbehn went on, were at first misunderstood by their audiences: an increasingly bourgeois public had hesitated to buy Rembrandt's works, thus rendering him a commercial failure; Beethoven had composed for listeners "often more deaf than he was—especially in a moral sense." In order to revitalize their common spirit, Germans had to overcome respectable reservations and learn to accept the leadership of artists regardless of how strange or shocking they were.[88]

Like Chamberlain, Langbehn equated the depth of Beethoven's works with Germanic *Staatsräson.* Linking Rembrandt's chiaroscuro to his opinion that the soul of a North German is "light and dark," Langbehn offered the murky generalization that while the German's "politics are light, as in Bismarck's; his art is dark, as in Beethoven's. . . . He is hard and tender; he drinks stout and ale. His soul is one of shadows, nuances, modulations. And he behaves the same with regard to state duties, desires, and actions. Sometimes he moderates himself, sometimes he acts decisively; in short, he gets by. He is elastic. He always has two irons in the fire. And that is an effective political method, because it is a rhythmic political method."[89]

Summing up this perplexing characterization of the ideal German race, Langbehn once more teamed Beethoven with Rembrandt as the type of genius Germans should choose as leaders. "The Nordic artist must wring his images from the fog which surrounds his homeland. It is because of this that the music of Beethoven as well as the paintings of Rembrandt express the dark rumblings of thunder. Some [contemporaries] spoke of Beethoven's music as 'unplayable' and Rembrandt's painting was likewise described as 'unenjoyable.' That which is mystical is often considered insane, and this is a terrible mistake. The deeper the personality, the more deeply it understands the world. Admittedly, not everyone is gifted with the ability to recognize the regulations [of the world], but the genius is."[90]

As historians of the politics of cultural despair have shown, Langbehn's *Rembrandt als Erzieher* became a textbook of volkish opinion; his ravings about dead German artists who could transmit the spirit necessary to save the nation from modernity became commonplace on the German extreme right.[91] Although it was not his primary intention, Langbehn also showed extreme right-wing politicians how to integrate Beethoven into their cultural symbolism. Later volkish thinkers would eliminate Rembrandt from the lesson plan and refer to Beethoven alone as the *Erzieher* who would teach Germans how to overcome the degenerate influences of modernism, socialism, and unwelcome races.

While volkish ideologues mentioned Beethoven in their critique of modern German culture, as well as in the prescriptions they offered to counter these problems, activists on the other side of the Wilhelmine political spectrum also included references to him in their promotions. We have seen that the socialist movement developed a program of cultural politics very early in its history; but it was not until the end of the century that an extensive policy of propagandizing through culture evolved. A founder and leader of the women's movement in Germany, Clara Zetkin, also worked to organize the cultural policies of the Social Democratic Party (SPD) under the reign of Wilhelm II. Leading the educational committee of the SPD, Zetkin undertook to educate common men and women so that they could better understand the ideas supported by the socialist party; to raise working-class consciousness Zetkin arranged the publication of books, the establishment of libraries, the development of courses, the performance of plays, and the production of musical events.[92]

In conjunction with Zetkin's efforts, Kurt Eisner—editor of the leading socialist newspaper, *Vorwärts*—encouraged the establishment of festivals that included cultural activities illuminating the ideals of Marxism for the general public. Under Eisner's leadership, the *Freie Volksbühne* was established in August of 1890. This organization produced plays and concerts that poorer members of German society could attend; its stated protocol was to "make the wage earner into a self-conscious, culturally aware, and creative personality, into a producer and critical consumer of art and literature."[93] These organizers of socialist culture sought to develop a centralized system of worker education: part of their policy was to gain control of already existing left-wing cultural organizations, including workers' choirs; these were now subsumed under the party's cultural organization and guided in their programming by leading socialist ideologues.[94]

Changes in the administration of left-wing cultural activities had powerful ramifications for the reception of Beethoven during the latter part of the Wilhelmine era. Administrators of socialist cultural politics, particularly Eisner and Zetkin, wanted to make Beethoven and his music into important symbols of their party's ideals. Eisner associated Beethoven's music with socialist theory and policy in his editorial essays for *Vorwärts*.[95] Arguing that only socialist culture "unites humanity and binds it into a community, . . . smashing the boundaries of hate and the misunderstandings of peoples," Eisner evoked the text of Beethoven's Ninth Symphony: the "heavenly mood of enthusiasm," created by Schiller's exhortation that the millions rejoice, "flames the serious, exhaustive work that will lead to the day of victory for the revolutionary alliance of the world," the day when "all mankind will be brothers."[96] Likewise did Zetkin consider Beethoven's last symphony prophetic of victory for her cause; in her view, the "elementary and colossal chorus"—*Freude, schöner Götterfunken*—"emerges from the tremendous rejoicing of a freed humanity."[97] Sharing the impulse to introduce Beethoven to the working class as a comrade, both of these cultural politicians incorporated his works into the socialist party liturgy.

This consolidation is most evident in the programs of mass rites arranged by Eisner. The major festival associated with the Social Democratic Party of the nineteenth century was the celebration of the workers' movement on the first of May. As originally conceived, May Day observances were silent affairs, somber ceremonies asking proletarians to contemplate their misery. But as the tradition progressed, organizers recognized that May Day rituals could have a more positive function.[98] A principal administrator of these events, Eisner contended that they should not just force workers to meditate on their desperate state, but motivate them to seek higher things. He complained that culture was, for the most part, beyond the reach of the real people; most of them lived and died within the space of a few kilometers without ever seeing the world. Under normal conditions, therefore, masterpieces like Beethoven's symphonies—though "composed for humanity"—served no purpose. However, Eisner rejoiced, with increased working-class self-consciousness "the cultural hunger of the rejected, as well as the determination to satisfy it" were growing; and this could be seen in gradual changes to the format of the May Festival of the International Proletariat. Until the SPD arranged more lively celebrations, the proletariat had been "robbed of a jubilant May," remaining incapable of enjoying the blossoms of art, thought, and entertainment. By partaking in enhanced versions of these events, however, Eisner felt that humanity would finally begin to "conquer life."[99] As his policy statements promised, changes Eisner made to ensure that May Day festivals would heighten the aesthetic awareness of the working class highlighted art music, especially Beethoven's. By 1905, May Day festivals included performances by workers' choirs and orchestras, who prominently played and sang works by Beethoven. By exposing the working class to this music, and thereby "raising their revolutionary consciousness," Eisner strove to guarantee that Beethoven—a revolutionary composer, as he saw him—had not worked in vain.

Apart from May Day performances, the German left included Beethoven's music in other events for the working class. In 1903, the SPD initiated a March Festival to commemorate the fifty-fifth anniversary of the 1848 uprisings. As had been the case in 1848–49, participants acted with Beethoven's music resonating in their ears. The highlight of this tribute to the failed German revolution was a "Beethoven Concert" by the *Freie Volksbühne* in the *Festsaal* of a brewery in Berlin-Friedrichshain.[100] Later, at the repetition of this festival in March of 1905, occurred one of the most dramatic performances of Beethoven's music put on by the growing workers' movement. Again held in the Berlin-Friedrichshain brewery, the 1905 *Revolutionsfeier* performance constituted, in Eisner's words, the first time that the Ninth Symphony had been played "by and for the working class."[101] In an article run immediately afterward in both *Vorwärts* and the *Freie Volksbühne* journal, Eisner stipulated the ideological significance of this event. Beyond relating the details of the performance, Eisner's report formalized as SPD dogma the revolutionary interpretation of Beethoven that had been implicit in the writings of the Romantics, the early socialists, and—to some extent—Nietzsche.

Eisner opened his account by suggesting that, while writing this symphony, Beethoven had been inspired by Kant's notion that ethical decisions should be guided by the "moral law in us and the starry

Fig. 6. Program cover featuring Max Klinger's sculpture of the composer, March Festival 1903, a Beethoven concert arranged by the Freie Volksbühne in the Berlin-Friedrichshain brewery. (Arbeiter Lieder Archiv, Akademie der Künste, Berlin)

heaven over us." So conceived, Eisner asserted, the Ninth pointed toward a "sun culture" that would allow the human species to free itself; Beethoven's creative goal was to fight against the "darkness and viciousness of the daily lives of the little people." The Ninth was therefore more than the expression of lonely struggle by an individual artist that bourgeois interpreters considered it to be: "all of humanity sings in the Ninth—a humanity that will evolve into a humanitarian society in the same lawful way [that governs] the movement of the stars and the music of the spheres." The Ninth Symphony, wrote Eisner, describes moral laws that make the "revolutionary mission of humanity into a duty that will not be fulfilled until the freedom of all is achieved."

Since its composition, however, the Ninth—like the rest of Western culture—had "spoken" in vain; none of its "tones" had become "living reality in human society"; art and artist, tragically, remained powerless in bourgeois civilization. Classic German art—the greatest being Beethoven's—should be considered a refuge from the "disgusting restrictions of bourgeois existence," a place of "asylum from an insupportable existence," a "home for the homeless," where humanity could prepare to fight for liberty. But few understood art in this way, complained Eisner. To most people—to the music "public"—art was only an intermezzo, not an experience; a way to kill off superfluous time, not the rejection of a distressed and stunted existence—in short, a simple source of entertainment.

Year after year, Eisner lamented, the Ninth had served merely to intoxicate musicians and music lovers who go into ecstasy over "elegant and temperamental conductors." But, he cried, the Ninth is "no pomp and circumstance for high society and gushing young ladies—it calls the *millions* to joy, it wishes to awaken humanity." Nevertheless, he regretted, most of "the millions to whom this work craves to speak" died without knowing that such magnificence had been created for them; written for humanity, the Ninth had only reached a "public." The masses "had no idea that they were heirs to such a rich legacy" because bourgeois society had surreptitiously stolen this treasure by deceiving the rightful owners: "strangled by the yoke of work, without light, eternally bent over in the trot of slaves, they crossed the earth, ignorant, hardened, shut off from the joy which should be the calling of humanity." By Schiller and Beethoven they were told "be embraced, ye millions"—only to receive "a hug of death" from their keepers.

"But then came socialism," Eisner rejoiced. "Out of beasts, humanity had finally emerged." This could be proven, because

> on 18 March 1905, in memory of the March Revolution and of Friedrich Schiller, in a brewery in the middle of the workers' quarter of Berlin, Beethoven's Ninth Symphony had been performed for *proletarians*—for the first time in history. Up to three thousand people sat noiselessly, pressing against one another in the hot, overfilled hall, endeavoring to comprehend. One can assume that all of them had sacrificed a considerable part of their measly wages

> to finally be able to hear the work. This event was not a charitable gift of patronizing bourgeois. The proletariat has become too mature and strong to submit itself to even well-intended welfare education about artistic matters. Everywhere it strives for the highest and reaches for the stars. In the fate of its class, it experiences the drama of humanity in the Ninth Symphony. And this feeling became all-powerful when, during the choral finale, human voices replaced the speech of the instruments. From the depths flowed the redeemed feeling of joy—the millions had found the way to the Ninth, and the Ninth had found its way to the millions!

Few knew of this event, Eisner admitted: for the "bourgeois press" it had no more significance than an automobile accident. But, he exclaimed, this concert represented tremendous progress: in attendance, "modern barbarians" had formed a "congregation for the greatest artistic creation." This enterprise, he felt, was of world-historical importance—more so even than the victories of the Prussian army. It signified that art was no longer "a place of flight from life" but intertwined with life itself. Now "*Götterfunken* of joy glowed in the violent class war of the proletariat"; someday all of humanity—freed and matured by the battle of proletarian socialism—would be educated by "the world-hymn of the Ninth." Once made "the catechism of their souls," Beethoven's art "will have returned to the home from which it escaped: to life."[102]

Perhaps this concert was not the world-historical event Eisner claimed it to be; yet it did have lasting influence on the history of Beethoven reception. Here Eisner crafted the interpretation of Beethoven and the Ninth Symphony that would henceforth prevail in the writings of the German left. His demand that Beethoven's work be used as the catechism of the revolutionary soul would resound in all subsequent leftist literature dealing with the composer. Moreover, by distinguishing between the "bourgeois" interpretation of Beethoven as a great individualist and the "revolutionary" view of his music as a beacon for the masses, Eisner made Beethoven into a primary example for aesthetic theories fundamental to left-wing cultural politics; once in place, revolutionary governments both inside and outside Germany would hold up Beethoven's compositions as models for "socialist-realist" expression in music.

Eisner was not the only socialist working to integrate Beethoven into the party liturgy at the turn of the century: Clara Zetkin was equally instrumental in arranging performances of Beethoven's music to accompany SPD events. Under her direction the SPD undertook intensive efforts to make cultural events available to the workers. Many included Beethoven's music. In October of 1908, the *Freie Volksbühne* arranged a special "Beethoven Evening" featuring the Berlin Blüthner Orchestra.[103] In 1909, Beethoven's *Fidelio* was among the operatic and dramatic productions Zetkin administered as part of her educational program.[104] In 1910, an SPD-organized "Beethoven Festival" had to be repeated because of overwhelming response from party members.[105] In 1913, the fourth party conference of the Social Democratic Party of Prussia included a performance of Beethoven's *Leonore* Overture, op. 72, no. 3, by a "professional" orchestra, unlike the workers' ensemble at Eisner's event.[106] Zetkin thus acted on the sentiments expressed in her statement about the Ninth Symphony, making its composer a central symbol of the socialist program. But neither her claim to his legacy, nor those of other political activists in the Second Reich, went unchallenged.

While both left-wing and right-wing extremists used Beethoven to fan flames meant to destroy prosperous Wilhelmine society, spokesmen for the privileged formulated interpretations of Beethoven that countered the cultural symbolism of radicals. As Kurt Eisner observed, commentators associated with the social and cultural elite prepared versions of the Beethoven myth that disassociated the composer from both contemporary political issues and the historical context of his lifetime. Efforts to distance Beethoven from the social realities of modern Germany evolved with the philosophical tradition of idealism; in many ways they were a manifestation of social and political conservatism. Primarily concerned with metaphysics of spirit and history, idealistic philosophies satisfied a desire to look away from harsh realities, to isolate oneself from the problems of the masses, and to rationalize the status quo.[107] All these themes can be perceived in interpretations of Beethoven that emerged from the elite sectors of Wilhelmine Germany. Gentrified publications such as *Der Kunstwart, Der Sturm,* and *Simplicissimus* emphasized Beethoven's personal and cultural achievements without mentioning his opinions about politics and society; there was no room in their interpretation for aspects of his biography that implicated the composer in the militancy of his day. Beethoven, their analyses implied, was a hero on the basis of his intellectual accomplishments alone—he was in no sense a "political man."

In a major two-part article printed in *Der Kunstwart* in June of 1907, for instance, the University of Leipzig historian Karl Lamprecht did to Beethoven exactly what Eisner accused the bourgeoisie of doing:

he designated the composer an exceptional individual—a genius who transcended common affairs—not a model for the masses. Nowhere did Lamprecht discuss those features of Beethoven's personality that might have been shared or even understood by the average German; he addressed only his achievements as "creator-philosopher."[108] Such interpreters never referred to Beethoven as a hero for the people. Lamprecht even refused to associate Beethoven with political personages such as Napoleon and Bismarck, referring to him solely in connection with other renowned cultural figures. Like Giotto, wrote Lamprecht, Beethoven "animated the typical forms of the original images in the Old and New testaments." Beethoven "resembled Michelangelo" because in the works of both, "sensation" becomes "agitation." Lamprecht paired the composer with Rubens because they had "the same energy for expressing their feelings, the same inexhaustible sense of fantasy." One can likewise compare Beethoven's Fifth Symphony, according to Lamprecht, with the stories of Faust and Wilhelm Meister.[109] Even in those instances when Lamprecht did link Beethoven to more contemporary affairs, he carefully limited himself to aesthetic comparisons. Beethoven's late style marked him as a precursor to the tendencies of impressionism and expressionism, as (one might assume) evidenced by Max Klinger's monument to the composer.[110]

Not even the Third Symphony, according to Lamprecht, followed a social, political, or historical program. Nowhere did the historian mention any connection between this music and Beethoven's opinions of Bonaparte; what was new about the Third Symphony was that it "cast off [all] social ties to any sort of special class, be it that of the aristocracy or the bourgeoisie." The hero of the Third Symphony, in Lamprecht's opinion, was an artist-thinker, not a military or political leader. Composing according to a "grand poetic plan," Beethoven had as his mission to describe an alternative "ideal world of tones" and to indicate the "path of the genius through [our] world of imperfection"; to represent the "heroic battle of his innermost existence and its effects, the moment of apparent defeat, then the joyous upswing and final victory."

The Ninth Symphony, to Lamprecht, constituted a missive neither to humanity nor to the Volk, but solely a "monument to Beethoven's personality." Beethoven's bliss—the joy he expressed in the Ninth—was that felt in the "stillest of solitudes, in the loneliness of the creator." The composer, he was sure, found happiness only in creative effort and in "thought of God." Arguing that Beethoven had manifested the tradition of "subjectivism" that ran from Schiller and

Goethe through Ludwig, Hebbel, and Nietzsche, Lamprecht countered the socialist claim that Beethoven was at home among the people: Beethoven's realm was that of the highest intelligentsia, his habitat the mountaintop of Zarathustra—not the valley of the ordinary man. In Lamprecht's idealistic words, Beethoven was one of the "earliest who raised his eyes to the new mountains"; his melodies would "lead humanity on its pilgrimage to these mountains, until they give way to the triumphal song" announcing that the summit has been reached.[111]

The music scholar Paul Bekker was another major interpreter who considered Beethoven a guide leading toward intellectual heights rather than to a workers' paradise. Yet his 1911 book, *Beethoven*,[112] initiated a controversy that continued into the Nazi era. The ongoing dispute over Bekker's analysis focused on its "subjective" or idealistic nature. Briefly, the trouble with Bekker was that he assumed a poetic style of interpreting music compositions. As did idealists in other disciplines, Bekker found inspiration in the works of the Romantics.[113] Like Lamprecht, who in his analyses of Beethoven's music evoked such Romantic images as "unheard depths of mood," "the eruption of a volcano," an "entanglement in infinity," and "the indication of infinity," Bekker modeled his interpretations partly on those of E. T. A. Hoffmann. All were very personal reflections on the structure and meaning of the work.

Critics rebuffed Bekker's intimate approach as incomprehensible to any but the most sophisticated readers. Even *Der Kunstwart* complained that the book was simply not accessible to a general audience (*volkstümlich*); its reviewer suggested that readers consult the scores of Beethoven's works while trying to decipher Bekker's erudite analyses.[114] In the eyes of activists, moreover, this esoteric interpretation of Beethoven developed by members of the educated elite was politically inspired. By arguing that the composer had absolutely nothing to do with politics, idealists seemed to reserve his music for their own enjoyment while deflating attempts to use it to communicate with the masses. Whereas leftists such as Eisner took issue with Bekker's distancing of Beethoven from the realities of the proletariat, extreme right-wing groups were disturbed by arguments that removed Beethoven from the domain of the German Volk. Later the National Socialists would suppress Bekker's work; in 1935 even program notes he wrote for the Berlin Philharmonic Orchestra would be replaced.[115]

The evolution of this idealistic interpretation verifies that during the reign of Wilhelm II most factions playing on the increasingly crowded German political field fought over the legacy of Beethoven. By 1914 was established a variety of Beethoven interpretations, each associated with particular political or social orientations: Wagner's nationalistic interpretation, an extreme volkish interpretation, a radical socialist interpretation, and a lofty idealistic one. As competition continued within Germany over the "true meaning of Beethoven and his music," another interpretation arose from outside the composer's *Heimat* to threaten all of these. Just as cultural pessimists in Germany looked to Beethoven for inspiration to regenerate their country, Frenchmen disturbed by problems they perceived in their nation chose, strangely enough, the same hero as a role model.[116] In response, all German factions united between 1914 and 1918 to defend "their" Beethoven against the claims of national enemies.

Beethoven in the First World War

Soon after the Great War broke out, Hermann Hesse entitled an essay with the first words of the Ninth Symphony: "Oh friends, no more of these tones!" (*O Freunde, nicht diese Töne!*). Beneath this admonishment, he berated fellow artists and men of letters for contributing to the war effort. By supporting boycotts of enemy cultural products, he contended, his colleagues—who should have remained outside the political struggle—were doing as much as politicians to heighten hostilities. Hesse accused his associates of inflaming German hatred for other European nations and "carrying the war into the realm of the spirit."[117] Despite this reprimand, martial tones thundered in the cultural atmosphere of wartime Europe. In Germany, the frequency with which works of the German masters were played as part of belligerent propaganda events justified Hesse's accusations against cultural authorities. By 1915 the *Neue Zeitschrift für Musik* had already noted that wartime concert programming had undergone a severe process of Germanification—a "retreat to the especially comfortable masters and an uncommon narrowing of the musical horizon"—that excluded the works of most foreign artists.[118] German forces marshaling to attack were accompanied by bands playing songs and marches of many composers, though it is difficult to determine precisely which ones. Soldiers surely left for the fronts humming *Heil Dir im Siegerkranz*, the *Pariser Einzugsmarsch, Die Wacht am Rhein*, or Wagner's *Kaisermarsch*[119]—and Beethoven's marches may have been included as well.[120] But in concert halls, we can be certain, it was primarily Beethoven's music that was synchronized with the German war effort.

The prewar tendency to program Beethoven's music excessively was exacerbated once the fighting had begun. Lists of concerts by the Berlin Philharmonic Orchestra from the 1914–15 season through that of 1918–19 reveal that his music had priority. During the war the orchestra performed 526 different programs in Berlin; of these, 201 included compositions by Beethoven. By comparison, the orchestra during the same interval presented 80 concerts with pieces by Wagner and 60 that included music of Mozart. Even more representative of Beethoven's wartime dominance: at least 66 performances at the Berlin Philharmonie in this period consisted of works by Beethoven alone![121] By the winter of 1915, one critic believed, Beethoven's works could be heard as often as three times a day in Berlin. This nationwide tendency provoked a debate on whether "too much Beethoven" was performed during the war.[122]

There were many reasons for this situation. To judge from articles protesting against it, emphasis on Beethoven's music resulted partly from a desire to avoid controversial pieces and entertain the largest number of people. Understaffed orchestras could easily arrange Beethoven concerts during the war, since all professional musicians knew the music. Further, it was generally held that Beethoven's "heroic music" was most fitting during wartime. Given this popular attitude, the policy of inspiring Germans to fight by programming Beethoven's compositions was an obvious measure for cultural authorities to take.[123] As a result, between 1914 and 1918 Beethoven's works became even more firmly associated with military values, nationalist goals, and wartime experiences. Combined with the proliferation of Beethoven concerts in the background of battle, this linkage was strengthened by music and nonmusic journals that fulfilled their propaganda duties in part by encouraging the populace to perceive his compositions in warlike terms.

Not unexpectedly, Houston Stewart Chamberlain was an enthusiastic war propagandist, and his broadsides show how Beethoven was integrated into wartime discourse. Immediately after the mobilization, Chamberlain commenced his contribution to the war effort—a series of articles. In essays for various journals, he continued his attempt to prove the superiority of German culture, explaining his plan for German domination over Europe by referring to the nation's cultural heroes.[124] "Deutschland," written on 21 October 1914, is representative of Chamberlain's patriotic rhetoric. To follow the new course of German politics, he felt, the Volk had to discard its "shortsighted" ways and operate according to a "world-historical perspective." Poetry such as Heinrich Heine's—"sickly sentimental"—was poison for young boys and girls. The "true poets and thinkers of Germany" did not stand apart from the warriors; indeed, Chamberlain had heard from a publisher that German soldiers on the western front were carrying copies of *Faust* into battle. The great poets, he contended, openly expressed their Germanness and the desire to see their nation become powerful. Likewise, Chamberlain's argument progressed, Beethoven had celebrated after Germans were victorious at Waterloo; and "it must certainly be noted, when such a man recognizes that 'power is the morality of persons who distinguish themselves before others.'" Beethoven, Schiller, and Goethe wanted peace, Chamberlain went on, but they knew that it could only be achieved under a strong Germany. The will for peace that Germany had preserved for the forty-four years since unification, Chamberlain concluded, was not sufficient to maintain it: "Peace can only be enforced by the supremacy of Germany, the only country in Europe that seriously wants peace."[125]

Once the war began (in the interest of peace?), volkish activists such as Chamberlain were not alone in counting Beethoven among the true poets and thinkers who would have German victory at all costs; even a liberal newspaper such as the *Berliner Tageblatt* favored using Beethoven's music to inspire wartime patriotism. Published only twenty days after war was declared, a *Berliner Tageblatt* essay describing "How Beethoven Sang of War and Victory" called for use of Beethoven's music in motivational pageantry. The author, Leopold Hirschberg, started by insisting that Beethoven had been strongly influenced by the nationalistic atmosphere of his time; the only classical composer to witness "the glorious emergence of the German Volk," Beethoven always felt himself "as one with it." Because of his infirmity, however, Beethoven could not take a weapon and participate in battle against Napoleon. Nevertheless, knowing that "the soldiers in the field required music as much as they needed nourishment and sleep," Beethoven "gave the brave fighters the best he had to give: his art." The military marches Beethoven composed for this patriotic purpose, not being his finest technical work, were usually neglected by scholars and performers. As enemies threatened Germany, however, Hirschberg believed that Beethoven's martial songs had to be "awakened from their deep slumber." He proposed mass distribution of Beethoven scores to mustering soldiers, perhaps from the air. "Hundreds of thousands of copies of the songs of the great master, who belonged to both Germany and Austria, should be distributed—in flying sheets (*fliegenden Blättern*)—to the two armies of brothers. Beyond the grave, Beethoven is with his courageous compatriots."[126]

Working to revive them, Hirschberg described a number of pieces Beethoven had composed in response to the Napoleonic invasion and the Wars of Liberation, including *Wellingtons Sieg*, the *Chor auf die verbündeten Fürsten*, and *Der glorreiche Augenblick*. Most prominent among these war tunes, in his opinion, were the Third and Seventh symphonies: in the "Funeral March" of the former he sensed Horace's fateful notion, *dulce et decorum est pro patria mori*; the Seventh, he argued, was prophetically written to commemorate the victory of the forces ranged against France (which did not occur until three years after the first performance of the symphony). Hirschberg put much effort into reinvigorating another song of victory that Beethoven had, in the composer's words, "laid on the altar of his love for the Fatherland." Referring to the 1814 defeat of France at Leipzig, Beethoven's incidental music for the Singspiel *Die Ehrenpforten*, WoO 97, included the triumphant line, "It is achieved, it is achieved!" Hirschberg "hoped and prayed" that Germans would not have to wait until 1915 to be able to sing this again, that they could hold a "secular celebration" of victory before the end of 1914.[127] This wish—expressed within Hirschberg's analysis of Beethoven's music—exemplifies the attitudes that prevailed in the Generation of 1914 that went to war expecting to get home by Christmas.[128]

Another example of the martial Beethoven interpretation cultivated in wartime Germany appeared in *Der Reichsbote* under the telling title "A Musical Enemy of France." Published six weeks after the start of the war, this essay also conscripted Beethoven for the operation in the West. After briefly reviewing the story of Beethoven's flight from Grätz Castle, his refusal to perform before French officers, and his statement that he would have defeated Napoleon had he known the art of war, the anonymous author of this patriotic tract brusquely concluded that "the great works of a Beethoven are doubly worthy of our attention in these times, because Beethoven was one of the fiercest haters of the French who ever lived." *Der Reichsbote* tried, furthermore, to convince contemporary artists to be as nationalistic as Beethoven had supposedly been. Like him, *Der Reichsbote* enjoined, they should participate in the war through their art: "today's artistic greats are far less nationally disposed" than Beethoven had been; unfortunately, they did not consider it a disgrace to play for French, English, or Russian guests as he did—a little more "Germanic feeling" in the art world would not hurt.[129]

The *Zeitung der 10. Armee* also integrated reference to Beethoven into its bellicose rhetoric. "As a monstrous time broke upon Germans, as a terrible world storm from East and West raged on German lands, and when every individual was forced to fulfill enormous duties," this military publication considered it proper to contemplate the music of Beethoven. At a moment when "power of feeling, purity of sensation, greatness, and willingness to sacrifice oneself had again become holy possessions," Beethoven was the "greatest expression of the time." His Third Symphony—referred to as the *Heldensymphonie* instead of the *Eroica*—and other works described as evincing violence, blood, conflict, and fighting communicated the values of wartime. By forcing Germans to conceive his music in this way, the article concluded, the "world war would clear away the last restrictions on a full understanding of Beethoven's originality: he lives in our time as the strongest expression of pure Germanness."[130]

On Beethoven's one hundred thirty-seventh birthday in 1917, the *Tägliche Rundschau*—newspaper to the Pan-German League—reminded Germans about the celebrations that had gone on near the end of the Franco-Prussian War. *Tägliche Rundschau* writer Hermann Pfaender felt it valid to celebrate Beethoven for the same reasons during the present battle. In time of war, he argued, it was natural to "lovingly and appreciatively honor" Beethoven, since his compositions were so "warlike." They had helped to defeat France in 1814 and 1870, Pfaender recalled, as well as bring about the process of German unification; perhaps they would have the same magic effect on the present struggle. Referring to Beethoven as a "German prince in the realm of tones" who "wound a spiritual band around all Germans," Pfaender reprinted the poem that Wilhelm Koffka had written after the Battle of Sedan in 1870:

> In this moment, when our Germany
> Raises itself over all other lands,
> Should we not honor a man
> Who achieved in art that which
> Heroes of war and rulers of state
> Only now carry forth:
> He led his Fatherland to victory.[131]

If nothing else, writing this article gave the Pan-German League an excuse to dust off such propaganda from 1870 and apply it in the context of the latest conflict; clearly, the broader intention was to embellish the culture of the new war with militaristic apotheoses of Beethoven, as during the last invasion of France.

Most such interpretations were formulated in coordination with propaganda concerts that included Beethoven's music. As during the Franco-Prussian War, many official events between 1914 and 1919 featured performances of his compositions. Aside from constant repetition of his works in standard concerts, Beethoven's pieces were regularly played at special war-related performances. The first concert by the Berlin Philharmonic after the outbreak of war, on 12 September 1914, was a benefit to raise funds for the struggle; it was also an all-Beethoven evening. A reviewer in attendance found the program of the *Coriolan* Overture, the Fifth Piano Concerto, op. 73, and the Third Symphony—arranged "under the protection of the Berlin magistrate" —to be "very appropriate" under the circumstances. So, apparently, did the crowd: "every number" was "received by the overfilled house with jubilant ovations, as they deserved," reported the critic. "The whole evening was dominated by a beautiful, spirited mood."[132]

After this auspicious start to the war propaganda effort, use of Beethoven's music at fundraising events continued throughout the conflict. The Franco-Prussian War policy of performing his pieces at *Kriegsfürsorgekonzerte* to raise money for the care of the wounded was expanded during this war. Other wartime charities aided by concerts of Beethoven's music included the Fund for the Support of Artists in Need during Wartime, the Fund for Suffering East Prussia, the Fund for the War Needy, the Fund for the Families of our Marines, the Fund for the Children of Reservists, and the Fund for the Aid of War Children. Two Concerts for the Fatherland (*Vaterländische Konzerte*) given by the Berlin Philharmonic in 1915 opened with the overture to *Egmont* and the "Turkish March" from the *Ruinen von Athen*, respectively; in 1917 a "Celebration of the Kaiser's Birthday" again highlighted Beethoven's "heroic" *Egmont* Overture; and Beethoven's music dominated a *Hindenburg Konzert* on the general's birthday in 1915—the Third *Leonore* Overture and the Violin Concerto, op. 61, were both played to honor the hero of Tannenberg.[133]

Given the tradition of associating Beethoven with the ideology of aggressive nationalism that already existed in Germany, learning that patriots promulgated a militaristic view of him during the war is no surprise. It is noteworthy, however, that scarcely anyone who had previously opposed jingoistic interpretations spoke out against using Beethoven to propagandize for the nation at war; very few voiced alter-

Fig. 7. A militaristic interpretation of the *Eroica* Symphony. (*Berliner Illustrirte Zeitung* [24 March 1927], courtesy of the Beethovenhaus, Bonn)

native interpretations, especially during the early years of the struggle. As will be shown, subtle resistance to the militarization of Beethoven's image did arise as the conflagration progressed, but through most of the conflict there existed a kind of united front of Beethoven interpretation, roughly corresponding to the temporary political concords of the time.

Aside from patriotic fervor, the one-sidedness of wartime Beethoven interpretations in Germany might have been the result of a perceived threat from foreign "usurpers" who charged that Germans had forfeited the privilege of enjoying Beethoven's music. Since before the turn of the century, some Frenchmen had considered Beethoven a role model who could guide them through a period of supposed cultural decline. During the First World War, use of Beethoven as a French national symbol was heightened in France's propaganda battle against Germany; articles in French newspapers charged that Germans had "lost the right" to play and listen to Beethoven because they were behaving immorally in the war. Some French music scholars, striving to validate use of Beethoven as wartime symbol for their own nation, tried to prove that the composer was not of German origin, but of Flemish or even French descent.[134]

German editors loved to find such articles in French papers and expose them to the German public, undoubtedly hoping to pique its anger toward the Western enemy. The *Neue Preußische Kreuz-Zeitung* of 8 November 1914 disclosed a French newspaper article which stated that Beethoven's "was the purest form of French genius." The French article opened by chiding Germans for not knowing the true origins of their culture; luckily, it continued, resourceful scholars in Paris could help "dumb Teutonic bears" overcome their ignorance. Beethoven, the French article proclaimed, "was in reality no German"—he came from Belgium—but Germans could no longer expect to steal the culture of France, because it was now shut off by a ring of military might.[135] By reprinting them, the *Neue Preußische Kreuz-Zeitung* must have assumed that German readers would at least laugh at such overzealous claims, and perhaps seek revenge for this raid on their cultural patrimony.

In November 1915 the *Berliner Börsen-Zeitung* replicated a French "Call for Beethoven." An article under this title reported that the French were debating whether German music should continue to be performed in the concert halls and theaters of Paris. There were three sides to the issue, the German paper stated: "steadfast" Frenchmen who wanted to proscribe all German music for the duration of the war, "reasonable" persons who considered art "immune from political passions," and a moderate group who wanted to bar most German music while retaining some carefully selected pieces. This moderate party, according to the *Berliner Börsen-Zeitung,* demanded continued performance of Beethoven's music in particular. Its journal, *La Revue Bleue,* defended Beethoven by contending that he was of "Belgian, or more exactly, Flemish origins"; although he was born and lived in German lands, he was not of "German stamp." To prove this, said the German report, "the *Revue Bleue* pointed out that in 1792, Beethoven had written in an album: 'Do all the good that one is capable of.—Love freedom above all else.—Never betray truth.' Can a German write such a thing? Unthinkable!" This "expression of true humanity," *La Revue Bleue* had argued, proved Beethoven to be the "opposite of German," making him "worthy of being heard by French ears" because the French "are themselves the living expression of true humanity."[136] Given this scuttlebutt about the French expropriation of Beethoven, German claims that he had been a "fierce hater of France" and a "musical enemy of Frenchmen" are less jarring, likewise the fact that objections to this nationalistic portrayal were rare.

While Beethoven served as a symbol of German superiority for those attending concerts at home during the war, his music also constituted a cultural weapon at the front. In May of 1915, the Berlin Philharmonic presented two all-Beethoven concerts in the Théâtre de la Monnaie of occupied Brussels. As reported in *Signale,* these performances of the song *An die ferne Geliebte,* op. 98, the Fifth Piano Concerto, and the Fifth Symphony were not intended to improve relations with the Belgians: despite reference in this report to the "conciliatory power of music," the goal of these performances was to extend occupation of Belgium into the spiritual realm. According to the story, entitled "Art Strategy," these concerts were given "if not on their initiative, [then] certainly not without the permission of the military authorities." "It goes without saying," said *Signale,* "that the military authorities expect much of them as valuable assistance in the moral conquest of Belgium." The article continued: "nothing is more welcome in music circles than such official recognition of the power of music. There is really nothing surprising in this because, since the first day of the war, the highest official representative of 'militarism,' our military *Oberkommando,* has proven that it does not intend to limit its concern to the fighting army, but that it is striving in all particulars to give the moral factors of the nation every possibility of conserving and multiplying their forces. In consideration of the inevitable reality that the moral conquest of Belgium cannot be brought about as quickly as the military, [the *Oberkommando*] has called on all-powerful German music as a most natural auxiliary troop."[137]

In addition to seeing action in concert halls just behind the lines, the image of Beethoven was present in the trenches themselves, brought there as a motivational figure by soldiers on both sides. Some Frenchmen went into battle carrying pocket editions of Romain Rolland's *Life of Beethoven* in their "dirty bread bag, right between the copybook and the flashlight," reading it—perhaps contrary to the wishes of its pacifist author—as inspiration for defending their country.[138] Letters from German students who fought and died in the war attest that these soldiers also remembered Beethoven's strength of will as they prepared to go over the top. To many young men, the music of the German masters was the highest manifestation of the cultural heritage they fought to defend.[139] Walther Harich used references to music when conceptualizing the nation for which he was sacrificing himself. Shortly before he died on the eastern front, Harich asked in a letter home, "When does the notion of the nation come to life, erupt, and drive roots into our innermost soul?" It was "always alive," he answered, in a "peculiar mixture of the titanic force of Beethoven" and "the pain raised to playfulness of Mozart."[140]

A student from Leipzig anonymously described the significance Beethoven's Fifth Symphony held for him as he served in the artillery near Soissons. His letter home was popularized during the war in the *Vossische Zeitung* and the *Deutsche Militär-Musiker-Zeitung* under the title "Beethoven's C Minor Symphony in the Trenches." The following passage warrants full reproduction.

> Recently during the night I have gone through the C Minor in my mind: that is truly the symphony of war. The introductory measures in fortissimo are the mobilization orders. Then the measures in piano: anxiousness before the tremendous [events ahead]. Then the crescendo and again fortissimo: the overcoming of all terror and fear and the summoning of courage and unity, rising to a unified will to victory. The second theme represents our loved ones at home, their worries, their pain, and their loving favors. In the bass of this section, the first theme [is recalled]: the faraway thunder of the battle on the border; the rise to fortissimo: the rejoicing of

> victory in the Fatherland. The second part of the first movement is the war itself, the great battles. The measures with the half-notes [describe] the long waiting in fortified positions, intermittently broken by the short first theme: the violent battles for the fortified positions, like those we go through here. Second movement: the work of love in the homeland and the sadness of those left behind. Third movement: the battle, the privations, the perseverance; the trio: the gayer side of life in the field. The transition from the third to the fourth movement: the final, decisive battle. The fourth movement: victory, rejoicing, and peace![141]

Of course, few soldiers on either side of the line were capable of associating Beethoven's music with the experience of battle in this way; even fewer had the wherewithal to analyze his piano sonatas during stand-downs, as musicologist Hugo Riemann did with fellow officers.[142] It is apparent, though, that many front soldiers reared in the musical culture of the German middle class did think of Beethoven and his compositions when articulating their feelings about modern war, and that propaganda authorities—newspaper editors in particular—wanted people at home to believe that soldiers were fighting for such high-cultural ideals.[143] During wartime much newspaper space was devoted to letters of this kind, and variations on its themes.

In July 1915 *Der Reichsbote* ran a story that had first appeared in a Swiss publication, the *Journal de Genève.* It reported that a French officer had written his parents about hearing, while trying to sleep at the front in Champagne, someone playing Beethoven's Sonata in C-sharp Minor, op. 27, no. 2 ("Moonlight"). He crawled through ruins to the house from which the music came and entered; there he found a mother and her blind, blond son who had refused to leave their home despite the terrible conditions. On a piano that survived with them, the son gave the officer a short recital of Beethoven's music. This experience made the French officer cry; he would never forget the blind, blond boy and his mother, who remained so far "above the war" and its destruction.

One is at first puzzled as to why *Der Reichsbote* published this article. Depicting a French officer so appreciative of Beethoven's music countered the usual patriotic themes. Yet the propagandistic justification for retelling this story is discernible in a detail: since the article repeatedly emphasized that the young musician was blond-haired, the reader might assume he was of German descent. In the midst of war, the blind, blond, German boy and his mother were maintaining the highest of cultural ideals by playing Beethoven's sonatas, thereby impressing a French officer. Like soldiers who supposedly hummed Beethoven in battle, this family was a useful symbol of German cultural prowess.[144]

Another article associated Beethoven with the war effort in an even stranger way. In 1917 German papers reported that a Landsturmmann Beethoven had died while performing his military service. Multiple articles told the story of Beethoven's great-nephew—the grandson of Karl—who died of blood poisoning in an army hospital.[145] A desire to insinuate that had Beethoven lived during the First World War, he would have joined in the fight as his relation did, might explain the extensive interest newspapers afforded this minor war tragedy. In any case, the story provided an excuse to place a military title—albeit a minor one—before Beethoven's name, thereby reinforcing other martial connotations projected on it.

Living under an unending barrage of such anecdotes and interpretations, Germans understandably associated Beethoven with nationalistic and militaristic notions during the war. Nevertheless, some Beethoven listeners did break from the united front to counter the official view of the composer and articulate a more cosmopolitan, even pacifist interpretation. Having referred to the Ninth Symphony when at the outset of the conflict he criticized artists who "carried the war into the realm of the spirit," Hermann Hesse later elaborated his idea of Beethoven's music as a symbol of peace. In an open letter "To a Cabinet Minister" in August 1917, Hesse recalled that one evening after a hard day's work, he had asked his wife to play a Beethoven sonata for him. "With its angelic voices the music recalled me from bustle and worry to the real world, to the one reality which we possess, which gives us joy and torment, the reality in which and for which we live." Later that night, while reading the Sermon on the Mount and the words "Thou shalt not kill," Hesse decided to write to an unnamed leader of the war effort. Troubled by a speech the official had given—one that dashed hopes for a negotiated truce—Hesse ironically blamed "Beethoven's sonata" and "that ancient book" for keeping him awake. "Beethoven's music and the words of the Bible told me exactly the same thing; they were water from the same spring, the only spring from which man derives good. And then suddenly, Herr Minister, it came to me that your speech and the speeches of your governing colleagues in both camps do not flow from that spring, that they lack what can make human words important and valuable. They lack love, they lack humanity." He went on:

> Perhaps you will call my reference to Beethoven sentimentality. You smile. Or perhaps you will say that you as a private citizen feel very close to Beethoven and to all that is noble and beautiful. And maybe you do. But my heartfelt wish is that one of these days, chancing to hear a piece of sublime music, you suddenly recapture an awareness of those voices that well from a sacred spring. . . . Oh, if this hour of music, this return to true reality, could somehow come your way! You would hear the voice of mankind, you would shut yourself up in your room and weep. And next day you would go out and do your duty toward mankind. . . . You would be the first among governing statesmen to condemn this wretched war, the first to tell his fellows what all feel secretly now: that six months or even one month of war costs more than what anything it can achieve is worth.[146]

Apart from Hesse, though, few opponents of the war articulated a connection between Beethoven and ideals of world peace.[147] Even members of the Social Democratic Party who resisted the war and ultimately formed the Spartakus League omitted references to Beethoven in their rhetoric. Surely peace activists such as Karl Liebknecht and Rosa Luxemburg had little opportunity, between periods of incarceration, to develop an effective cultural-political program. Still, considering that both were honored by a fanfare of his music after the war,[148] it is remarkable that neither they nor their comrades reinvoked the image of Beethoven as cosmopolitan reconciler that had been developed by the SPD before 1914.[149]

Wartime criticism of the Wagnerian tradition of Beethoven interpretation came instead from the German cultural elite, in the context of debate over excessive playing of his music. Opprobrium appeared in the major music journals of Germany as early as the first months of battle. At that time, however, such grievances were lodged in wholly apolitical terms: some concertgoers were simply tired of hearing so much music by Beethoven. In November of 1914 a Herr Marschalk wrote to *Signale* worrying that dominance by the wartime "Beethoven cult" was detrimental to contemporary composers. *Signale* dismissed Marschalk's concerns: in times of war "artists must avoid the dangerous mines of modern works which appear on the threatening open sea of musical art and seek refuge in the safe harbors of our classical greats."[150]

After a year and a half of bloodshed, though, this issue was discussed in terms that communicated growing reservations about both the martial interpretation of Beethoven and the war itself. In March 1916 another article in *Signale* protested the "all too one-sided use of Beethoven" in war. This critique pointed out that conductor Arthur Nikisch, a noted supporter of leftist causes,[151] had warned against performing Beethoven's music to excess. A recent event had convinced the writer that Nikisch was right. The yearly concert for the pension fund of Berlin Philharmonic musicians usually involved highly innovative programming, stated the reviewer, but in March 1916 the orchestra merely repeated a previously arranged "Beethoven Evening." This was the last straw. Recognizing that the immoderate programming of Beethoven was the result of "coercion" (*Zwang*) by the "pressure of the war" (*Kriegsdruck*), this critic felt the policy had gone far enough. This music had been so incessantly associated with the war that a concert without a composition by Beethoven would have seemed a sign of coming peace. In an ironic tone, he predicted that audience members would "shout with joy, jubilant as children, over the prospect of having their musical bread served without Beethoven," inferring from this sign that "spring and peacetime" had arrived. "Would friends of music not welcome" a Beethoven-free concert "as a reference to the return of better days, as a presentiment of the joy to come with relaxation of the coercion which has been applied even to things musical on account of the pressure of war?" About wishing for peace "no one need be ashamed," the critic went on, nor need one feel guilty for condemning the overplay of Beethoven's music; these compositions contained something that would be of value in the difficult days after the war. "For this reason it is valid to warn the leaders of our Philharmonic concerts not to spend all the Beethovenian currency that we possess, but rather to hold some in storage—as the *Reichsbank* does with pretty gold coins."[152]

Guarded criticism of what the *Signale* reviewer obviously considered a formal policy reveals a growing inclination to question the militaristic implementation of Beethoven's music; beyond announcing that he was tired of hearing Beethoven, this critic quietly suggested that the music contained more meaning than was being attributed to it. Without forthrightly rejecting the martial interpretation of Beethoven's works, he implied that they might also be associated with notions of peace. Coupled with his open assertion that it was not shameful to wish for an end to the war, these statements indicate that a pacifistic view of Beethoven was germinating halfway through the war.

Within a year's time this seed of discontent had developed into more extensive repudiation of the official views of Beethoven and his music. Again, the growth of an alternative interpretation was not cultivated by active dissidents, but by members of the German scholarly community.[153] Eugen Schmitz, musicologist, composer, and onetime director of the Mozarteum in Salzburg, had earlier delineated the "warlike" aspects of the *Missa Solemnis*, op. 123, for a military journal.[154] By comparison, his 1917 essay "Understanding Beethoven's *Eroica*" revealed a stark change in opinion. Though writing for the *Allgemeine Musik-Zeitung*, among the most conservative of German music journals,[155] Schmitz modified his previously bellicose views: after three years of conflict, Nietzsche's Beethoven competed in his mind with the Wagnerian hero. Schmitz's immediate goal was to counter an argument of fellow idealist Paul Bekker. In his controversial book, Bekker had suggested that the two middle movements of Beethoven's Third Symphony could be inverted in order to more easily follow the work's "inner idea"; against this suggestion, Schmitz defended the accepted order of performance. For our purposes, the music-theoretical details of this controversy are not important—Schmitz's description of the "inner lines" of the Third Symphony is, however, of great interest.

In the first part of his article, Schmitz maintained the idealistic view of Beethoven's music as an entity resting beyond the realm of common concerns; denying that the subject of the Third Symphony was a politician or a warrior, but rather the artist-as-hero, Schmitz contradicted conceptions of the *Eroica* as a "symphony of war." He then argued that the second movement was modeled on the French operatic tradition, particularly the works of Rameau, before discussing the broader influence of French culture on Beethoven. "The intimate contact Beethoven had with the French memories of his Bonn period is easily sensed in his masterworks." Writing for a conservative German music journal, Schmitz practically verified the French claims on Beethoven; moreover, by presenting Beethoven as a product of French culture, Schmitz promoted a major tenet of the Nietzschean interpretation.

Schmitz revived other notions formulated by Nietzsche; describing the meaning of the "Funeral March" of the Third Symphony, he cited a passage mourning the sacrifices made by a creative hero. "In resignation, the hero sings a grave-song [full of] his passion and joys: 'O you visions and apparitions of my youth! O all you glances of love, you divine moments! How quickly you died. Today I recall you like dead friends. From you, my dearest friends among the dead, a sweet scent comes to me, loosening heart and tears. Verily, it perturbs and loosens the heart of the lonely seafarer. I am still the richest and most enviable—I, the loneliest!' "[156] This description of the pain felt by a hero when confronted by death was a quotation from the "Tombsong" of Nietzsche's *Also sprach Zarathustra.* Arguing that it best communicated the emotion expressed in this music of Beethoven, Schmitz implicitly disputed the glorification of self-sacrifice made in most wartime interpretations of the *Eroica.* Discussing the third movement, Schmitz again invoked Nietzsche: repeating the philosopher's call for "affirmation of life" (*Lebensbejahung*), he projected onto the music an image of the artist-hero standing on a mountain and laughing at the absurdity of the herd below.

Schmitz refused to associate the *Eroica* with literal experiences of war. Arguing that it had "in no way been the warlike or militaristic" aspects of Napoleon's character that had originally impressed Beethoven, but rather Bonaparte's "artistic" will to success, he contended that the first movement represented "not a battle, as is so often asserted, but a struggle in the soul." It was the "struggle against oneself, one's surroundings, and one's passions that the hero, the person striving after greatness," must endure.[157] Thus did Schmitz reject the martial interpretations of this symphony so prevalent during the war. Contrary to prevailing opinion, he concluded that the "Heroic" Symphony was an idealistic "apotheosis of artistic ability," not a graphic celebration of bloody battle. This article indicates that some Germans, namely those of high-cultural background, subtly asserted a Nietzschean-Cosmopolitan interpretation of Beethoven instead of the Wagnerian-Germanic one preferred by the military establishment.

By 1917 Schmitz was not alone in questioning the legitimacy of using Beethoven's music as symbolic justification for prosecuting the war. The ongoing dispute over wartime performances of Beethoven raised so much controversy by the penultimate year of the war that the conservative *Allgemeine Musik-Zeitung* ran a series of letters debating whether "too much Beethoven" was indeed being performed by Berlin orchestras.[158] Extending over three issues, this series mainly rehashed arguments that had been voiced as early as 1914. Critics of the tendency questioned whether the cultural-political demands of wartime should be given precedence over the "cultural-educational" duties of the music establishment;[159] recognizing the present demand for the "inspiration to high deeds" found in Beethoven's compositions, they still feared that the rest of the repertoire was being undermined.[160] Defenders of the policy reviewed the need for noncontroversial entertainment, easily arranged performances, and Beethovenian themes of willpower and stamina.[161]

Nonetheless, the last letter of this 1917 series did raise an issue that had not yet been openly debated, though it had been slumbering ever since the beginning of the war and the induction of Beethoven into the propaganda effort. Through most of his letter, Hans Mersmann acceded to the policy of emphasizing Beethoven's works in the troubled times, although he "didn't like too much of a good thing." In concluding, however, Mersmann wondered if it would not be appropriate to stop playing at least Beethoven's Ninth Symphony for the duration of the conflict. "Shouldn't we defer the Ninth? It has already been [played] many times this winter. I attended one of these performances, watched the public that filled the Philharmonie, and quietly asked myself whether there was no one in this large crowd, so ready to give ovations, in whose ear this highest apotheosis of joy sounded like a screaming disharmony."[162]

By pointing out the hypocrisy of partaking in the joyful celebration evoked in Beethoven's Ninth Symphony while thousands of friends and loved ones were perishing in the trenches, Mersmann voiced more loudly a notion that had remained a mere undertone since the beginning of the war. An ensemble of artists had, to be sure, sounded the same alarm as early as 1915—to no avail. In October of that year, members of the Leipzig Gewandhaus Chorus had refused to perform Beethoven's Ninth Symphony during the war, offering the following explanation: "That one should not perform Beethoven's Ninth Symphony at this time—who would dispute this? In this time when many German families are in deep mourning, we cannot strike up Schiller's hymn to joy in the closing movement. Schiller's thoughts about the coming together of humanity as brothers, which even in peacetime seem 'almost too beautiful,' must now seem even more foreign."[163] Despite this plea, the significance of the Ninth Symphony that this small group of singers attempted to impress on their fellow countrymen did not register. As Mersmann's letter attests, performances of the *Ode to Joy* continued throughout the conflagration; few seem to have considered them inappropriate, despite the humane efforts of a few scholars, critics, and artists.

Proof that the militaristic interpretation of Beethoven and the Ninth Symphony dominated until the end of the war is found in a

Fig. 8. A post–World War One *Simplicissimus* cover: Beethoven transcending a battlefield. (*Simplicissimus* 25, nr. 38 [1920], courtesy of the Beethovenhaus, Bonn)

remarkable source from 1918. Just fourteen days before hostilities ceased, the *Deutsche Militär-Musiker-Zeitung* proposed that Beethoven's Ninth Symphony be used in advertising to exhort people to contribute to the ninth "war loan" (*Kriegsanleihe*). An article entitled "Should the Ninth Advertise for the 9th?" presented the results of a survey of leading persons in the German music world. This survey had asked if such a use of Beethoven's music would be proper. The responses confirm that the patriotic version of the myth of Beethoven was firmly entrenched in the German mind. The composer Engelbert Humperdinck answered: "The Ninth Symphony as incidental music for the ninth war loan? Why not? Why not use all nine symphonies, one after another?" The conductor Siegfried Ochs wrote: "This is more than a question of the Ninth, or of art, it is a question of the existence or nonexistence of our Fatherland. . . . 'The Ninth' can and must advertise for the ninth war loan." Hugo Bock, head of the Bote and Bock music publishing house, contributed the following verse:

> The "Ninth" with its tones of violence
> Has often raised our hearts.
> The young and old, the weak and powerful,
> Have always listened, enthralled.
> Now we must consider this highest pleasure
> Which the most German tone-master created for us
> In terms of the Fatherland.
> Let your thoughts become absorbed
> With the powerful symphony of battle
> Now being waged by Hindenburg and Ludendorff.[164]

It was not until the war ended and Wilhelmine cultural institutions crumbled that interpretations of Beethoven contrary to those preferred by staunch patriots were openly professed. Although some artists and scholars courageously yet meekly voiced them during the war, most suggestions that Beethoven's music, even the Ninth Symphony, contained messages of international reconciliation were suppressed or rejected. Two months after the armistice, Arthur Nikisch conducted a performance of the Ninth Symphony in a concert dedicated to "Peace and Freedom." Beginning at midnight, 31 December 1918, this concert was meant to usher in a new era of political accord and, one might surmise, agreement over the "meaning" of the Ninth Symphony. Both of these assumptions were inaccurate: in the bourgeois press the following morning, Nikisch was criticized for having participated in this event. By performing this concert, terrified middle-class critics scolded, Nikisch and his musicians might have inspired "the proclamation of a soviet republic by revolutionary sailors!"[165] The war in Flanders had ended; but the struggle for political power and the battle over the "rights" to Beethoven within Germany had only begun.

3

The Weimar Era

When was the memory of an artist ever celebrated in such a way? Every political party, every confession counted him as one of their own; all of them fought tooth and nail to demonstrate that he belonged exclusively to their circle.
VÖLKISCHER BEOBACHTER

The streets of Berlin were chaotic in the revolutionary winter of 1919. Because of strikes, the city lay in darkness and no public transportation was available; bullets whizzed down Unter den Linden. Nevertheless, reported the conservative *Deutsche Rundschau,* the show at the Singakademie went on through one of those "sinister" nights. Cut off from electricity, the music stands in Schinkel's classically designed music hall glowed by candlelight; yet the house was filled to the last seat. Berliners had braved the dark and avoided barricades to attend this concert—of Beethoven's chamber music. "Neither power outage nor machine guns," the reviewer remarked, "could block this audience's way to Beethoven."[1]

The *Deutsche Rundschau* critic presumed that for audience members this was "much more than a concert, more even than a church mass." To these music lovers, he felt, it was a "confession to the all-powerful creative spirit in its highest form; it was like a solemn oath in which the will was pledged to overcome all hindrances and unpleasantness and gain the prize of holy genius." Performed amid "unforgettable silence and the shimmering of candles," the music "consecrated the room and the soul." At this moment critic and crowd knew what this composer and his works meant to them: "Beethoven signifies for us an educator (*Erzieher*) who will lead us beyond the wonderful garden he designed to a tremendous height with an unlimited view." There "we will feel secure about ourselves and develop, on learning his teachings, the power to control our own lives; the miracle of his existence is our most precious legacy."[2] If the views of their spokesman were accurate, this opportunity for prosperous Berliners to listen to Beethoven symbolized the hope of returning to the garden of peace and order that had existed, for them at least, before the war.

However, the high-cultural paradise envisaged by this idealistic Beethovenian and his flock was lost. The political strife threatening them would not soon end, and the vision of Beethoven as a guru who could calm modern disturbances would not be accepted by all their fellow citizens. In coming years the streets of Berlin would remain disorderly and the struggle over the precious legacy of Beethoven would reach its peak. At the same time that the good burghers of Berlin used Beethoven to symbolize their yearning for tranquility, other factions promoted less bourgeois interpretations of the composer—and used them in efforts to revolutionize German society.

In Munich on 17 November 1918, ten days after the putsch that made him prime minister of Bavaria, Kurt Eisner organized another of his revolutionary festivals, this time to mark the establishment of a Bavarian republic. Eisner was determined to inspire public order and confidence in the new government.[3] He did so with his usual theatrical flair, by arranging a performance of Beethoven's *Leonore* Overture, op. 72, no. 2, in the National Theater. For a man with such strong opinions about the meaning of Beethoven's music, a simple performance would have been an insufficient observance of the recent political transformation. Therefore, as the piece ended and the sound of the trumpet (announcing, in Beethoven's opera, the arrival at the prison of the minister of justice) still echoed in the theater, the curtains parted and Eisner stepped forth. "My friends, the tones which penetrated your souls portray the enormity of a tyrannical absurdity; the world appears sunken and shattered in the abyss. Suddenly, out of the darkness and despair there is heard a trumpet fanfare which announces a new world, a new mankind, a new freedom. In this way Beethoven saw the fate of the world. And for this reason his heart was heavy with longing through the times of his oppressed life." After this assessment of the political inspiration behind the opera, Eisner directly correlated Beethoven's overture with the revolutionary events of 1918. "The work which we have heard created in prophetic foresight the reality which even now we are experiencing. At the moment when the senselessness of the world had appeared to reach the peak of horror, new hope, new confidence is announced by the distant fanfare of the trumpets. Friends, what we have experienced in these days is a fairy tale becoming reality. . . . All who are of pure heart, clear spirit, and firm will are called to take part in the new work. . . . Freedom raises its head. Follow its call!"[4]

After this straightforward politicization of Beethoven's music, Eisner's revue continued with a scene from Goethe's *Epiminedes Erwachen* and a portion of Handel's *Messiah;* it concluded with a rendition of the *Egmont* Overture.[5] With his selection of music, as well as his excited commentary, Eisner's *Revolutionsfeier* for 1918 revived themes of Beethoven's political significance that the poet-politician had publicized long before. In remission during wartime, the association of Beethoven with revolutionary ideals and the integration of his music within the symbolism of the socialist movement had not completely died out; Eisner's dream that Beethoven would return home from the peaks of elitist cultural experience to the world of the German proletariat was realized, at least for a short time.

It was not only Eisner's erudite reveries that linked Beethoven's music to the November Revolution and the postwar workers' movement. On 2 February 1919, members of the newly founded Communist Party of Germany (KPD) made a straight connection between Beethoven's work and the harsh realities of class war. Two and a half weeks after the murders of Karl Liebknecht and Rosa Luxemburg—once the revolutionary situation calmed—their comrades gave them a memorial. In the building that housed the teachers' organization of the KPD, a room was decorated with portraits of the Spartacist leaders, as well as the death mask of Liebknecht. Inside it KPD survivors performed a service that included the recitation of a poem in honor of their fallen leaders, the recognition of all others killed in the recent fighting, and the reading of a statement by Karl Radek. To end the ceremony, the Blüthner Orchestra played the "Funeral March" and the fourth movement of Beethoven's *Eroica* Symphony in homage to the dead revolutionaries.[6]

The Singakademie chamber concert, Eisner's *Revolutionsfeier*, and the tribute for Liebknecht and Luxemburg together confirm the accuracy of an observation later made in the Nazi *Völkischer Beobachter:* all the political factions of the Weimar era endeavored to prove that Beethoven belonged exclusively to their circle.[7] After the First World War, interpretations of Beethoven that had dominated prewar German culture fragmented when every political group active in the new republic formulated its own variation. Competing for the first time in open democratic systems, each party designed cultural-political programs meant to attract voters. All these programs, including those fashioned by the Communist Party (KPD) and the Socialist Party (SPD) on the left, the German Democratic Party (DDP) and Center Party in the middle, the German Peoples' Party (DVP) and the German National Peoples' Party (DNVP) on the right, and the volkish and National Socialist (NSDAP) parties on the extreme right, contained passionate claims to the "precious legacy" of Beethoven's music.[8] Moreover, most of these groups took advantage of new technological means to spread their views of Beethoven; henceforth, German ideologues broadcast their notions about the composer via every modern medium of mass propaganda.

Leftist Claims on Beethoven

In formulating their version of the myth of Beethoven, members of the SPD and KPD, along with independent left-wing intellectuals,[9] repeated many pre-existing themes: according to their articles, speeches, lectures, and broadcasts, Beethoven had neither aristocratic nor bourgeois leanings; rather, he had been a staunch democrat and active revolutionary who sought to reform the inequities of the ancien régime and enhance lower-class living conditions. What was new about the leftist assessment of Beethoven after the war was not its ideological line but the assiduousness with which it was argued. The general assertions of Friedrich Engels, Kurt Eisner, and Clara Zetkin about the composer's life and art as revolutionary were sharpened with increased biographical detail and somewhat deeper analysis of his compositions.

That Weimar leftists refined their interpretation is discernible in their criticism of the Romantic vision of Beethoven. Before the war the left had upheld portraits sketched by E. T. A. Hoffmann and Bettina Brentano, because they depicted Beethoven as uncomfortable in respectable society and revolutionary in musical matters. Indeed, the left would never eradicate all aspects of the Romantic portrayal; articles in left-wing journals often alluded to the legends initiated by Brentano. But Weimar leftists did censure the lyricism of Romantic writing about Beethoven because it clouded the relationship between hero and historical reality. According to Willi Münzenberg's *Arbeiter-Illustrierte-Zeitung,* Beethoven's work did not conjure "some sort of 'timeless' phantoms" but "mirrored the life and struggle of his time."[10] The goal of his art, said the Austrian social-democratic *Arbeiter-Zeitung,* had not been a "cloudy and unattainable distance"; Beethoven did not strive to be "the Romantic artist or the Romantic man, but rather the new man who felt himself part of a whole."[11] Not just the achievements of a lonely, idealistic dreamer, Beethoven's titanic deeds originated from a "political yearning," asserted the Communist

Party daily, *Die Rote Fahne.*[12] By standing the Romantic portrait of Beethoven on its head, the left removed whatever similarities existed between its interpretation and the idealistic version preferred by the elite of Weimar society.

After the war, leftist critics launched a virulent attack on what Kurt Eisner had in 1905 delineated as the bourgeois interpretation of Beethoven. The *Rote Fahne* denounced the bourgeoisie for misrepresenting him as a "good-natured Philistine."[13] Rebuffing associations of Beethoven with bourgeois respectability, the leftist press denied that he exhibited any middle-class characteristics. According to one leading Weimar music critic, writing for the *Weltbühne* of Siegfried Jacobsohn and Kurt Tucholsky, his rough appearance would have shocked the shopkeepers. "How did this person whom the bourgeois public has made into its musical and human idol really look? . . . This broad and rough Beethoven with the mighty frown, the thick nose, the aggressiveness of a beast of prey, contempt for all authority not earned by spirituality: today he would be held suspect as an extreme danger to the state. . . . If members of the public had the misfortune to meet him, they would take to their bourgeois heels at the sight of this horror, this brutal fellow who could smash this era of scoundrels with a single blow from his hard fist."[14]

Leftists likewise discarded the supposedly bourgeois notion that Beethoven had been an individualist. In their opinion it was specious to idolize him as a Great Man concerned only with achieving aesthetic goals and expressing personal emotions.[15] The themes of his compositions, said the *Arbeiter-Zeitung,* "did not represent a single man, but all humanity." This paper even denied the importance of biographical information: anecdotes and legends about Beethoven and his work "are not worth the trouble" involved in repeating them, since the composer was of no interest as an individual, but only as the "representative of a community."[16] The tendency to deny the ideological content of his music, to describe it as "pure" or "objective," and to protest against reading into it "content of thought and feeling" was a cover-up;[17] his deeds were impelled by a political impulse to promote revolutionary ideology, not an aesthetic urge to create art for art's sake.[18] Of course, left-wing Beethoven lovers also rejected signs that he had been comfortable with the feudal aristocracy; suppressing all indications of Beethoven's "noble pretense," the left highlighted stories of his egalitarian behavior toward nobles to insinuate that he rejected aristocratic society outright.[19] Articles in *Vorwärts* reveled in the fact that Beethoven's late circle of friends had agreed on the "foolishness and stupidity" of the nobility, without noting that the evidence was drawn solely from a particular time in Beethoven's political development—under Metternich's restoration.[20]

Beyond specifying what he had not been, left-wing cultural propagandists also made many assertions about who, in their opinion, Beethoven was. Featuring his interest in government affairs, all left-wing literature designated him an advocate of political and social reform. Typical headlines in leftist journals read "Beethoven as Republican"[21] and "Beethoven: The Man, the Artist, the Republican."[22] Under such titles, Beethoven was portrayed as a "committed adherent to the republican form of government"[23] who "raised republican morale."[24] Variations on this theme introduced Beethoven as a "democrat,"[25] a "democrat of the heart,"[26] or the "Tone-Poet of Democracy."[27] To certify his worthiness of the titles bestowed on him, those leftists still interested in biographical information dug deeply into Beethoven's life story to find indications of his progressive opinions. Left-wing newspapers highlighted Beethoven's youth in the Josephinian atmosphere under Elector Maximilian Franz, saying he then took the ideas of the Enlightenment and the French Revolution for his own and "structured his subsequent life according to them."[28] Beethoven's early cantata in honor of Joseph II was evidence of his youthful political awareness, inspired by the emperor's struggle against the fanaticism of the ancien régime.[29]

Even smaller details garnished the leftist interpretation during the Weimar era. Arguing that Beethoven was a "democrat of the heart," the novelist and playwright Herbert Eulenberg reported incorrectly that the only decorative item Beethoven carried with him through all his changes of residence was a small bust of "the ideal republican," Marcus Brutus.[30] The *Illustrierte Reichsbanner-Zeitung,* a publication of the SPD's paramilitary organization, the *Reichsbanner* (*Schwarz-Rot-Gold*), noted that the composer had written a letter to his nephew mentioning Cato's struggle against Caesar and interpreted this as verification of Beethoven's republican tendencies.[31] Progressives also underscored records of Beethoven's interest in the English parliamentary system.[32] Oddly (because English liberalism was scarcely a model for most German leftists), both *Vorwärts* and *Kulturwille,* another leading journal of left-wing cultural politics, delighted in the fact that he considered the English system his political model and desired to visit the House of Commons.[33]

Indeed, the republican and democratic aspects of the left-wing Beethoven myth seem rather tame when one considers that they were publicized in some of the most ardent revolutionary organs of Weimar Germany. In many cases, however, these publications went further and promoted the opinion that the composer had been a revolutionary activist. More radical leftist mythmakers likewise bestowed upon Beethoven appropriate titles such as "eternal rebel,"[34] "son of the revolution,"[35] and "revolutionary at heart."[36] Some even described him as having proletarian roots,[37] as a "great man of the working class."[38] Shirking responsibility to prove such anachronistic suggestions, others contended that if the workers' movement had existed in his own lifetime, Beethoven would have enlisted without hesitation.[39] Leftist critiques implied that whether a card-carrying comrade or not, Beethoven had "manifested the revolution founded by philosophers and demanded by poets" in his music.[40] Beethoven was not an artist to be enjoyed, but a revolutionary leader to be followed toward a workers' utopia.[41]

Radical interpreters gleaned proof of Beethoven's activism from records of his relations with Eulogius Schneider[42] and his experiences at the time of the French Revolution.[43] They also gave much attention to his friendship with the revolutionary General Bernadotte, contending that their bourgeois counterparts "completely overlooked the political significance of this relationship when they represented it as having been founded on purely human-musical grounds."[44] Because Bernadotte recklessly projected his convictions, one had to assume that his relationship with Beethoven was based on shared political ideas, not just musical and personal tastes. "Whoever trafficked with him had to be of similar political persuasion."[45]

Leftists also discussed extensively Beethoven's association with Napoleon. Their deliberation over this issue entailed—primarily—dissociating the composer from Bonaparte's tyrannical characteristics. The *Rote Fahne* argued that Beethoven had esteemed Napoleon as a hero of the revolution who waged progressive wars against the feudal monarchies; for this cause the composer "treasonously" supported Napoleon's campaigns against Austria.[46] What impressed Beethoven about Napoleon, said *Kulturwille,* was his "battle against tyranny."[47] According to the *Illustrierte Reichsbanner-Zeitung,* Bonaparte was Beethoven's political hero because he raised the republic, "the most noble form of government," to new heights.[48] Leftist stipulations that Beethoven celebrated the "republican Bonaparte"[49] may seem commonplace, but comparison with assertions by other Weimar political groups reveals their pertinence; debate over Beethoven's attitudes toward Napoleon was of great strategic significance in the interwar fight for his legacy.

Another tactic deployed by the left to certify Beethoven's rebellious inclinations was constantly to retell Bettina Brentano's version of the Teplitz Incident.[50] Aware that the authenticity of Brentano's letters was in question, leftist interpreters still continued to use them to demonstrate Beethoven's defiance of aristocratic society; many presented the story of his untamed behavior in front of Goethe as proof that Beethoven had been a "revolutionary at heart."[51] While few who reproduced the anecdote bothered to defend its use, most leftist writers would have agreed with the rationale proposed by the musicologist Karl Nef. Nef argued that although the authenticity of the letter to Brentano was doubtful, "genuine or not, it did not come out of thin air"; true or false, he insisted, "the sense and spirit of Beethoven correspond to this scene."[52] In spite of its dubious origins, therefore, Brentano's tale remained an integral part of the leftist interpretation of Beethoven.[53]

Alongside their versions of Beethoven's life, leftist intellectuals popularized ideas about his music that served their cultural-political purposes. In general, Beethoven's music was interpreted by leftists as having been democratic or revolutionary because it "raised the spirits of all peoples," including the struggling and the poor,[54] and glorified a "general love of mankind."[55] This broad politicization of Beethoven's music was explained, by some, in musicological terms. More sophisticated analysts such as the composer Kurt Weill, writing for the *Sozialistische Monatshefte,* maintained that Beethoven's was "music of freedom" because he had burst the conventional sonata form, thereby freeing music from the constraints of classical structure and opening the way for modernist expression.[56] Other leftists—following the interpretive lines laid by Kurt Eisner—did not hesitate to project more literal political messages onto the compositions of Beethoven. Rejecting as bourgeois the assumption that music was an art whose "material, political, and economic background is not easily established," they theorized that the musician's power to create was "determined by and dependent on the real world in which he lived and worked."[57] Thus did most leftist cultural politicians consider it valid to associate Beethoven's music with political ideas and events, with or without evidence that the artist intended to make such connections.[58]

Liberated from methodological reservations, Weimar radicals proclaimed that the source of Beethoven's sensitivity was the social

Fig. 9. Thomas Ring, illustration for Kurt Weill article, "Beethoven und die Jungen," *Sozialistische Monatshefte* (March 1927). (Courtesy of the Beethovenhaus, Bonn)

idealism of his day; they insisted that his free use of musical forms was equated in his mind with the struggle for freedom from political slavery.[59] More precisely, said the *Arbeiter-Illustrierte-Zeitung*, his music was the "perfect expression of the most important epoch of history: the French Revolution."[60] Why had the composer not more explicitly explained that he considered his music a medium for spreading political ideology? Under the repression of the Metternichean system, the *Rote Fahne* divulged, Beethoven and others like him expressed their revolutionary impulses in music because they would have been punished had they put them in writing.[61]

Leftist interpreters elucidated specific compositions in comparable terms. The focus of many discussions in left-wing publications was his Third Symphony. Assuming that Beethoven had wanted to honor Bonaparte as a hero of freedom, leftists represented the *Eroica* as a revolutionary work.[62] Throughout their references to the Third, leftist journals implied that the "program" of the symphony was purely political. According to the *Rote Fahne*, this symphony can be correctly understood only in relation to the following "fundamental ideas." In the first movement, "the stormy, eventful battle of the revolution is characterized with powerful, manly rhythms and violent fanfare." Here and there these recede to allow "timid moments of stillness and retreat, only to scream forth all the more stormily" later. The "Funeral March" expressed "grief over the fallen victims of the revolution" although, in the midst of the mourning, "the victorious idea of their struggle is announced and the path to new battles breaks open." Interwoven with popular dance tunes, the third movement depicts "something of a rest period for the revolutionaries amid the joyous Volk." Finally, "the closing part is an energetic cry of jubilation upon the success of the revolt" in which "the wild revolutionary melody of the *Carmagnole* sounds unmistakably" (although Beethoven changed it somewhat—"as a precaution against the Austrian censors").[63]

Reference to the political significance of the Third Symphony required additional comment on the legend of its rededication. Left-wing mythmakers were happy to repeat Beethoven's outraged reaction to Bonaparte's self-crowning: his subsequent rechristening of the work changed nothing, it was still written "to a hero of freedom."[64] Some on the left, however, felt it imperative to remind people that it was not Beethoven, the German nationalist, but Beethoven, the political reformer, whose ideals Napoleon had betrayed.[65] Again, the reason leftists reiterated this will become clear below, when the explanations of other Weimar ideologues are discussed.

A left-wing elucidation of the Fifth Symphony illustrates how Weimar radicals refined interpretations by earlier leaders of the workers' movement. In an article marking Beethoven's one-hundred-fiftieth birthday, the *Rote Fahne* suggested that when Friedrich Engels wrote about Beethoven in his "Notes on Germany," he had been waiting for the poetic or visual expression of the revolutionary impulse of his time. While listening to Beethoven's music, Engels perceived that "the great longing of the eighteenth and nineteenth centuries would not be fulfilled in poetry," even though it was the richest and most versatile genre of art. Rather, "titanic expression of the not yet comprehensible perceptions of the time" came in music. "I heard Beethoven! It was tremendous!" wrote Engels upon realizing this, according to the *Rote Fahne* article.[66] Closer investigation reveals, however, that while enthusiastic about Beethoven's compositions, especially the Fifth Symphony, Engels had been ambiguous about the political significance he attributed to the music. In "Notes on Germany," Engels had expressed admiration for Beethoven's ability to create while his people were "under the yoke of the Emperor Napoleon," but he did not discuss Beethoven as a harbinger of revolutionary ideology. By implying that Engels thought Beethoven had understood the basic emotional content of the socialist program before a written doctrine existed, *Rote Fahne* writers exaggerated their precursor's interpretation.

Another work leftist interpreters declared prophetic was Beethoven's Ninth Symphony. According to *Vorwärts,* the Ninth was the "last confession of a man of freedom, driven by the highest of social impulses," a dream that "all mankind will become brothers."[67] In the pages of the *Arbeiter-Illustrierte-Zeitung,* the Ninth was the work of a "proud freedom fighter" of proletarian origins who "suffered under the 'holy' world order until his death."[68] *Kulturwille* deemed the *Chorale* Symphony a strong expression of egalitarian principles, since it suggested that even the *Wurm* would attain joy.[69] *Die Menschheit* assessed the Ninth as the "prelude and harbinger of a time yet to come, of a great future for humanity."[70] If the leftist interpretation were accurate, though, the great future predicted in the Ninth would not be enjoyed by all members of German society: only "brothers" of proletarian origins could join the *Wurm* in Beethoven's utopia. To clarify this distinction on the one-hundredth anniversary of the work's premiere, *Vorwärts* disclosed that the royal box of the Vienna Kätnerthortheater had remained empty during the first performance. By reporting this fact, the socialist paper implied that the music was so critical of monarchy that the royal family would have been uncomfortable had it attended the concert. Without mentioning that he had dedicated the Ninth Symphony to Friedrich Wilhelm III of Prussia, *Vorwärts* insisted that Beethoven had "no respect for monarchical thrones" and had not composed the work for the enjoyment of the aristocracy.[71]

Still, purveyors of these views admitted that even the working class had to wait to experience the jubilant scenes and sensations presaged in the Ninth Symphony. A millennial view of the Ninth was often articulated in the writings of the left. The Viennese *Rote Fahne* warned that only after struggling relentlessly, applying the willpower of a Beethoven, and overcoming manifold difficulties would humanity "first be able to truly experience this music."[72] The *Vorwärts* article commemorating the centennial of the premiere also promoted this notion: "We have no reason to give up our joy of life. The torch of the Ninth Symphony of Beethoven will light our way. Whenever and wherever people gather in the honor of Freedom, it will remain lit, until a larger, better portion of the world is freed from drudgery, misery, and need, and until we can all risk, knowing in our conscience that we have done our social duty, calling out to Joy: 'Drunk with fire, oh heaven-born goddess, we invade thy holy realm' (*Wir betreten feuertrunken, Himmlische, dein Heiligthum*)."[73]

The revolutionary composer Hanns Eisler—onetime student of Arnold Schönberg—expressed this idea potently in an oft-cited article on Beethoven for the *Rote Fahne.* "When this powerful Hymn to Joy bubbles up, climbs, and ends in jubilation, every class-conscious worker, filled with strength and confidence, can and must say to himself that these tones which now provide fighting workers with energy will only truly belong to us when we defeat the ruling class. Then the masses of oppressed millions will cheer with Beethoven's song of triumph: Be embraced, ye millions! (*Seid umschlungen, Millionen*)"[74]

Besides the major symphonies, other works by Beethoven were also associated with revolutionary ideals; emphasized were the composer's best-known compositions, but no composition was immune to politicization. *Fidelio,* said to depict the "action of the French Revolution,"[75] was tagged a "manifesto against the feudal aristocracy."[76] The *Egmont* Overture was touted as the "true high-song of freedom" for describing the liberation of a people.[77] Many of Beethoven's songs, including the *Opferlied,* op. 121b, and *Der freie Mann,* WoO 117, were said to represent the composer's republican tendencies.[78] Even late works such as the *Missa Solemnis*[79] and the last quartets, usually neglected by politically oriented interpreters, were mentioned in Weimar descriptions of Beethoven as a revolutionary pathbreaker in music.[80]

The goal was twofold: to anchor leftist doctrine in German cultural tradition and to transform stories about Beethoven and his compositions into symbols communicating the basic tenets of social-democratic, socialist, and communist ideologies. Once Beethoven's music was widely understood in these terms, it would motivate audience members to act out the prescribed political plans. Leftist journals did much to guide the working-class music listener, telling proletarians exactly what to feel upon hearing Beethoven's music. Based on the oft-heard declaration, triumphantly voiced by Hanns Eisler, that "his music belongs to us"[81] and not to "those who try to appropriate him on the basis of their economic and political hegemony,"[82] leftist interpreters assured that the proletariat was "closer" to Beethoven than to any other composer.[83] If the general populace were given opportunities to hear Beethoven's art, it would help unite the working class into a community—just as chorales did in the churches.[84] Listening to and following the ideals supposedly expressed in Beethoven's music, workers would march toward a new and joyous future. In their present state they could experience joy only vicariously in Beethoven's music, but if they contributed to the revolutionary effort they would soon have it in their own lives.[85]

Successful execution of this cultural-political master plan demanded more than simply laying out its thematic framework in articles and essays. Left-wing organizations strove to transmit their propagandistic interpretation of Beethoven by every means at their disposal; they provided their followers with many performances of Beethoven's music, supplementing these with introductory lectures, educational programs, instructive speeches, and radio broadcasts. Since the turn of the century, a majority of workers' choirs had been incorporated into the centralized organization of the Association of German Working-Class Singers (*Deutsche Arbeiter Sängerbund,* or DAS). After the war this organization continued its tactic of appropriating the "best" traditional German music for use in revolutionary political culture.[86] Throughout the Weimar era, choirs under its authority added more and more classical music to their repertoire. By 1933 the DAS had entered a large number of Beethoven's songs and choral works onto its lists, some with texts altered to be more "pertinent." The "worker-poet" Ernst Preczang provided new words for the song *Die Ehre Gottes aus der Natur* (The glorification of God by nature), op. 48, no. 4, renaming it a "Hymn to Life."[87] Other compositions printed by the DAS publishing house and performed by its choirs—in original or adulterated form—included Beethoven's *Gesang der Mönche,* WoO 104, *Opferlied, Bundeslied,* op. 122, *Elegischer Gesang,* op. 118, *Der freie Mann, Ruinen von Athen, Der glorreiche Augenblick, Christus am Oelberge,* op. 85, and the Mass in C Major, op. 86.[88] DAS choirs also performed Beethoven's larger vocal works regularly; often joining with established groups such as the Blüthner Orchestra in Berlin and the Gewandhaus Orchestra in Leipzig,[89] workers' choirs pooled resources to present major pieces such as the *Missa Solemnis* and the Ninth Symphony.[90]

Proletarian audiences also had access to Beethoven's instrumental music. Organizations dedicated to the education of workers, such as the *Volksbühne* and the *Arbeiter-Bildungs-Institut* (ABI), produced

Fig. 10. The Lichtenberger Propaganda Orchestra of the German Communist Party on an outing to Hölzern See. (Arbeiter Lieder Archiv, Akademie der Künste, Berlin)

chamber and full orchestral concerts for their memberships; these included complete cycles of Beethoven's sonatas, quartets, and symphonies.[91] Even the *Rote Frontkämpferbund*—the Fighting Alliance of the German Working Class—arranged evenings of Beethoven's chamber music for its members.[92] Moreover, persons of the working class, especially youths, were encouraged to make music themselves. "Workers Symphony Orchestras," such as the Lenin-Orchestra in Hamburg, the Karl-Liebknecht-Orchestra of Berlin, and the Lichtenburger Propaganda Orchestra of the Communist Party, were founded in the twenties and thirties, and Beethoven's music was an important part of their repertoire. The Lichtenberger Propaganda Orchestra played mainly workers' songs on mandolins, guitars, trumpets, and violins, but it also arranged pieces by Mozart and Beethoven for performance on these instruments.[93]

In addition to concerts for the entertainment and general enrichment of the working classes, the revolutionary vanguard devised rites and festivals of chiefly political import. Beethoven's music was a prominent element in these ceremonies too. Important examples, including the *Friedens- und Freiheitsfeier* conducted by Arthur Nikisch, the inaugural celebration of the Bavarian Republic produced by Kurt

Eisner, and the memorial for Karl Liebknecht and Rosa Luxemburg, have already been mentioned. Records of other symbolic leftist events featuring Beethoven's music confirm that this was a general practice. SPD festivals in smaller towns, especially party "youth consecrations" (*Jugendweihen*), were often enhanced by Beethoven's chamber music; in large cities these rituals were backed by full orchestras.[94] In 1919 the *Volksbühne* established a tradition practiced in German leftist circles until at least 1989: New Year's Eve performances of Beethoven's Ninth Symphony to ring in the coming (revolutionary) year.[95] On 21 September 1920 a concert featuring Russian songs from the Revolution of 1905 began, curiously, with the playing of a Beethoven quartet.[96] Throughout the Weimar era, the conductor Rosebury d'Arguto —whose essays often appeared in the communist journal *Weltrevolution*—arranged concerts for the benefit of political prisoners. In them d'Arguto performed songs of Beethoven augmented with more "relevant" political texts from his own pen.[97] And starting in 1925, the DAS instituted a new *Revolutionsfeier,* this time to mark the anniversary of the November Revolution of 1918: each year the culmination of this festival was a performance of Beethoven's Ninth Symphony.[98]

Apart from revising the texts of his songs, leftist promoters tried to control audience comprehension of Beethoven's music by supplementing performances with written or spoken commentary. Organizers regularly provided concertgoers with program notes insisting on the revolutionary significance of the compositions. Moreover, they frequently arranged "lectures on the work and significance of the master" to precede the performances.[99] Aiming at the same goals, leftist parties proposed extensive music education programs. The *Volksbühne* was the leading organization in this effort. Leo Kestenberg, among other things an important *Volksbühne* director during the Weimar era, considered his mission to be the introduction of music to those who had no regular access to serious compositions. In his opinion, serious music had been needlessly separated from the populace during the feudal and bourgeois epochs; his goal was to form a broad community on the basis of common musical experiences, thus overcoming the individualistic culture of the bourgeoisie and contributing to the development of a socialist society.[100] Kestenberg considered Beethoven's music crucial to this effort: it was he who argued that shared experiences of Beethoven's compositions, like church chorales, could unite people into a community.[101] A primary job of the *Volksbühne* was, therefore, to make Beethoven's "language" accessible to the poor and burdened; in this way, everyone could develop some of the courage demonstrated by the composer.[102] Only when this was achieved, Kestenberg felt—referring to the text of the Ninth Symphony—would the "kiss" of Beethoven and Schiller finally touch the whole world.[103] To realize this goal, Kestenberg exhorted the *Volksbühne* to induce the whole working class to participate in festivals of Beethoven's music. Concerts, he decreed, had to mitigate the formal aspects of the classical music world and make working-class citizens feel welcome; lectures and program notes were to emphasize Beethoven's "thoughts of community." At the same time, Kestenberg planned People's Music Schools, People's Singing Schools, and Young Persons' Music and Orchestra Schools.[104]

Kestenberg and others like him carried out some of these designs in the activities of leftist party organizations, but real opportunities to apply such notions came when the left wing attained positions of political leadership in Weimar Germany. When the SPD headed the government, as in 1920, socialists instituted educational reforms on a nationwide basis. That year the Ministry of Education ordered the establishment of music-education programs—including festivals of Beethoven's music—in all German schools.[105] Kestenberg ultimately advanced to the Prussian Ministry of Science, Culture, and Education, where he instituted a series of modifications still known in German music-educational circles as the Kestenberg Reforms. That these reforms were oriented to leftist political aims is evident in the response of opponents who derided them as "social-democratic cultural politics."[106]

Intense efforts by left-wing groups to expose the German public to their version of the Beethoven myth occurred in 1927. During the centennial year of the composer's death, German political parties deployed every possible means to substantiate their contradictory claims to the legacy of Beethoven, prompting the observation that "every political party, every sort of confession" competed to count him as one of their own. Left-wing exertions in this competition were strenuous; the above discussion of how leftists regarded Beethoven is based largely on essays and articles produced by revolutionary journals in this effort. To commemorate the anniversary, moreover, the *Volksbühne* sponsored numerous performances and educational events: in Breslau, the Ninth Symphony was performed after an introductory lecture;[107] in Solingen and Barmen-Elberfeld, Beethoven's quartets were played for workers attending classes at the *Volkshochschulen*.[108] Most dramatic were performances of Beethoven's works arranged by the DAS. Throughout the nation in March of 1927, German workers' choirs gathered to form mass choruses and sing Beethoven's choral works for huge audiences: in Erfurt, a thousand "proletarian singers" performed his music on the steps of the cathedral before many thousands of listeners;[109] in Schmalkalden, DAS choirs sang in the marketplace;[110] in Stuttgart, six hundred members of the DAS gathered to present their rendition of the Ninth Symphony to an audience of over ten thousand.[111] The journal of the DAS, the *Deutsche Arbeiter-Sängerzeitung*, reported on more than seventy Beethoven festivals arranged and performed by workers' music groups across the land between March and May of 1927.[112]

Not all the *Todestag* commemorations arranged by leftist organizations went smoothly. On 26 March 1927 a performance of Beethoven's *Bundeslied* by the Berlin chapter of the DAS was to occur on the steps of the Reichstag. But the concert had to be moved to the Altes Museum in the Lustgarten because the minister of the interior, a member of the conservative DNVP party, forbade the use of the Reichstag for this event; he claimed that the facility was reserved for parliamentary business alone. Shortly before, however, this minister had allowed rightist paramilitary groups to honor General von Hindenberg with a ceremony there. This inconsistent application of the law infuriated left-wing music organizations; journals decried this "blockade" as a cultural-political maneuver by reactionary imperialists (*Schwarz-Weiß-Rotern*).[113]

In those locations where parties on the left were in control, however, government-sponsored events promoted leftist interpretations. Evident in celebrations throughout Germany, this trend was especially evident in neighboring Austria where the Social Democrats governed in 1927.[114] Under their authority the date was observed almost as a national holiday: the Austrian centenary lasted six days and included many concerts, exhibitions, and colloquia;[115] Austrian schools were advised to organize lectures on Beethoven and, when possible, performances of his music;[116] government offices were closed and adorned with national flags.[117] Central was the opening ceremony in Vienna's Großer Musikvereinssaal, where representatives of thirteen nations gathered to praise Beethoven. Published in Austrian and German newspapers, these statements were all colored by the national interests of the officials who formulated them: the French socialist minister of education, Edouard Herriot (himself an author of works about the composer), announced his conviction that France had the same passion for freedom that Beethoven had expressed in his music; the Italian representative, Pietro Mascagni, used the opportunity to

Berlin
den 9. April 1927

Illustrierte Reichsbanner Zeitung

Preis 25 Pf.

Erste republikanische illustrierte Wochenschrift

4. Jahrgang
Nr. 15

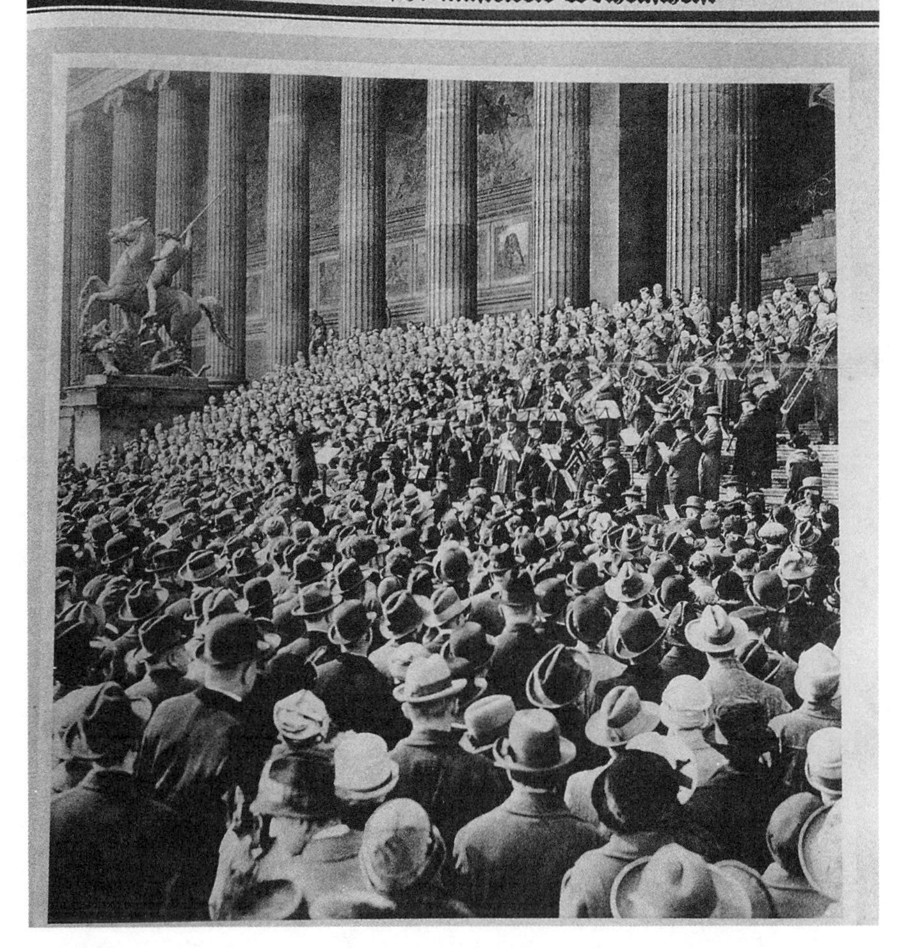

Fig. 11. German Working-Class Singers Association (DAS) observing the one-hundredth anniversary of Beethoven's death on the steps of the Altes Museum in Berlin, *Illustrierte Reichsbanner Zeitung* (9 April 1927). (Photo: Mark Knoll)

praise his country's leadership by declaring that *Il Duce* had, among his other gifts, deep understanding of music and therefore genuine respect for Beethoven.[118]

Likewise the Austrian hosts took this opportunity to connect their platform to the Beethoven celebrations; representing a government that supported a foreign policy of reconciliation and cooperation, Austrian spokesmen communicated a benevolent message to their guests.[119] The Social Democratic mayor of Vienna, Karl Seitz, spoke of Beethoven's music in toto as a "Song of the Love of Man," while asserting that the Viennese would live up to the honor of being caretakers of the "holy ground" upon which the "Composer of Freedom and Love" had walked.[120] Federal President Michael Hainisch made his hopes for international cooperation even clearer: "After the destruction of the war and a long period of conflict, mankind looks with all its heart for any chance of true unity"; music is one unifying element, "especially Beethoven's music, which expresses a universal ethos in its highest form." "Men like Beethoven do not belong to Vienna or to the German Volk alone, but to all mankind."[121] As will be seen, Pan-German nationalists would attack Hainisch's association of the composer with "internationalist" views as a grossly inaccurate politicization of Beethoven's "message"; opposing Hainisch meant rejecting his interpretation of Beethoven as well.

Members of the Austrian left broadcast their ideas about Beethoven to the public by the most modern means available, radio. Radio transmission made Beethoven concerts, along with the speeches at the Großer Musikvereinssaal, accessible to the broadest possible public—in Austria and Germany both. This programming received rave reviews in the *Arbeiter-Zeitung*. The workers' paper rejoiced that hundreds of thousands of Germans and Austrians had experienced the celebration over the airwaves. Many, the *Arbeiter-Zeitung* surmised, had probably heard the *Missa Solemnis*, the Choral Fantasy, op. 80, the Fifth Symphony, and *Fidelio* for the first time in their lives on these broadcasts: "radio and the cultural policies of the Social Democratic government" had "brought Beethoven to the masses." Together they had "overcome reactionary opposition" to make Beethoven into what he had most wanted to be: "a purveyor of art for the people."[122]

Over the radio, through publications, at concerts, in classrooms, and in speeches, leftist politicians ensured that German-speaking multitudes experienced the 1927 Beethoven celebrations. Throughout the interwar period, socialist and communist cultural politicians did everything they could to "bring Beethoven to the masses." It

Fig. 12. Italian politicians at Beethoven's gravesite during the Vienna commemorations of the composer's one-hundredth Todestag. (*Illustrierte Kronen-Zeitung* [30–31 March 1927], courtesy of the Beethovenhaus, Bonn)

was not, however, the historical Beethoven whom they introduced to the people, but a portrait designed according to their propagandistic needs. No one could deny that the composer's recurring "revolutionary fever" had inspired some of his music, but left-wing ideologues introduced such compositions without indicating that Beethoven made statements and produced other works that communicated contradictory political attitudes. Though not wholly inaccurate, the leftist presentation of Beethoven's life and music was carefully formulated to serve party interests. It did not stand unopposed.

Centrist Idealizations of Beethoven

Just months before his murder, in his first speech to the Reichstag on assuming the position of foreign minister in February of 1922, Walther Rathenau also made a powerful reference to Beethoven. Explaining his policy of fulfilling the terms of the Versailles Treaty (*Erfüllungspolitik*), the former head of the *Allgemeine Elektrizitäts-Gesellschaft* (AEG) and leader of the German Democratic Party (DDP) reminded his audience of the question that Beethoven had written over the last movement of his String Quartet in F, op. 135: "Must it be?" Without saying that Beethoven had posed the question in jest over the payment of a small debt, Rathenau projected serious meaning onto this programmatic heading.[123] Just as the composer had to struggle with the terrible personal and professional hindrance of deafness, Rathenau implied, Germans were destined to comply with Allied terms. Like Beethoven, Germans had to answer "It must be!" and resign themselves to pay all war reparations. "Whoever approaches his task without that 'It must be!'" Rathenau concluded, is only half committed to solving Germany's problems.[124] Rathenau's use of Beethoven's words to symbolize the theme of stoicism was a common practice of parties in the center of German politics during the Weimar period. Germans who feared the specter of revolution—Bolshevik and otherwise—preached the need for patience and endurance, apparently hoping to stem further insurrection.[125] Reversing the propaganda project undertaken by the Weimar left, parties such as the DDP and the Center Party employed the myth of Beethoven to inspire political *inaction.*

The interpretation of Beethoven favored by republicans of reason (*Vernunftrepublikaner*) was the idealistic version developed in the years preceding the First World War.[126] Once more, this esoteric interpretation can be seen as a counter to views of Beethoven proposed by radicals; instead of highlighting the composer's concern for the issues of his day, the idealistic interpretation contained little discussion of Beethoven's political outlook. Duplicating abstract arguments of the prewar cultural elite, Weimar-era high society presented Beethoven as a model for spiritual strength in difficult times, but not as a man who had notions about social reform. Sophisticated Weimar publications such as *Der Querschnitt, Der Kunstwart, Der Reichsbote, Westermanns Monatshefte, Germania,* the *Berliner Tageblatt,* the *Vossische Zeitung,* the *Berliner Börsen-Zeitung,* and the *Deutsche Reichs-Zeitung* introduced Beethoven as a "poet in tones,"[127] a "magician,"[128] a "musical philosopher,"[129] even a "priest of true religion,"[130] but never as a political activist. His "deeds" were of hallowed aesthetic or philosophical significance, not strategic value. "Like Goethe, Nietzsche, and in a certain sense Tolstoy," said *Germania,* the main journal of the Center Party, Beethoven's principal achievement was to "channel human desire into ideal metaphysical fulfillment." His "musical consignment" (*musikalische Sendung*) did not include the power to affect history or achieve practical results, but rather to "shape the ethos of humanity, to rupture material inhibitions," thereby revealing the "absolute essence of appearances" and the "final sense of all things."[131]

In a 1920 speech on "Beethoven and German Idealism," the musicologist Arnold Schering put this visionary interpretation into somewhat less ambiguous terms. He reduced the idealist view to two major points: first, Beethoven tried to relate in music concepts that came to him "in a poetic way"; second, he set goals or ideals for himself and strove to live up to them in his art and life. Both of these tendencies marked him as a "German idealist."[132] Thus did Schering try to clarify some of the more nebulous references to the artist's inspirational sources and "moral system"; but he did not overcome the tendency of like-minded interpreters to represent Beethoven as an unearthly creature instead of a human being. Beethoven, the historical persona, was very difficult to perceive in idealist treatises; most described him as having existed somewhat outside the realm of common experience. In an article imprecisely titled "Beethoven: The Person," the *Deutsche Reichs-Zeitung* argued that data about his life and works should not be considered as mere biographical information, but as "metaphysical facts" that represented the "human overcoming the human."[133] Other idealists referred to the composer as a "notion" instead of a living man: the *Berliner Illustrirte Zeitung* insisted that the word "Beethoven" no longer signified a name or a person; having risen to the state of "the incomprehensible and indescribable," it had become a "concept."[134]

Though sometimes vague, idealistic Beethoven conceptions did constitute an implicit attack on more literal interpretations of the composer. When considered within the Weimar political context, their value as a means to undermine representations of the composer made by extremists becomes more apparent. Most important in this sense was the centrist denial that Beethoven had concerned himself with social and political issues. Those elite journals that did treat the biography of Beethoven in historical terms rarely referred to his political sentiments or activities; when they did, it was usually in order to contradict assertions made by other factions.[135] *Der Querschnitt* criticized interpreters who considered Beethoven's ethical behavior a manifestation of political conviction. He was conscientious, this sophisticated publication argued, because he had "to overcome his personal infirmity" (deafness) by being a good person, not because he wanted to serve as a political role model. The idea that Beethoven's "ethical sensitivity" arose from democratic convictions was an untruth designed "for today's party purposes" and exaggerated according to the needs of the "most radical" elements of Weimar society.[136]

Renunciation of arguments that Beethoven had been rebellious was vehement in the journals of high society. *Der Querschnitt* unequivocally rejected the main themes of leftist interpretations. "The political label of revolutionary at any price is false!" To contradict assumptions that he had been oriented toward the political left, this journal highlighted stories of Beethoven kowtowing to royalty. *Der Querschnitt* reproduced a letter in which Beethoven appealed for financial support from the king of Naples; taken alone, it portrayed him as deferential to monarchs. The journal's commentator haughtily sharpened the point, finding it "simply remarkable that this 'democrat' so gruffly refused to be counted among the plebes, that he preferred the company of 'higher persons'—aristocrats—and that he could plead so humbly when it was a question of business interests."[137]

Moderate interpreters contested some of the Beethoven anecdotes most beloved of leftists. First on their list for eradication was the Teplitz Incident. Under the title "Goethe and Beethoven: On the Question, What is the German Worldview?" the *Berliner Börsen-Zeitung* recounted the artists' relationship without mentioning their supposed encounter with aristocracy on the *Spaziergang* in Teplitz. The issue was addressed only later in the article, when Bettina Brentano's account of Beethoven's behavior was dismissed as the fantasy of a "fanatical democrat." According to the idealistic view, the German *Weltanschauung* represented by Goethe and Beethoven consisted of polytheistic religious beliefs and a Romantic relationship with nature; it had nothing to do with politics.[138]

Repudiating Brentano's youthful reveries was child's play for established critics; but some even argued that Beethoven's anger over Napoleon's Caesaristic behavior was fictitious. The *Berliner Illustrirte Zeitung* assumed a sarcastic tone in discussing this affair: "How manly was the Republican Beethoven's conduct when he tore the title page from the draft of the *Eroica* with its dedication to Napoleon, shredding and stomping on it in senseless fury after the consul Bonaparte had named himself emperor! Too bad for sensitive souls that all of this and much like it has been fabricated from start to finish." This iconoclastic report continued, "Yes, the copy of the *Eroica* with its dedicatory title is still available today. Even if Beethoven had wanted to erase the word 'Bonaparte,' it still stands there clearly legible."[139] Knowing that few readers would consult the original autograph of the *Eroica* to analyze how Beethoven had belabored its dedication, the *Berliner Illustrirte Zeitung*'s blunt—though legitimate—rejection of the usual version of this story was doubtless an effort to disturb "sensitive souls" who believed Beethoven had righteously denounced the tyrant.[140]

Another aspect of Beethoven's image that German economic leaders tried to polish was his reputation as an unethical businessman. Responding to exposés of Beethoven's business dealings as unscrupulous, leading financial papers defended him against his creditors. A *Berliner Börsen-Zeitung* article, "Beethoven as Capitalist," vindicated the composer by establishing that he had not misrepresented his financial situation to the London Philharmonic Society shortly before his death.[141] Similarly, an article on "Beethoven and Inflation" in the *Berliner Montagspost* depicted him as a man with refined taste and sincere interest in financial matters, especially during the period of inflation that struck Austria in the first part of the nineteenth century. Unlike most, this paper did not consider Beethoven's habit of counting his coffee beans each day a sign of stinginess; the *Montagspost* regarded this eccentricity as proof that he was a shrewd consumer, willing to pay extra for real instead of *Ersatzkaffee*, but concerned about the cost of this luxury.[142]

Capitalist interpreters sneered at the idea that Beethoven had been a member of the working class, countering that he had been a respectable burgher. In the view of *Der Querschnitt* and the *Frankfurter Zeitung und Handelsblatt*, he had a "bourgeois sense of order."[143] The *Berliner Illustrirte Zeitung* agreed that Beethoven was a role model not just for artists but for all humanity, because he had been an "upright, upstanding citizen."[144] The *Berliner Tageblatt* also specified Beethoven's exemplary traits in bourgeois terms. In its pages, three features of Beethoven's character were said to give him the power to "shine as a model": his "respect for his art," his "responsibility as an artist," and his "creative honesty."[145] Certainly respectfulness, responsibility, and honesty were not just qualities that German industrialists perceived in Beethoven's biography, but also traits they wanted to inculcate in their workforce.

The trait that leading bourgeois journals most strongly endorsed through their depiction of Beethoven's life was stoicism. Politically moderate writers often referred to him the way Walther Rathenau had: as one who recognized that life was as "it must be." Beethoven's work, said the *Westermanns Monatshefte*, was a great expression of "yea-saying" (*Lebensbejahung*): though he faced obstacles and disappointments, Beethoven ultimately accepted life as it came to him. Without despairing or seeking radical alterations of his fate, he composed music that "strengthened the feeling for life and the consciousness of existence."[146] In spite of all the adversities with which life burdened him, the *Berliner Illustrirte Zeitung* insisted, "he went his own way unbent."[147] To capitalist leaders asking people to sacrifice in an era of economic difficulty, the image of Beethoven as one who accepted life as a vale of tears was a useful propaganda tool.

Upholding basic premises of the idealistic interpretation, German sophisticates rarely claimed that such slogans sounded in Beethoven's music itself. Significantly, when high-society journals did discuss the "meaning" of Beethoven's compositions in literal terms, their goal was usually to dispel political associations suggested by other groups. Unlike those of the left and other activist segments of the political spectrum, urbane publications such as *Der Kunstwart* defended the "purity" of Beethoven's music, insisting it should be accepted simply for what it was: musical expression unencumbered by the mundane. The only persons who really understood Beethoven's compositions, *Der Kunstwart* insisted, were musicians who looked for nothing more in them than aural artistry.[148]

In most cases, the genteel press preferred the philosophical readings of Beethoven's music, highlighting his metaphysical *Weltanschauung* as opposed to his politics. The *Deutsche Reichs-Zeitung* contended that the "program" of the Third Symphony traced an "idea of the hero much broader and more comprehensive" than that of Napoleon alone: Beethoven's hero was the "creative ideal person (*Idealmensch*), the bringer of a new, true culture." To explain this, the *Deutsche Reichs-Zeitung* cited one of the principal formulators of the idealistic tradition. The hero's "significance lies in Paul Bekker's reference" to Prometheus—the transfigured hero who "whizzes down with his holy fire of spirit" and founds "the cosmos of new human culture"—a "myth of true Beethovenian, sublime naivete!" In the same vein, the Fifth Symphony was said to describe the "deepening of ethical pathos in a religious way" as the "anthropocentristic standpoint of the Enlightenment gradually and unconsciously gave way to the organic thoughts of Romanticism and post-Kantian German idealism." Finally, this representative *Deutsche Reichs-Zeitung* article designated the Ninth a "synthesis" of the *Eroica* and the Fifth symphonies. "In a philosophical sense it remains a powerful torso, a staggering monument to a time when both the obvious metaphysical quality of unity and the optimistic focusing of view of the Enlightenment, which had engendered a complete organism in the Fifth, was lost."[149]

Arguments of this profundity appeared in widely distributed daily newspapers associated with the Center and German Democratic parties.[150] Nonetheless, while exposing the public to such ponderous notions, these papers did not strive to make Beethoven's music more accessible to the masses. The message implicit in their erudite interpretation was that only the educated elite could fully appreciate Beethoven's music. The *Berliner Illustrirte Zeitung* stated it gruffly: "Is he popular? Nothing is further from the truth. What do the broad masses know about him? Little more than nothing."[151] Still, parties in the political middle did not passively observe the jousting for Beethoven's legacy that went on during the Weimar era: the champions of the Center Party were instrumental in arranging some of the most important *Todestag* observances of 1927, for they headed the national government at the time. Indeed, it is in the records of a major commemoration directed by the leaders of the German center—at Beethoven's birthplace—that the political significance of the ambiguous idealistic interpretation becomes explicit.[152]

The 1927 celebrations in Bonn were designed by Carl Heinrich Becker, a notable scholar of the ancients, at that time Prussian minister of culture. Although not a member, Becker was closely associated with the Center Party and mapped out its cultural-political programs.[153] In a statement issued to the *Berliner Tageblatt* when the festivities began, Becker stipulated the objectives he and his associates sought in marking Beethoven's death in 1927. He explained that the commemorations would operate on two levels, external and internal. In his opinion, the external aspects—performances, broadcasts, and exhibitions—were inconsequential; more important, in Becker's view, was how the "inner life" of the nation would be affected. The true goal of the festivals was neither to make Beethoven more popular, nor to render his music "part of daily experience," nor to propagate his music "in an uncontrolled fashion," but to encourage a deeper "engagement with the art" on the part of the participants.[154] The contrast between Becker's designs for the *Todestag* events and those of leftist cultural politicians such as Leo Kestenberg and the administrators of the Vienna celebrations is glaring: whereas left-wing organizers sought to transmit their message about Beethoven's art as broadly as possible, Becker strove to protect his legacy for the privileged, seeking only to deepen comprehension of the music for those who were already aware of it—namely, the educated elite.

The 1927 Beethoven Festival in Bonn was indubitably the work of privileged society in Weimar Germany. The commemorative program for the event—richly printed and bound on fine paper by a former royal publishing house—listed all the members of the organizing committee. Every level of German political and cultural hierarchy was represented on this "Roll of Honor": at the top stood the name of Reich Chancellor Wilhelm Marx of the Center Party, then those of the Prussian minister-president, the president of the *Reichstag*, and the president of the Prussian *Landtag*. Five tightly printed pages followed, showing the names of each cultural, economic or political authority associated with the event, including Carl Heinrich Becker himself, Reichstag representatives, state finance office heads, mayors, church leaders, bank directors, union bosses, telegraph inspectors, industry and trade officers, post office directors, and university presidents, to name a few. To leave no doubt about the privileged place of this celebration within the general observance of Beethoven's death, the Bonn festival was held "under the protection of Herr Reich President von Hindenburg."[155]

In contrast to the holiday atmosphere of the Vienna celebrations, the Bonn festival was subdued; ceremonies were limited to masses in the churches, speeches on the Münsterplatz, and a "gala" breakfast. At this last, honored guests received commemorative cups from the Prussian state (formerly "royal") porcelain factory and the mayor of Bonn sent a telegram of thanks to President von Hindenburg. There were concerts of Beethoven's music, yet little of the fanfare of events organized by the left disturbed the village quiet of Bonn.[156] However, speeches by Becker and Reich Chancellor Marx betrayed the political significance of the ceremonies. Their statements confirmed that the leadership of the Center Party preferred the idealistic interpretation, authorizing it as the official version of Beethoven's "meaning."

In his speech, later published as a small book, Becker argued that Beethoven had overcome his fate through inner strength, not external action. Opening with an expression of religious awe before Beethoven —"Take off your shoes, this is holy land"—Becker insisted that if pilgrims were ever to "find him," it would be only in the "deepest depths of [their] own souls." He continued, "The way to Beethoven leads over the mountains of purification, but as in the case of Dante, it is a trip to

General-Anzeiger
für Bonn und Umgegend.

58. Jahrgang. Nr. 12627 · Bonn, Montag, 23. Mai 1927. · Gründungsjahr des Verlags 1725.

Deutsches Beethovenfest 1927 Bonn.
Erster Tag.

Fig. 13. Newspaper coverage of the 1927 Beethoven festival in Bonn. (*General-Anzeiger* [23 May 1927], courtesy of the Beethovenhaus, Bonn)

the interior, a path into the depths." Thus did Becker dismiss the "external" political analyses of Beethoven that pervaded the commemorative discourse of other political elements, especially the left. Instead, he elucidated the placating theme of stoicism. "Beethoven had little joy in the external sense of the word. But his life must nevertheless have been filled with scarcely imaginable richness which allowed him to forget all bitterness, physical hindrances, material need, and professional disappointment." Communicating another major facet of the ideology of the Catholic Center Party, Becker closed his appeal for patience with a Christian notion: the "bridge" that carried Beethoven through his torments was religion; in his last quartets and the *Missa Solemnis*, the "foundations of the miraculous Beethovenian religiosity were firm and clear, like the inside of a Gothic cathedral." Christian piety, Becker implied, was the basis for Beethoven's inner peace, his "holy yes" to life. Passing over "holy ground," his listeners were obviously expected to follow the same path of resignation through their own sorrows.[157]

In his Bonn address, Reich Chancellor Marx likewise emphasized the inexpressibility of Beethoven's significance, but added the notion that the composer was a role model mainly because of his will to work. "I do not want to attempt to explain these ideas in detail: how the fullness and breadth of the Beethovenian spirit, the depth and power of his sensitivity, the incomparable unity of violent temperament and iron self-discipline can and should be characteristic of the German essence or stand as models for the ideal German personality; because every one of us has a special relationship with Beethoven." Marx also made it plain that he considered Beethoven's art the domain of a privileged few. "Each of us links with his works memories of holy moments of soulful and spiritual exaltation. What Beethoven is to us, we need not say to one another. His personality is alive in each of us and his work belongs to the best-known and loved provinces in the realm of our glorious German culture."[158] The "us" to whom the leader of the Center Party referred—those already imbued with the glory of German high culture—left out most of the German population; the Reich chancellor and his colleagues were not much concerned with heightening knowledge about Beethoven in the minds of the masses.

Articles in upper-class publications expressed contempt for popular festivals more explicitly. *Der Querschnitt* condemned the Vienna celebrations of 1927: "Flags and emblems were lowered before the grave site, wagonloads of laurel leaves and battalions of children were mobilized, radio receivers reveled in excesses of Beethoven—this overflowing stream of honors gave the impression that it originated from feelings of bad conscience."[159] The *Berliner Tageblatt* suggested an alternative way to observe the anniversary of his death: the proper way to honor Beethoven was to read through the score of one's favorite composition by the composer. "Such a festival would be best celebrated by each in the quiet of his own room and in his own way. One might think of the E-flat Major Cavatina from the B-flat Major Quartet, op. 130; another, the Andante of the slow movement of the Ninth Symphony; this person may [contemplate] the transfigured lyricism of the great masses, while that one may prefer [the score] of *Fidelio*."[160] A Beethoven "festival" of this sort was reserved for an erudite minority of the German population—the economic and political elite was in no hurry to change this situation.

Right-Wing Evocations of Beethoven

If *Vernunftrepublikaner* refused to do so, leftist organizations were nevertheless not the only ones to discern powerful political connotations in the music and legends of Beethoven; those further to the right formulated a much more aggressive Beethoven myth than did moderate elites. Disillusioned patriots in the German Peoples' Party (DVP), stubborn monarchists in the German National People's Party (DNVP), writers for antirepublican newspapers such as *Der Tag*, the *Neue Preußische (Kreuz-) Zeitung*, the *Tägliche Rundschau*, the *Fränkischer Kurier*, and the *Deutsche Allgemeine Zeitung*, and others disturbed by conditions in interwar Germany, drew a portrait of Beethoven as having been an active *counter*revolutionary, a nationalistic enemy of France, and even a militaristic leader.[161]

Just as they held other ideological convictions in common, including devotion to private enterprise and a strong sense of patriotism,[162] some aggressive rightists shared idealistic ideas about Beethoven with more moderate members of the German elite; articles in right-wing publications also represented him as a "starry-eyed idealist"[163] or a "timeless" entity[164] operating "above all knowledge and philosophy."[165] As in the case of moderates, right-wing linkage of Beethoven with the abstract principles of German idealism can be seen as an attempt to wrest his legacy from the revolutionary tradition. However, many who were unsatisfied with the postwar status quo insisted that the life and music of Beethoven had more literal political significance than was allowed in the idealistic approach; in contrast to their relatively content centrist counterparts, most right-wing ideologues endorsed the notion that Beethoven had been conscious of political issues.

Still, rightists launched fierce attacks on those who "draped the red mantle of a political revolutionary" around Beethoven.[166] While admitting that the composer had lived during a revolutionary age and therefore his political and social views "cannot be grasped without the background of the French Revolution," rightists insisted that "he was himself no revolutionary."[167] The "Marxist" position was "no longer valid," said *Der Tag*—owned by nationalist Alfred Hugenberg—in unison with other right-wing papers.[168] Rightists assaulted both left-wing arguments about Beethoven and the individuals who formulated them:

> On the 17th of November 1918 in Munich's Royal Theater, Kurt Eisner, whose real name as everyone knows is Solomon Kosma-

> nowsky, had the great *Leonore* and *Egmont* overtures played to glorify the successful revolution. This was to be expected, since Eisner had already in 1905 tried to give the Ninth Symphony a meaning which suited him personally: he celebrated it then as the high-song of class warfare. . . . His use and interpretation of this work, however, do not coordinate with the thoughts of its poet and composer. . . . Undeniably, the young Beethoven was filled with the ideas of the revolutionary epoch. . . . But it was up to Eisner and his admiring comrades to agitate politically with [his music].[169]

Grounds for nullifying the leftist portrait, right-wing interpreters argued, were signs that Beethoven had been respectful of the aristocracy. "He was no revolutionary," said the musicologist Adolf Sandberger, because "in principle" he recognized "the old social order"; he did not scorn princely and royal employment and he enjoyed being included in the circles of the noble class.[170] Some rightists, partially accepting Beethoven's own noble pretense, held that he had many aristocratic characteristics, including contempt for the masses. "Following his innermost convictions," argued Sandberger, Beethoven "thought in an aristocratic way." He stood among those "who distinguish themselves from others," since he felt himself "one of a select few, a chosen instrument of higher powers"; "seeking the goal of humanity in run-of-the-mill masses was the last thing on Beethoven's mind."[171] *Der Tag* contradicted the presumption that he had been a democrat by arguing that "Beethoven, the proud and lonely one, was an aristocrat through and through"; the motto "*Odi profanum vulgus et arceo* (I dislike and spurn the ordinary masses) was deeply fixed in his blood." It is for this reason that he "fought like a lion" in the proceedings against his sister-in-law to prove that the "van" in his name was a noble title; when his nobility was legally denied, he called it a "terrible event" that robbed him of "all his senses." Therefore, enjoined *Der Tag*, "let him live on in our thoughts" as an "aristocrat of purest stamp."[172]

The German right wing also found onerous the thought that Beethoven had been influenced by French culture. To zealous German nationalists, allegations made during the Great War that Beethoven had been of French or Belgian origin were particularly irritating; after the war these views continued to appear in representations of Beethoven as an adherent to French revolutionary ideals.[173] Angry rightists undertook to dispel them once and for all. Referring to the issue as Beethoven's "nationality problem," the right launched an attack on the writings of Romain Rolland, who had suggested in his *Life of*

Beethoven that the composer's grandfather might have been Flemish. Criticizing all of Rolland's biography as full of "poetic inaccuracies," German nationalists condemned as products of "war psychosis" those passages which dealt with Beethoven's ancestry.[174] In articles such as "Beethoven, the German" in the *Deutsche Allgemeine Zeitung,* right-wingers combated the nationality problem by arguing that the "Nether-German Germanness" (*Niederdeutsches Deutschtum*) inherent in the Bonn native "marked his character in all of its gnarledness and cheerfulness, its robustness and charm." Moreover, "the great, creative German individual"—more than any other genius of any other country—works under a sense of the "highest moral responsibility," and this was most true in Beethoven's case: the "concept of art as play has very little meaning for him, in contrast to those of the Roman race"; art "is for him always an expression of deep, soulful experience." In this sense, concluded the *Deutsche Allgemeine Zeitung,* Beethoven was the "most German of all creative musicians."[175]

While negating "enemy" insinuations about his heritage, German rightists also stipulated that Beethoven had spurned the French. "Quite obviously," remarked *Der Tag*—ridiculing a statement made by the French minister of education, Herriot—"it did not escape Beethoven's attention how France's campaign of robbery through Germany, Italy, and Holland sharply contrasted with its sermons of freedom, brotherhood, and equality."[176] It was "completely logical," noted another right-wing interpreter, that "our master turned away from the French and wanted to expel them from those places where they did not belong."[177]

Treatment of this issue led to discussion of the Third Symphony dedication. Some on the right allowed that Beethoven had originally dedicated the *Eroica* to Napoleon, but others presented different versions altogether. "In reality, it has nothing to do with Napoleon," wrote one patriot. "It was composed, rather, to honor the death of the English General [Ralph] Abercromby," a German ally.[178] Even rightists who admitted that the Third had once been called the *Bonaparte* Symphony differed with the left and center on why Beethoven had so named it. The composer, argued *Der Tag,* had been disappointed in Bonaparte not for raising himself up to the status of royalty, but for *lowering* himself *down* to that level. "He admired this man of strength and deed because he, like himself, was a self-made man. This explains his deep disappointment when he learned that Napoleon had climbed down from his proud, lonely heights to join the ranks of other kings and princes . . . Is this democratic thinking? I think it highly aristocratic."[179] According to right-wing interpreters, then, Beethoven esteemed Bonaparte's leadership qualities, not his republican ideals; unlike the left, rightist interpreters constantly reminded Germans of Beethoven's wish that he had known the art of war as well as the art of music, so that he could conquer Napoleon himself.[180] In this way, ardent nationalists tried to convince their readers that Beethoven changed the title sheet not because the Corsican had betrayed democratic ideals, but because he had invaded the Fatherland.[181]

Building on this concept of the composer as national leader, right-wing ideologues during the interwar period sustained the image of Beethoven as a military symbol. The *Fränkischer Kurier* argued that the warlike atmosphere of his lifetime had deeply influenced Beethoven's art.

> The greatest genius of German statesmanship, the Prussian King Friedrich II, had awakened in his Volk self-consciousness of its power for the first time. On the battlefields of Hohenfriedburg and Hochkirch he sowed into the German earth the seeds that germinated a half a century later into the most powerful spiritual and moral movement of freedom ever to break forth from a people, that of Scharnhorst, Blücher, Fichte, Arndt, and Körner. In the meantime flowed the stream of blood that [resulted from] the French Revolution. From its waves emerged Napoleon I, the Antichrist, [who contradicted] all notions of human worth and rights, who silenced the spiritual life of Europe under the rhythm of his marching men. This spiritual and political atmosphere . . . is decisive in judging and determining the meaning of Beethoven.[182]

Concurrently, the right rekindled legends of the association between Beethoven and Bismarck. The *Tägliche Rundschau* linked Beethoven's music with the Iron Chancellor, as it had in the Second Reich. "When he had Keudell play music for him on the decisive winter evenings in Versailles from 1870 to 1871, he said, 'If I heard this music often, I would always be very brave.' In saying this, Bismarck did not mean that he needed this music to be brave, but that he experienced it as an expression of the heroic so powerful that it raised heroism into the realm of the supermanly (*Übermenschlich*) . . . This is what the music of Beethoven meant to Bismarck, which he specifically ordered played by an orchestra in his chancellor's palace on the eve of the declaration of war."[183] The right wing also recalled the importance of Beethoven as a military symbol during the First World War. "A powerful tie binds the citizens of the Weimar Republic with Beethoven: the same moral idealism that led them to war and victory in 1914."[184] Others reinstated the Wagnerian tradition that had been demoted at the end of the First World War. Papers and publishers associated with the right, such as the *Neue Preußische (Kreuz-) Zeitung* (still printed under the motto "Forward with God for King and Fatherland!") reproduced Wagner's essays linking Beethoven to politics and military conquest, implying that his music could again lead Germany to victory.[185]

Understood as a product of his troubled times, Beethoven was constantly acclaimed in right-wing literature as a "fighting man" (*Kämpfer*). The *Neue Preußische (Kreuz-) Zeitung* observed that the composer's struggle against deafness exemplified his fighting nature.[186] His was the "music of a German man, which means that of a fighter," exclaimed the *Deutsche Allgemeine Zeitung*.[187] "He is the man of victory," wrote the conductor Wilhelm Furtwängler in *Der Tag*. "All the battles that filled his life stemmed from his absolute and unconditional will to victory. . . . To be a man means to be a fighter. And Beethoven proved this in heroic dimensions. He was a fighter who 'grasped Fate by the throat,' a hero who defied the demons, a victor who raised himself with wings of Daedalus over the suffering world. For all the troubles that occasionally filled his breast, he never became an impeacher of the godhead, a quarreler with fate, or a pessimist full of gloomy resignation."[188] Furthermore, Furtwängler continued, Beethoven was a model for strengthening German art and spirit in the present era of troubles. "This Beethoven who, in a time of humiliation, preserved the pride of his people against the Corsican oppressor, refused to follow him, and continually demonstrated the indestructible strength of the German spirit—how he now admonishes us Germans in this, our own fateful time: 'Care for German art! Strengthen German spirit! Maintain and contribute to German culture! That is the way to new heights, to a new future of greatness.' "[189]

Thus did the Weimar right present Beethoven as an "admonition in this time of gloom" when, they felt, Germans were succumbing to mistreatment at the hands of the French.[190] Unambiguously, rightists endeavored to renew his value as a Germanic hero who would help the country overcome problems they perceived in the Weimar system. "To honor Beethoven is to honor a German hero, a knight without fear or reproach such as Germany and the world have never seen."[191] By contemplating Beethoven's deeds and their place in world culture, insisted the *Fränkischer Kurier*, Germans could regain the national pride they had lost in military defeat and economic downturn. "In the misery of the present, in the despair over our own impotence, in view of the abrupt downfall and destruction of all ethics, memories return of men to whom we owe the spiritual and moral greatness of our Volk. And among these the name of Beethoven today sounds from the past as [a symbol of] redemption and promise."[192]

By emulating Beethoven, bitter nationalists insisted, Germans would find the strength to resist the external enemies of the nation and overthrow the republican system. All should consider Beethoven's music, said the musicologist Sandberger, in the same way Germans living "under foreign flags" in the demilitarized Rhineland did: "as a refuge of German culture, as a major bastion in the fortress that the spiritual Rhineland built against the West, the fortress that no Versailles Treaty is capable of destroying." Beethoven's work, Sandberger went on, should be considered inspiration for the effort to reconstitute "a poorly led, torn-apart, and very sick Volk." "The fist that Beethoven raised in his last battle against death shines today as a symbol, saying, 'Shame if you betray the great and true, if materialism, mechanization, orientalism, Americanism, and internationalism finally change your nature. My work remains in all its strength and glory; you, however, are emasculating yourselves.' . . . So it is: the German Volk must now decide."[193] Arguing, as did one writer for *Der Tag,* that if Beethoven still lived he would have admired Mussolini just as he had respected Napoleon,[194] some rightists perceived in the composer's character the kind of Führer they sought in lieu of a restored monarch.[195]

Conceiving of Beethoven's compositions as nationalistic and militaristic theme songs, rightist interpreters highlighted motifs of heroism and war in their explications of his music.[196] Some developed intricate arguments about the composer's deceptively contributing to the national cause through his art. According to Arnold Schmitz's 1927 analysis of the Romantic portrait of Beethoven, he had patterned some of his works after pieces the French composers Méhul and Grétry wrote for revolutionary festivals. However, Beethoven's choice of French revolutionary songs as models did not reflect his political leanings, in Schmitz's view, nor the true meaning of his works. Having "no sympathy for the revolution," Beethoven borrowed French musical methods with the intention of turning them against the French themselves and thereby "defeating them with their own weapons"![197]

This interpretation placed great weight on those works Beethoven wrote in response to the Napoleonic Wars. Unlike leftist analysts, writers for journals such as the *Deutsche Militär-Musiker-Zeitung* discussed at length Beethoven's "battle music," including *Wellingtons Sieg* and *Der glorreiche Augenblick;*[198] but they conceived other works as useful "against Germany's enemies" as well. Rightists introduced the Third Symphony as a "fighting symphony" meant to "celebrate the striving of a victorious champion and other fallen heroes"[199] and impart the idea that "to be a man means to be a fighter."[200] The Seventh Symphony was supposed to have a "spiritual relationship to the German freedom movement," serving as a "call to the German nation."[201] Likewise the music for *Egmont* was the work of "a German musician standing up against the oppressor of personal and national freedom, armed with weapons that came partly from the arsenal of the enemy himself."[202] Journals such as *Der Tag* delineated the Ninth Symphony as "the ultimate song of victory" marking the conquest of the German people over its enemies.[203]

Since right-wing parties such as the DVP and the DNVP controlled neither the national government nor the principal institutions of the German cultural world, it was rarely possible for them to organize major events at which to promulgate their views of Beethoven.[204] Through most of the period, rightists expressed their ideas about him mainly in newspaper and journal articles—often in essays criticizing how he was depicted by their opponents, especially the socialists. When rightist publications attacked leftist cultural-political organizations and the *Musikpolitik* of the Weimar government, a frequent complaint was that they were spreading offensive notions about Beethoven.

Disparaging all interpretations of Beethoven "from the left," *Der Tag* berated Leo Kestenberg and the *Volksbühne* specifically. "What does the man want?" *Der Tag* asked.

> The center of his considerations is the *Volksbühne.* He expects it to organize Beethoven celebrations and thereby educate people about art. . . . This will be achieved by the People's Theaters, People's Music Schools, and People's Singing Schools, etc. . . . Herr Kestenberg wants to make the German people into a race of composers. Thank God things like this do not happen quickly. This fantasy is just as crazy as the nonsense about pacifism with which a number of fools and swindlers try to becloud the minds of their neighbors. Pacifism contradicts a law of nature, because wherever we turn in the world of animals and plants we run into a gruesome, merciless battle in which only the strongest survives. And should mankind stand outside natural law? A similar law applies to the relationship between men and art. There are two kinds of men, artistic and non-artistic, whose characteristics are fixed at birth. Just as one cannot

make a goose out of a horse, one cannot make an artist out of a nonartistic man. No, Kestenberg's dream is nothing, this shimmering image is sheer rhetoric: a soap bubble which bursts when you touch it with your finger. . . . Kestenberg is just trying to use Beethoven for the benefit of the rattletrap of social democracy.[205]

The *Fränkischer Kurier* also expressed distain for Kestenberg's reforms. "Leo Kestenberg, the Prussian general of music . . . hopes that the whole country will take part in the graces of creative experience, that individual achievement will be replaced by the 'collective.' This *proletarian cultural politics* becomes most clear when one considers [his] 'modern' portrait of Beethoven, as it is expressed in the criticism of certain daily publications." Further on, this *Fränkischer Kurier* critique of the socialist portrait shifted into an attack on the republican system itself. As proven by the cultural policies of its leftist administrators, Weimar Germany was an "anti-Beethovenian state" ruled by "a handful of little men who cannot keep up with their responsibilities, but who know how to use the political situation for their own purposes."[206]

The Weimar right also communicated its discomfort with the anti-Beethovenian state through the channels of the German academic system. Like numerous German academics, many Beethoven experts were unhappy with the state of affairs in the Weimar Republic.[207] When such scholars produced serious studies for professional journals and books, they attempted to maintain historical and musicological objectivity; when writing exegeses of Beethoven for the journals of political organizations, however, some allowed their negative opinions of republican rule to show. Many of the right-wing interpretations of Beethoven discussed above originated in the work of experts including Arnold Schmitz, Hans Joachim Moser, and Adolf Sandberger.[208] Lectures by such men were among the few events that communicated right-wing interpretations of Beethoven to broad audiences in ways comparable to the festivals arranged by centrists and leftists: Sandberger expounded his view of Beethoven's art as a spiritual fortress against the Versailles Treaty in a *Festrede* arranged by the Beethovenhaus Society during the 1927 celebrations;[209] besides his venomous articles in the newspapers of Alfred Hugenberg, Moser declared his right-wing views in a speech for the 1927 celebrations at the University of Heidelberg.[210]

Yet disgruntled academics were not the only detractors of postwar Germany to scorn the revolutionary portrait of Beethoven projected at *Todestag* observances. Right-wing publications generally decried the celebrations in republican Germany, and Austria, in 1927. In the Catholic *Gregoriusbote* one reactionary critic attacked them as "godless and mendacious" machinations of the left; in his view, the policy of "opening art events to the mob" had to be stopped—police were needed to protect art works from the masses. This skeptic took heart only from his opinion that Beethoven would have scoffed at the manner in which common society was celebrating him.[211]

Particularly disturbing to rightists was the commemorative speech given by the Social Democratic mayor of Vienna. *Der Tag* characterized as "false speechifying" Seitz's promise to be the "caretaker of the holy ground" where the "Composer of Freedom and Love" had walked; by promoting the idea of a Beethoven whose music "constantly ignites revolution," his statement contributed to the "electioneering that his party was carrying on all over the city."[212] The *Wiener Reichspost* condemned other "Marxist" observances: "Until recently in the Schubert Park, at the onetime grave site of Beethoven, there shone a wreath with a glaring red bow on which one could read the ingenious inscription, 'To the great revolutionary—from the Workers' Choral Group of Vienna.' . . . Our Marxists do not even balk at outraging, for their party-political purposes, this honorable place which every German . . . should consider a 'Sanctissimum.' Beethoven . . . earned better thanks than to be claimed as a spiritual comrade of the party of upheaval in this most shallow and materialistic [way]." Behind such "hollow" actions and phrases, this counterrevolutionary paper warned, existed a "musicology" of "Marxist music-ignoramuses" (*marxistische Musikignoranten*) intent on poisoning Germanic society. This "red musicology" had to be combated by all possible means.[213]

Warnings against the left's politicization of Beethoven did not go unheeded. We have seen that one reactionary who wielded authority in 1927 did all he could to stop a left-wing "outrage" against Beethoven in Berlin. Walther von Keudell, once an active participant in the Kapp putsch, in 1927 was the German interior minister.[214] A leading member of the DNVP, it was he who blocked the performance of Beethoven's *Bundeslied* by the Deutsche Arbeiter Sängerbund on the steps of the Reichstag.[215] Others simply ridiculed the *Todestag* celebrations in 1927. A cartoon in the Austrian *Kronen Zeitung* depicted a bedraggled Beethoven looking down on all the commemorative rituals, speeches, and concerts, muttering "Today it is good that I am deaf."[216] But rightists used the 1927 commemorations to do more than just protect the deaf composer against misuse by their enemies. In ways reminiscent

Fig. 14. Cartoon criticizing 1927 Todestag observations: "Today it is good that I am deaf!" (*Illustrierte Kronen-Zeitung* [27 March 1927], courtesy of the Beethovenhaus, Bonn)

of the turn-of-the-century politicians of cultural despair, reactionaries communicated broader political themes in their interpretations of Beethoven: Weimar society itself was "godless and mendacious," a fact that could be verified by considering the republican depiction of Beethoven as a progressive. To counter the degeneration of the German nation, right-wingers exhorted their countrymen to conceive of Beethoven, instead, as a model for the leader who could make Germany great again. Nostalgic to regain Germany's feudal stature, one put it in verse:

> He was a Siegfried who, in swordplay,
> Most daringly fought for the prize.

This artist leapt after the most noble goals,
Carrying others along in his flight.

If you, Germany, want to win the world again,
Do not lean on the handle of your sword.
You must brandish your weapon more boldly.
Send Beethoven ahead as your duke:
The strength of his nine symphonies
Each ensures a victorious battle![217]

Extreme Right-Wing Visions of Beethoven

Fantasies of Beethoven as a daring knight who might return to save his nation in distress were often conjured in the writings of Germans captivated by volkish mythology. On 11 December 1919, Houston Stewart Chamberlain wrote a letter to King Ferdinand of Bulgaria describing the grief he suffered on the German defeat. Looking back over the previous year, though, Chamberlain remembered that he had found solace in belief that the lost war had been part of a grand plan designed to forge the German nation. "My thoughts were somewhat as follows: Since it had become clear that the German Volk—without whom the whole plan was unthinkable—was not yet ripe for the fate that had been conceived for it, it seemed from a wider perspective—let us say through God's eyes—that it was not impossible that the present setback could have had the sense of a *réculer pour mieux sauter,* and that therefore one did not have to give oneself up to complete despair." Proclaiming that a supreme German nation could emerge if led by modern Teutons, this volkish mythmaker found reassurance in the text of Beethoven's song *An die Hoffnung,* op. 94: "[I] consider it possible that the united powers of some most-noble men—of which Germany always has many—could bring forth a better Germany. . . . I know, of course, what little value such speculations possess; but as it says in the glorious song of Beethoven: man must hope, not question."[218]

Many on the extreme right agreed with Chamberlain's revelations: his dream of Germany's future, his vision of a new class of heroic leaders, and his evocation of Beethoven as a motivational figure. According to the volkish journal *Deutsches Volkstum,* the Beethoven interpretation that Chamberlain had outlined in *The Foundations of the Nineteenth Century* was the "most beautiful" of all.[219] Like Chamberlain, this important publication of the radical right felt that readers living in "a time without gods" (*entgötterte Zeit*) should "direct their feelings" toward Beethoven's "Germanness" as inspiration for building a new nation according to volkish design.[220]

The extreme right-wing interpretation of Beethoven shared many features with the portrait conceived by less radical reactionaries. Like the propagandists of the DVP and the DNVP, ideologues of the more disparate far right such as the *Tat-Kreis,* the *Stahlhelm,* and the Pan-German League presented him as counterrevolutionary, Francophobic, and ultranationalistic. But depictions of Beethoven published in extreme right-wing sources, including *Deutsches Volkstum, Die Tat, Der Stahlhelm, Hammer, Gewissen, Deutschlands Erneuerung,* and *Muttersprache,* had characteristics that distinguished them as products of volkish ideology: associations of Beethoven not with the German and Austrian nations as they were, but with the volkish state as it might become, and allusions to "Germanic" attributes that integrated composer and music into the symbolism of racist ideology.[221]

More strongly than right-wing journals, volkish publications blanched at any insinuation that Beethoven "betrayed" his nation by admiring the French. *Hammer,* the journal of leading volkish publicist Theodor Fritsch, insisted that Beethoven was the "furthest thing from Francophile (*französenfreundlich*)," since he would have fought Napoleon had he known the art of war.[222] Especially vindictive were extreme right-wing attacks on Edouard Herriot's speech at the 1927 celebrations in Vienna; for arguing that Beethoven had shared a "Napoleonic-French vision of a united Europe," the French socialist was reproved by *Gewissen,* the influential volkish journal of Heinrich von Gleichen, as having the "narrow perspective of someone living according to the ideas of 1789."[223]

Gewissen also contradicted suggestions that Beethoven did not respect nobility, saying that "the Viennese aristocracy secured his external existence, making it possible for him to follow the call of his interior life." While deprecating Herriot's speech, *Gewissen* turned discussion of this issue into a tirade against the Versailles Treaty, upbraiding the Frenchman for "forgetting that this 'peace treaty' has destroyed the conditions necessary" for music creation of Beethoven's quality. "It has annihilated those very social levels of Vienna which supported the old artistic and musical culture. Not only the aristocracy has disappeared, but above all that cultivated German bourgeoisie which cared for fine old *Hausmusik.*" "With the creation of today's Austrian state," *Gewissen* concluded, the patrons of high musical culture in Vienna had disappeared or descended into the proletariat—and this was the fault of France: "under French leadership this German capital has practically become . . . a Jewish-Slavic *Balkanstadt.*"[224]

Volkish mythmakers also linked Beethoven compositions to notions of military heroism, particularly those personified by Bismarck. *Der Stahlhelm,* journal of the veterans' organization of the same name, insisted that Beethoven's music should be understood in the way Bismarck comprehended it—as an expression of "the heroic and the demonic."[225] To depict him as a nationalist, the self-appointed caretakers of the German language who wrote for *Muttersprache* even dug up the argument that Beethoven must have been patriotic because he favored German music terminology instead of Italian.[226]

The trait that the extreme right stressed most emphatically in its depiction of Beethoven was, simply, his Germanness (*Deutschtum*). As we have seen, discussions of Beethoven's German origins were prevalent in the publications of right-wing parties—especially debates over his "nationality problem." But extreme right-wing references to Beethoven's Germanness went beyond merely determining his national allegiance; volkish allusions to his "Germanic" features integrated composer and music into racist symbolism. According to journals such as *Der Stahlhelm,* Beethoven and his works epitomized the Nordic race and culture. "The fate of Beethoven is not only symbolic of the Nordic worldview (*nordische Weltanschauung*), it is also symbolic of the means by which it expresses itself; it gives us a last look at the formal conditions [required] of German art." Thus did volkish propagandists present Beethoven as a reminder of the creative forces that supposedly stirred in the blood that coursed through German veins. "The Germanic impulse to defy and move forward toward the horizon manifests itself most strongly in the personality of the greatest of composers, whose creativity grew to the most monumental of proportions while he was going deaf."[227]

Volkish activists expected the image of Beethoven, along with his music, to quicken the pulse of all Germans, inciting them to form a new state. Fully experiencing Beethoven, argued *Gewissen,* did not mean just listening to his music but working to strengthen the German Volk. "Simply enjoying his symphonies and quartets, quietly listening to concerts of his sounds, or losing oneself in the ecstasy of playing his works: such disinterest in worldly matters is unacceptable today." To "experience his rhythm as deed and his beauty as a challenging summons, to strain oneself while listening: this is a true celebration of Beethoven" and the way to progress "from dream to Volk, from the soul to the state."[228] Some on the extreme right considered

Beethoven the herald and even the Führer of the new German empire. "Every genius," *Gewissen* asserted, "seeks his Volk. And Beethoven's genial abundance of volkishness is to us a form of anticipating and heralding his Volk. In the one hundred years since his death great music has died out. But he will remain the model of the power of genius in music, so long as his Volk does not hypocritically allow him to be violated."[229] This conviction that Beethoven prefigured the Führer sought by volkish dreamers was perhaps most clearly stated in a poem published in *Propylaen* in 1921:

> We who wanted to found a world empire
> But who are now the mere plaything of other countries,
> We Germans look up to him proudly,
> To the man who created the highest of art
> Out of the deepest necessity,
> To the man who is our consolation,
> To the man who is our Führer,
> To the man who will lead us
> To true domination of the world,
> To the man who will lead us
> To spiritual domination of the world.[230]

Like the various *Bünde* that concocted them, volkish Beethoven myths contained many incongruous elements. One volkish thinker, however, concatenated the principal notions of the radical right-wing Beethoven interpretation. A leading writer for the publishing house of Eugen Diederichs, Richard Benz was a prolific analyst of German cultural matters, especially music, which he cast in the mystical terms of volkish ideology.[231] *Die Tat,* another Diederichs publication, described Benz's approach in a review of his book *Die Stunde der deutschen Musik* (The hour of German music): "Music is not valued by him as a technical product, but rather it is understood as a spiritual mystery on whose preservation or dissipation hangs the fate of all Germans." Presenting music "as the key to apprehending a unified German worldview, this book aspires not only to inform but to give rise to deeds: it demands a renewal of culture through the spirit of music and thereby demonstrates the possibilities of a reformation of church, state, and school."[232]

Central to Benz's plans for reforming these German institutions was the "spiritual mystery" of Beethoven's music. Besides lengthy chapters on Beethoven in his books on Germanic culture, Benz produced articles such as "Beethoven's Spiritual Message to the World,"

"Beethoven as the Measure of Our Time," and "Beethoven and the Turning Point of Culture." These writings all gave Beethoven a prominent place in Benz's vision of a volkish future.[233] In them Benz engendered the Beethoven myth most popular among Germanic ideologues of the Weimar era: along with *Die Tat,* many other journals of the far right reproduced Benz's articles and excerpts from his books; some described his interpretation of the composer as the best since that of Houston Stewart Chamberlain.[234]

Many right-wing and volkish themes underlay Benz's Beethoven analysis. According to Benz, the modern age—when "culture-negating communism" threatened to dominate the world—had produced inaccurate readings of the composer and his works. Some considered Beethoven the great representative "of individualism, of hubris, of a spirit which is no longer bound by belief or community." Others portrayed Beethoven as a Romantic revolutionary, seeing his "power of expression as uncontrolled passion, his pronouncements of the last secrets of the soul as a lack of moderation, his struggling and suffering as a lack of happiness and greatness, his will to communicate . . . as a tendency to seduce the Volk. To them he seems to have anticipated not [just] individualism, but the liquidation of European culture by communism." Portraits of the composer as bourgeois or as socialist, Benz asserted, were products of minds that had "broken with the spirit of Beethoven"; instead of providing insight into him, Benz chided, they "tell us more about the people who formulated them."[235]

Having thus dispensed with views promoted on the center and the left of Weimar politics, Benz wove notions borrowed from earlier volkish Beethoven worshippers—mainly Houston Stewart Chamberlain and Julius Langbehn—together with cryptic concepts of a Nordic religion, to synthesize an alternative Germanic interpretation. If people would stop listening to Beethoven's art for entertainment and understand it as "spiritual experience," Benz suggested, they would recognize that his "tonal language" expressed a "new Nordic-Germanic feeling for the world." Beethoven's was the art form that would best motivate Germans to overcome political divisions; common awareness of this Nordic feeling among Germans would reconcile all ideological conflicts, which in any case were foreign to the Germanic worldview.[236]

Hearing the composer's "Nordic products," Benz held, the listener became a member of a broad Germanic community that Beethoven had himself "yearned to be part of and wanted to help to establish." Because of the political circumstances of his time, he never experienced volkish togetherness; as consolation, he created a "feeling of the Volk" in his music so that later men would sense their duty to form it in reality.[237] Doing so, Beethoven acted as a medium between spirit, nature, and the Volk. His music was the "national language of the Germans"; by linking them to their landscape and their past, it would "finally and forever overcome the old powers of Antiquity and Christianity."[238] Resonating with the "primal poetry" (*Urdichtung*) of earliest German tribal origins, Beethoven's music constituted a "new mythology" upon which a vigorous German society could be founded. Thus was Beethoven the "Creator of a New Mythos," the "Founder of a New Humanity"[239]—a Nordic prophet. But, Benz warned, in Beethoven's case the term "prophet" was to be understood not in the "Jewish-Christian" sense, but as it was used in the "old-German sagas":[240] "unlike Buddha and Christ, who announced the teachings of a distant god, Beethoven was himself a creator, one who made order out of chaos."[241]

Once properly understood, Benz insisted, Beethoven would emerge as the greatest Germanic hero, leading efforts to establish a "new German world." However, he could take things only so far: having demonstrated through his music the joys and comforts of a united community—to be attained in a truly volkish state—Beethoven's message to the world (*Weltbotschaft*) was complete. It was then up to audience members to execute the "assignment demanded of us in this art—to create this community [and] found this cult."[242] Benz urged all Germans to take up these spiritual and political tasks with constant reference to Beethoven. "In this world crisis . . . let us follow Beethoven. Let us carry in our hearts the sound of the *Eroica,* this heroic song of a new era for the Volk: he sings neither of individual domination over the globe nor of communist destruction of the earth's culture—he rings in a new age: he prepares souls for world domination by the German spirit."[243]

Other volkish leaders also considered Beethoven's music an essential ingredient in the political spell they wished to cast on the German nation and beyond. While Benz heard ominous messages in Beethoven's Third Symphony, the head of the Youth Music Movement (*Jugendmusikbewegung*), Fritz Jöde, had faith that music could render a simple crowd of people (*eine Masse Mensch*) into a German Volk. In educational programs meant to indoctrinate a generation that would lead Germany out of its desperate postwar state, Jöde encouraged group singing of folk music to instill feelings of comradeship. He also presumed that study of the music and biographies of serious composers would contribute to this process, since these figures represented "timeless, universal ideals that should be emulated by every generation." To unite German youth into a committed community, a true Volk, the movement required inspirational focal points; Jöde thought of German music masters as symbols ideally suited for this purpose.[244]

Although other composers were included in Jöde's hall of heroes—Haydn for representing "fatherly good and diligence" and Mozart for demonstrating "respect for the mysterious power of God"—Beethoven was highlighted in his educational schema, for personifying "heroic struggle."[245] In an article on "Beethoven and Us," Jöde announced his conviction that "should today's youth meet and look him in the eyes," they will recognize that Beethoven must be their "true Führer"; before the composer "we will stand quietly for a while, eye to eye with him, and recognize the demonic and the incomprehensible suffering of his heroism, and we will bow in awe before him, who with a bleeding soul sought his Volk . . . but never found it."[246] Besides imagining scenes that eerily resembled the *Blut-Fahne* ritual performed by another Führer, Jöde transmitted his ideas about Beethoven through Youth Music Movement events. His stated goal in organizing festivals of Beethoven's music—as were held by the Youth Music Movement in 1927—and observances of Haydn, Mozart, and Beethoven—as in 1932—was not just to honor great men of the past but to inspire work toward developing a new Germany. "We are not here, in these deafeningly uncertain times, to give ourselves up to a tired cult of the divine. So often in recent years we have had to observe escapism in Germany. Some celebrate the past [because] they do not comprehend duty to the present, because they do not expect anything from the future. We however understand duty, and know that what is at stake is a new Germany. To keep our powers ready for this, to awaken and arouse them if they still slumber, so that they are effective within us—that is what now fills all our days and that is why, I hope, we have met here today."[247]

In spite of such high hopes expressed in what contemporary critics derided as "labyrinths of word and thought," the "dark oracles" of the extreme right had limited means by which to diffuse their Beethoven *Mythos*.[248] Apart from the rituals of the Youth Music Movement, their primary method of propagating ideas about Beethoven as Germanic prophet was to influence public reception of ceremonies arranged by other groups. *Deutschlands Erneuerung*, an important organ of volkish thought published by J. F. Lehmann, expressed support for all the celebratory events of 1927, even those arranged by left-wing or foreign organizations. By spreading the music of Beethoven, *Deutschlands Erneuerung* surmised, each would bind Germans—including those who called themselves "Dutch"—more closely to their *Heimat.* "The fact that awe for Beethoven reaches to the Netherlands" provides a "welcome opportunity to clarify the ancient unity of this place with the Reich."

Deutschlands Erneuerung also enjoyed the spectacle of other foreigners paying homage to a German artist, since this experience would prove to them the superiority of German culture. "Seen from a patriotic standpoint, such a truly loving festival gives an impression that makes one very proud. Where did the symphony originate and develop? In German lands. Which other Volk has a musical personality of Beethoven's standing to show for itself? None. Where is the name of Beethoven [being celebrated]? Throughout the whole world. A statesman who understood something of the spiritual could call on Beethoven inconspicuously but effectively as a political propaganda instrument: the Volk from which he arose must really be worth something."[249]

Deutschlands Erneuerung's recognition of Beethoven's usefulness as a foreign political propaganda instrument was unique among extreme right-wing journals; most volkish publications derided celebrations organized by other groups and nations, as shown by the attacks on Edouard Herriot's statements. A further example of this tendency was the action taken by an extreme right-wing group in Austria. In 1926 the Tyrolian *Landtag,* dominated by the Christian-Social Party (*Christlichsoziale Partei*), known as a "black" party of the far right,[250] refused to accept funds from the Austrian government designated for arranging a local Todestag celebration. These Tyrol extremists decided that there was "nothing in Beethoven for them": celebration of him was something arranged by and for intellectuals and politicians of the city; in their opinion all the fuss about such matters was just an excuse for "one Jew to plagiarize from another."[251] Complete refusal to honor Beethoven was not typical of extreme right-wing cultural politicians; many Germanic ideologues wanted to use Beethoven as a symbol for their volkish movement, even as an idol for their Nordic religion. Yet the actions of the *Tiroler Landtag* show that representatives of the extreme right were not content with celebrations arranged by other parties, and, more important, that racist hatred could threaten the status of even so great a *nordisches Heldenbild* as Beethoven.

Nazi Exploitation of Beethoven

Like all major parties involved in Weimar politics, the National Socialist German Workers' Party (NSDAP) exploited the life and music of Beethoven to convince the public that he had held opinions comparable to those of its leadership. Arguing that he hated the French, feared revolutionary disorder, and supported authoritarian rule, National Socialists evoked Beethoven to legitimate Hitler's platform of rejecting the Versailles Treaty, combating communism, and installing strong-armed leadership in Germany. And to the Nazis, the vigor of Beethoven's music symbolized one thing above all: the energy of their movement. In his propaganda, the self-proclaimed party philosopher Alfred Rosenberg equated the vim of Beethoven's symphonies with the verve of the Nazi *Bewegung* and the victory he assumed it would obtain.[252] Thus did National Socialists integrate Beethoven into the arsenal of symbols they wielded during their "era of struggle" and lay the basis for using him as a centerpiece of their *Kulturpolitik* after 1933.

More than any other German political organization—even other volkish groups—the NSDAP injected race issues into the process of Beethoven reception.[253] Indeed, dictates of racial anthropology nearly nullified the composer's value as a party hero. Stirred by the same bigotry that swayed the *Tiroler Landtag,* the Nazis almost rejected Beethoven as a symbol of their movement simply because his physical appearance disquieted theorists who contrived National Socialist "racially determined music politics" (*rassisch bedingte Musikpolitik*).[254] While portraits and observations of Beethoven by his contemporaries differ tremendously, all reveal that he had few of the physical characteristics associated with "Aryan" stereotypes.[255] Noticing this, a handful of pseudoscientists concluded during the Weimar era that Beethoven was of impure blood: careful analysis of his portraits, they said, led to the discovery that although his eye color may have been blue (it was not), he was short, dark-haired, and swarthy. Based on these findings, racist savants such as Hans F. K. Günther and Ludwig Ferdinand Clauß determined that Beethoven's genetic background was mixed.[256]

Although their ideology rested on the tenets of racial science, most National Socialist propagandists were not willing to accept that Beethoven had been of impure racial stock. Upholding such a position would have required discarding his music as "alien," whereas many in the party designated Beethoven's art a musical symbol of how the German Volk would thrive under Hitler's rule. To National Socialist cultural politicians, Beethoven's legend was simply too valuable to repudiate. The *Völkischer Beobachter* therefore recognized its duty to decontaminate him for National Socialist applications. Edited by Rosenberg, the principal Nazi paper vouched for the composer's racial purity; during the Weimar era, a number of articles produced with the obvious intention of cleansing Beethoven of his apparent physical flaws appeared in its "Art and Culture" section.

One of these, "Portrait of His Heredity" (*Erbbild*), stressed indications that his paternal grandfather was of Germanic ancestry. "In the portrait of Ludwig van Beethoven's grandfather by Radoux, the court painter in Bonn, we see a conspicuously Nordic head of the finest racial stamp."[257] Another, "His Outward Appearance" (*Erscheinungsbild*), did the same for the composer. This report cited Anton Schindler's contemporary depiction of Beethoven's stocky physique, overbearing laugh, and unruly hair; but the Nazis revealed their ulterior motive with a telling alteration of Schindler's recollections. To his statement that Beethoven's "forehead was high and wide, his brown eyes small" the *Völkischer Beobachter* added in parentheses the question, "blue?" In this way the paper insinuated that Schindler, Beethoven's reverent secretary, had described his hero's eye color inaccurately. Thereafter, the passage continued without annotations in a way that nevertheless indicated why the *Völkischer Beobachter* had reproduced it: "The tint of Beethoven's face was yellowish. He usually lost this, however, through his wanderings in free nature during the summertime, when he received a good tanning and his skin came to be covered with a fresh varnish of red and brown." In all probability this passage was reproduced to discount reports that Beethoven was a "dark" racial type, since it implied that his skin was tinted by the sun. Confirmation of this assumption came in the next paragraph, which opened with the revelation that "Friedrich August Klöber, the sculptor who made a bust of Beethoven in 1818 and who also painted [him], reports to us in words and in images that *Beethoven's eye color was gray-blue.*" The *Völkischer Beobachter* then denounced racial scholars who had raised questions about Beethoven's genetic purity: *"Dr. Hans Günther errs decidedly when . . . he characterizes Beethoven as predominantly Eastern."*[258] Thus did Nazi propagandists try to eradicate signs that Beethoven might not have been worthy of leadership status in the racially pure Volk they fantasized.

In this coverup designed for public consumption, the Nazis apparently did not consider it necessary to formulate sophisticated explanations of the discrepancy between Beethoven's appearance and his required significance as a Nordic hero. For a mass audience, the propaganda method of the "big lie" sufficed: the *Völkischer Beobachter* simply insisted that Beethoven was of Aryan descent and justified its position by misrepresenting contemporary descriptions and portraits of him.

A more persuasive argument was necessary to quiet the concerns of those who called for strict adherence to racial criteria in choosing Nazi *Helden.* A secondary school teacher and would-be musicologist from Bochum, Richard Eichenauer, provided the racial-scientific assessment needed to justify the use of Beethoven as a party symbol. A volkish enthusiast whose poems and essays had appeared in extreme right-wing publications, Eichenauer was not a trained scholar of music.[259] However, his book *Musik und Rasse* (Music and race), issued in 1932 by the extreme right-wing J. F. Lehmann Verlag, synthesized racist and Germanic ideology with music history in a way National Socialist propagandists would find useful. Republished after the Nazis achieved power, Eichenauer's book later became the Third Reich's most influential guide to applying racial theory to music and musicians; in 1938 it was recommended as background reading for a National Socialist musicological congress that carried the same name (*Musik und Rasse*).[260]

Opening his chapter on Beethoven, Eichenauer admitted that he had once agreed with the negative evaluations of the composer's racial ancestry by Günther and Clauß. Reconsidering this "racial-scientific representation while writing this book," however, Eichenauer felt himself "required to deviate in many ways from the views" he had expressed earlier. In the rest of his discussion he labored to fashion Beethoven onto the National Socialist paradigm of racial acceptability. Eichenauer's efforts to reinstate the composer began with a partial retraction of the view he had shared with other racial scholars: he had never said that Beethoven's spirit or "world of tones" were racially compromised, only his physical qualities. Beethoven's attitudes, actions, expressions, and art were clearly not Eastern. In fact, his Germanic fighting nature was greater than that of any purely Aryan composer, including Schütz, Bach, Handel, Gluck, and Haydn. This was because, Eichenauer argued (citing Richard Benz, incidentally), Beethoven had fought "like the descendant of a dragonslayer" to overcome his racial impediment and create the greatest of Nordic music. Since Beethoven had struggled to overcome his mixed nature, Eichenauer felt he should be considered even *more* Nordic than the other composers. He concluded: "We believe that we have shown that

Beethoven's non-Nordic inheritance worked, in the highest sense, not as a limitation, but as a steady impetus for raising himself to become Nordic. So he is to us, in spite of his undoubtedly impure Nordic nature, one of the most stirring developers of the inner soul—a Nordic fighter and hero."[261] Thus did Eichenauer help to save Beethoven's legend from extermination by the most fanatical among racists.

Despite such reevaluations of his heredity, the case of Beethoven remained problematic for the NSDAP. Though he could, with some reservations, be counted as a member of the German race, certainly Beethoven had exhibited quasi-socialist tendencies. This fact necessitated a parallel process of purification purging his image of contamination by leftist political ideology. The Nazis had to enter into competition over Beethoven's legacy with the ideologues of the socialist and communist parties. To minimize Beethoven's enthusiasm about the French Revolution and the rise of Napoleon, National Socialists borrowed themes from their right-wing and volkish counterparts: although Beethoven had been exposed to French revolutionary (in their words, "cosmopolitan" and "internationalist") political ideals, he was "always a Rhinelander" at heart. When it came to defending his nation against French rule, the *Völkischer Beobachter* held, Beethoven had always sided with Germany; though he temporarily suffered from "revolutionary fever," his heart remained with his German *Heimat*.[262]

Substantiation of these assertions was offered in various forms. One essay in the *Völkischer Beobachter* reviewed the story of the Grätz Castle incident, when Beethoven fled the country home of Prince Lichnowsky after refusing to perform on the piano for guests who included French officers. Significantly titled "The Patriot," the Nazi version retold the legend without mentioning the standard explanation of Beethoven's anger on this occasion—that his artistic pride had been affronted—and implying instead that he had acted on nationalistic impulse alone.[263] Another *Völkischer Beobachter* story, "The Great Pathfinder," reproduced the most jingoistic passages of Richard Wagner's 1870 essay on Beethoven's significance during the Franco-Prussian War. While Germans were feeling the effects of the Versailles Treaty, Wagner's assertions complemented perfectly the depiction of Beethoven as a Nazi fellow traveler.[264] Finally, in articles like "The Words of Beethoven," National Socialist journalists ripped citations out of context—including Beethoven's jest that power was his morality and his angry wish that he could meet Napoleon on the battlefield—and presented them as evidence that the composer had been a fierce enemy of the French.[265] Carefully selected and doctored stories, essays, and quotations suited Nazi use of Beethoven to fuel bitterness against the enemy to the West. In the words of another Nazi publication, the *Deutsche Arbeiterpresse* of Vienna, all Germans had to fight along with the National Socialists to protect Beethoven from the French. "Woe if his spirit is ever stolen from us, since that would mean ultimate defeat—because this spirit is *German* spirit."[266]

A confirmed enemy of France, Beethoven naturally appeared in Nazi propaganda as a fighter. Like other activists on the right, Nazis revitalized the legend of Bismarck's feelings about the *Appassionata* to display Beethoven as a *Kämpfer*.[267] To this end, they also recast the obscure First World War anecdote about the fate of Beethoven's grand-nephew. The *Völkischer Beobachter* article, "Landsturmmann Beethoven: A Wartime Memory," related the story of the German officer who trained the ill-fated grandson of Karl, with sentimental embellishment at the conclusion. "Dismissing my squad, I squeezed Beethoven's hand with particularly heartfelt feelings. Tears rolled down his cheeks. Half a year later he was no longer among the living. He died in a garrison hospital of blood poisoning caused by a leg wound that he had neglected. The sad end of *Landsturmmann* Beethoven. The last descendant of the creator of the 'Ninth'!"[268]

As in the original versions of this report, implicit is the notion that Beethoven would have fought in the First World War like his distant relation, and could therefore be considered a symbolic flag bearer in future battles. The *Deutsche Arbeiterpresse* hoped that his biography would convince German youth that military strength was necessary and desirable. "Let youth embrace the spirit of Beethoven, and thereby learn and comprehend in the deepest sense that life means *struggle*."[269] Beethoven's current German admirers, the journal added, should emulate him not as an artist but as a warrior, for that was what Germany and the Nazi Party required at the time. "To love Beethoven means to love battle and to honor the essence of heroism. We need this."[270]

Also like other right-wing organizations, but more emphatically, Nazis rejected any suggestion that Beethoven had been a supporter of modern democratic ideals. They asserted instead that he recognized the need for autocratic leadership and would have seconded their call for the strong hand of a Führer. Richard Eichenauer came up with a way to dismiss rumors that Beethoven had been a democrat. "If one calls Beethoven a 'democrat,'" he contended, "one must be aware of the difference in the meaning of the word between then and now. God knows he was never a representative of sentimental feelings for the masses; even the 'Be embraced, ye millions' makes him less a democrat in this sense than the spiritually related Schiller. He had wished to honor outstanding men in Napoleon. As soon as he found him to be a small man, he ripped up his dedication. That is representative of a wholly aristocratic outlook."[271] The *Völkischer Beobachter* similarly stipulated that Beethoven had "no absolute hatred of aristocrats," then went on to point out that the composer had been enthralled with Napoleon's charisma and domineering tactics: what made him enthusiastic was that the Corsican had "with a strong hand transformed the chaos of the gruesome revolution into state order." Ultimately, this paper argued, Beethoven feared chaos brought on by revolution, thus recognizing that authoritarian rule was occasionally necessary. "He did not close his mind to understanding that in special times of anarchical uprising an oligarchic aristocracy had its attractions."[272]

After its composer was deemed politically sound, Beethoven's music was also incorporated into National Socialist propaganda. Nazi cultural politicians extolled his works as exemplifying the greatness of Germanic art—and the German race itself. Beethoven's music is "indisputably Nordic," said Eichenauer; after all, "the greatest Nordic poetry of all times and peoples" (specified as the works of Homer, Euripides, Shakespeare, Cervantes, Goethe, and Schiller) influenced him directly. *Fidelio,* Eichenauer asserted, "should be seen as the first truly Nordic opera." All his symphonies were renditions of "Nordic-colored heroism."[273] Beethoven's music did not describe the struggle against Fate understood in universal, abstract terms: the fate that Beethoven worked to surmount was "his own racial background, and it is for this that he should be celebrated."[274]

The most important image projected by the Nazis onto the music of Beethoven was that of the National Socialist movement itself. In his own contribution to the *Völkischer Beobachter* apotheosis of Beethoven, Alfred Rosenberg reminded all Germans that in an "era requiring spiritual struggle" his music was a perfect source of inspiration. Of course, he added, participants in the National Socialist movement would derive the most from this store of strength. "Whoever has a notion of what sort of nature operates in our movement knows that an impulse similar to that which Beethoven embodied in the highest degree lives in all of us: the [desire] to storm over the ruins of a crumbling world, the hope for the will to reshape the world, the strong sense of joy that comes from overcoming passionate sorrow." When National Socialists achieved victory in Germany and throughout Europe, Rosenberg continued, they would owe thanks to Beethoven for motivating them. "One day we will permit ourselves the heart-warming consciousness that the German Beethoven towers over *all* the peoples of the West. . . . Then we will want to remember that Beethoven can and must pass to us the ability and the will of *German* creation. We live today in the *Eroica* of the German Volk. We must make use of it!"[275]

During their *Kampfzeit,* however, the Nazis did not make use of Beethoven's music as effectively as Rosenberg hoped. Like other opposition parties, Nazis could not diffuse their ideas about Beethoven through major concerts and ceremonies; they presented their views mainly in journal and newspaper articles. The Nazis did, however, have important allies among Beethoven scholars. Ludwig Schiedermair, professor at the University at Bonn and head of the Beethoven-haus Archive, provided much copy for *Völkischer Beobachter* commemorations of Beethoven. Throughout the Nazi period, Schiedermair would remain in these positions and continue to publish material about Beethoven. It was in his interest to ensure that the composer was counted among Nazi heroes—as Beethoven's myth went, so went Schiedermair's job. But professional motives are not the only reason to suppose that Schiedermair shared the National Socialist worldview: his major work, *Beethoven und das Rheinland,* was an extensive effort to prove Beethoven's Germanic racial roots; other essays, including "The Formulation of *Weltanschaulicher* Ideas in the Folk Music of Beethoven" and "Beethoven's Parents,"[276] as well as speeches he gave during the Second World War,[277] were also tainted by his "brown" political tendencies. Indubitably, Schiedermair deserved the honors he later received from the cultural authorities of the National Socialist regime.[278]

Despite this important contact in the world of Beethoven scholarship, the Nazis were not in a position to force their interpretation on the nation during the Weimar period. They could do little more than berate observations of the composer's birth and death organized by opposing groups.[279] That the Nazis had plans to alter the situation, however, is evident in an essay by the man who would later become president of the principal National Socialist music organization in the Third Reich, Peter Raabe. In 1920, as conductor of the Aachen orchestra, Raabe expressed his feeling that during the "present state of calamity," when Germany was facing a debt to France of "between 1,320 and 50,000 billion marks" and the French were threatening to take everything else (including 810,000 milk cows) "so that the child-mortality rate in Germany will rise immeasurably, so that tuberculosis spreads, and so that we become weaker and less dangerous business competitors," Beethoven's music was not being played enough. Instead of maintaining the "one thing which, in spite of all the enslaving they are doing, they cannot take away from us"—the compositions of the German masters—orchestras programmed the degenerate music of contemporary composers to excess: the "measureless overestimation" of new music was "a cancer in our program of music cultivation which causes much harm." If, he contended, "one pushes Beethoven aside simply because one wants to perform something new, then one sins against German art." Such "miserable trash" could not help the German nation in distress; only powerful German treasures such as Beethoven's works could inspire national regeneration. "If there is *anyone* who, through the power of his language, can turn our people to good and at the same time comfort and delight them, it is Beethoven."[280]

Consequently, Raabe called for censoring modernist culture, increasing the Volk's knowledge of traditional German music, and enforcing performance of the classics—especially Beethoven.

> Very incisive measures must be taken. I know of [some] that will lead to the goal: close all the cinemas, which are plague-ridden hells that infect the taste of the Volk irrecoverably, in which "detective dramas" allow eighteen-year-old dwellers of big and small cities . . . to study theft from the ground up. Dam up the operettas, which are nuisances! Outlaw sentimental Kitsch! Protect the sensitivity of pure, decent, sensitive people through legislation, through the strictest censorship! A tenth of the millions that are given out for miserable trash would be enough to make the best German music, the friendliest and most serene art, accessible to the Volk in excellent productions. And a Volk to which one only offers good things will certainly no longer ask for bad.

"The spirit of Beethoven will have conquered," Raabe concluded, if the German government would only do such things. "In distress as we are now, we *need* this music more than almost anything else in order to break free of servitude, stupidity, and self-inflicted suffering! Beethoven, the Seer, knew that his music could be used for these purposes when he said, more than one hundred years ago, 'Whoever understands my music must become free of all the misery that burdens others.'"[281]

With its anxious references to cancerous elements that threatened the health of the German Volk and had to be eliminated by "incisive measures," one might, in retrospect, fairly designate Peter Raabe's tirade the *Mein Kampf* of music politics. Like the work of the prisoner in Landsberg, this diatribe was written in anger over the defeat of the German armies, the terms of the Versailles Treaty, and the supposed downfall of traditional German culture. It also formulated and outlined plans that, on first appearance during the republican era, seemed ridiculous—but were ultimately put into practice.

4

The Third Reich

> We will continually achieve success if we stride forward on the high points of our spiritual heritage . . . if we stride forward from Beethoven to Hitler.
>
> EUGEN HADAMOVSKY
> Reich broadcast chief

Ten years after the one-hundredth anniversary of Beethoven's death, Julius Nitsche, a music critic for the *Völkischer Beobachter,* remembered the observances in an article entitled "Jonny against Beethoven: Memory of a Centennial That Took Place during Confused Times." In 1927 Nitsche had been enthusiastic about the Todestag events; after attending a concert in Munich, he and a friend traveled to Leipzig to partake in the festivities there. Bemoaning the noise and confusion that inundated the city's "modern" streets, the two found a café and sat down. Reading the newspapers, they noticed that all contained articles commemorating the composer. "Beethoven was everywhere," Nitsche remembered. "Each newspaper, domestic and foreign, carried appreciations of Beethoven." Nitsche had wondered, "When was the memory of an artist ever celebrated in such a way? Every political party and every sort of confession counted him as one of their own; all of them were fighting tooth and nail to demonstrate that he belonged exclusively to their circle of life." To what extremes, he asked, could this process of appropriation lead? Moments later he found his answer: the Leipzig newspaper announced that *Jonny spielt auf*—Ernst Krenek's *Zeitoper* highlighting jazz rhythms and a leading man in blackface—was opening that evening.[1]

In his 1937 article, Nitsche reflected on this experience as a sign of how degenerate life had become in the Weimar era. It was so bad in the *System-Zeit,* he wrote, that people were capable of performing a "nigger operetta" on the day of Beethoven's death. In what was then the recent past, Germans had placed "next to the purest, the dirtiest; next to the deepest, the most shallow; beside the most spiritual, the most lacking in spirit; and next to that of eternal content, the most ephemeral." Even on the day for honoring the creator of the *Missa Solemnis* and the Ninth, people had been willing to perform a show headlining "a devilish Negro who lured the hearts of all women and girls." It had been, in his opinion, a thoroughly "confused time."[2]

All was not dreary, though; writing four years after Hitler's accession to power, Nitsche could report change. As the National Socialist regime achieved mastery, all interpretations and uses of Beethoven by progressive artists, leftist politicians, and non-Germans were overruled. In the Third Reich, Beethoven was again recognized in ways acceptable to Nitsche: "Today Jonny no longer plays for us. Gone is the hell's spittle that deified the Negro hopping around like a horny he-goat. Through us, art has gone far in the conquest of the simply sensual and generic."[3] Because the Nazis could now enforce their aesthetic standards, Nitsche implied, Beethoven's music and all other fine German art would henceforth be appreciated in the fashion they deserved. The German people could rest assured that they now lived in a new millennium of stability, respectability, and good taste.

The National Socialist Beethoven

One can understand why in 1937 this Nazi cultural politician viewed the future of Beethoven reception in Germany confidently. Once the National Socialist Party seized the political and cultural administration of the nation, its version of the volkish Beethoven image dominated all others. A few pockets of resistance sustained opinions of Beethoven's music as symbolizing leftist, idealist, humanitarian, and other such "confused" ideals within the Third Reich, despite enforcement of Nazi interpretations. But as the *Völkischer Beobachter* critic asserted, between 1933 and 1945 the fight over Beethoven was—temporarily—won by the extreme right. This victory of the volkish Beethoven interpretation was achieved because Peter Raabe and those who shared his views were able, after Hitler's ascension to power, to take the "incisive measures" they had designed to purify the German music world. Once in control, the NSDAP developed a more extensive program of music politics than had ever been implemented by a national government. The manner in which the National Socialists seized and coordinated the world of music performance, education, and criticism demonstrates the importance they accorded their policies of *Musikpolitik*—particularly efforts to impose on the German public their views about specific compositions, including Beethoven's.

All professional organizations of musicians in Germany were subsumed under the Law for the Restoration of the Civil Service, imposed on 7 April 1933. Jews, political nonconformists, and supporters of musical modernism were eliminated from positions as conductors, players, and administrators; hundreds were affected, including notables such as Bruno Walter, dismissed from the Gewandhaus Orchestra in Leipzig, and Otto Klemperer, ousted from his post as conductor of the Staatsoper in Berlin. By 1934 Nazi-administered organizations vied for authority over the music world. Most significant were Rosenberg's Fighting League for German Culture (*Kampfbund für deutsche Kultur*), later restructured as the NS Cultural Community (*NS Kulturgemeinde*), and the Reich Music Chamber (*Reichsmusikkammer*) within Joseph Goebbels' Reich Culture Chamber (*Reichskulturkammer*). The Reich Music Chamber that eventually prevailed was designed to manage all branches of music, including folk music and entertainment music, as well as the classical music establishment. According to Raabe, its president after 1935, music under control of the Reich Music Chamber was "to serve a social function, to be clearly defined in subordination to the general aims of National Socialism, and to be denied traditional autonomy."[4] All music performing groups thus became instruments of the Hitler state: the Berlin Philharmonic Orchestra performed throughout Europe as a cultural ambassador for National Socialism; other orchestras and ensembles enhanced the pageantry of party rallies and state functions. Throughout Hitler's rule, programs of all performances were carefully monitored according to the dictates of Nazi tastes and the needs of party propagandists.

Even more important to National Socialists than controlling music performers was mastering those who determined how music was conceived—scholars and critics, for they could ensure that Germans would interpret music as the Nazis wished. Stringent control of critical and scholarly institutions was pivotal to the Nazi policy of projecting onto music preferred political meanings and adjusting audience perceptions accordingly. Under the legal and administrative pressure applied by the party, it was the "expert" community that politicized, or nazified, the processes of music reception in Germany. Music scholars and educators were subjected to the same measures that affected academics in other fields; none could publish work contrary to the National Socialist line and expect to retain his or her position. Music critics and other commentators were swiftly subordinated as well;

journals of music criticism and scholarship were either transformed into organs of Nazi music policy or eliminated. After 1933 the progressive music journal *Melos* was repeatedly attacked until its chief editor was dismissed; in 1934 *Melos* was withdrawn, thoroughly nazified, and reissued as the *Neues Musikblatt.* Likewise *Die Musik* was subjugated. Its editor, respected for balanced treatment of modernist trends, was forced out by June 1933 and replaced by a party hack; thereafter the journal became a mouthpiece for Rosenberg's NS Culture Community. During the war *Die Musik* and the *Neues Musikblatt* were consolidated with the ever-conservative *Allgemeine Musik-Zeitung* and *Zeitschrift für Musik* to form a single publication entitled, tellingly, *Musik im Kriege.*[5]

Thus did Goebbels, Rosenberg, and other Third Reich culture authorities appropriate the machinery necessary for disseminating music criticism suitable to the regime. With control of the institutions of music performance, and especially music analysis, each set out to mold this art form into a powerful propaganda tool. The contribution scholars and critics made to the new government, willingly or otherwise, involved more than adjusting interpretations of music to comply with volkish and racist theories in general; in studies of composers and their works, they explicitly associated music matters with party policy. According to National Socialist pamphleteers, atonal composition was not just "alien" (*artfremd*) music, as earlier music conservatives had argued, but "musical bolshevism" created by internationalist Jewry to cause worldwide chaos in preparation for revolution. Supporters of progressive music trends were branded enemies of German society who diffused works meant to weaken the will—and blood—of the Volk. Yet the German masters were deemed heroes not just on account of their "Aryan" background or their native (*arteigene*) styles of musical expression, but because they supposedly shared Hitler's worldview. No matter how anachronistic, signs were sought in the lives and art of the important German composers that each would have supported at least the spirit of the Führer's nationalist, militarist, and anticommunist directives.[6] We have seen that these methods of propagandizing through music were innovations neither of the Nazi party nor of the Hitler state. At least in the case of Beethoven, such procedures had been undertaken well before the *Machtergreifung* by every major group in the German political spectrum. What is unique about Nazi *Kulturpolitik* is the extent to which it was enforced. With Hitler's accession to power, the NSDAP was able to refine and expand these techniques without restriction. The National Socialists' manipulation of the myth of Beethoven typifies their grand cultural-political scheme, aimed at presenting the movement as respectable and surrounding it with an inspirational aura.

The Beethoven image that the regime thrust on the German public was derived from that designed in the Weimar era by party propagandists; few alterations were made to this portrait after the Nazis took power.[7] Some controversy over his genetic background did continue after 1933, but as we will see doubts about his fitness as a hero of the German race were subdued, Beethoven was accepted into the Nazi *Gemeinschaft,* and his music became an integral part of its rituals. The main difference between previous promotions of Beethoven as a symbol of volkish ideals and efforts in the Third Reich was the effectiveness with which his nazified image was publicized. Unlike earlier exploiters of the Beethoven Mythos, the Nazi regime had complete control of every medium of communication within Germany and used all of them to promote its version.

While doing so, Nazis undertook to end all argument about the suitability of Beethoven as a National Socialist idol. Taking up the job Alfred Rosenberg had started, music-political functionaries set themselves to cleansing Beethoven of biological blemishes once and for all. One aspect of the continued effort to sanitize Beethoven for propaganda use was an intensive campaign to remove doubt that he had been German born. An excess of articles appeared in Nazi-controlled journals rejecting the notion that Beethoven was of Flemish background: in spite of arguments made by "foreigners who had found their way to his door" during the "era of occupation" (*Besatzungszeit*), Nazis defended Beethoven's Deutschtum as irrefutable.[8] "The roots of his whole being lay along the Rhine," Ludwig Schiedermair insisted in numerous essays and speeches; "he never forgot this."[9] His spirit was full of "Nordic depth," affirmed another expert on such matters, Hans Joachim Moser.[10] The regime, held Walther Vetter (another music historian who contributed to this effort) could confidently hold up Beethoven as a "representative of his Volk; as the highest embodiment of his race."[11]

Nevertheless, diligent wardens of the so-called Aryan community were troubled by another aspect of Beethoven's family background: his father.[12] Since Johann van Beethoven had been a heavy-drinking, mean-spirited character, some National Socialists had difficulty correlating the life of Ludwig with their theories of inheritance. If blood and family background were the basis for acceptance in the Nazi

Gemeinschaft, Beethoven could not be one of its icons—his father's record was wholly unacceptable. Manipulative Nazi scholars had to come to the composer's rescue again. Some brazenly defied the historial record by contending that Beethoven's father had not been an unruly sort at all. In an article entitled "The Truth about Beethoven's Father," *Die Musik* presented Johann as having had "a heroic fighting nature of Nordic essence." By trying to establish a "German theater" in Bonn, *Die Musik* averred, Johann had attempted a "nationalistic act." Therefore, this nazified journal concluded, the heroic aspects of Beethoven's works could be seen as "racial-spiritual monuments" to the deeds of his father.[13]

Schiedermair also concocted a remedy for this blot on his hero's background. In a 1935 *Völkischer Beobachter* article, "Beethoven's Parents," he argued that it was unjust to damn Beethoven's father: persons who condemned him as a drunk did not understand the importance of alcohol in Rhenish culture. The idea that Beethoven derived from a "family swamp" (*Familiensumpf*) was absurd, Schiedermair avowed, because this would "contradict biological laws." Since Beethoven was a great German artist, he simply could not have come from inferior stock; therefore the father must have been sound. Having deftly resolved the problem, Schiedermair went on to suggest that his solution invalidated arguments by those who opposed legal measures of sterilization or castration. Some, he said, contested such legislation by referring to Johann van Beethoven; within its strictures, they contended, he would have been castrated and his renowned son never born. Schiedermair considered this stance preposterous because he was sure Johann had been fit and therefore would not have been subject to sterilization under National Socialist law. About the legislation itself he had no qualms.[14] So did the head of the Beethovenhaus continue to ingratiate himself with party authorities.

Others maintained that Beethoven's father was in fact an unsavory figure, and the composer had hated him. Intimating that he was more attached to his mother than to his father, Nazi literature stressed Beethoven's love for her. Much was made of the fact that upon her death Beethoven had written: "She was such a good mother, so worthy of love. She was my best friend. Oh, who was as lucky as I when I could still cry out the sweet name 'Mother' and it would be heard." Magdalena van Beethoven was esteemed in National Socialist culture as a traditional mother-type, tending the kitchen and providing refuge from the father.[15] By so depicting her, the Nazis achieved two goals:

Sippschaftstafel Beethovens.

Corneille van Beethoven 1641—1716 Tischler (?) in Mecheln	Catherine van Leempoel 1642—	Louis Stuyckers Bäckermeister in Mecheln	Magdeleine Goussau	Tillmann Westorff Zollinspektor in Engers

Michel van Beethoven 1684—1749 Bäckermeister und Gemäldehändler in Mecheln	Marie Luise Stuyckers 1685—1749	Johann Heinrich Keverich Hofkutscher in Ehrenbreitstein aus Leiwen-Köverich (Mosel)	Eva Katharina Alber 1664—1753 geb. Trier (89 Jahre alt)	Jakob Westorff Kaufmann in Koblenz seit 1690 geb. Engers	Maria Magdalena Schettert T. des Schiffsreeders, Kaufmanns u. Ratsherrn J. Franz Schettert aus Traben u. Maria Magd. Beeker

Ludwig van Beethoven 1712—73 (Großvater Beethovens) Hofkapellmeister (und Weinhändler) in Bonn Gestalt: klein, gedrungen Gesicht: länglich Stirne: breit Augen: hell, sehr lebhaft Hautfarbe: dunkel	Maria Josepha Poll 1714—75 (aus Kur-Köln)	Heinrich Keverich 1702—59 Oberhofkoch und Admoniator des Kurfürstl. Hofküchenwesens in Ehrenbreitstein	8 Geschwister (Näheres unbek.)	Anna Clara Westorff 1705—68 geb. Koblenz	Maria Magd. Westorff × Georg Ad. Daubach Hofkoch in Ehrenbreitstein u. Schöffe

Maria Bernardina Ludovica van Beethoven 1734—35	Markus Josephus van Beethoven 1736—? (früh verst.)	Johann van Beethoven 1739—92 Hoftenorist in Bonn Gestalt: mittelgroß, breitschulterig Gesicht: länglich Stirne: breit	Maria Magdalena Keverich verw. Leym 1746—87 Gestalt: schlank, mager Gesicht: länglich Augen: dunkel Haare: wohl dunkel	Joh. Peter Keverich 1734—1807 Karmeliterpater	1 Tochter (Näheres 2 Söhne unbekannt)

Ludwig Maria van Beethoven geb. 1769, † 1769	Ludwig van Beethoven 1770—1827 Gestalt: klein, stämmig, breitschulterig Gesicht: ziemlich breit Augen: blau Haare: schwarz oder schwarzbraun Hautfarbe: dunkel	Kaspar Anton Karl van Beethoven 1774—1815 × (Johanna Reiß) K. K. Staatsbankkassier Gestalt: klein Haare: rot Karl van Beethoven 1806—58 (× Karoline Adamberger) K. K. Offizier (Zahlreiche Nachkommen)	Nikolaus Johann van Beethoven 1776—1848 Apotheker und Gutsbesitzer (× Therese Obermeyer) kinderlos Gestalt: ziemlich groß Haare: dunkel Gesicht: schmal	3 frühverstorbene Kinder geb. 1779—1786

Fig. 15. Table of Beethoven's genealogy, *Volk und Rasse* 9 (1934) 201. Under the composer's name: "Build: short, husky, broad-shouldered. Face: rather broad. Eyes: blue. Hair: black or dark-brown. Skin tone: dark."

they insinuated that Beethoven had received a greater amount of his mother's more respectable blood and they promoted their notion of a woman's place in family life.

Any residual doubts about Beethoven's background were abolished in 1934 when *Volk und Rasse*—the "Journal of the Reich Committee for the Volk's Health Service and the German Society for Racial Hygiene"—gave him a clean bill of racial health. In "Racial Features of Beethoven and His Nearest Relatives," Walther Rauschenberger verified and sharpened Eichenauer's earlier justification of the composer's status as Nordic hero.[16] In spite of his mixed racial appearance and imperfect family background, this article reiterated, Beethoven had created compelling Germanic art. "Nordic are, above all, the heroic aspects of his works which often rise to titanic greatness. It is significant that today, in a time of national renovation, Beethoven's works are played more often than any others, that one hears his works at almost all events of heroic tenor."[17] Thus did an official institution of racial hygiene guarantee Beethoven's eligibility for Nazi hero status and deem his music appropriate for performance at National Socialist events.

Once determined to be no risk to racial security, Beethoven was promoted in the Third Reich as having shared National Socialist political ideals. Nazi interpreters continued after 1933 to attack any notion that Beethoven had been a revolutionary; while admitting that he had been influenced by "French political ideas" during his youth, they claimed that these notions faded as he matured. Beethoven, according to a 1937 biographical sketch for young people, "drowned out the battle-thunder of Napoleon with a thunderstorm that came down to him from heaven"; a patriotic Rhinelander, he had done all he could to "counter the Great Terror and the despotic Moloch"—Napoleon.[18] Moser compared this Beethoven—the musical warrior triumphing over the enemies of the German people—to "Parsifal at the Round Table of King Arthur."[19] In Moser's opinion, Beethoven's works were sacred, since the "holy circulation of the Volk's blood pounds in the music."[20] By listening to them, said the *Westdeutscher Beobachter* in Bonn, Germans would sense the "roots" and demands of the Fatherland" and thereafter use the "power of the Heimat" to achieve world-historical status, as Beethoven had.[21]

The idea of Beethoven as "world conqueror" was an important element in the Nazi edition of his Mythos.[22] Perhaps borrowing the concept from right-wing and volkish poems, Rosenberg had hinted at it in his 1927 article, when he described his vision of "the German Beethoven towering over all the peoples of Western civilization." Later Nazi propagandists, such as the musicologist Walther Vetter, expanded this theme. "The Beethoven portrait of our time should in no way be limited or stunted; . . . only then will it do justice to the great man's power to have political effect, which shows itself in the fact that all the peoples of the earth it has peacefully subjugated consider his art an admirable manifestation of German style. . . . It is Beethoven that we have to thank for founding a musical world-literature of German-national origins. The only comparable spiritual domination of the world to spread from Germany was that of Goethe."[23]

Such descriptions of Beethoven as conqueror were part of an effort to associate him with Adolf Hitler. Rejecting all former interpretations of Beethoven as a democrat—or even an aristocrat—as the outmoded thought of "parliamentarians," Nazi-era studies of his political views said he had sought the guidance of a "Führer-personality":

> A spiritual and cultural revolution . . . has been achieved. To use expressions out of the vocabulary of the parliamentarians to denote Beethoven's art today would be an invalid and frivolous masquerade. Today's politicization of the spiritual man does not allow a Beethoven to sink back into what was once considered political. It commands rather that one develop political thought to a spiritual level at which an exchange with Beethoven's spirit first becomes possible. . . . We will today no longer speak of a "democratic folk-overture to *Egmont*." Instead we will fully agree that, in a critical period of total misery for his race, Beethoven felt his heart yearning for a born Führer-personality and communicated this feeling clearly in a great work, the *Eroica*.[24]

National Socialists even intimated that the composer was himself a Führer-type, both artistic and political. According to Schiedermair, "Beethoven appears to us today from the German past as one of the artistic Führer of epochal dimensions who maintained German ideals against ephemeral political and artistic trends."[25] In this capacity, Vetter supposed, Beethoven had assigned the German people a duty: "to seek unity in multiplicity, to trace the forceful spiritual-soulful powers behind that unity, and to point out the link between these powers and the movements and currents [running toward] the Beethovenian future." Beethoven himself had been unable to complete this mission; and nineteenth-century Germans had failed to unify the Volk.[26] But by following the newest Führer, Germans could finally reach the "Beethovenian future." According to Eugen Hadamovsky, Reich broadcast chief (*Reichssendeleiter*), "we will continually achieve success if we stride forward on the high points of our spiritual heritage . . . : if we stride forward from Beethoven to Hitler."[27]

Along with biographical writings, Nazi interpretation of Beethoven's music alluded to the supposed link between the composer and Hitler. According to Arnold Schering, another important scholar who fell under the sway of the new regime, "the vague sense of *per aspera ad astra* in the Fifth Symphony" could be understood as a depiction of the "fight for existence waged by a Volk that looks for its Führer and finally finds it." If this view were popularized, Schering went on, the Fifth could be transformed into a symbol that would "illuminate contemporary Germans in the purest light of day."[28] Nazi ideologues were very open about this process of appropriating Beethoven's music. Writing for the *Kölnische Zeitung*, the critic Walter Jacobs forthrightly recommended that National Socialist *Musikpolitiker* use the Third Symphony as a sonic emblem of the new Reich: "The *Eroica* will be very useful to musicians as well as the musical Volk as a political symbol, as a sign of the state order that will care for national treasures of life and art."[29]

Strangely, the Ninth Symphony was not immediately highlighted in Nazi culture. Some National Socialists considered it suspect because the idea of all men becoming brothers did not sit well with party ideology.[30] In contrast to Beethoven's so-called heroic symphonies—the Third and the Fifth—hard-liners such as Jacobs regarded Beethoven's "kiss for the whole world" as "shameless." During the Weimar era, "political-republican" ideals had tainted the Ninth, according to Nazi radio officials; performances of it then had been in "crass discord with human and artistic feelings."[31] When hearing the "Chorus of Joy" at that time, a *Völkischer Beobachter* reviewer reminded, the "contradiction between ideal and real" verified that "humanity was not yet worthy of following its fighting prophets."[32] Until the German Volk was reunified and disturbing conditions in modern Germany were rectified, it was advisable to concentrate on Beethoven's other works.[33] Of course, once the processes of coordination (*Gleichschaltung*) were under way, supporters considered Hitler's Germany much closer to manifesting the dream of the Ninth than the republic had been: in 1935 the *Völkischer Beobachter* could claim that "today the German Volk again stands united—Schiller's and Beethoven's high ideal of humanity is starting to be fulfilled. The band of joy is again wrapping itself around the nation."[34] Nonetheless, before it could become a major part of the Nazi liturgy, the Ninth Symphony had to be reinterpreted in purely German terms. Throughout the Hitler era, Nazi ideologues worked to eradicate earlier "internationalist" interpretations of the Ninth.[35] Moser's contribution to the effort went as follows: "His 'kiss for the whole world' (*Kuß der ganzen Welt*) means anything but a desire to fraternize with every Tom, Dick, and Harry, as it was too often misunderstood back in Germany's red years"; it was much more an expression, Moser held, of "glowing devotion to the notion, the dream, the simple idea of a humanity conceived in as German terms as possible (*so deutsch wie möglich gedacht*)!"[36]

As this and other examples attest, once in power the Nazis constantly promoted the notion most essential to their ideology—the need to establish a united community, or *Volksgemeinschaft*—in their interpretations of Beethoven. They also used composer and music to convey a sense that Hitler's rule would reestablish the stability missed since the First World War. By playing often the traditional works of Beethoven and other composers, the Nazis hoped Germans would "feel at home" when they heard "their music"—or at least more secure than they had during the *System-Zeit*, when unsettling styles of progressive musical expression had flourished.[37] A 1938 article in *Die Musik* put it this way: "Every German able to listen to and explain musical experience profoundly . . . will run up against something in the Ninth Symphony that is perhaps best described as a 'sense of the homeland': the individual feels secure, as if 'at home.' He feels warmly surrounded by old friends, [not only] because this type of music is familiar to us, but because something of the blood and race of our own nature lives in it."[38] Like the Ancient Oak, the Holy Flame, and references to the medieval past, Beethoven's music became a symbol meant to root the National Socialist state in a longstanding tradition of Germanic strength and order.

Little of the Beethoven interpretation promoted during the Third Reich was new; National Socialists in power popularized many of the same ideas they had emphasized during the *Kampfzeit*. Now, however, they had access to every means of publicizing their Beethoven myths. Insisting that all members of the *Volksgemeinschaft* could appreciate this music—"because something of the blood and race of our nature lives in it"—Nazi cultural politicians diffused their ideas about Beethoven's compositions as widely as possible.[39] National Socialist control of newspapers and journals compelled writers and editors to present the party's ideas about Beethoven and other German artists. Pressure on the institutions of German scholarship was similarly effective; many important German music scholars did their duty for the Third Reich by propagating the Nazi image of Beethoven in their scholarly writings and lectures. As we have seen, prominent facets of the Nazi *Beethovenbild* were first formulated by musicologists including Hans Joachim Moser,[40] Walther Vetter,[41] Max Unger,[42] Arnold Schering,[43] and, of course, Ludwig Schiedermair.[44] Perhaps these experts felt it necessary to contribute to Nazi propaganda in order to maintain their positions; but the enthusiasm with which they did so is a blot on the history of Beethoven and general scholarship only now being confronted in Germany.[45]

Adults were not the only ones force-fed Nazi Beethoven myths; National Socialists felt it crucial to educate German children about their ideals and plans, since they would carry out the program in the coming thousand years of the latest Reich. An excellent example of Beethoven's portrait in didactic literature appears in *Unseren Jungen: Ein Buch zur Unterhaltung, Belehrung, und Beschäftigung* (Our youth: a book for entertainment, education, and general interest). Published in 1937, *Unseren Jungen* was a collection of stories and anecdotes about exciting adventures, natural wonders, and important persons compiled for the edification of German children. It included chapters on "Boxing: The Fighting Sport of Our Youth," "Africa," "The Hero from Kolberg," "Old Frederick" ("The Sergeant King"), "The Birth of Radio," and "Ludwig van Beethoven."

The chapter on Beethoven contained elements typical of a biographical sketch for pedagogical purposes. It depicted him as having been a very hard worker, especially as a young man: to overcome his lack of classical education he read the major poets and writers on his own initiative, even underlining a passage by Homer which said that sleeping too much is shameful. "Above all," *Unseren Jungen* informed, Beethoven "never whined": even when going deaf, "he took courage in his pain until his heroic will helped him to get over this terrible turn in his fate and he was able to return to his work." Beethoven's self-discipline and intensive work habits were highlighted in this publication for young people—but that was not all. Rehashing the National Socialist versions of Beethoven rededicating the Third Symphony and fleeing from Grätz Castle, *Unseren Jungen* led young readers to believe that the primary significance of his music, especially the *Eroica,* was its contribution to the defeat of Napoleon. "In this work everything that the enslaved German people struggled to express is represented through titanic waves of music and a powerful language that carried away and angered its listeners."[46] Thus were German youths taught to perceive Beethoven's symphonies as nationalistic fight-songs.

Young people under Nazi authority were constantly told that the composer himself symbolized the heroic ideals advocated by the party. In an article entitled "Let's Ask the Young Generation: Beethoven? Yes, Beethoven!" *Deutsche Musikkultur* argued that this composer perfectly personified traits that German children should cultivate in the new era: "heroic behavior, cognizance of life's tragic nature, and sincere faith." To prove "how heroically Beethoven can make one think, feel, and act," *Deutsche Musikkultur* told of a First World War fighter pilot who was shot down. For three days, this knight of the air struggled against death; but when the moment came, he died with the word "Beethoven" on his lips.[47] Stories like these goaded German youths to emulate the composer in the way this warrior supposedly had.

Journals of the National Socialist Teachers' Union (*National-Sozialistisches Lehrerbund*) encouraged educators to read the latest literature on Beethoven and consider his works as "depictions of Nordic fate" (*nordische Schicksalsbilder*).[48] One Nazi pedagogue treasured Beethoven as the "schoolmaster of the nation."[49] That teachers enthusiastic about Nazism introduced him into the curriculum is certain; in the *Zeitschrift für Musik* one described how Beethoven's music affected her pupils. After listening to Beethoven in her class, Ida Deeke reported, one boy was deeply stirred. On the following day he came in with a "brooding face," his eyes "inner directed"; he worked "furiously, feverishly," without speaking to his comrades until the afternoon, when he broke down and cried. The next morning, however; "It was as though light were emitting from him. His eyes gleamed like suns, his brow was clear and free, his boyish mouth laughed proudly, victoriously, while his hands worked with inexhaustible diligence, not bitterly like the day before, but with joyous, jubilant, victorious power. He had heard Beethoven for the first time in his young life and only in the second night thereafter grasped its strength and triumphant, exultant joy."[50]

Evidently this boy was ready to participate in some of the Beethoven-related activities that Nazi cultural authorities arranged for him and his classmates, for instance, a Beethoven Festival administered by the Hitler Youth organization. Part of a larger program of music education undertaken by the group,[51] the 1938 "Beethoven Festival of the Hitler Youth" at Bad Wildbad in the Black Forest epitomized the National Socialist use of Beethoven's music to motivate young persons. Five hundred members of the Hitler Youth (HJ) and the League of German Girls (BDM) came together for a three-day festi-

Fig. 16. Arthur Haelßig conducting the Staatliche Kurorchester at the Beethoven Festival of the Hitler Youth in Bad Wildbad, May 1938. (*Zeitschrift für Musik* 105 [1938] 729)

val of Beethoven's works. In that time, all of Beethoven's symphonies (except the Ninth), three of the piano concertos, the Violin Concerto, both romances, five overtures, and a handful of chamber works were performed by members of a "state orchestra." In addition, "lively directives about the life and fate of Beethoven" were given to the children as preparation for understanding him as a role model.[52]

The tenor of these directives was unambiguous. The pianist who performed the concertos for the festival—Elly Ney, a staunch supporter of *NS Musikpolitik*—inaugurated the program by declaiming:

> Beethoven for the Hitler Youth! Lively young Germans, you are being carried away by the fire of enthusiasm. In you the desire for beauty, truth, and heroism awakes and urges you to action. How beautiful it is for the participating German musicians to bring you closer to Beethoven. The incomprehensible miracle of the work of this great German master shakes the soul. Powers and forces threatened him terribly—but he found redemption in his art. . . . Heroism is the essence of Nordic art. Here it lives in every tone. . . .

> And this holy fire should ignite the hearts of youths, awaken a sense of responsibility, strengthen them in battle, comfort them in distress. Come then, young Germans! Leave daily concerns behind! In these days and hours we want to open ourselves to the soulful powers of our Volk. May great and enlightened deeds in the service of the Führer arise from this![53]

The next speaker, music scholar Max Strub, also encouraged the young audience to think of Beethoven in heroic terms during the marathon. Not superficial entertainment, his music should "ignite fire in the souls of the men" while providing young women with "an ideal model of womanhood, to which Beethoven created an eternal, virtuous monument in his opera *Fidelio*."[54] Later the organizer of this festival, Arthur Haelßig—who also conducted the orchestra—looked back on the event very proudly. It was aimed at developing, he stated, a generation "artistically and spiritually aligned with Beethoven." In this way would evolve "a German man, a man who is freed of all liberal and foreign influences and legacies, the National Socialist man, the generation that will carry the future." As Haelßig saw it in 1938, moreover, the National Socialist future required that children quickly obtain the attributes of a warrior. This generation "will carry out the struggle even faster if we keep it from becoming infected by cowardice, tempted by exhaustion, and enticed by flaccid, timid passivity; if we strengthen its understanding of the joy to be experienced in fighting this battle." And these goals were all achieved by exposing young Germans to Beethoven's music. "At this decisive moment I have forged a weapon, in the form of this Beethoven Festival. With this weapon youth will prosecute the war. . . . Since the Wildbad Beethoven Festival of the HJ, my mind has been at ease: because through it youth grasped these ideas."[55]

To complement its journalistic, scholarly, and educational features, Nazi propaganda also manipulated the newest technologies of mass communication. In keeping with Goebbels' sophisticated ideas about modern publicity techniques, the NSDAP developed radio broadcasting as a powerful method of propagating ideology. By orchestrating common cultural experiences on the radio, the Nazis would draw the German Volk closer together than ever before. Writing about Beethoven's role in this process, *Deutsche Musikkultur* claimed that radio was "born with us" (meaning the NSDAP). "Like National Socialism, it is the carrier and herald of an idea that demands neither individuals nor classes, neither high nor low, poor nor rich, but rather the

Gemeinschaft, the whole, undivided Volk." The "political mission" of Nazi-controlled radio, then, was "to reestablish a completely united Germany."[56]

Beethoven was assigned an important role in this effort; programmers extolled the suitability of his music for National Socialist broadcasting. According to Johann Georg Bachmann, author of a *Deutsche Musikkultur* mission statement for the airwaves (aptly titled "Radio: 'Beethoven for Everyone?' ") the *best* way for radio to contribute to the volkish experiment was to disseminate Beethoven's music. Though Goebbels commanded that radio entertain the German people, Bachmann assumed that the propaganda czar did not want radio broadcasts to be pedestrian; while it should not present "high-brow" material alone, radio should provide quality entertainment and education. Sending Beethoven's works over the airwaves was the perfect way to do both. "The important thing is whether the broadcast resonates in the soul of the hearer, whether it releases free, joyous, and festive feelings. That a Beethoven symphony can achieve this is self-evident, and will be constantly proven by the radio. . . . Beethoven for everyone? Absolutely! . . . In selecting this healthy, constructive, positive material, we have made radio what it should and must be: a source of strength for a Volk of seventy million people which fights under its Führer in a hard struggle for its daily bread and for the place in the sun it deserves."[57] The radio trade journal *Der Deutsche Rundfunk* seconded this policy statement: "Beethoven will bring the Volk together. Let his works sound in every house over the magnificent medium of radio!"[58]

Working from these assumptions, Nazi radio authorities programmed a great deal of Beethoven's music;[59] his work was often featured on the most popular of the Nazi radio programs, "Concerts by Request" (*Wunschkonzerte*).[60] But the first and most dramatic examples of this propaganda technique were the "Beethoven Reich Broadcasts" (*Beethoven-Reichssendungen*) of January 1934. Transmitted nationwide through the coordinated efforts of regional broadcast groups, this series was designed to symbolize the start of a new phase in German radio history.[61] Each night between January 14 and January 25—beginning at 9:00 p.m. so that working people could listen—a Beethoven symphony was broadcast live, along with a selection of chamber works; *Fidelio* was also featured.[62] According to the Reich Radio Corporation (*Reichsrundfunkgesellschaft*) that governed the new era of German standard-wave broadcasting, the cycle was a huge success. "The Beethoven Week has been an incomparable achievement. It has contributed to radio's effort to conquer the whole German Volk. It has also helped to forge the unfailing instrument that the Führer needs to remain close to his Volk."[63] Reich broadcast chief Hadamovsky applauded the cycle for having contributed also to the regime's foreign-policy efforts. "Just as in Germany, Beethoven was heard in the rest of the world. From Japan, over Finland, to North and South America, the broadcast companies of the world tuned to our station and transmitted these German artworks to their listeners. . . . Even if politics was not mentioned once in these broadcasts, and the word 'propaganda' never used, they were still a cultural advertisement of the greatest style and deepest effect. The fact that Beethoven's heroic German music was made accessible to foreign peoples, awoke understanding for the German nature, and thereby must have offset base lies, was a great achievement of this project."[64] Following up on this success, state radio in Cologne (*Reichssender Köln*) broadcast a tour of the Beethovenhaus led by Ludwig Schiedermair; the program ended with a performance on Beethoven's original quartet of instruments and was transmitted to the United States via the National Broadcasting Company.[65]

Beethoven's music was also an important feature of motion pictures produced for the Nazi propaganda blitz. Concerts by eminent German orchestras were filmed and shown in movie houses, among them a performance of the Ninth Symphony conducted by Wilhelm Furtwängler;[66] newsreels acclaiming the achievements of Führer and party were introduced each week by the music of Beethoven's *Weihe des Hauses;*[67] a newsreel covering the 1937 "Great German Art Exhibition" in Munich had no narration—it was accompanied only by a recording of the first movement of Beethoven's Second Symphony, op. 36. This synchronization of Great German Art with Great German Music, Berthold Hinz later noted, contributed to the "sacred aura" of the Munich exhibition.[68]

Nazis also integrated Beethoven's works into feature movies. A popular 1936 Ufa film, *Schlußakkord,* portrayed the troubled marriage of a fictional music director of the Berlin Philharmonic Orchestra. Stormy scenes of marital conflict are backed by Beethoven's music and set in rooms where busts and statues of the composer seem to frown from every wall. The most dramatic use of Beethoven occurs in the film's opening sequences. In faraway New York City a young German woman—who eventually becomes the conductor's lover—succumbs to life in the decadent jungle of jazz, drink, and corruption. Upon learning of her husband's murder, she collapses and is placed under the care of an American doctor. In his home she remains prostrate, until he tunes his radio to receive a Berlin Philharmonic concert broadcast. From the next room the patient hears Beethoven's Ninth Symphony; the first three movements awaken and draw her out of delirium. Noticing this the doctor moves the radio to her bedside: the choral finale completely revives her and motivates her to return to the fatherland. The healing powers of German culture, in the form of Beethoven's music, have worked again.[69] Beethoven's piano music was also an important motif in a wartime film named for the radio program, *Wunschkonzert*. This 1940 epitome of Nazi kitsch portrayed a music student performing a Beethoven sonata for his roommates just before marching off to war; the musician-soldier later dies while playing Bach's music as if possessed, on the organ of a Gothic church under bombardment.[70]

Along with modern media, National Socialist cultural-politicians implemented traditional methods of honoring Beethoven while associating him with the new Reich. In 1934, shortly before he emigrated from Germany, photojournalist Alfred Eisenstaedt did a story on the Beethovenhaus in Bonn. Having climbed the narrow steps of the apartment, he prepared to take a shot of the cramped attic room where the composer was born. "By sheer coincidence," in his words, "the Nazis came into the room . . . and laid a wreath with a swastika at the base of [Beethoven's] bust in honor of the Führer's birthday. After they left, I took the picture both with and without the swastika. I was a little afraid to remove it, but I was willing to take a chance for a good picture."[71] The photograph that resulted bears witness to the National Socialists' persistent attempts to appropriate memorials of Germany's creative genius as monuments to their party and its leader.[72] The symbolic seizure of the *Geburtshaus* bust was part of a grander effort to link Beethoven's visual image with the party; had the Nazis completed all their plans for monumental construction in the "thousand-year Reich," Bonn and Frankfurt would have each gained new sculptures of the composer. Even before the *Machtergreifung*, plans had been drawn up for an additional *Beethoven-Denkmal* in Bonn, fashioned in the austere style characteristic of National Socialist design.[73] Later, when the funds for this project ran out, 22,000 Reichsmark were donated from Hitler's private account, earning the Führer grateful thanks in the press for supporting the project.[74]

Most important among Nazi efforts to connect the music of Beethoven with their political liturgy were live performances. Often produced under the auspices of a party patron and certainly attended by

Fig. 17. Alfred Eisenstaedt, Beethoven's bust, Beethovenhaus, Bonn, 1934. Just before Eisenstaedt took this picture of the room where the composer was born an SS troop entered to place a wreath at the base of the bust. The ribbon reads "In memory of Ludwig van Beethoven on the birthday of the Führer, Cologne, 20 April 1934, Medical Section of the 58th SS Regiment." (Photo: Alfred Eisenstaedt, *Life Magazine* © Time Warner Inc.)

Fig. 18. Peter Breuer's model for a Beethoven monument in Bonn. Despite direct financial support from Adolf Hitler, this statue was never completed. (Courtesy of the Beethovenhaus, Bonn)

political leaders, many traditional concerts of Beethoven's music took place within the Third Reich.[75] Events such as the 1937 *Beethovenfeier in Lauenburg,* the 1939 *Badener Beethovenfest,* ongoing festivals in Bonn, and a multitude of other performances of his works were relatively free of political significance. Nevertheless, even in the case of conventional events, not everything was normal: as noted above, all Jewish musicians had been removed from German orchestras; those who remained in the country were allowed to play only for symphonies associated with the *Jüdischer Kulturbund* (Jewish Cultural Organization). Significantly, Beethoven was the first composer whose music the *Jüdischer Kulturbund* orchestras were barred from playing.[76]

Of greater interest to Nazi propagandists than patronizing some standard events and proscribing others was arranging performances of Beethoven's music as part of party pageantry. Throughout the Nazi era, his compositions were enlisted to serve as inspirational elements in National Socialist ceremonial events. A few crucial examples signify that this process was the culmination of the National Socialist politicization of Beethoven and his music. Within the Third Reich, it was common practice to perform Beethoven's *Weihe des Hauses,* as well as the *Coriolan* and *Egmont* overtures, at ceremonies inaugurating cultural and political institutions.[77] The November 1933 opening of the Reich Culture Chamber itself was marked—just before Goebbels' speech on "German Culture at a New Beginning"—with a performance of the *Egmont* Overture by the Berlin Philharmonic under Wilhelm Furtwängler.[78] For the "Cultural Day of the Party Congress" in 1935, Hitler himself requested that the Fifth Symphony be played at the Apollo Theater in Nuremberg. This time Furtwängler, the scheduled conductor, talked his way out of performing, so Peter Raabe instead directed the *Egmont* Overture.[79] The crowning event of the musicological conference associated with the Düsseldorf exhibition of "Degenerate Music" in 1938 was a performance of the Ninth Symphony after speeches by Goebbels and the composer Richard Strauss, who had preceded Raabe as head of the Reich Music Chamber.[80]

At the opening ceremonies of the 1936 Olympics in Berlin, moreover, the *Schlußchor* of the Ninth Symphony was performed in the stadium. Even within this context it was not intended to symbolize international accord; organizers considered it a "proclamation of the Nazi *Volksgemeinschaft.*"[81] The Third Symphony also had a part in the Olympic festivities. The conductor of the military band (!) that performed it hoped his rendition of the *Eroica* would convey the following images to the international audience watching the Olympics: "The first movement should be a portrait of battle, the second should evince lamentations of death, the third should depict a bivouac"; in his opinion, "Beethoven had wanted to paint battle alarms, cries, and piercing screams" in this work.[82] Presumably, this man's interpretation coordinated with Hitler's intention to use the Olympics to demonstrate German athletic (in his mind, military) supremacy.

The most conspicuous use of Beethoven in the liturgical events of the National Socialist religion was the playing of his music on Hitler's birthday, both live and on the radio. In 1937, at Goebbels' request, Furtwängler conducted the Ninth Symphony to honor the Führer. (Apparently controversy over the meaning of the Ninth had been settled, at least to Goebbels' satisfaction.) Playing this music was the perfect way to mark the day, according to Goebbels' newspaper, *Der Angriff,* because "with its fighting and struggling" the work denoted the Führer's capacity for "triumph and joyous victory."[83] In 1938, Herbert von Karajan led his Aachen orchestra in a performance of *Fidelio* to mark

Hitler's birthday;[84] a later commentator reminds us that the Führer was not, as might be assumed today, to be identified with Pizarro the jailer—rather, with Fidelio the savior![85] Goebbels would link these compositions with the Führer's birthday to the bitter end.

The effect of Beethoven's music in National Socialist rituals can only be imagined; not even film records convey the potency of these rites. Perhaps William Shirer best described the emotional content of Nazi cultural-political *Gesamtkunstwerke.* Shirer attended an NSDAP spectacle embellished with Beethoven at the 1934 national rally in Nuremberg. Afterward he admitted: "I'm beginning to comprehend, I think, some of the reasons for Hitler's astounding success. Borrowing a chapter from the Roman church, he is restoring pageantry and color and mysticism to the drab lives of twentieth-century Germans." The rest of his description warrants full reproduction because it powerfully conveys the function of music in the spectacles of the Third Reich.

> This morning's opening meeting in the Luitpold Hall on the outskirts of Nuremberg was more than a gorgeous show; it also had something of the mysticism and religious fervor of an Easter or Christmas mass in a great Gothic cathedral. The hall was a sea of brightly colored flags. Even Hitler's arrival was made dramatic. The band stopped playing. There was a hush over the thirty thousand people packed in the hall. Then the band struck up the *Badenweiler Marsch,* a very catchy tune, and used only, I'm told, when Hitler makes his big entries. Hitler appeared in the back of the auditorium, and followed by his aides, Göring, Goebbels, Hess, Himmler, and the others, he strode slowly down the long center aisle while thirty thousand hands were raised in salute. It is a ritual, the old-timers say, which is always followed. Then an immense symphony orchestra played Beethoven's *Egmont* Overture. Great Klieg lights played on the stage, where Hitler sat surrounded by a hundred party officials and officers of the army and navy. Behind them the "blood flag," the one carried down the streets of Munich in the ill-fated putsch. Behind this, four or five hundred S.A. [Stormtroop] standards. When the music was over, Rudolf Hess, Hitler's closest confidant, rose and slowly read the names of the Nazi "martyrs"—brownshirts who had been killed in the struggle for power—a roll call of the dead, and the thirty thousand seemed very moved. In such an atmosphere no wonder, then, that every word dropped by Hitler seemed like an inspired Word from on high. Man's—or

at least the German's—critical faculty is swept away at such moments, and every lie pronounced is accepted as the truth itself.[86]

Besides including inspirational performances at rallies within Germany, Nazis exploited Beethoven's music as a foreign propaganda instrument. In September of 1937, for instance, the Reich Culture Chamber arranged a "Celebration of Germanism" in Paris. Under the patronage of Reich Culture Chamber vice president Walther Funk, this project coordinated with the World Exhibition where the French film community acclaimed Leni Riefenstahl's film *Triumph des Willens*.[87] The nine days of Funk's "German Exhibition" climaxed with a concert of Beethoven's Ninth Symphony by the Berlin Philharmonic under Furtwängler's baton. Audience members received a program in which Funk explained the intentions behind the event: "to give National Socialist Germany a chance to present to the world a portrait of its accomplishments" and "to give an accurate idea of life"—especially cultural activity—"in the Reich of Adolf Hitler."[88] As the performance commenced, French dignitaries watched their "hosts" rise to give the Hitler salute while the *Deutschlandlied* and the *Horst Wessel Lied* were played as preludes to Beethoven's symphony. Back in Germany, Nazi newspapers heralded this spectacle as a significant foreign propaganda victory. The *Völkischer Beobachter* reported that the concert had been sold out and a traffic jam had occurred because the crowd was so large—it had been "the most powerful and successful cultural event to happen in Paris since the [First World] War." Realization that German art and German artists had achieved this "great victory over French culture" filled NS reviewers with pride and joy; the evening had been "an important page in the history of German-French relations."[89]

Not all Beethoven concerts in or near foreign lands were produced to tighten international ties in this way. The image of Beethoven was often evoked to justify more aggressive aspects of Nazi foreign policy. In July of 1938 occurred a performance of *Fidelio* in Burg Monschau, on the border south of Aachen near Eupen and Malmédy—towns made part of Belgium by the Versailles Treaty. A reviewer for the *Kölnische Volkszeitung* observed audience members who had crossed the frontier from the Eupen-Malmédy region and compared them to the opera's captives. He insinuated that the "border people" felt as though "we are these prisoners, we people of Eupen-Malmédy, from whom the light of life, the dear homeland, has been stolen; who are blocked off from freedom, from unity with our brothers on the other side of the border! Now we enjoy a couple of hours of freedom and light, reunited with our brothers. But soon we must return to the dungeon, to servitude."[90] Thus did this opera buff fuel the Nazi drive to permanently liberate "prisoners" of the *Diktat.*

As Nazi aggression intensified, justification via Beethoven became more explicit. In March of 1938, during the weeks leading up to the Anschluß, Nazis arranged a flash of propaganda aimed at highlighting the Germanness of Austrian life. Leaders in the arts were asked to provide evidence that Germany and Austria were historically and culturally unified, thereby rationalizing annexation and promoting Austrian support for it. Representatives of the music world, including Peter Raabe and Karl Böhm, were among those who did so—many made reference to Beethoven in their statements.[91] Beethoven's name even came up when Hitler personally threatened the head of the Austrian government. On 12 February 1938 at Berchtesgaden, as Hitler harassed the Austrian chancellor, Kurt von Schuschnigg remonstrated that his nation had made a unique contribution to history and suggested that the Nazi leader "take, for instance, a man like Beethoven." Hitler replied indignantly, "Oh—Beethoven? Let me tell you that Beethoven came from the lower Rhineland."[92] Hitler thus used the composer's name to justify his territorial cravings. All "Austrian culture," including Beethoven's music, belonged to Greater Germany.

When Nazi Germany marched, Beethoven's music accompanied: *Fidelio* was performed in Vienna two weeks after the Anschluß. Reviewing the show—which Field Marshal Hermann Göring attended—the Austrian edition of the *Völkischer Beobachter* linked Beethoven's opera to the consolidation of *Großdeutschland* by proclaiming that *Fidelio* was "a prophecy of the escape" of this southern portion of the German nation from incarceration by international powers; following the libretto one could "relive the individual phases and the final victory of the National Socialist revolution" in Austria. According to this review, the Vienna production was "an uplifting festival of liberation, a religious service thanking the Creator for bestowing the Führer's genius on this poor, small, tormented people."[93]

As the Führer's interest turned toward the Sudetenland, references to Beethoven appeared in Nazi claims against Czechoslovakia. Shortly before Hitler forced the Sudetenland into the Reich, the *Deutsche Militär-Musiker-Zeitung* hinted that the plan to incorporate Bohemia was proper, since Beethoven had often visited the resort towns of the area. Because of their association with the composer, Teplitz, Karlsbad, and Franzensbad were integral parts of German cultural territory—at least according to the military musicians who would provide music to accompany the invasion.[94] Further along in his campaign, Hitler personally requested that Wilhelm Furtwängler lead a performance of Beethoven's Fifth Symphony prior to a Führer-speech at the "Party Conference on Peace" (*Reichsparteitag des Friedens*) on 1 September 1939. Perhaps to Furtwängler's relief, but certainly to no one else's, this peace rally was canceled because of the attack on Poland which commenced that day.[95]

Beethoven in the Second World War

Once the war broke out, Nazi efforts to use Beethoven as an inspirational hero were greatly intensified. Visions of Beethoven as an "announcer of fate" (*Schicksalskünder*) were emphasized as never before.[96] "In these decisive days," said the *Allgemeine Musik-Zeitung*, "Beethoven, the hard-tested herald of fate, speaks his *amor fati* to fighting men who are brave enough to look death and ruin in the eye."[97] To keep morale high, music scholars such as Erich Schenk, Walther Vetter, and Ludwig Schiedermair produced wartime articles and lectures exhorting people to consider Beethoven a motivational figure in battle. According to Schenk, "in the life of no other composer did the experiences of war play as significant a role" as they did in Beethoven's.[98] Vetter felt that the "politics and war-making of his time" belonged among the influences that Beethoven "forged with the heat of his genius into motivating forces."[99] Schiedermair concluded that the "heroic *Wehrmacht*" could interpret Beethoven's "tragic" symphonies as "example, encouragement, admonition, and assurance of victory over the dark demons that are circling German life."[100]

To help Germans meet their national responsibilities and contribute to the war effort, Schiedermair suggested that soldiers and workers listen to Beethoven's music because it provided "stamina": both the Third and Fifth symphonies expressed the need for personal fortitude, he explained. Of course, the Third had always been considered the symphony of heroism, but the Fifth had previously been understood as a "song of fate"—implying passivity. The war, however, convinced Schiedermaier that the Fifth was really a "battle song." "It is a call to war, a challenge, a call to battle stations." As in the Third, "everything flows into a thrilling *trionfale* which has no trace of the resigned, fatalistic attitude of a Werther and which banishes all darkness and demons with one blow." In the end, Schiedermair finished, the Ninth Symphony could also be considered an important symbol of the war effort, since it too "mirrored human fate and tragedy" before expressing the joy that one felt on acting for the community and not just for oneself.[101]

Hitler himself referred to Beethoven in his wartime rhetoric. Speaking in a Munich beer hall, he argued that "one German, Beethoven, achieved more musically than all Englishmen of the past and present put together."[102] Several articles followed his line of argument, pointing out the irony that Germany's enemies continued to enjoy performances of Beethoven while trying to destroy his homeland. "Americans, Englishmen, and Jews scream that they wish to fight to protect the greatest creations of humanity, but the only things of eternal value to which they can refer were created by the Volk they aspire to exterminate."[103] To counter this state of affairs Richard Wagner's writings about Beethoven were mustered to intensify hatred for Germany's enemies. His 1870 essay was often reproduced during the war, while "A Pilgrimage to Beethoven" was directly distributed to soldiers—in 1943 and 1944 reproductions of this short story with its uncomplimentary depiction of a British aristocrat were printed for the *Hyperion-Bucherei: Feldpostausgabe, Bertelsmann-Feldpostausgabe, Karlsbader-Feldpostausgabe,* and *Die bunten Hefte für unsere Soldaten.*[104] Indeed, Wagner's "Pilgrimage to Beethoven" was even made part of school curricula; children were taught that the Englishman in the tale represented the worst aspects of the nation that the *Luftwaffe* was bent on destroying.[105]

Meanwhile, Nazis were claiming to have "rediscovered" Beethoven's military music. As had happened between 1914 and 1918, a spate of wartime articles extolled Beethoven's "lost" marches: the *Kriegslied der Österreicher,* the *Abschiedsgesang an Wiens Bürger,* the *Yorcksche Marsch,* the *Marsch zur großen Wachparade,* the *Karussel Märsche,* and the *Türkische Marsch* from the *Ruinen von Athen* were all dusted off and played frequently by Wehrmacht bands.[106] Also as during the First World War, Beethoven's other compositions were preponderant in wartime concert programs. In 1943 the *Zeitschrift für Musik* produced a statistical overview of performances in the previous year: during this representative wartime season, Beethoven's Third, Fifth, and Ninth symphonies were the three most-played works of the repertoire.[107] Apparently no dissent against "too much Beethoven" was voiced in Germany during the Second World War. "Strength through Joy" concerts for soldiers and workers often highlighted Beethoven's works: in 1940 the Berlin Philharmonic Orchestra performed for "the men in field-gray" in The Hague, Amsterdam, Brussels, Utrecht, Antwerp, Lütich, Ghent, Bruges, Ostend, Lille, Paris, Versailles, Fontainebleu, Metz, and Strassburg a concert series that repeated Beethoven's Second and Seventh symphonies.[108] In the program notes for these concerts, the Seventh was described as a "victory symphony," the "expression of a humanity which had finally triumphed over life and battle."[109] Outside Germany, these concerts were strictly reserved for German nationals, especially when they included a performance of the Ninth Symphony; with its message of brotherhood, live concerts of the Ninth were forbidden to the populations of occupied areas, particularly Eastern territories.[110]

During wartime the NSDAP continued to mark the eve of Hitler's birthday with broadcasts of Beethoven's music. On 19 April 1942, just after Hitler personally assumed the Wehrmacht command in Russia, Goebbels arranged a special birthday celebration to announce the Führer's new role. The culmination of the ceremony was a performance of the Ninth Symphony. In a speech given just before the music, Goebbels orchestrated the emotions he expected this selection to stimulate:

> If ever the German nation felt itself united in one thought and one will, then it is in the thought of serving and obeying [Hitler]. This time, the sounds of the most heroic music of titans that ever flowed from a Faustian German heart should raise this realization to a serious and devotional height. When, at the end of our celebration, the voices and instruments strike the tremendous closing chord of the Ninth Symphony, when the exhilarating chorale sounds joy and carries a feeling for the greatness of these times into each and every German cabin, when [Beethoven's] hymn resounds over all distant countries where German regiments stand guard, then we want everyone, whether man, woman, child, soldier, farmer, worker, or civil servant, to be equally aware of the seriousness of the hour and to experience the tremendous happiness of being able to witness and take part in this, the greatest historical epoch of our Volk.[111]

Another common wartime propaganda technique was to publish letters by soldiers explaining the reasons why they were fighting. Under the title "We Are Protecting Beethoven: A Soldier's Letter Accounts for the Meaning of the War," *Die Musik Woche* reprinted the letter of a soldier posted on the English Channel in 1941. This soldier described defending the western coast against an air attack just after hearing a broadcast of Beethoven's Violin Concerto. At that moment, he had understood the "meaning of the war."

> You ask me what all this has to do with the music I just heard. Let me say to you that a statement of the Führer struck me at that moment. He said that a single great German, Beethoven, had achieved more for human culture than all the British plutocrats put together. This pompous clique sends its machines over here supposedly in order to save culture and civilization. In truth, however, they attack in desperate fury against the victorious storm of a new, better world that is shaking their decayed world apart. Weren't you, as I, seized by a fanatical eagerness to fight when agitated by the sounds of the Violin Concerto? At the time I thought of innumerable testimonials to our German culture; I thought of the thousands of events in which this culture has been brought to life in the consciousness of the *Volksgemeinschaft;* and I saw the simple comrades of the Volk thankfully surrendering themselves to this music which German [National] Socialism made accessible to them. With the notion of this better and more beautiful world, [though,] I also linked thoughts of that spirit which rejects it and believes it can destroy [it] with blockades and bombs. We, however, are opposing this attempt with our grenades night after night. Do not laugh if it seemed to me in these minutes as if we had to defend Beethoven, who, himself unhappy, gave us the "Hymn to Joy" and taught us what it meant to fight.[112]

The contents of this letter, and others like it, certify that the process of politicizing Beethoven both before and during the war did transform his music into a symbol of National Socialist ideology in the minds of some Germans.[113] Nevertheless, evidence exists that others maintained and expressed views counter to the requisite volkish version. External factors might have had some influence: in Paris in 1933, the *Association des Anciens Combattants Volontaires Juifs,* the *Comité de Défense des Juifs Persecutés en Allemagne,* and the *Ligue internationale contre l'Antisemitisme* decried the Berlin Philharmonic Orchestra's practice of playing Beethoven as part of the National Socialist foreign propaganda; members threw leaflets from music hall balconies asking concertgoers to help fight against the regime in Germany.[114] In 1936 a group of "Anti-Fascist Musicians" resisted the Berlin Philharmonic in London by distributing a flier that read:

> The concerts begin with the *Egmont* Overture, and we cannot but have in mind those men who have had to die during the past two and a half years and have to die today because they have fought for

> that very liberty which was Beethoven's inspiration in the *Egmont* Overture. Progress and Liberty stand today in such danger that we must not forget, in listening to the glorious march of the *Egmont* Overture, the hundreds of thousands of upright men confined in the horrible gaols of German fascism, tortured by loneliness and terror. . . . Let the musical experience of hearing the Berlin Philharmonic Orchestra be a commemoration of these anti-fascist heroes. Honor by your applause the unknown antifascist, whether he sits before you at this moment among the orchestra, or whether he is carrying on in Germany, Italy, Austria, etc. his dangerous underground work against War, Reaction, and the Destruction of Civilization. Honor the unknown antifascist and you honor yourself. Become a member of the growing army against fascism and retrogression.[115]

Moreover, the British Broadcasting Corporation used tones resembling the four notes opening Beethoven's Fifth Symphony as its call signal for wartime transmissions into the continent. Because of this practice, some Germans came to perceive the sound of this phrase as a sign either that Allied forces would be victorious or that someone in their neighborhood was listening to foreign broadcasts illegally. Tales of how the BBC chose this signal vary. In 1970 *Der Spiegel* investigated the matter and reported that the broadcasts did always begin with the moving "Tam-tam-tam-ta," but this phrase was not originally intended as a reference to Beethoven's symphony. The producer of the BBC "Free France" program, Victor de Lavelaye—a Belgian—sought a sonic signal that both Flemish and Walloons would understand. He suggested the resistance symbol of the "V"—since it commenced the French word *victoire* and the Flemish *vrijheid.* A "V" in Morse code is three times short, one time long, and this signal was pounded out on kettledrum. Only by chance was it then compared to the first beats of the Fifth Symphony.[116] Whether the broadcast signature was Morse code inspired or not, German listeners clearly perceived it as Beethovenian. Some who lived in the Nazi era admit that, to this day, whenever they hear the first notes of Beethoven's Fifth Symphony on the radio, they reflexively wonder who is listening to proscribed broadcasts. During the war the BBC became aware of this danger; consequently, Radio London always warned, "Attention! Control the volume of your speaker. The transmission contains music. Attention! We are switching on."[117] Another technique that might have influenced the wartime interpretation of Beethoven was the Russian practice of broadcasting propaganda over huge speakers on the eastern front. As part of their effort to convince German soldiers to defect, aid in destroying the fascist regime, and establish "a better world system," the Russians often transmitted the music of Beethoven at full volume.[118]

Whether these international antifascist interpretations of Beethoven influenced reception within National Socialist Germany is difficult to determine; but there are slight indications that a resistance view of the composer did survive in the Third Reich. These are found in records of left-wing choirs that operated underground in Nazi Germany. Though these singing groups were former outlets of socialist propaganda, National Socialist authorities did not immediately consider them a threat; some were able to disassociate themselves from their leftist origins early enough to become integrated into the Nazi musical administration without changing their composition. In this guise—when not under direct observation by Nazi authorities—such groups performed music that reminded them of the ideals they had promoted before 1933. Indeed, many works that had been on the socialist and communist *Liedertafeln* were included in Nazi songbooks as well. In this case the choirs did not interpret the songs as the Nazis desired; singing them was a subtle way to express their determination to resist the regime.[119] Proof exists in *Gestapo* files reporting that in August of 1938 the "Male Choir of Berlin Friends of Song 1879" (*Männerchor Berliner Liederfreunde 1879*), formerly associated with the SPD, performed the "Prisoners' Chorus" from *Fidelio,* which includes the verse:

> O, what desire to breathe happily
> In free air.
> Only there, only there is life.
> The jail is a grave.
> Quietly, quietly, be careful!
> Eyes and ears are watching and listening.

As this was sung, the room broke out in stormy applause and resounded with cries of *da capo.* At this point, the Gestapo burst into the room and made arrests. The choir was dissolved.[120]

The practice of adhering to National Socialist dictates that encouraged the playing of Beethoven's music while thinking of it in terms of resistance also went on in concentration camps. In the camp at Sachsenhausen, a choir performed Beethoven's song *Das Glück der Freundschaft,* op. 88, with new words: instead of singing "Friendship is the source of true happiness," prisoners shouted "Friendship! Com-

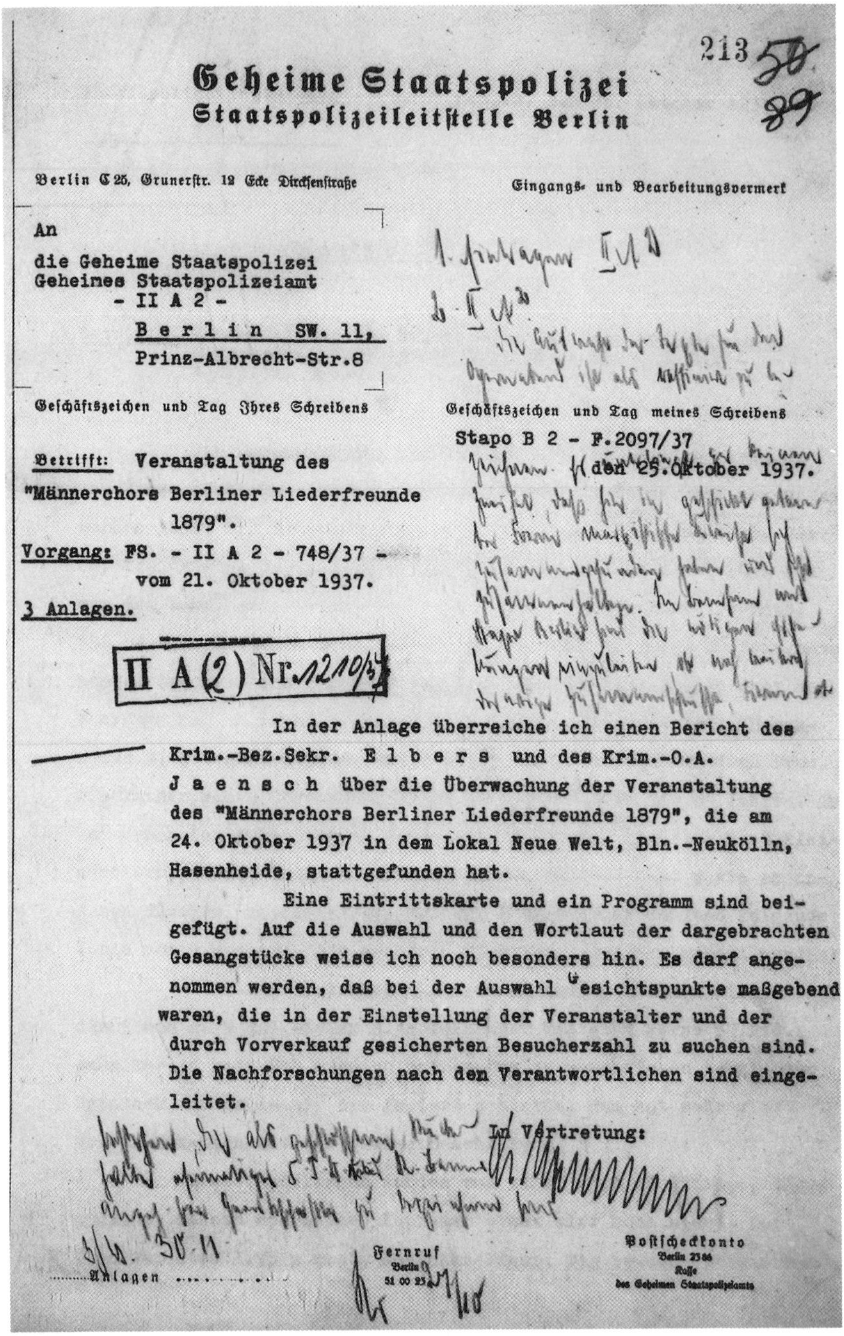

213

Geheime Staatspolizei
Staatspolizeileitstelle Berlin

Berlin C 25, Grunerstr. 12 Ecke Dircksenstraße

Eingangs- und Bearbeitungsvermerk

An
die Geheime Staatspolizei
Geheimes Staatspolizeiamt
- II A 2 -
B e r l i n SW. 11,
Prinz-Albrecht-Str.8

Geschäftszeichen und Tag Ihres Schreibens

Geschäftszeichen und Tag meines Schreibens
Stapo B 2 - F.2097/37
den 25.Oktober 1937.

Betrifft: Veranstaltung des "Männerchors Berliner Liederfreunde 1879".
Vorgang: FS. - II A 2 - 748/37 - vom 21. Oktober 1937.
3 Anlagen.

II A (2) Nr. 1210/37

In der Anlage überreiche ich einen Bericht des Krim.-Bez.Sekr. E l b e r s und des Krim.-O.A. J a e n s c h über die Überwachung der Veranstaltung des "Männerchors Berliner Liederfreunde 1879", die am 24. Oktober 1937 in dem Lokal Neue Welt, Bln.-Neukölln, Hasenheide, stattgefunden hat.

Eine Eintrittskarte und ein Programm sind beigefügt. Auf die Auswahl und den Wortlaut der dargebrachten Gesangstücke weise ich noch besonders hin. Es darf angenommen werden, daß bei der Auswahl Gesichtspunkte maßgebend waren, die in der Einstellung der Veranstalter und der durch Vorverkauf gesicherten Besucherzahl zu suchen sind. Die Nachforschungen nach den Verantwortlichen sind eingeleitet.

In Vertretung:

Fernruf
Berlin
51 00 23

Postscheckkonto
Berlin 2386
Kasse
des Geheimen Staatspolizeiamts

Anlagen

Fig. 19. Gestapo file reporting surveillance of the "Männerchor Berliner Liederfreunde 1879." This left-wing choir continued to operate underground until August of 1938 when the Gestapo raided a concert just after the group performed the "Prisoners' Chorus" of Beethoven's *Fidelio.* (Bundesarchiv, Potsdam)

raderie! Solidarity!"[121] In her memoir *Sursis pour l'orchestre* (translated into German as *A Women's Orchestra in Auschwitz*), Fania Fénelon—a French singer and antifascist—described an incident when her orchestra of captives was ordered to play Beethoven for camp guards. She acted as if all she could orchestrate was the first movement of the Fifth Symphony. As they played, she found it ironic that her musicians were forced to perform Beethoven's music which, to them, communicated thoughts of freedom and liberty. "It was a rare joy for me! [Our guard] did not notice the joke behind it, nor did the SS leadership. In no way did they make the connection between [the work] and the call signal of the BBC's 'Free France' broadcasts. To the Germans Beethoven is a god, a monument of German music, which they listen to respectfully, with expressions of amazement. One more minute and their seriousness would have affected me too. What a grand joy it was, though, when our orchestra played this movement. One of the most enjoyable moments of my life."[122]

Despite intermittent acts of musical-political resistance, the importance of Beethoven and his music as symbols of the National Socialist movement continued unabated even as the tide of war turned. As his "great historical epoch" became more and more desperate, Goebbels continued to program Beethoven's works for symbolic occasions: on 12 February 1944, he had the Berlin Philharmonic play works including Beethoven's Fifth Symphony in the Berlin Cathedral as a "public demonstration against the barbarity of the Western plutocrats," because the dome of the church had been destroyed in a bombing raid.[123] On 21 October 1944, Nazi bureaucrats were still seeking ways to perfect the biography of Beethoven as a symbol of their ideas. Even so late in the war, the head of the music section in Alfred Rosenberg's office, Herbert Gerigk, generated a memo asking if rumors that Beethoven had been a Freemason were true—one can only wonder what Gerigk would have done if this were the case, or how his Beethovenian boss would have reacted.[124]

On 11 April 1945, eleven days before the Russians took Berlin, a concert was given in honor of Albert Speer. The program opened with music from Richard Wagner's *Götterdämmerung,* included Anton Bruckner's Fourth Symphony, and closed with Beethoven's Violin Concerto. This last concert orchestrated by the Nazi cultural authorities symbolized the fact that along with Wagner and Bruckner, Beethoven was an honored member of the Nazi *Walhalla,* even as it went up in flames.[125] Nine days later, a last celebration for the Third Reich's self-styled Siegfried, now living underground like a Niebelung, was also marked with Beethoven's music. On 20 April 1945, Beethoven's Seventh Symphony—supposedly the "Symphony of Nazi Victory"—was played over the radio in honor of the Reich chancellor's last birthday. Finally, on 30 April 1945, German radio announced the death of Adolf Hitler. In his honor were read a few lines by the First World War writer Walter Flex:

> He lived
> He fought
> He fell
> And he died
> For us.[126]

As accompaniment to this poem, the music of Beethoven was pressed into one last service for the Third Reich: for this broadcast, the "Funeral March" of the *Eroica*—composed "to celebrate the memory of a great man"—was forced to serve as a requiem for the Nazi Führer.[127]

5

Germany Divided, and Reunified

"I find," he said,
"that it is not to be."
"What, Adrian, is not to be?"
"The good and noble,"
he answered me,
"what the ecstatics exul-
tantly announced. That is
not to be. It will be taken
back. I will take it back."
"I don't understand,
dear man, what will
you take back?"
"The Ninth Symphony,"
he replied . . .
THOMAS MANN
Doktor Faustus

For many who experienced the horrors of the Third Reich and the Second World War, the idea that the music of Beethoven should have been "taken back" from humanity in general—but especially from the German people—was a powerful one. In March of 1945, the conductor Carmen Weingartner-Stüder, living in exile in Switzerland, had demanded in an open letter to the cultural community that Beethoven's music not be played at least until the end of the war, and perhaps longer. "Beethoven, the living symbol of the struggle for freedom of the spirit, should not be played until the cruelties are ended and we can all again stand before his image with a clear conscience."[1] Even before publishing the devastating scene from *Doktor Faustus* cited above, Thomas Mann had expressed this conviction in correspondence. In September 1945, he wrote to upbraid Walter von Molo, former president of the Prussian Writers' Academy, for remaining in Germany and maintaining his membership in the Nazi-controlled institution. In his letter Mann asked: "How could it happen that Beethoven's *Fidelio,* this opera destined for the day of German self-liberation, was not forbidden in the Germany of the last twelve years? It is a scandal that it was not forbidden and that highly cultured performances were given, that singers could be found to perform, musicians to play, a public to listen. For what utter stupidity was required to be able to listen to *Fidelio* in Himmler's Germany without covering one's face and rushing out of the hall."[2] After the era of Nazi terror, it is no surprise that some Germans lost hope of achieving the ideals of brotherhood and peace they thought to be expressed in Beethoven's music; nor is it strange that they believed the right to perform and enjoy his works had been forfeited by their nation altogether. As it turned out, this pessimistic attitude did not prevail for long. Beethoven's art was not taken back from the Germans; it remained a fundamental part of cultural—and political—life in postwar Germany.

In the initial period after the war, Beethoven's image was stripped of the trappings projected on it by National Socialist cultural politicians. Rejecting the volkish portrait, some presented composer and music as transcending nationalism, promoting them instead as symbols of the universal need for tolerance and cooperation. As before the Hitler era, many associated Beethoven with notions of international brotherly love. A December 1945 article on "Beethoven and Our Time" in the *Tägliche Rundschau*—then printed under the authority of Soviet occupation forces—exemplifies this immediate postwar attitude. According to the music critic Karl Laux, Beethoven belonged to all nations—"he who spoke of the great dream of all persons becoming brothers in his Ninth Symphony, he who offered his music to 'the whole world,' he who gave a fiery kiss of joy, he, the citizen of the world, the fanatical representative of an honorable *humanitas.*" The Hitler regime, Laux continued, did all it could "to disavow the notion of Beethoven as a citizen of the world and to transform his work into exclusive nationalistic propaganda"; but when Germans read that even during Hitler's war Beethoven was, after Tchaikovsky, the most-played composer in Russia, or that a French minister president, Edouard Herriot, wrote one of the best books on Beethoven, then "we realize that the East and the West honored this master" as much as Germany did.[3]

Beyond depicting him as a symbolic citizen of the world, Laux and others looking forward from "zero hour" also believed that the *Mythos* of Beethoven would be of use in forming another New Germany, designed to overcome the division and strife that the last three had caused. "We Germans are today called on to undertake a great work of reformation." To overcome the most disgraceful epoch of German history, a spiritual rebirth was necessary; this meant, Laux insisted, that Germans had to be "on the lookout for those forces of the past that should remain a part of our being." Beethoven, in his opinion, stood for the best of these. "Scarcely any other name shines so brightly, with such an unbroken gleam, as that of *Ludwig van Beethoven.*"[4] Nevertheless, hopes for a utopian solution to the problems of European and German nationalism were not soon realized. The dream that, according to Mann, a few ecstatics perceived in the Ninth Symphony was achieved neither in Europe nor in Germany after the Second World

War. Even consensus that Beethoven's life and art were of universal, humanitarian significance was not long prevalent in German minds. As two separate German nations developed in the atmosphere of the cold war, approaches to Beethoven also diverged.

For some time—though conflict between the Soviet and Western zones was leading to construction of a wall splitting German lands and culture—Beethoven's music was used to signify the German people as a whole. At the first three Olympics to occur after the war—at Melbourne in 1956, at Rome in 1960, and at Tokyo in 1964—the famous melody of the Ninth Symphony's finale served as the anthem for the combined German teams. But this policy was discarded at the 1968 Olympics in Mexico City; by then each German country had its own team, wanted its own Olympic anthem, and complained about using the Ninth to represent both.[5] This cultural-diplomatic breakdown reflected the fact that at least until 1989, German interpretations of Beethoven corresponded to the division of the nation: in the German Democratic Republic (GDR), the view of Beethoven as a social revolutionary reigned as long as the communist-controlled Socialist Unity Party (SED) maintained power; in the Federal Republic of Germany (FRG), a psychological analysis of the composer—along with increasing commercialization of his music—countered notions of the composer as a sensible "political man."

Beethoven in East Germany

Cultural authorities of the GDR never accepted the pessimism about Beethoven that Thomas Mann expressed in *Doktor Faustus*. An article on "The Meaning of Beethoven for the Socialist National Culture of the GDR"—part of an official report on the commemorations of Beethoven's two-hundredth birthday in 1970—argued that Mann's "nihilistic" view of the composer's place in postwar German life represented the "crisis of bourgeois culture in the twentieth century"; it had no significance for members of a revolutionary society that had done nothing to invalidate its prerogative to take pleasure from Beethoven's works. The author, vice chairman of the Ministry of Culture Werner Rackwitz, believed that Beethoven should be revoked from the "barbaric and antihumanist imperialists" in the bourgeois sector of German society. According to the cultural politicians of East Germany, the German middle class had lost the right to enjoy Beethoven because of its alleged support of National Socialism.[6] Of course, the postwar revolutionary vanguard did not feel this to be true for the proletarians who supposedly governed East Germany; like other traditional German heroes, GDR ideologues used Beethoven to symbolize their social and political ideas.[7]

As had been the case in National Socialist Germany, exploiting Beethoven as a political symbol of the GDR did not require fabricating a new interpretation. East German propagandists repeated legends about the composer highlighted by earlier ideologues of the left with embellishment, but without much revision. As in the Third Reich, the major difference was that these ideas were now forced on the people through a totalitarian cultural system.[8] To popularize the revolutionary idea of Beethoven, SED activists simply republished articles in which their predecessors had discussed the composer's socialist tendencies. Throughout the existence of the GDR, remarks about Beethoven by Friedrich Engels, Clara Zetkin, Kurt Eisner, Hanns Eisler, and others discussed above were reproduced.[9] East German political leaders also associated Beethoven with early leaders of the workers' movement by claiming that his music had been an "inexhaustible source of energy" for their struggles.[10]

While miming previous formulations of leftist Beethoven myth, GDR propagandists undertook to eliminate all conceptions of the composer that National Socialists had promoted—now rejected as "hopeless, sad *Quatsch.*"[11] Beethoven was quickly readmitted into the ranks of major social revolutionaries. Just as political leaders were given exalted titles of rank,[12] he was introduced to East German citizens as "Ludwig van Beethoven: the Great Musician, the Revolutionary of Music, the Passionate Humanist and Democrat, the Fighter for Freedom and Progress in Life and in Art, the Musical Herald of Humanist-Revolutionary Ideals of Mankind."[13] To demonstrate that Beethoven was worthy of such an impressive title, East German cultural functionaries scoured the previous literature for evidence—now familiar to the reader—that he was uncomfortable with the aristocracy and the bourgeoisie, cared for the poor, respected revolutionary France, resisted the authority of Metternich, and was an active revolutionary. They then propagated it by every medium at their disposal.[14]

The GDR pamphleteers did add a few original themes to the existing leftist interpretation of Beethoven's life. Kowtowing to the Soviets, they made much of the fact that Lenin had mentioned Beethoven's music. Few articles or speeches produced in East Germany concluded without noting that Lenin "loved Beethoven's music,"[15] having once said to Gorki: "I know of nothing more beautiful than the *Appassionata* and could listen to it every day. . . . Hearing it I think with pride, perhaps naive pride, Look, people really can create such masterworks!"[16] The GDR literature also frequently mentioned that Lenin had opened the way to including Beethoven's works in revolutionary culture when he stated that the workers' movement should appropriate the best of bourgeois art for its own purposes.[17] One might conjecture that harping on this point was a way for GDR propagandists to cover themselves in case the anomaly of using music dedicated to Viennese aristocrats as a symbol of proletarian revolution was denounced.

To associate him more directly with SED ideology, East German scholars scrutinized Beethoven's music for connections—no matter how tenuous—with Marxist ideas. The leading journal of music studies in East Germany, *Musik und Gesellschaft,* regularly alleged that facets of Beethoven's art "anticipated" the theories of Marx. According to a report on the findings of a 1970 Beethoven conference in Potsdam, many elements of Marxist theory—"particularly the Feuerbach Theses"—were anticipated by Beethoven in his works and "in his practical relationship to reality."[18] Explaining how to make the "Marxist image of Beethoven" recognizable to the largest number of people, another *Musik und Gesellschaft* article suggested that cultural authorities emphasize how the composer "reached the threshold of Marx's teachings" by virtue of his progressive conceptions of the role of creative individuals in society. "Completely in accord with the eleventh Feuerbach Thesis of Marx," Beethoven wanted not just to represent the world in his music, but to change it, to have direct effect on society through it. He considered writing music a "revolutionary, practical-critical deed" of the sort Marx denoted in his first Feuerbach Thesis.[19]

Also fresh were direct associations of Beethoven with the social system erected in East Germany after 1945. On the eve of the founding of the SED in April 1946, party delegates were entertained with a performance of the Ninth Symphony.[20] Subsequent propaganda tightened the symbolic link between his music and the German Democratic Republic. Again highlighting the "anticipatory content" of his music, East German *Musikpolitiker* asserted that just as Beethoven had sensed the "coming victory of the forces of freedom, proving his deep understanding of social necessity"[21] when he wrote the Seventh Symphony while Napoleon was still at large, he had also predicted the founding of the GDR: as music he formulated ideas that "became reality only through the victorious struggle of the working class and its associates to erect our socialist social order."[22] Hansjürgen Schae-

Fig. 20. Pamphlet produced by the East German National Front in 1952 linking Beethoven to the conspiracy theories of the GDR regime: "American generals are having the Loreleifelsen rigged with explosives; the roads along the Rhine, the viaducts and bridges, are all being made ready for destruction upon their command. . . . If these generals go through with their plans, the lovely Rheinland, the homeland of Beethoven, will no longer exist." (Courtesy of the Beethovenhaus, Bonn)

fer, one of the most prolific critics in the GDR,[23] explained this point further.

> His music has its secure place in our socialist community . . . because its creator not only thought of the issues of his time, but because his conceptions reached widely into the future, into our days. . . . One can say without exaggerating that the real humanism of our society is the target, the "final goal" which the revolutionary composer and thinker Beethoven already strove for in his day, with unerring artistic consistency. In the portrait of a free, equal people aware of their worth and power, which he formulated in his heroic symphonies, his opera, and many other works, . . . we find representation of the essential characteristics of the image of the socialist in our epoch. In the real humanism of our society, the fighting humanism of Beethovenian music—always aiming for progressive change—is uplifted and proves its aesthetic power over life.[24]

Another East German patriot who wrote for *Musik und Gesellschaft,* Frank Schneider, put it this way: "We do not honor him because he was a great German . . . or because of his great creative achievements." Instead, "it is because we know he was one of the early fighters for the principles and ideals that we have made reality in the conditions of the socialist society. Since we have achieved that which Beethoven preconceived in his music . . . he is legitimated as a comrade and fellow traveler . . . just as, on the other hand, we legitimate ourselves by administering his legacy carefully and using it actively as a source of inspiration and productive power for our further work."[25] East Germany, such cultural-political activists constantly asserted (echoing Kurt Eisner's somewhat more sophisticated view in 1905) was the "home of Beethoven."[26] "Beethoven belongs to us," wrote the GDR's minister of culture, Klaus Gysi (perhaps citing Hanns Eisler's 1927 essay) because "he too struggled inexhaustibly against the injustice and arbitrariness of the ruling classes."[27]

As in all other politicized Beethoven interpretations, these political notions about the man were also applied to his compositions. The *Grundstudium für Kulturfunktionäre* (Primer for cultural functionaries) was a 1965 source from which GDR pedagogues were expected to learn all they needed to know about "Beethoven: Fighter and Teacher" before indoctrinating East German children. It presented the Third Symphony as a device for making the ideas of the Enlightenment and the French Revolution "operative" in the minds of students, since Beethoven's placement of movements and themes constituted a "musical application of dialectical thought" meant to represent social conflict. The "Funeral March" of the *Eroica,* according to this source, had been written for neither Napoleon Bonaparte, Prince Lichnowsky, nor General Abercromby: the notion that the death of one man inspired the Second Movement is "too limited"; one must see in it rather a "funeral for all heroes who were sacrificed in every battle ever fought to liberate humanity from slavery." The GDR functionaries were ordered to delineate the third movement as a joyous celebration on the victory of the "ideas of the French Revolution, dressed in the garment of folk music." The finale, said this primer, is an artistic transformation of the notion of Prometheus, also a hero of the GDR cultural authorities: "the symbol of liberation from the yoke of absolutism," the "bringer of freedom, who means deliverance, culture, freedom, and independence."[28]

Of course, the Ninth Symphony was also interpreted in revolutionary terms in the GDR. It was Beethoven's response to the reactionary atmosphere of the Metternichean era. "Prince Metternich destroyed progressive reforms that had been very carefully attained. In Beethoven he confronted a passionate enemy who, with his life and work, staunchly defended the progressive ideas of his time against dark reaction. The Ninth Symphony climaxed in the recognition of a brotherhood that included all men."[29] This view was widely held in the GDR. Written at the time of Metternichean reaction, Schaefer announced, the Ninth had anticipated the "antifeudal front" by presenting a portrait of a truly free society in which brothers found their brothers.[30]

Walter Ulbricht, the "father" of East German society, had ideas about the significance of the Ninth that were, well, a bit more up to date. In a 1970 speech given just before a performance of the work on New Year's Eve—traditional in German leftist culture—the first secretary of the SED gave his version of the "deep meaning" of this symphony. "The humanistic hopes and dreams of many generations of our people, expressed in works of German classicism, have, through the strength of the united German workers' movement, been made firm reality in our socialist German state. All men can now become brothers because the working people have been freed from the chains of imperialist profiteers and oppressors and have taken their fate into their own hands."[31] Thus did Ulbricht exhort "his" people to interpret the Ninth as a visionary depiction of the GDR.

Along with the symphonies, *Fidelio* was said to represent the "Jacobin-revolutionary stance of Beethoven";[32] likewise the *Egmont* Overture was held up as a "revolutionary vision of the future."[33] Even

Beethoven's piano sonatas were revealed by GDR scholars to have been originally conceived as works of leftist propaganda: in composing the *Hammerklavier* Sonata, op. 106, Beethoven—"the revolutionary Jacobin"—was resisting the reactionary social developments of his time "with fighting strength."[34] While working toward their stated goal of disseminating a "Marxist-Leninist Beethoven portrait," the self-styled "cultural functionaries" and "music propagandists" of the GDR regime projected their ideological conceptions onto every one of Beethoven's works.[35] With full command of the scholarly and journalistic instruments of the state, they ensured that this view of Beethoven was the only one to be communicated publicly in East Germany. Confirmation can be found in almost any book, article, program note, lecture, speech, film, radio program, or television broadcast about Beethoven's music produced in the GDR.

East German cultural functionaries intended to establish among proletarians a sense that Beethoven's music had been written for them. They expected this belief to have tremendous effect when Beethoven's compositions were performed at concerts for workers; hearing them, East Germans were supposed to be inspired to contribute to the further development of the new nation. Many scholars, journalists, and politicians worked to inculcate these notions in the minds of East German inhabitants. According to Ministry of Culture vice chairman Rackwitz, "Beethoven's symphonies and concertos are the most oft-played works in our musical life, his great vocal compositions and his chamber music sound regularly in many places, [his] work enjoys wide dissemination through radio, television, and record albums, it is played in schools and music schools, it is performed by all choruses and amateur orchestras. [Because] for many workers the name Beethoven has a sound of trustworthiness."[36]

Reviewing socialist cultural tradition, East German propagandists insisted that the workers' movement had a relationship with Beethoven's music which was stronger than that with any other composer. The many performances of Beethoven's music in the GDR—supposedly arranged by and for the working class itself—"proved the desire of the working people for education, for a deeper worldview."[37] In "every city and village" people showed their affection for Beethoven by arranging—supposedly on their own initiative—"innumerable events, contests, and exhibits."[38] One such series was covered in a publication for farmers, *Der freie Bauer:* "At first there were doubts when some really small-town cultural groups of the Union of Mutual Farmers' Aid (VdgB) came up with the plan to entertain our farmers with Beethoven concerts. 'The music is much too difficult,' the skeptics said. Yet when the performances began, they quickly learned better. Small booklets published by the Thüringer People's Press eased things immensely for everyone. . . . Through them farmers in many districts of the GDR were prepared for hours of edification and joy."[39] All this, said the nation's leaders, symbolized the strength of the "spiritual-musical life of the GDR."[40]

Echoing Kurt Eisner, boasts about the quantity of Beethoven concerts in the GDR aimed to convince people that the revolutionary government had given workers who had been "shut out" of cultural events under the capitalist system the chance to "appropriate the art of the past and present."[41] In return, East German cultural authorities charged workers and farmers to improve and defend the GDR. "On the way to a socialist-humanistic community, Beethoven's work is our guide. Let us use the power of his music which unites strength and beauty," said one.[42] Another exhorted: "Let the powerful melody of the Ninth Symphony guide the national struggle of the [East] German people against the foreign tyrants who want to plunge our Volk and the world into a new war!"[43]

This reference to Beethoven as a symbolic leader to be followed in case of conflict with the West was of immense significance to East German reception. A crucial aspect of the GDR interpretation was the difference East German cultural functionaries perceived between it and views developed in the Western Sector. According to GDR ideologues, a gap existed between Eastern and Western interpretations of Beethoven because each side had reached different world-historical stages. In their view, an "unbridgeable abyss" lay between the "reception and cultivation of Beethoven in our socialist state and in the state-monopolistic Federal Republic": the fact that each German state existed in an "objectively and historically different epoch" necessarily resulted in "completely diverging relationships to Beethoven's work."[44]

Probably based on their own methods and experiences, GDR cultural propagandists operated under two fundamental assumptions about West German Beethoven reception: first, that there existed an official Western interpretation; second, that the authorities of the FRG were somehow afraid of the Beethoven conceived by East Germans. In the Federal Republic "a politics of culture and art is operated against the people," wrote Hansjürgen Schaefer. There, Beethoven was used as an "advertising symbol for this politics." Moreover, the Beethoven image manipulated in the Federal Republic was completely one-sided

Fig. 21. Wilhelm Pieck, president of the GDR, inaugurating East German commemorations of the one hundred twenty-fifth anniversary of Beethoven's death. (*Musik und Gesellschaft* 2 [1952] 106)

because it left out democratic-revolutionary thoughts which East Germans "find impossible to overlook in his music."[45] In the opinion of GDR analysts, aspects of the official FRG interpretation reflected the problems of Western society in general: even a "cursory view of the results of theoretical and the practical study of Beethoven" in the FRG confirmed the "social relations that condition them." Western, "late-bourgeois" notions "are objectively stamped with contradictions of various sorts, above all between economic-political discretionary power and spiritual-cultural aimlessness, between technological prosperity and ideological regression. Within these margins, late-bourgeois Beethoven reception is a true expression of social crisis, alienation, decadent consciousness, and final collapse."[46] In criticizing the "West German Beethoven," therefore, East German leaders surreptitiously attacked the Federal Republican government itself.

The most problematic aspect of Western Beethoven interpretations, in the minds of East German authorities, was their tendency to neutralize him, to represent him as an apolitical artist. This endeavor consisted of "de-ideologizing" (*entideologisieren*) Beethoven, said important GDR music scholars, thereby robbing people of the revolutionary education that they gained from the East German version.[47] At a major conference of Beethoven experts in Bonn in 1970, Georg Knepler, a leading GDR musicologist, voiced this opinion in a skirmish with West German scholars, including Carl Dahlhaus and Hanns-Werner Heister. Knepler said he wished to prevent the separation of music studies from the social sciences that he considered to have occurred in the West, because he believed musicology "free from ideology is no science." In his mind, the "party orientation" of Beethoven analysis in the GDR was a sign of "socialist progress" while the de-ideologized views of the West marked late-bourgeois decline.[48] According to East German scholars, their FRG counterparts were trying to depoliticize Beethoven by concentrating on inconsequential biographical details without linking them to his social and political background. Finding it remarkable how "factual research (*Faktenforschung*) dominates" in the West, they allowed that this positivistic approach laid the foundation for "precise analysis of historical-cultural-creative relations" within individual works. But they considered the value of such scholarship limited, since "the integration of these facts into a total [read "political"] portrait of Beethoven is never achieved."[49]

Another facet of Western Beethoven reception that angered GDR scholars was the propensity to present the composer as something less than the heroic character whom they visualized. Fans of Beethoven complained bitterly about the psychoanalytical interpretations that arose in the West during the 1960s. The best-known example of this approach, *Beethoven and His Nephew,* by psychoanalysts Editha and Richard Sterba, was derided in East German literature as scholarship based on "little scandals instead of the truth." Hansjürgen Schaefer held that "by gossiping and implicating him in scandals both major and minor," such analysis tried to "disqualify Beethoven the person," making his worldview appear unimportant. "We stand," Schaefer averred, "before a falsification that serves the goal of keeping Beethoven's music acceptable for the salons of the imperialist system, while at the same time upholding the 'modern' critical attitude of impiety which is now popular." The psychoanalytical approach, he concluded, was another example of West German "fear of Beethoven!"[50]

East German operatives also considered connections made in the West between Beethoven, modernism, and popular culture as signifying elements they wanted to combat in their society. Modernist celebrations of Beethoven's two-hundredth birthday in 1970—particularly a film by Mauricio Kagel and a "performance event" by composer Karlheinz Stockhausen—were judged in the GDR to reveal more about "all that is nihilistic, derisive, and decadent" in West German society than about the composer. Echoing earlier critics of modernist expression (Peter Raabe, for instance), these cultural politicians attacked such productions for combining Beethoven's music with "that which is absurd, inhuman, filthy, and hideous."[51] Pop-cultural ways of honoring him in 1970—especially the mixing of Beethoven's melodies into rock-and-roll songs—were derided in the GDR as a "falsification of the revolutionary meaning of the composer." Here, blurted *Musik und Gesellschaft,* "Beethoven's revolutionary Jacobinism" is transformed into a substitute for "the delights of hashish."[52]

Above all, East German cultural authorities were disdainful of the Western tendency to commercialize Beethoven's music. This aspect of Beethoven reception was proof of endemic corruption in West German society. The chairman of the East German Council of Ministers, Willi Stoph, summarized this view—ubiquitous in GDR cultural officialdom—when he opened a Beethoven bicentenary conference.

> Is anyone still surprised that West German capitalists, hungry for profit, have appropriated Beethoven's music in order to earn millions? [One is shocked], however, by the unscrupulousness with which this occurs, by the lack of any moral sensitivity for things artistic which this development reflects. It is a macabre spectacle of the ruin of Western imperialist culture. The denial and falsification of humanistic traditions, the ever more apparent and unrestricted destruction of all ethical and moral values of art and culture, cannot be covered up by representative events highlighting famous performers, which are only accessible to an exclusive public. The legacy of Beethoven has long left his city of birth, Bonn. It cannot be maintained by a state which has nothing to do with humanistic ideas, to which measureless quest for profit means

everything, and in which reactionary imperialistic powers still influence political life decisively.[53]

East German leaders regularly mentioned Beethoven in their most serious and threatening anti-Western rhetoric. According to propagandistic sources, West Germany—led by the United States—was planning a war, and inspiration from Beethoven's music would help the GDR win it. East German officials typically used Beethoven celebrations and performances as opportunities to warn against the conspiratorial government in Bonn. On the one-hundred-twenty-fifth anniversary of Beethoven's death in 1952, the Central Committee of the SED itself issued a statement that directly connected the event with cold war politics: "This commemoration takes place in a time when the American imperialists are preparing a new war and militarism is rising again in West Germany. This means civil war, destruction, and death for our people. Thus is the existence of the German nation seriously threatened. In order to achieve their goals, the American imperialists are trying to poison our national consciousness, to destroy German culture and especially our national cultural legacy. But this attempt will be countered by Germans who fight for the reconstruction of our homeland." What all this had to do with Beethoven, the Central Committee went on to explain: "That which Beethoven fought for, that which he foresaw for the future, was made possible through the power of the Soviets attained in the great socialist October Revolution. . . . But Bonn is trying to force a foreign power onto millions of Germans, to cause war among brothers, to crush Beethoven's demands for freedom and friendship among peoples under its feet. Bonn is trying to create a new regime of terror that will muzzle every freedom-loving and democratic German in West Germany through police violence and martial law."[54]

A pamphlet produced by the Presidium of the National Front in the same year agreed that thoughts of Ludwig van Beethoven "remind us what course official Bonn steers today." In honor of the composer, the Presidium exhorted, "let us realize that a poisonous wind is blowing decay and putrefaction" through Bonn, the "headquarters of the warmongers." This Todestag eulogy then connected Beethoven and his hometown to the deepest conspiratorial fears of the GDR regime: "Let the German people know of the conspiracy against its life. Not even a speck of dust will be left of the honorable Beethovenhaus in Bonn. The German people must now remember that the American generals are having the Loreleifelsen rigged with explosives, that the roads along

Fig. 22. Cartoon from an East German newspaper: Beethoven and Goethe overlook divided Germany. (*Sonntag* [23 March 1952], courtesy of the Beethovenhaus, Bonn)

the Rhine, the viaducts and bridges, are all being made ready for destruction upon their command. . . . If these generals go through with their plans, the lovely Rheinland, the homeland of Beethoven, will no longer exist."[55]

Thus was the idea promoted within the context of Beethoven reception in the GDR that—given the corrupt and threatening nature of the West—the outbreak of World War Three was a distinct possibility. In such a case, Beethoven was to have an important function in the defense of the Soviet Zone: once the war had begun, his "humanistic work, his powerful music, his fighting example" would "spur us to the highest achievements in the righteous battle for our Volk."[56] Beethoven's works would be the "inaugural music of our fight for unity and peace," stated the National Front.

> The powerful melody of the Ninth Symphony will lead the national battle of the German people against the foreign tyrants who wish to drag our people and the world into a new war. The music of Beethoven, his *Fidelio* and his *Egmont,* will now become the songs announcing triumph by our Volk in the war against the dark powers of destruction. The *Missa Solemnis* will consecrate our righteous struggle for the inner and outer freedom of Germany! . . . The hour is no longer distant when Beethoven's music will sound in a free, united, peace-loving, and democratic Germany and when all Germans will be inspired to honorable deeds of peace. Beethoven wished it so! Beethoven fought for this! But we will execute his will![57]

Although this conflagration never occurred, such themes were repeated throughout the years of communist rule in East Germany. Every means of communication was employed to instill in East Germans belief in the validity of Marxist-Leninist ideology, confidence in the strength and purpose of the East German nation, and fear of attack from the West. And each of these points was made at some time with reference to Beethoven. In the scholarship produced under state control, in the literature of organizations devoted explicitly to propaganda, in recordings of music ensembles, in program notes for concerts, in publications for educational use, in broadcasts of government radio, and in television spectacles highlighting the nation's renowned performing artists, the "Marxist-Leninist image of Beethoven" was consistently evoked in order to clarify the fundamental tenets of East German ideology. And most prominent among these musical-political routines were official statements by the SED and the national government. Communiqués from the party's Central Committee, the Council of State (*Staatsrat*), the Council of Ministers (*Ministerrat*), as well as lengthy speeches by major figures including Walter Ulbricht, Otto Grotewohl, and Wilhelm Pieck contained far more than passing reference to Beethoven as a cultural hero.[58] At the culmination of the century-long tradition of leftist reception, these proclamations exhaustively evoked the image of Beethoven as a social revolutionary and closely linked his legacy to the fate of the German Democratic Republic. East German authorities even made mention of Beethoven when erecting their "antifascist protection wall." In 1961, as the Berlin Wall was completed, Ulbricht promised that within the so-called protected area East Germans "would always walk in the spirit" of the composer, "parading in celebration of achievements by the first workers' and farmers' state on German soil."[59]

Beethoven in West Germany

Such propaganda was not received only by the people enclosed within the Wall. Much of it was picked up and analyzed by Western observers of East Germany and its cultural politics. West German cold warriors were angered by the GDR's use of Beethoven. A report from the Federal Ministry for General German Issues (an interest group incensed by the division of the nation) complained that East German application of the Beethoven myth was directly comparable to the techniques of Nazi propaganda: GDR authorities who depicted Beethoven as a revolutionary activist and employed his music as an instrument of "totalitarian *Kulturpolitik*" applied the same methods as had the brownshirts, misusing the German cultural heritage to prove their "doubtful" legitimacy. "The cultural functionaries in the Soviet Zone operate according to the same principles as the National Socialists used in their ideology; instead of a 'Germanic Superman,' however, they are developing in their Beethoven image an anti-Western popular tribunal [*sic*] that uses music as a political propaganda tool."[60]

In reaction, cultural-political leaders on the Western side of the Iron Curtain might have formulated their own politicized version of the Beethoven myth to counter the Marxist-Leninist rendition. This process did occur to a limited extent. However, the main tendency in West German reception of Beethoven from the end of the Second World War until the end of the cold war was—as East German critics claimed—to "de-ideologize" the image of the composer and interpretations of his music. Appalled by the jingoistic version purveyed by the Nazis and embarrassed by the revolutionary portrait promulgated in the GDR, West German scholars, journalists, and even political leaders stressed objective musicological study of his compositions and close psychoanalysis of his character.[61] If Beethoven's music and image were exploited for nonscholastic or nonartistic purposes in the FRG, it was mainly for the profit of individual entrepreneurs who incorporated them into the commercial culture of Western capitalism, not to further grand political plans.

One might correlate the emergence of many dissimilar interpretations of Beethoven with the establishment of a democratic political system in the Western Sector. As in the Weimar Republic, interpretive diversity in the reception of Beethoven could be attributed to the multiplicity of political groupings in the Federal Republic. To be sure, no state interpretation was enforced from above; but one can press this argument only so far. It is very difficult to discern links between the *Faktenforschung* of Beethoven's life and music preferred by West German scholars and the ideologies of specific FRG political organizations. One could also deem the variety of Beethoven interpretations in West Germany a political manifestation in the inverted way devised by propagandists of the GDR. As noted above, East German critics described the cultivation of manifold interpretations of Beethoven as a symptom of Western "aimlessness." "Their research shows no interest in a modern, unified image of Beethoven. Their achievements are to dissociate, individualize, and splinter in an extreme fashion. The overlapping, methodologically united collective work which is the only way of mastering Beethoven cannot be realized under the social conditions [of West Germany]. In contrast to [our] high degree of social reception capability they offer either none at all or markedly individualistic, subjective conceptions." East German ideologues perceived "neutral" interpretations by Western scholars as an organized coverup of Beethoven's political tendencies that "helped the imperialistic and bourgeois ruling classes" undermine revolutionary ideology.[62] If, according to this mindset, Western interpretations did not emphasize Beethoven's role as a revolutionary, they had to be the products of reactionary ideological thought—whether overtly or not. Yet, hard as one might look for signs that the proliferation of Beethoven interpretations in West Germany constituted a conspiracy against Marxist-Leninist ideas, proof is difficult to discern; the most conspicuous aspect of Beethoven portraits popularized in West Germany was their lack of ideological coloring. Most who promoted positivist analysis, psychological study, and commercial exploitation of Beethoven and his art in the FRG seem to have operated without political intent. Apathy rather than activism marks their reception.

Indubitably, some discussions of Beethoven in the West were motivated by hostility toward the GDR and its exploitation of the composer. Western newspapers frequently printed and ridiculed East German statements about Beethoven.[63] "The holy state-idol that the Soviet Zone has created for itself" out of Beethoven "does not have much in common with the man who died in Vienna on 26 March 1827," chortled a staunchly anticommunist publication.[64] Even *Vorwärts*—still the banner of the SPD in West Germany—acknowledged that despite GDR claims and those of its own early leaders, "neither Marx, Engels, nor Lenin concerned themselves more than casually with Beethoven."[65] In 1970 *Der Spiegel* responded to minister of culture Gysi's assertion that Beethoven "belonged" to the GDR with telling evenhandedness: "Fine—but not exclusively."[66] To balance the record, many Western journals did highlight biographical material which dispelled notions that Beethoven had been a single-minded revolutionary. For instance, in commemorating his two-hundredth birthday, *Der Spiegel* contended that Beethoven had been a "republican," but no model revolutionary. "This man who enjoyed the favors of nobles was a republican who mistrusted the Hapsburgers, but who nevertheless would have gladly become a servant in the royal house. He was a petit-bourgeois who lived off the nobility and who scolded the bourgeoisie and the aristocracy equally with his big mouth (*böses Maul*). He is reputed to have been a revolutionary, but not a very convincing one."[67] Therefore, some interpreters of Beethoven in the FRG did contradict ideas dear to ideologues across the Wall. But it seems they did so less in the interest of their nation—that is, to protect the FRG from the political rhetoric of the East—than in the interest of Beethoven—that is, to defend him against East Germany's unidimensional political characterizations. "The dead Beethoven is powerless against their claims," *Die Welt* alerted.[68] West German interpreters did raise the issue of Beethoven's politics, but it was usually in order to answer this call to guard the composer against the one-sided claims of GDR propaganda, not to further the interests of the FRG. "Beethoven wrote not for, but also not against, society," argued *Die Welt*; he "considered music an unengaged art."[69]

Complete lists of publications on Beethoven compiled in the *Beethoven-Jahrbuch* between 1945 and 1983 contained few titular references to politics in West German sources.[70] Nor did contributions to major Beethoven conferences.[71] Instead of debating his party affiliations, scholars in West Germany aimed primarily to dispel the "Promethean *Mythos*" and reveal "poor Beethoven" beneath. Recognizing that the Romantics had overlaid his image with mythological coloring, priority was given to rediscovering Beethoven, "the whole human being," including his all-too-human flaws.[72] In this quest, many Western analysts admitted that Beethoven was not the paragon the Romantics had made him out to be; in reality, they conceded, he was a troubled man.

Psychoanalytical interpretations declared that Beethoven had deep emotional problems: he was a "selfish narcissist," he arranged shady financial dealings, he engaged in less-than-elegant sexual encounters, and he exhibited a homosexual attraction toward his nephew. Rather than epitomizing moral and artistic integrity, psychoanalysts argued, he may have been "the victim of the degeneration of his ethical structure." Based on the "latest research," *Der Spiegel* disclosed that Beethoven had exhibited a "good portion of hatred for his fellow man," perceived intrigues all around him, was distrustful to the point of madness, and terrorized his servants.[73] Such disparagement of the composer's character, for whatever reason, represented a significant shift in the history of Beethoven reception in Germany. Until this time almost every interpretation, political or otherwise, had accepted the basic premise that Beethoven had been a Great Man, defined in Romantic terms. Now, instead of authenticating his sublimeness, Beethoven interpreters highlighted the darker sides of his personality; his greatness was limited to his achievements as an artist, as a man he was at best *allzumenschlich.* Perhaps marginal vis-à-vis the history of the politicization of Beethoven's image, this shift did represent a growing indifference to his ideological outlook.

Beethoven's representation in West Germany as something larger than life did not occur in political-ideological campaigns: it was in the commercial propaganda of business that the Promethean myth was perpetuated. East German observers were accurate when they assessed the commercialization of Beethoven in the capitalist West. In the Germany that enjoyed the "economic miracle," people made money by stamping Beethoven's image on practically anything that could be marketed, and by playing his music in advertisements for literally anything that could be sold.[74] Nonetheless, within the context of West German political culture, evidence indicates that a conscious effort was made to minimize crass exploitation of Beethoven's art. Perhaps in order to avoid committing acts comparable to the *Kulturpolitik* of the Third Reich, FRG governments implicitly yet extensively promoted an "international" or "universal" view of Beethoven that exalted his music not as a treasure of German society, but as the common property of humanity. Even the anticommunist Federal Ministry for General German Issues, which so vehemently attacked the GDR interpretation of Beethoven, stipulated that he "belongs to no political order . . . he belongs to the world."[75]

One significant exception to this altruism was a performance of Beethoven's music that marked the founding of the West German state. During the first meeting of the Bundestag on 7 September 1949, a chamber orchestra sat before the podium in the new parliamentary

Fig. 23. Constituent Assembly of the Bundestag in Bonn on 7 September 1949. To open the proceedings the orchestra seated beneath the presidium performed Beethoven's *Weihe des Hauses*. (Courtesy of ECON Verlag, Düsseldorf)

room. To open the ceremonies, Beethoven's *Weihe des Hauses* was performed.[76] Later the newly appointed federal president, Theodore Heuss, made reference in his inaugural speech to Goethe, whose bicentenary had just been observed, and to Beethoven, in whose hometown the government sat. "In these two men from German soil were developed world values from which we can proudly derive strength and comfort in the convulsions of time."[77] Certainly, these were attempts to associate Beethoven with the new government in the Western Sector. Yet the West German government did not thereafter reserve the legacy of Beethoven for its own propagandistic applications. In 1967 West Germany cooperated in making the Ninth Symphony's "melody of joy" into the anthem for the North Atlantic Treaty Organization; in 1972 the FRG was instrumental in appointing the same phrase as a hymn for the European Economic Community.[78]

As had every government since Bismarck's, the West German state also produced performances of Beethoven's music within the context of its foreign policy. The Berlin Philharmonic Orchestra continued after the war to perform German music, including Beethoven's compositions, throughout the world. Unlike earlier manifestations of this policy, however, these tours were not meant to vaunt the superiority of German art over the host cultures; the intent behind them was plainly to establish warmer international relations. In 1969—at the height of both the Vietnam and cold wars—the Berlin Philharmonic gave a series of concerts in Moscow. Because of West Germany's continued close association with the United States, this visit might have been seen as a propaganda ploy on the part of the Western powers. However, a West German politician present at the performances—which included Beethoven's Fifth Symphony—announced to the press that it had been "a victory of the music over politics," not a victory of German music over Russian culture.[79] Here Beethoven might be said to have served as an emissary anticipating *Ostpolitik* instead of the flagbearer of violent conflict he had so often been portrayed to be.

Similarly, events arranged by West German cultural authorities on the one-hundred-twenty-fifth anniversary of Beethoven's death in 1952, his two-hundredth birthday in 1970, and the one-hundred-fiftieth Todestag in 1977 were marked by a lack of patriotic innuendo. Such celebrations were indeed stamped by commercialization: book publishers caused a "boom" of Beethoven literature and manufacturers produced mountains of Beethoven bric-a-brac.[80] However, these commercial appropriations of the composer were undertaken for personal, not political, gain. An observer of the ceremonies in 1952 was pleased that, unlike East German officials, West German authorities did not attempt to link Beethoven to present-day political conditions.

> We are simply registering the paradox that in [East Germany] . . . the composer from Bonn is depicted as a national hero while the . . . Federal Republic honors him without a trace of inappropriate pathos. In Bonn one has enough tact not to drag the famous son of the city into the fight over political opinions. Here one is so "laid back" as to pass up an obvious opportunity for state public relations persons to make propagandistic capital. If they had applied the [GDR] methods, they would have made him out to be the prophet of the United Nations and the pathfinder for Dr. Adenauer; and they would have attributed the inspiration of the *Eroica* to *Yankee Doodle Dandy*. But here such counterfeiting was waived. A wreath on the monument, cathedral bells, a speech—for the rest, one played music.[81]

Nor did the 1977 observations trigger a dramatic struggle among political factions over the legacy of Beethoven, as had been the case fifty years earlier. Todestag rites exemplified the West German indifference to Beethoven's politics. Federal president Scheel did participate in the festivities in Bonn, but only under the proviso that he simply lay a wreath at the foot of the statue in the Beethovenhaus without making a speech.[82] This Todestag was to be observed in a quiet, reverent way, government organizers stipulated: "it was not to be a state function."[83]

Despite a growing feeling among Germans that Beethoven had bequeathed his legacy to *alle Menschen* regardless of national or political orientation, the struggle over the "rights" to it did not subside after Nazi claims had been negated. As Thomas Mann had suspected, "the good and noble that human beings had fought for and stormed citadels for, that the ecstatics exultantly announced" did not come about in Germany between 1945 and 1989. During the cold war, the pessimism that Mann expressed through his character Adrian Leverkühn was justified: hope for coalescence communicated in the Ninth Symphony was realized neither in the political sphere nor in Beethoven reception. In Germany divided there raged competition between those who wanted to free the composer of political significance and a regime that enforced precisely such an interpretation. However, achievement of the good and noble connoted in the Ninth—the "coming together of brothers," at least within Germany itself—was not far off.

Beethoven and the Reunification of Germany

The history of the reception given Beethoven and his works by German politicians is the story of a battle that raged from his lifetime on. Ever since his death, ideas about this artist have developed in such close relation to national developments that, viewed critically, they seem to mirror the contours of modern German political thinking itself. With the possible exceptions of the First World War, when a common front of interpretation developed, and the Nazi era, when only one view was permitted, the struggle within Germany over the "meaning of Beethoven" has been almost as fierce as the history of the nation. But during the transformation (*Wende*) of postwar politics that occurred in 1989, the German people did—at least momentarily—come to agreement on the "universal" and "humanitarian" interpretations affirmed by a minority throughout the annals of thought about Beethoven.

On the evening of 9 November 1989, the Central Committee of the Socialist Unity Party of the GDR announced new travel laws that effectively punctured the Iron Curtain. In the days and nights thereafter, hundreds of thousands of East and West Germans flooded the west side of Berlin, converging on the Kurfürstendamm and the Breitscheidplatz surrounding the Kaiser Wilhelm Gedächtniskirche. Observing them, one could not but reflect that this had been the site of many milestones in German history: troops of the kaisers marched over it; early socialists met in the surrounding cafés; Karl Liebknecht and Rosa Luxemburg led rallies there; Nazis paraded by torchlight along this way; American and British fliers bombed it. But few of these events compared in magnitude, either physical or emotional, with the congregations that gathered there over that autumn weekend in 1989. The Volk had impressed its will on the nation; all but a tiny minority were elated by the decision of the SED to open the Wall. Most significant, this had been achieved by peaceful means. East Germans and West Germans had overcome both the concrete Wall that had separated them physically and, for the time being, the ideological Wall that divided them spiritually. The citizens of "West Berlin" and the citizens of the "Capital of the GDR" were no longer enemies: they were again simply *Berliner*.

Given the history related in this study, only one cultural metaphor could have matched the momentousness of the occasion. No product of German art, whether painting, sculpture, essay, novel, poem, film, or song, could capture the emotion of the "reunification" as well as Beethoven's Ninth Symphony—especially its finale. The only appropriate way to enhance these celebrations would have been to position speakers on the rooftops surrounding the *Ku'damm* and direct the tones of the *Schlußchor* into the crowd—as if from beyond the starry canopy. For within the multitude, the dream of reconciliation many Germans have perceived in this composition became reality. Weeks of marching in the streets of Dresden, Leipzig, East Berlin, and the rest of the GDR had given the German people, divided for forty years, a chance to reunite. As the headline to the "Special Edition for the Opening of the Wall in Berlin" of the *BZ* (*Berliner Zeitung*) read: "A new and great feeling of togetherness animated all hearts in the city."[84] The sound of people milling around each other, regarding each other, greeting each other, laughing with each other, was itself a hymn of joy.

While this spontaneous "freedom festival" went on through the weekend, some participants set up stereo equipment in order to broadcast music to accompany it. For the most part, they chose to play contemporary popular music. Given that these songs were products of the Western music business and thus symbolized the desire of East Germans for consumer goods, this selection of consecratory music was not unfitting. However, a more decorous musical observance of the "Revolution in the GDR" was soon arranged. On Sunday morning, 12 November 1989, the Berlin Philharmonic Orchestra held a special concert for East German citizens to solemnize their deliverance. The response to this "spontaneous gift of music" from the orchestra was powerful. "They came from Potsdam, from Klein-Machnow, Marzahn, East Berlin, and even from Rostock over the freshly opened crossing at Potsdamer Platz—whether young with children or older persons who knew Berlin before the construction of the Wall. Everywhere were expectant, excited, happy faces. Couples hugged each other as they received their tickets. Some who had not been convinced by press, radio, and television reports were simply astounded to receive this concert as a gift."[85] The music performed at this event, which East Germans experienced "as in a dream," was that of a single composer: led by Daniel Barenboim, the orchestra played Beethoven's First Piano Concerto and Seventh Symphony. Interviews conducted with several audience members afterward indicate that on that day the debate over the political meaning of Beethoven's music in Germany paused in accord.

East German interviewees agreed that the program harmonized perfectly with the emotional circumstances. According to a woman who said her husband and son had both been musicians and died in the Second World War, the choice of Beethoven's music had been most appropriate (*angekommen*). In the opinion of another, this event signified the "reconciliation of the German people," and the selection of Beethoven's Seventh Symphony was perfect because "it is a happy piece for a happy event, since there was something of a carnavalesque feeling to it." Finally, an East German man said that this event symbolized the reestablished "unity of the German people"; Beethoven's was the "best possible music for marking this occasion." But he added that while aware of technical difficulties that made it impossible on such short notice, he felt the orchestra should have played the Ninth Symphony instead of the Seventh—since "we are now brothers again."[86]

During the weeks that followed the initial crumbling of the Wall, and as the East German regime continued to disintegrate, other references to Beethoven appeared in German newspapers. In its first editorial response to the breach of the border, *Die Welt* referred to *Fidelio* extensively. Using the plot of Beethoven's opera as a metaphor for the process of revolution in the GDR, the paper expressed its hope that developments would ultimately lead to free elections. According to *Die Welt,* on the opening of the Berlin Wall the story had "only reached the first act": only if "all democratic social suggestions" can be discussed in the GDR, "only if citizens have the possibility of voting freely and secretly," would the editors feel it appropriate to quote the prisoners of *Fidelio*—"O nameless Joy." "The last days have a great power to persuade, and nothing seems impossible," *Die Welt* closed. "At least the chorus can now decide whether the piece will be sung to its end."[87]

In addition to exhortations for further revolutionary action on the part of the East German "prisoners," Beethoven's music was featured in liberation celebrations throughout the next weeks. On 18 December 1989, the violinist and conductor Yehudi Menuhin gave a concert to benefit the "reconstruction of the historical city-center of Berlin" that featured Beethoven's *Egmont* Overture and Fourth Symphony, op. 60.[88] On 19 December 1989, the violinist Norbert Brainin and the pianist Günther Ludwig played three Beethoven sonatas at the Berlin Hochschule für Musik "out of joy over the developments in the GDR."[89] After two centuries in which his music had been politicized in Germany, thoughts of Beethoven came quickly to the minds of those who experienced the "peaceful revolution" in 1989.

The ultimate association of Beethoven's music with the Wende came later in the year. Upon the fracture of the Wall, the German pianist, conductor, and impresario Justus Frantz and the American conductor Leonard Bernstein conceived of a pair of Berlin Celebration Concerts.[90] When their plan was carried out, the wish expressed by some East Germans on 12 November—that the Ninth Symphony be played to symbolize their liberation—was granted in the fullest possible way. On 23 December 1989—the day after the opening of the Brandenburger Gate—and again on Christmas morning, Beethoven's Ninth was performed in the (West) Berlin Philharmonie and the (East) Berlin Schauspielhaus, respectively. Through modern video technology, both concerts were broadcast to audiences massed on the Breitscheidplatz and the Platz der Akademie. There banks of audio speakers and large video screens were erected so that multitudes could take part in this cultural-political ritual. The concerts were also transmitted to thirty-six other nations by satellite, thereby including the world community in this festival of liberty.

Before leading the orchestra, which consisted of musicians from each of the major powers involved in the Second World War, Bernstein released a statement that made the association between Beethoven's music and the recent events in the GDR most explicit: "There is apparently conjecture that Schiller may have produced a second sketch of his poem, 'Ode to Joy,' which carried the title 'Ode to Freedom.' Most researchers today are of the opinion, however, that this rumor is

Fig. 24. Leonard Bernstein and an orchestra of musicians from the major combatant nations of the Second World War receive an emotional response after performing Beethoven's Ninth Symphony in the Berlin Schauspielhaus to celebrate the opening of the Iron Curtain in 1989. (Photo: Ludwig Schirmer, Deutsche Grammophon Gesellschaft, Hamburg)

a fraud originated by Friedrich Ludwig Jahn. Whether true or not, I believe that this is a heavensent moment when we should sing the word 'Freedom' wherever the score reads 'Joy.' If there ever were a historical moment in which one can neglect the theoretical discussions of academics in the name of human freedom—this is it. And I believe that Beethoven would have given us his blessing. Let freedom live!"[91]

Interviews conducted at these concerts confirm that Germans in attendance did consider Beethoven's music the finest expression of the emotions they were feeling at the time. An East German couple who had traveled from Freiberg to partake in the spectacle under the Gedächtniskirche said that "you couldn't find a more appropriate work for this festive occasion than the Ninth Symphony because it expresses our present feelings of joy." A West Berlin couple agreed, "because the *Schlußchor* is the song 'To Joy' and we are all joyous that the border has just become passable and the Brandenburger Gate has just been opened." A man who cried through the whole performance agreed. "I find that just this Symphony of Freedom has a very particular meaning in this moment. This music fits like no other with the bonding of people to one another that is now occurring—I don't think we have any other music for such an event, do we?" A nearby woman felt this was an appropriate selection because the Ninth "belongs to both German nations, doesn't it?" "Yes, exactly," interrupted a man from the GDR, "but I think it should touch [people] not only in the German Democratic Republic and the Federal Republic, but also in all of Europe and the whole world."[92]

These statements, along with reviews in East and West German newspapers, show that Bernstein's revision of Beethoven's Ninth Symphony was considered valid by most. As the West Berlin *Tagesspiegel* put it, "The public, above all those who crowded under the Gedächtniskirche and on the Gendarmenmarkt in front of the video screens, seemed to share his conviction."[93] An East German man who attended the Schauspielhaus concert asked: "Did you notice what Bernstein did with the theme? There were many of us here who had taken part in the [reform] movement. . . . For us this had great significance."[94] Even arch-*Musikpolitiker* Hansjürgen Schaefer, reviewing the concert for *Neues Deutschland,* the principal newspaper of the SED, agreed: "The fact that the conductor replaced Schiller's 'Joy' with 'Freedom' belonged to this beautiful and fascinating concept . . . of celebrating a great festival of brotherhood, democracy, and peaceful togetherness."[95] A reporter from the *Neue Osnabrücker Zeitung* captured the general emotional response to the Christmas performance in the Schauspielhaus:

> *Freiheit, schöner Götterfunken,* Leonard Bernstein had them sing. And only literature professors winced at the alteration of Schiller's ode. Musicians and public were of the same opinion as the conductor, that "Beethoven would have given us his blessing in this heavensent moment." *Alle Menschen werden Brüder:* many in East Berlin shed tears unashamedly. A young woman next to me gave up trying to save her makeup. Even Bernstein and the musicians, overwhelmed by . . . the profundity of the moment, played with an intensity, a fervor, as if they were hugging the world. Beyond the music itself, one could trace the . . . idea of the thinking man as the crown of creation awakened in the revolution of 1789, the notion of *humanitas* in the Weimar Republic, the utopian idea of freedom. Bernstein raised the finale to a dionysian ecstasy. One moment of silence: and then all people jumped jubilantly from their seats and fell into one another's arms.[96]

With these events strife over Beethoven ended, for a short time at least. As in German politics, a compromise was reached during the revolution of 1989 with regard to the "meaning of Beethoven." Considering the future of the newest Germany, one cannot assume that this harmony will last. Contending interpretations will continue to proliferate and incite ongoing competition over Beethoven's "legacy." For now, all Germans can choose freely which Beethoven they want to hear—among others, the nationalistic conqueror, the revolutionary activist, the bourgeois entertainer, the herald of international cooperation. They may hearken to the Beethoven of reconciliation some sensed in late 1989, looking down on the *Ku'damm* from beyond the starry canopy. *That* Beethoven might inspire Germans to become brothers—not only with fellow nationals but with all peoples of Europe and the world.

Notes

All translations are the author's unless otherwise indicated.

1. Beethoven in German Political Culture

1. Based on interviews conducted by the author and tape-recorded at the Berlin Philharmonie, 12 November 1989, Ira F. Brilliant Center for Beethoven Studies, San Jose State University, San Jose, California. See further discussion in Chapter 5.

2. As George L. Mosse has shown, even before the unification of the German state "cultural experience was a political reality in central Europe." The political philosophies of Ernst M. Arndt, G. W. F. Hegel, and Friedrich L. Jahn all reflected the tendency of Germans to conceive of politics in cultural terms; each asserted that "ideas of beauty and of the soul" were integrally related to objective political realities (*The Nationalization of the Masses: Political Symbolism and Mass Movements in Germany from the Napoleonic Wars through the Third Reich* [New York: Howard Fertig, 1975], 214). Josef Chytry substantiated these observations of the cultural component of German political philosophy in his book on *The Aesthetic State: A Quest in Modern German Thought* (Berkeley: University of California Press, 1989). There he traced the German quest for "a social and political community that accords primacy, although not exclusiveness, to the aesthetic dimension in consciousness and activity," pursuing the "ideal of that community as it was developed by German thinkers from the mid-eighteenth to the late twentieth century" (xii).

3. In Mosse's words: "During the last two centuries the masses of the population were emerging as a political force and had to be integrated into the national community. Ritual, songs, and national symbols were used to shape the crowd into a disciplined mass in order to give it direction and maintain control; they nationalized the masses" (*Confronting the Nation* [Hanover, Md.: for Brandeis University Press by University Press of New England, 1993], 2).

4. Mosse, *Nationalization of the Masses*, 215. Particularly—but not exclusively—on the right wing, the result was "a theology which provided the framework for national worship," Mosse argued. "As such, its rites and liturgies were central, an integral part of a political theory which was not dependent on the appeal of the written word. Speeches fulfilled a liturgical function rather than presenting a didactic exposition of the ideology. What was actually said was, in the end, of less importance than the setting and the rites which surrounded such speeches" (ibid., 9).

5. Mosse, *Confronting the Nation*, 3.

6. Mosse holds that through the *Gründerjahre* and after, German nationalism evolved into a "civic religion"—the "continuation from primitive and Christian times of viewing the world through myth and symbol, acting out one's hopes and fears within the ceremonial and liturgical forms" (*Nationalization of the Masses*, 214).

7. Hermann Glaser, *Die Kultur der Wilhelminischen Zeit: Topographie einer Epoche* (Frankfurt am Main: S. Fischer, 1984), 223. Historian of what he calls the ideology

of nineteenth-century philistines, the *Spießer-Ideologie,* Glaser has shown that "heroes from yesterday and long ago were taken from the historical arsenal and placed on the pedestal of national glorification—as signposts for present and future orientation. The selection process was broadminded, since there were many in the schools, academies, universities, and churches who would undertake whatever ideological reinterpretation was necessary, *ex cathedra.* Festivals and celebrations, as well as the parades of the epoch [were] full of national and nationalist pretention—the Wilhelminian Baroque provided for a luxurious and refined decor that satisfied all the senses, and thereby reconciled them with sovereign duty. Merry, joyous national festivals secured German unity and solidarity" (ibid., 222).

8. As Celia Applegate argued in a thought-provoking piece on German identity, "music was of central importance to the spread of German national feeling in the nineteenth century, quite possibly of more importance than German literature" ("What Is German Music? Reflections on the Role of Art in the Creation of the Nation," *German Studies Review* [Winter 1992], 25).

9. Mosse, *Confronting the Nation,* 13–26.

10. In Applegate's words, "Music became a metaphor for the nation, in which a natural diversity was overcome in joyful togetherness"; further, "Music, German music, became for nineteenth-century Germans a direct expression of their national identity, . . . a cultural form through which they could participate actively, regularly, and intensively in a nation" ("What Is German Music?" 29–30).

11. Again, Applegate: "Beethoven has been, and always will be, many things to many people, but to Germans in the nineteenth century he was the very embodiment of their greatness as a people. . . . Beethoven's humanism, his individualism, his roughness, his transcendence, and his deafness have all, on one occasion or another, been taken to be expressive of the German condition" (ibid., 29).

12. Robert Schumann, *On Music and Musicians,* ed. Konrad Wolff, trans. Paul Rosenfeld (Berkeley: University of California Press, 1983), 61.

13. Julius Nitsche, "Jonny neben Beethoven: Errinerung an eine Jahrhundertfeier in wirrer Zeit," *Völkischer Beobachter* (Berlin), 26 March 1937.

14. Indeed, important music scholars, even Beethoven authorities, were involved in integrating his life story and music into the ideological symbolism of political movements and regimes. When such scholars produced serious studies for professional journals and books, they usually maintained historical and musicological objectivity; when writing exegeses of Beethoven for the journals of political organizations, however, some allowed their proclivities to show forth. Even taking into account the pressure that they felt under parties and regimes striving for total control of culture, the enthusiasm some exhibited in their efforts to render Beethoven and his music instruments of political indoctrination is a consistent problem in the field of musicology and music history in Germany.

15. Because of the worldwide appeal of Beethoven's music and mystique, analysis of their place in the political cultures of other nations would certainly be rewarding. The scope of my work is limited, however, to records of Beethoven's reception in German-speaking areas. Exceptions occur only when, as during the two world wars, "foreign" interpretations influenced analysis of Beethoven within German lands. I have included references to some sources originating in Vienna to bolster evidence on how Beethoven was received by large political elements (communists, socialists, National Socialists, etc.) that were represented in Austria as well as Germany; in these cases, I see no indication that Austrian versions differed greatly from those of the associated German parties.

16. Robert C. Holub delineated the principles underlying histories of reception in *Reception Theory: A Critical Introduction* (London: Methuen, 1984). For Holub, reception theory refers to "a general shift in concern from the author and the work to the

text and the reader" (xiii), from a "concern with production and presentation to a concentration on effect and response" (11).

17. See Christopher Ballantine's distinction between these fields in *Music and Its Social Meanings* (New York: Gordon and Breach Science Publishers, 1984), xv.

18. Maynard Solomon, "Thoughts on Biography," in Solomon, *Beethoven Essays* (Cambridge, Mass.: Harvard University Press, 1988), 103. Solomon cited psychoanalyst K. R. Eissler in this statement on method.

19. Maynard Solomon, *Beethoven* (New York: Schirmer, 1977), 212.

20. Ibid.

21. Carl Dahlhaus, *Nineteenth-Century Music,* trans. J. Bradford Robinson (Berkeley: University of California Press, 1989), 75, 76, 75.

22. Alessandra Comini, *The Changing Image of Beethoven: A Study in Mythmaking* (New York: Rizzoli, 1987), 14, 1.

23. Leo Schrade, *Beethoven in France: The Development of an Idea* (New Haven: Yale University Press, 1942), ix.

24. Leo Schrade, "Das französische Beethovenbild der Gegenwart," in Arnold Schmitz, ed., *Beethoven und die Gegenwart: Festschrift des Beethovenhauses-Bonn* (Berlin: Ferdinand Dummler, 1937), 58.

25. Schrade, *Beethoven in France,* x.

26. Peter Schnaus, *E. T. A. Hoffmann als Beethoven-Rezensent der Allgemeinen Musikalischen Zeitung* (Munich: Emil Katzbichler, 1977), 35–36, 45.

27. E. T. A. Hoffmann, review of Beethoven's Fifth Symphony, *Allgemeine musikalische Zeitung,* 4 and 11 July 1810, trans. Arthur Ware Locke, *Musical Quarterly* 3, no. 1 (January 1917), reproduced in Thomas K. Scherman and Louis Biancolli, eds. *The Beethoven Companion* (Garden City, N.Y.: Doubleday and Doubleday, 1972), 577–579.

28. Arnold Schmitz, *Das Romantische Beethovenbild: Darstellung und Kritik* (Berlin: Ferdinand Dummler, 1927), 178.

29. Ibid., 1–6.

30. In Comini's view, this legend "could not fail to fascinate an age [when] many Europeans had begun to question the rights and even the very existence of the aristocracy." In it "the plain, dark overcoat, which he had buttoned up defiantly, made this unfettered god of music a man of the people—perfect symbol for the battle against tyranny." The anecdote was transfigured into a "myth," she goes on, because of "the pre-1848 revolutionary mood of Europe that was disposed to see in Beethoven a fellow fighter against repression" (*Changing Image,* 17–18).

31. Ulrich Schmitt, *Revolution im Konzertsaal: Zur Beethoven-Rezeption im 19. Jahrhundert* (Mainz: Schott, 1990), passim.

32. Ibid., 68–70, 112–121.

33. Ibid., 206. Schmitt directed this criticism mainly at Arnold Schmitz, who worked to demonstrate the origins of many Beethoven compositions in French Revolutionary song.

34. Ibid., 145–179.

35. Press notice republished in Hugo Dinger, *Die Weltanschauung Richard Wagners in den Grundzügung ihrer Entwicklung,* vol 1., *Richard Wagners geistige Entwicklung* (Leipzig: F. W. Fritzsch, 1892), 178n1.

36. Ibid.

37. Gustav Adolf Kietz, *Richard Wagner in den Jahren 1842–1849 und 1873–1875: Erinnerungen* (Dresden: C. Riessner, 1905), 84.

38. Cited in Klaus Kropfinger, *Wagner und Beethoven: Untersuchungen zur Beethoven-Rezeption Richard Wagners,* vol. 29, *Studien zur Musikgeschichte des 19. Jahrhunderts* (Regensburg: Bosse, 1975), 44–47.

39. Richard Wagner, *Braunes Buch,* 8 May 1849, cited in Kropfinger, *Wagner und Beethoven,* 44.

40. Schmitt, *Revolution im Konzertsaal,* 131.

41. Schmitt's explanation of this is worth reading: "The interpretation of Beethoven's compositions as revolutionary music was not induced by a revolutionary vocabulary, through the use of military signals, through triadic melodies or march-like intonations; its basis was rather the [growing] capacity for panoramic listening, in which the hearer did not concentrate on individual motives and themes. The abundance of motivic material, the mingling of details, the abrupt transitions, the harsh modulations, the dynamic climaxes, the 'robust' instrumentation: all of these caused the modern hearer to eagerly become intoxicated by the total combination. This *Klangreiz*—in modern terms: this sound— . . . is what was revolutionary about Beethoven's music, and awakened corresponding associations in the modern hearer. In this sense, the catchword 'élan terrible'—the frightful energy in Beethoven's music—was the heart of the matter. But one must not allow oneself to be misled into seeking this élan terrible in specific (French) motives, in short passages, march rhythms, bugle calls, or triadic melodies. . . . What about such short motives, torn out of context, could possibly sound revolutionary? [What is revolutionary about] three fortissimo eighth-notes followed by half-notes down a third, as in the measures 1–5 of the Fifth Symphony? If anything at all, it is the symphony as a whole that sounds revolutionary, not merely a specific point in the first passage" (ibid., 207).

42. Ibid., 97–99. To understand how they felt when first confronted by Beethoven's sonic engines, Schmitt insisted, the modern researcher need merely take a "fleeting peek into the notes or, even better, simply listen to some works." This will leave "no doubt that the keywords of contemporary reception, such as abundance of ideas, abruptness, loudness, etc., accurately describe essential structural moments of this music" (ibid., 134).

43. Ibid., 99.

44. Robert Schumann, "Monument für Beethoven" in *Gesammelte Schriften über Musik und Musiker,* ed. Martin Kreisig, 5th ed., 2 vols. (Leipzig: Breitkopf & Härtel, 1914), 1:134.

45. Robert Schumann, "Neue Sinfonien für Orchester," in *Gesammelte Schriften,* 1:424.

46. Kropfinger, *Wagner und Beethoven,* 62.

47. Richard Wagner, *My Life,* 2 vols. (New York: Dodd, Mead and Co., 1911), 1:36.

48. Richard Wagner, "Eine Pilgerfahrt zu Beethoven," in *Sämtliche Schriften und Dichtungen,* 6th ed., vol. 1 (Leipzig: Breitkopf & Härtel, 1907), 90–114.

49. Kropfinger, *Wagner und Beethoven,* 76.

50. Frank Josserand, *Richard Wagner: Patriot and Politician* (Washington, D.C.: University Press of America, 1981), 33–34. According to Josserand: "The reason for choosing an Englishman as the butt of his humor is something which Wagner did not choose to reveal. One possibility is that he felt the need to deliver himself of some xenophobic sentiments, yet could not offend the French by making his 'companion' a Frenchman. After all, the article was to be published in a French journal." Kropfinger, however, argued that the presentation of the Englishman may have been based on an equally unflattering portrait of the British in a work by Heinrich Heine, "Florentinische Nächte II" (*Wagner und Beethoven,* 75).

51. Kropfinger, *Wagner und Beethoven,* 44–47.

52. Wagner communicated comparable themes in an essay of that name. According to Kropfinger, Wagner insisted in *Art and Revolution* that "with Beethoven's last symphony, music had finally fulfilled its artistic 'world-historical task'; from it the creation of the 'artwork of the future' was an inevitable last step. . . . Wagner saw himself, in this sense, as Beethoven's successor and 'heir,' not only because of the genial sense of

empathy and resolve which revealed to him the dramatic intentions of the composer: beyond this he was Beethoven's heir because they shared a conception of art and historical philosophy. Beethoven had taken the decisive step in the direction of the drama of the future, toward the 'end of history,'" which Wagner would ultimately bring about (*Wagner und Beethoven,* 278).

53. Richard Wagner cited in *Cosima Wagner's Diaries,* trans. Geoffrey Skelton, 2 vols. (New York: Harcourt Brace Jovanovich, 1978–80), 1:246.

54. Schmitz, *Beethovenbild,* 11.

55. Richard Wagner, *Beethoven,* trans. Edward Dannreuther (London: W. M. Reeves, 1903), 112–113. Emphasis in original.

56. Hans Heinrich Eggebrecht, *Zur Geschichte der Beethoven-Rezeption* (Mainz: Akademie der Wissenschaften und der Literatur, 1972), 41.

57. Heribert Schröder, "Beethoven im Dritten Reich: Eine Materialsammlung" in Helmut Loos, ed., *Beethoven und die Nachwelt: Materialien zur Wirkungsgeschichte Beethovens* (Bonn: Beethovenhaus, 1986), 187–221.

58. Glaser, *Kultur der Wilhelminischen Zeit,* 222–223.

59. See Karl Robert Mandelkow, *Goethe in Deutschland: Rezeptionsgeschichte eines Klassikers* (Munich: Beck, 1980).

60. Mosse, *Nationalization of the Masses,* 87–89.

61. Steven E. Aschheim, *The Nietzsche Legacy in Germany, 1890–1990* (Berkeley: University of California Press, 1992), 231.

62. See William J. Weber and David C. Large, eds., *Wagnerism in European Culture and Politics* (Ithaca: Cornell University Press, 1984). In addition to Wagner reception by German nationalists and National Socialists, this anthology reviews it among Italian futurists, British decadents, American trancendentalists, the Ballet Russe, Jungian psychologists, vegetarians, supporters of free love, and black magicians.

63. To my knowledge, no major work has compared the *Wirkungsgeschichten* of the music masters in German political life. Concentrating on Beethoven, I have not undertaken a comparative analysis of these reception histories, since thorough treatment would require at least a book-length study. I do hope that my coverage of Beethoven reception helps establish the groundwork for such an important project. Having paid some attention to other examples, I can report that while references to the lives and music of Bach, Haydn, Mozart, Weber, Schubert, Schumann, Wagner, Mahler, Bruckner, and Schönberg, among others, do appear throughout modern German political discourses, no composer is so ubiquitous in this context as Beethoven.

64. As Robert C. Holub pointed out, this emphasis on biography is not unique to the reception history of Beethoven. Reception theorists have marked the impact of legendary biography on the perception of art works: "[We] must consider how the poet's biography operates in the reader's consciousness. While the actual biography or curriculum vitae may be interesting as a cultural phenomenon, only the legend of the author's life, the 'ideal biography,' is important for the literary historian. The reader's image of Pushkin, Rousseau, or Voltaire, for example, is instrumental in an interpretation and evaluation of their works. . . . An adequate reading of a given writer is, therefore, not solely dependent on analyzing formal devices; from the reader's perspective, the ideal biography is an essential mediating element between text and audience" (*Reception Theory,* 20).

65. Within the political discourse cited in the following chapters, Beethoven's Ninth Symphony, op. 125, is mentioned forty-five times; the Third Symphony, op. 55, twenty-five times; the *Egmont* Overture, op. 84, sixteen times; the Fifth Symphony, op. 67, fifteen times; *Fidelio,* op. 72, fifteen times; the *Missa Solemnis,* op. 123, seven times; the Seventh Symphony, op. 92, six times; the Violin Concerto, op. 61, four times; the Singspiel *Ruinen von Athen,* op. 113, four times; the overture *Weihe des Hauses,* op. 124, four times; "string quartets" in general, four times; the *Coriolan* Overture, op. 62, three times; the *Leonore* Overture op. 72, no. 3, three times; the cantata *Der glor-*

reiche Augenblick, op. 136, three times; the *Appassionata* Piano Sonata, op. 57, three times; "chamber music" in general, three times; "piano sonatas" in general, three times; the Second Symphony, op. 36, twice; the Fifth Piano Concerto, op. 73, twice; *Wellingtons Sieg,* op. 91, twice; the *Opferlied,* op. 121b, twice; the *Bundeslied,* op. 122, twice; the First Piano Concerto, op. 15, once; the *Moonlight* Piano Sonata, op. 27, no. 2, once; *Die Ehre Gottes aus der Nature,* op. 48, no. 4, once; the *Waldstein* Piano Sonata, op. 53, once; the Fourth Symphony, op. 60, once; the Sixth Symphony, op. 68, once; the Choral Fantasy, op. 80, once; the Oratorium *Christus am Oelberge,* op. 85, once; the Mass in C, op. 86, once; the song *Das Glück der Freundschaft,* op. 88, once; the song *An die Hoffnung,* op. 94, once; the song *An die ferne Geliebte,* op. 98, once; the *Hammerklavier* Sonata, op. 106, once; the Piano Sonata in A-flat, op. 110, once; the *Elegischer Gesang,* op. 118, once; the String Quartet in B-flat, op. 130, once; the String Quartet in F, op. 135, once; the *Leonore* Overture op. 72, no. 2, once; the song *Germania,* Werk ohne Opuszahl (WoO) 94, once; the *Chor auf die verbündeten Fürsten,* WoO 95, once; *Es ist vollbracht,* finale to *Die Ehrenpforten,* WoO 97, once; the *Gesang der Monche,* WoO 104, once; the song *Der freie Mann,* WoO 117, once; the *Abschiedsgesang an Wiens Bürger,* WoO 121, once; the *Kriegslied der Österreicher,* WoO 122, once; the *Yorcksche Marsch,* WoO 18, once; the *Karussel Märsche,* once; the *Marsch zur großen Wachparade,* once. While dependent on my selection of sources and passages, the statistics do confirm this tendency.

66. This observation about the reception of Beethoven in German political culture holds true for many of the "mythological" views on him. According to Carl Dahlhaus: "The works on which the Beethoven myth thrives represent a narrow selection from his complete output: *Fidelio* and the music to *Egmont;* the Third, Fifth, and Ninth Symphonies; and the *Pathétique* and *Appassionata* sonatas. It is not a fact in support of the Beethoven myth that these works are 'representative,' but rather one of the claims that make up the myth. . . . To the same extent that the myth was abstracted from the music, the reception of the music was tempered by the myth. And if myth, once it impinges on biography, transforms anecdotes into allegorical ciphers, it also creates an order that separates symbolic works from nonsymbolic ones. Of course, there is little point in trying to argue that the *Pathétique* and *Appassionata* sonatas are 'major' works against which 'minor' works such as op. 7 and op. 90 pale by comparison. Yet, beyond a doubt, they belong to the symbolic works that sustain the Beethoven myth and that in turn owe their pride of place to that myth" (*Nineteenth-Century Music,* 76).

67. See Christopher Ballantine, "Beethoven, Hegel and Marx," in Ballantine, *Music and Its Social Meanings,* 30–48.

68. Aschheim, *Legacy of Nietzsche,* 155.

69. Thomas Mann, *Reflections of a Nonpolitical Man,* trans. Walter D. Morris (New York: Frederick Ungar, 1983), 24.

70. Sieghard Brandenburg, foreword to Brandenburg and Helga Lühning, eds., *Beethoven zwischen Revolution und Restauration* (Bonn: Beethovenhaus, 1990), 1.

71. Solomon, *Beethoven,* 40.

72. Brandenburg, foreword to *Beethoven zwischen Revolution und Restauration,* 1.

73. Solomon, *Beethoven,* 34; Martin Cooper, *Beethoven: The Last Decade 1817–1827* (Oxford: Oxford University Press, 1985), 87; and Sieghard Brandenburg, "Beethovens politische Erfahrungen in Bonn," in Brandenburg and Lühning, *Beethoven zwischen Revolution und Restauration,* 5–12.

74. According to Solomon, "the notion of an aristocratic redeemer remained central to Beethoven's belief until his last years—which observation may enable us to understand some of the contradictions in his later political utterances" (*Beethoven,* 38–39). Martin Cooper expressed this point as follows: "He was a typical man of the Enlightenment rather than of the French Revolution; an admirer of a benevolent despotism like that of Joseph II rather than a republican; an enemy of feudal privilege and a believer

in *la carrière ouverte aux talents* rather than a democrat in any but the vaguest sense of the word" (*Beethoven: The Last Decade,* 88–89).

75. Solomon, *Beethoven,* 35–40; and Brandenburg, "Beethovens politische Erfahrungen," 34–49.

76. Brandenburg, "Beethovens politische Erfahrungen," 13–34.

77. Solomon, *Beethoven,* 38.

78. Beethoven to Franz Anton Hoffmeister, 8 April 1802, *The Letters of Beethoven,* ed. Emily Anderson, 3 vols. (London: Macmillan, 1961), no. 57.

79. Solomon, *Beethoven,* 57–66.

80. Schmitt, *Revolution im Konzertsaal,* 231–237.

81. Jean Massin and Brigitte Massin, "Beethoven et la Revolution Française," *L'Arc* (1970): 9–10.

82. Beethoven to A. Vocke, 22 May 1793, *Letters,* no. 4.

83. Beethoven to Franz Anton Hoffmeister, c. 15 January 1801, *Letters,* no. 44. See Solomon, "Beethoven's *Magazin der Kunst,*" in Solomon, *Beethoven Essays,* 193–204, for discussion of whether or not "Beethoven's visionary recommendation [has] sources in the writings of the forerunners of modern socialism and, more particularly, in eighteenth-century French utopian thought."

84. Beethoven, *Der freie Mann,* WoO 117, translation in Frida Knight, *Beethoven and the Age of Revolution* (London: Lawrence and Wishart, 1973), 20.

85. Solomon, *Beethoven,* 39.

86. Massin and Massin, "Revolution Française," 3–4.

87. Maynard Solomon, "The Ninth Symphony: A Search for Order," in Solomon, *Beethoven Essays,* 22.

88. Solomon, *Beethoven,* 132–142.

89. Beethoven to Nikolaus Simrock, 2 August 1794, *Letters,* no. 12.

90. Beethoven to Nikolaus Zmeskall, 1798, *Letters,* no. 30.

91. Beethoven to Karl Amenda, 1 July 1801, *Letters,* no. 53.

92. Solomon, *Beethoven,* 87.

93. Beethoven, *Abschiedsgesang an Wiens Bürger,* WoO 121, translation in Knight, *Beethoven and the Age of Revolution,* 39.

94. Beethoven's attitudes toward his household help, in Cooper's words, "do no credit to his love of humanity, and often reveal a quite unregenerate ancien régime conception of the relationship between master and servant. According to him, servants were all, without exception, rogues and 'cattle,' who must be schooled by fear since they understood no other motive. He was free with verbal abuse, though very close with the housekeeping money, and not above resorting to physical violence, even with the women" (*Beethoven: The Last Decade,* 90). In Solomon's opinion, "Beethoven idealized, not actual nobles, but the concept of nobility itself. Conversely, he despised the common citizen—the burgher—with an aristocrat's disdain for the lowborn and the money-grubbing" (*Beethoven,* 88). Elsewhere Solomon writes, "He regarded the ordinary burgher as unworthy for him to associate with, preferring the company and status of 'higher men' " ("Beethoven and Schiller," in Solomon, *Beethoven Essays,* 203).

95. For in-depth analysis of other possible reasons for Beethoven's ongoing delusion that he was a member of the aristocracy, including confusion about his birth records and psychological problems stemming from abuse by his father, see Solomon, *Beethoven,* 2, 21, 23–24, 87–90, 244–245, 255, 275, 285–287.

96. Walther Nohl, ed., *Ludwig van Beethoven Konversationshefte* (Munich: Allgemeine Verlaganstalt, 1924), 288.

97. For concise reviews of Beethoven's oft-discussed regard for Napoleon and insightful explanations of the rededication of his Third Symphony, see Maynard Solomon, "Beethoven and Bonaparte," *Music Review* 29 (1968): 96–105, and "Bonaparte: The Crisis of Belief," in Solomon, *Beethoven,* 132–142.

98. Basing his version on Ignaz Seyfried's recounting, Alexander W. Thayer reported that Beethoven's flight from Grätz Castle occurred under the following circumstances: "Once when spending the summer [of 1806] with a Maecenas at his country-seat, he was so pestered by the guests (French officers) who wished to hear him play, that he grew angry and refused to do what he denounced as menial labor. A threat of arrest, made surely in jest, was taken seriously by him and resulted in Beethoven's walking by night to the nearest city, Troppau, whence he hurried as on the wings of the wind by extra post to Vienna" (Thayer, Hermann Deiters, and Hugo Riemann, *The Life of Ludwig van Beethoven,* trans. Henry Edward Krehbiel, 3 vols. [New York: Beethoven Association, 1921], 2:68).

This incident is commonly included in Beethoven biographies to exemplify his reluctance to be treated by the nobility as a common performer. The usual explanation for the fury Beethoven exhibited on this occasion is that Prince Lichnowsky, the "Maecenas" of Thayer's version, jested that he might force the composer to play for the guests. Affronted by this teasing, Beethoven fled, leaving behind a letter containing the famous line: "Prince, what you are, you are by accident of birth; what I am, I am through myself. There have been and will still be thousands of princes; there is only one Beethoven." As discussed in Chapter 3, the causes for Beethoven's action have been the subject of much debate.

99. Beethoven cited in Thayer et al., *The Life of Beethoven,* 2:146.

100. Barry Cooper, ed., *The Beethoven Compendium: A Guide to Beethoven's Life and Music* (London: Thames and Hudson, 1991), 251.

101. *Germania,* WoO 94, includes the stanza: "Germania! Germania! Wie stehst du jetzt gewaltig da. Nennt deutscher Mut sich deutsch und frei, klingt Friedrich Wilhelm Dank dabei, ein Wall von Eisen stand er da. Preis ihm, Heil dir, Germania!"

102. *Der glorreiche Augenblick,* op. 136, exhorts: "O seht es über jenem Kreise der Kronenträger glänzend stehn! . . . O knieet, Völker, hin und betet zuerst zu dem, der euch gerettet!"

103. *Es ist vollbracht,* WoO 97, concludes with the lines: "Es ist vollbracht! Der Fürsten treu Zusammenhalten, ihr ernstes, rechtes, frommes Walten gab uns den Sieg, nächst Gottes Macht. Es ist vollbracht. Gott sei Dank und unserm Kaiser! Es ist vollbracht!" For a full discussion of Beethoven's personal and professional involvement in this victory festival unparalleled for its Old World grandeur, see Michael Ladenburger, "Der Wiener Kongreß im Spiegel der Musik," in Brandenburg and Lühning, *Beethoven zwischen Revolution und Restauration,* 275–306.

104. Beethoven to *Wiener Zeitung,* December 1813, *Letters,* appendix H (6), III.

105. According to Solomon, Beethoven and his circle "were disenchanted and dismayed by the regressive aspects of imperial rule, which could no longer be disguised as patriotic prerogatives" (*Beethoven,* 260). Cooper wrote: "Beethoven and his friends were still living in the world of Joseph II, where reason, humanity and tolerance were the ideals. . . . They rejected the paternalistic Austrian police-state organized by Metternich, his secretary Gentz, and his censorship chief Sedlnitsky" (*Beethoven: The Last Decade,* 93).

106. From Friedrich August Kanne, "Academie, des Lud. van Beethoven," *Wiener allgemeine musikalische Zeitung* 8 (1824); and an anonymous "Konzertbericht aus Vienna," *Der Sammler* 16 (1824): 232, both cited in Schmitt, *Revolution im Konzertsaal,* 46–48.

107. Knight, *Beethoven and the Age of Revolution,* 168.

108. Solomon, *Beethoven,* 256.

2. The Second Reich

1. "Beethoven als Patriot: Das Festspiel von J. Rodenberg zu der Dresdner Beethoven-Feier," *Allgemeine musikalische Zeitung* 6 (June 1871), 170–171.

2. Ibid., and Hermann Pfaender, "Beethoven-Feiern in Kriegszeiten: Erinnerungen an des Meisters hundertjährigen Geburtstag 1870," *Tägliche Rundschau* (Berlin), 16 December 1917.

3. *Ludwig van Beethoven: Ein dramatisches Charakterbild in vier Aufzügen mit einem Epilog zur Feier von Beethovens hundertjährigem Geburtstage am 16. Dezember 1870: Von einem Bonner* (Leipzig: Oskar Leiner, 1870).

4. Pfaender, "Beethoven-Feiern in Kriegszeiten."

5. The largest Beethoven bust created for the 1870 birthday celebrations was fabricated in Vienna; there, a colossal twenty-foot-high reproduction of his head was transported to various concert halls for the celebration ("Die Beethovenfeier in Wien," *Signale für die musikalische Welt* [hereafter cited as *Signale*] 2 [January 1871]: 1).

6. "Wohl die originellste Beethovenfeier," *Signale* 2 (January 1871): 25.

7. See "Dur und Moll," *Signale* 2 (January 1871): 21–23; *Neue Zeitschrift für Musik* 66 (1870): 452, 463, 481; and *Neue Zeitschrift für Musik* 67 (1871): 33.

8. Pfaender, "Beethoven-Feiern in Kriegszeiten."

9. "Barmen," *Neue Zeitschrift für Musik* 66 (1870): 463. See also "Laibach," *Neue Zeitschrift für Musik* 66 (1870): 452. In 1871 the queen of Prussia sent two gold medals graced with portraits of the king to the writer and the composer of *Wacht am Rhein* as a sign of "joyous and thankful emotion over the victories of our army" (*Signale* 38 [1870]: 599).

10. See Hermann Glaser, "Geschichte als Umzug," in *Die Kultur der Wilhelminischen Zeit: Topographie einer Epoche* (Frankfurt am Main: S. Fischer, 1984), 215–262.

11. Ibid., 222. Glaser noted that Beethoven's music was often an important component of "Schiller Festivals" held during the Bismarck era; he discussed these parades and concerts as a primary means by which the new nation sought to represent and legitimate itself culturally.

12. Maximilian Harden, "Beethoven-Bismarck," *Neue Freie Presse* (Vienna), 27 March 1927, 2.

13. Emil Ludwig, *Bismarck: The Story of a Fighter*, trans. Eden Paul and Cedar Paul (Boston: Little, Brown, 1928), 18–19.

14. Robert von Keudell, *Fürst und Fürstin Bismarck: Erinnerungen aus den Jahren 1846 bis 1872* (Berlin: W. Spemann, 1901), 1–2.

15. Bismarck, cited in R. Sternfeld, "Bismarck-Beethoven," *Der Tag* (Berlin), 25 December 1912, 2.

16. Ibid.

17. Keudell, *Fürst und Fürstin Bismarck*, 64.

18. Ibid., 260–261.

19. See Harden, "Beethoven-Bismarck"; Ludwig, *Bismarck*; Houston Stewart Chamberlain, *Die Grundlagen des neunzehnten Jahrhunderts*, 5th ed., 2 vols. (Munich: Bruckmann, 1904), 1:510; Adolph Kohut, "Bismarcks Verhältnis zur Musik," *Die Musik* 14 (1914–15): 200; Friedrich Rießler, "Bismarck und Beethoven," *Tägliche Rundschau*, 29 March 1927; "Goethe und Bismarck über Beethoven," *Völkischer Beobachter* (Berlin), 26 March 1927; Hermann Unger, "Wenn ich Beethoven höre, werde ich tapferer," *Deutsche Militär-Musiker-Zeitung* 64 (5 July 1942).

20. Cited in Sternfeld, "Bismarck-Beethoven," 1.

21. Max Dessoir, *Der Tag* (1912), cited in Sternfeld, "Bismarck-Beethoven," 1.

22. Cited in Sternfeld, "Bismarck-Beethoven," 1.

23. Rießler, "Bismarck und Beethoven": "Bismarck's relation to Beethoven's music

was such that on the eve of the declaration of war he had an orchestra play [the Fifth Symphony] in the chancellor palace." See also Friedrich Rießner, "Bismarck und die Musik," *Der Stahlhelm* (Berlin), 27 March 1927.

24. P. Martell, "Die Musik-Sammlung der Staatsbibliothek zu Berlin," *Allgemeine Musik-Zeitung* 57 (28 March 1930), 327.

25. Alfred Becker, "Statten deutscher Musikkultur," *Deutsche Musikkultur* 2 (June/July 1937). The Bonn Beethovenhaus was preserved in 1889; chamber concerts were put on by the Verein Beethoven Haus after 1890; the Beethovenhaus Archive, however, was not dedicated until 1927.

26. Alessandra Comini, *The Changing Image of Beethoven: A Study in Mythmaking* (New York: Rizzoli, 1987), 349.

27. Hermann Glaser, *Spießer-Ideologie: Von der Zerstörung des deutschen Geistes in 19. und 20. Jahrhunderts* (Freiburg: Rombach, 1964), 133.

28. *Allgemeine musikalische Zeitung* (March 1889), reproduced in Peter Muck, ed., *Einhundert Jahre Berliner Philharmonisches Orchester,* 3 vols. (Tützing: Hans Schneider, 1982), 1:124.

29. Max Schwarz, "Deuter, Dichter, Denker: Zu Beethovens 100. Todestag," *Tägliche Rundschau,* 25 March 1927; and Munter, "Hans von Bülow und Beethoven," 131–154.

30. Hermann Freiherr von der Pfordten, "Beethoven und Wir," *Tägliche Rundschau,* 6 October 1907.

31. Cited in Friedrich Munter, "Hans von Bülow und Beethoven," *Neues Beethoven-Jahrbuch* 7 (1937): 154.

32. Hans von Wolzogen, "Richard Wagner über Beethoven," *Musikalisches Wochenblatt* 2 (1871): 145.

33. Hans von Wolzogen, *Großmeister deutscher Musik* (Regensburg: Bosse, 1897), 156.

34. Hans von Wolzogen, "Ein ungedruckter Schluß des 'Beethoven' von Richard Wagner," *Bayreuther Blätter: Deutsche Zeitschrift im Geiste Richard Wagners* 29 (1906): 1.

35. Friedrich Engels, in Karl Marx and Engels, *Über Kunst und Literatur,* 2 vols. (Berlin: Dietz, 1968), 2:485.

36. Friedrich Engels, "Notizen über Deutschland," in Engels and Karl Marx, *Über Deutschland und die deutsche Arbeiterbewegung,* vol. 1, *Von der Frühzeit bis zum 18. Jahrhundert* (Berlin: Dietz, 1982), 566.

37. R. Hildebrandt, "Ferdinand Lassalle und die Anfänge der modernen Massenpublizistik," (Phil. Diss.: Berlin [West], 1961), 202.

38. George L. Mosse, *The Nationalization of the Masses: Political Symbolism and Mass Movements in Germany from the Napoleonic Wars through the Third Reich* (New York: Howard Fertig, 1975), 161–167; and Friedrich Knilli and Ursula Münchow, *Frühes deutsches Arbeitertheater, 1847–1918: Eine Dokumentation* (Munich: C. Hauser, 1970), 341–342.

39. Herbert Birtner, "Zur deutschen Beethovenauffassung," in Arnold Schmitz, ed., *Beethoven und die Gegenwart: Festschrift des Beethovenhauses Bonn* (Berlin: Ferdinand Dummler, 1937), 14.

40. Friedrich W. Nietzsche, "Beethovens Tod," in *Jungendschriften, 1861–1864,* vol. 2, *Friedrich Nietzsches Werke: Historischkritische Gesamtausgabe* (Munich: C. H. Beck'sche Verlagsbuchhandlung, 1934), 322–325.

41. Birtner, "Zur deutschen Beethovenauffassung," 23.

42. Nietzsche, *Menschliches, Allzumenschliches I,* part 4, vol. 2, *Nietzsche Werke: Kritische Gesamtausgabe,* Giorgio Colli and Mazzino Montinari, eds. (Berlin: Walter de Gruyter, 1967–), 147.

43. Nietzsche, *The Birth of Tragedy and The Case of Wagner,* trans. Walter Kaufmann (New York: Vintage, 1967), 37.
44. Birtner, "Zur deutschen Beethovenauffassung," 23.
45. Nietzsche, *Birth of Tragedy,* 31.
46. Nietzsche, *Nachgelassene Fragmente,* part 3, vol. 3, *Nietzsche Werke: Kritische Gesamtausgabe,* 335–337.
47. Nietzsche, *Der Fall Wagner,* part 6, vol. 3, *Nietzsche Werke: Kritische Gesamtausgabe,* 24.
48. Peter Bergman, *Nietzsche, "the Last Apolitical German"* (Bloomington: Indiana University Press, 1987); and Thomas R. Hinton, *Nietzsche in German Politics and Society, 1890–1918* (Manchester: Manchester University Press, 1983).
49. Nietzsche, *Menschliches, Allzumenschliches II,* part 4, vol. 3, *Nietzsche Werke: Kritische Gesamtausgabe,* 289.
50. Nietzsche, *Nachgelassene Fragmente,* part 8, vol. 3, *Nietzsche Werke: Kritische Gesamtausgabe,* 40.
51. Nietzsche, *Nachgelassene Fragmente,* part 7, vol. 2, *Nietzsche Werke: Kritische Gesamtausgabe,* 152.
52. Nietzsche, *Die Unschuld des Werdens (Nachlass I),* vol. 83, *Nietzsches Werke: Kröners Taschenausgabe,* (Leipzig: Alfred Kröner, 1926), 437.
53. Nietzsche, *Nachgelassene Fragmente,* part 7, vol. 3, *Nietzsche Werke: Kritische Gesamtausgabe,* 309.
54. Nietzsche, *Jenseits von Gut und Böse,* part 6, vol. 2, *Nietzsche Werke: Kritische Gesamtausgabe,* 196.
55. Hans von Bülow, *Höhepunkt und Ende, 1886–1894,* vol. 7, *Briefe und Schriften* (Leipzig: Breitkopf & Härtel, 1896–1908), 380.
56. Ibid., 381.
57. *Allgemeine musikalische Zeitung* (1 April 1892), reproduced in Muck, *Berliner Philharmonisches Orchester,* 1:157.
58. Bülow, *Höhepunkt und Ende,* 383. In the original German, this text contained a pun on the name Bismarck, which was italicized. See fig. 1.
59. *Allgemeine musikalische Zeitung* (1 April 1892), reproduced in Muck, *Berliner Philharmonisches Orchester,* 1:157.
60. *Neue Berliner Musikzeitung* (1892), reproduced in Muck, *Berliner Philharmonisches Orchester,* 1:155.
61. *Neue Zeitschrift für Musik* (April 1892), reproduced in Muck, *Berliner Philharmonisches Orchester,* 1:157.
62. Ibid.
63. Concert review, *Allgemeine Musik-Zeitung* 19 (17 June 1892): 306.
64. Franz Herre, *Kaiser Wilhelm I: Der letzte Preuße* (Cologne: Kiepenhauer und Witsch, 1980), 428.
65. Karl Julius Mueller, *Die Berliner Centanär-Feier für Kaiser Wilhelm den Großen vom 21. bis 23. März 1897: Denkschrift* (Berlin: Aktiengesellschaft Pionier, 1897).
66. Jacques Barzun, *Darwin, Marx, Wagner: Critique of a Heritage,* 2nd ed. (Garden City, N.Y.: Doubleday Anchor, 1958), 293–294.
67. Glaser, *Kultur der Wilhelminischen Zeit,* 239.
68. Freiherr von der Pfordten, "Beethoven und Wir."
69. *Neue Zeitschrift für Musik* (1 April 1914), reproduced in Muck, *Berliner Philharmonisches Orchester,* 1:427.
70. "Über das Beethovenfest in Bonn," *Allgemeine Musik-Zeitung* (21–28 August 1903), 28, 173, 383, 397, 526, 779, 743.
71. "Das Beethovenfest in Eisenach," *Neue Musik-Zeitung* (1901), 248, 270. This review highlighted the significance of a Beethoven Festival situated in Eisenach: "What

a collection of fond memories and poetic images are evoked by the name of this place, with its Wartburg at the entrance of the romantic Waldgebirge!"

72. "Das Haydn-Mozart-Beethovendenkmal in Berlin," *Allgemeine Musik-Zeitung* (1 July 1904), 489, 520.

73. The *Neue Zeitschrift für Musik* reported that popular concerts had been given in the halls of the city's breweries during the summer of 1912 (articles reproduced in Muck, *Berliner Philharmonisches Orchester,* 1:415).

74. *Neue Zeitschrift für Musik* (1 April 1914), reproduced in Muck, *Berliner Philharmonisches Orchester,* 1:427.

75. "Beethoven und das deutsche Volk," *Neue Preußische Kreuz-Zeitung* (Berlin), 27 September 1912.

76. "Ludwig van Beethoven: Symphonie in D-Moll: Ein Beitrag zur Schiller-Feier," *Deutsche Wehr* 15 (5 May 1905).

77. A. Döring, "Ludwig van Beethoven: Zum achtzigjährigen Gedächtnisse seines Todestages," *Deutsch-Soziale-Blätter* 22 (27 March 1907).

78. Houston Stewart Chamberlain to Wilhelm II, 4 February 1903, in *Briefe, 1882–1924: Und Briefwechsel mit Kaiser Wilhelm II,* 2 vols. (Munich: Bruckmann, 1928), 1: 171–172.

79. Houston Stewart Chamberlain to Graf L., 8 March 1910, in *Briefe,* 1:192.

80. Chamberlain, *Grundlagen,* 22.

81. Ibid., 537, 510.

82. The term is Fritz Stern's. See his *Politics of Cultural Despair: A Study in the Rise of the Germanic Ideology* (Berkeley: University of California Press, 1961); and George L. Mosse, *The Crisis of German Ideology: Intellectual Origins of the Third Reich* (New York: Schocken, 1981).

83. "Beethoven und das deutsche Volk," *Neue Preußische Kreuz-Zeitung.*

84. Ludwig Woltmann, *Die Germanen und die Renaissance von Italien* (Leipzig, 1905), 107–166.

85. Ludwig Woltmann, *Die Germanen in Frankreich* (Jena: E. Diederichs, 1907). For more on Woltmann and his "anthropological" theories, see Jürgen Misch, *Die politische Philosophie Ludwig Woltmanns: Im Spannungsfeld von Kantianismus, Historischem Materialismus und Sozialdarwinismus* (Bonn: Bouvier, 1975).

86. "Genie und Rasse," *Mitteilungen aus dem Verein zur Abwehr des Antisemitismus,* 24 January 1906.

87. See Stern, *Politics of Cultural Despair,* 97–182.

88. Julius Langbehn, *Rembrandt als Erzieher: Von einem Deutschen,* 61st ed. (Leipzig: C. L. Hirschfeld, 1925), 55, 64, 71, 86.

89. Ibid., 241.

90. Ibid., 330.

91. Stern, *Politics of Cultural Despair,* 97–182; and Mosse, *Crisis of German Ideology,* 39–46.

92. Knilli and Münchow, *Deutsches Arbeitertheater,* 419.

93. "Das Gründungsprotokoll der Freien Volksbühne," reproduced in Knilli and Münchow, *Deutsches Arbeitertheater,* 14. See also Inge Lammel, "Zur Beethoven-Rezeption in der deutschen Arbeiterbewegung," in H. A. Brockhaus and Konrad Niemann, eds., *Bericht über den Internationalen Beethoven-Kongreß in Berlin 10 December 1970* (Berlin: Verlag für Neue Musik, 1971), 156.

94. Knilli and Münchow, *Deutsches Arbeitertheater,* 341–342.

95. See Kurt Eisner, *Taggeist: Culturglossen* (Berlin: Edelheim, 1901), 224, 281.

96. Kurt Eisner, "Die Wahlnacht," *Feste der Festlosen: Hausbuch weltlicher Predigtschwinke* (Dresden: Kaden, 1905), 241; originally published in *Vorwärts* (Berlin), June 1903.

97. Clara Zetkin, "Kunst und Proletariat," in *Über Literatur und Kunst* (Berlin: 1955), 111.

98. Mosse, *Nationalization of the Masses,* 167–170.

99. Kurt Eisner, "Maienrauss," in *Feste der Festlosen,* 64; originally published in *Vorwärts,* 1904.

100. "Program zur Feier des 18. März 1903, des 55. Jahrestages der Berliner Revolutionskämpfe von 1848," reproduced in Inge Lammel, *Arbeitermusikkultur in Deutschland, 1844–1945* (Leipzig: VEB Deutscher Verlag für Musik, 1984), 77 [#D 106].

101. Lammel, *Arbeitermusikkultur,* 77–78; and Lammel, "Beethoven-Rezeption," 158.

102. Kurt Eisner, "Heimat der Neunten," in *Feste der Festlosen,* 291–294, originally published in *Vorwärts,* March 1905; and *Freie Volksbühne* 8 (1905).

103. Lammel, "Beethoven-Rezeption," 156.

104. Knilli and Münchow, *Deutsches Arbeitertheater,* 419.

105. Lammel, "Beethoven-Rezeption," 156.

106. Ibid.

107. Gordon Craig, *Germany, 1866–1945* (New York: Oxford University Press, 1978), 33; Fritz Ringer, *The Decline of the German Mandarins: The German Academic Community, 1890–1933* (Cambridge, Mass.: Harvard University Press, 1968), 80, 102, 120–121; W. H. Bruford, *The German Tradition of Self-Cultivation: Bildung from Humboldt to Thomas Mann* (Cambridge: Cambridge University Press, 1975); and George L. Mosse, *The Culture of Western Europe: The Nineteenth and Twentieth Centuries* (Chicago: Rand McNally, 1974), 131–142.

108. For more on Karl Lamprecht as a purveyor of "idealistic" thought as political evasion, see Ringer, *Decline of the German Mandarins,* 302–303.

109. Karl Lamprecht, "Beethoven," *Der Kunstwart* 20 (2 May 1907 and 1 June 1907).

110. See Comini, *Changing Image,* 397–403, for discussion of Max Klinger's sculpture as symbolizing views of Beethoven from the perspective of the early-twentieth-century cultural elite.

111. Lamprecht, "Beethoven."

112. Paul Bekker, *Beethoven* (Berlin: Schuster and Löffler, 1911).

113. Mosse, *Culture of Western Europe,* 131.

114. Hermann Freiherr von der Pfordten, "Paul Bekkers *Beethoven,*" *Der Kunstwart* 25 (1 June 1912).

115. "*Festkonzert zur 100. Aufführung der IX. Symphonie von Beethoven,*" Berlin Philharmonic program, 30 October 1935, Staatliches Institut für Musikforschung, Preußischer Kulturbesitz, Berlin. This was the program produced to mark the one-hundredth time that the Berlin Philharmonic played the Ninth Symphony; it also marked the first appearance of program notes for the Ninth Symphony by Robert Oboussier, replacing those of Paul Bekker. Bekker's Jewish heritage undoubtedly brought on suppression of his work, but the idealistic tone of his interpretations surely bothered Nazis as well.

116. Leo Schrade, *Beethoven in France: The Development of an Idea* (New Haven: Yale University Press, 1942), passim.

117. Hermann Hesse, "O Freunde, nicht diese Töne," *Neue Zürcher Nachrichten,* September 1914, reproduced in *If the War Goes On . . . Reflections on War and Politics,* trans. Ralph Manheim (New York: Farrar, Straus and Giroux, 1973), 9–14.

118. *Neue Zeitschrift für Musik* (1915), reproduced in Muck, *Berliner Philharmonisches Orchester,* 1:436–437.

119. Modris Eksteins, *Rites of Spring: The Great War and the Birth of the Modern Age* (New York: Doubleday, 1989), 55–64.

120. Indeed, in 1860 the *Pariser Einzugsmarsch* was erroneously attributed to Bee-

thoven in a collection of military marches for the Prussian army (*Beethoven: Das Genie und seine Welt* [Wiesbaden: R. Löwit, 1961], 71). Many soldiers might, therefore, have thought they were listening to a work of Beethoven as they drilled to the sound of this popular march.

121. These statistics were compiled by the author from listings of programs in Muck, *Berliner Philharmonisches Orchester,* 3:152–184. I have included only concerts performed in the Philharmonie, not travel dates.

Year	*Total Programs*	*Including Beethoven*	*Including Wagner*	*Including Mozart*	*Beethoven only*
1914–15	90	41	17	7	19
1915–16	104	41	21	12	9
1916–17	109	37	16	16	11
1917–18	129	44	15	16	13
1918–19	94	38	11	9	14
Total	526	201	80	60	66

Of course, it is not fair to compare concert-hall performances of Beethoven's work with those of Wagner's compositions, since Wagner wrote mainly operas. However, this fact does not diminish the importance of Beethoven's music in German concert life at this time.

122. R. Sternfeld, "Zu viel Beethoven?" *Allgemeine Musik-Zeitung* 44 (20 February 1917).

123. Ibid.; Wilhelm Klatte, "Zu viel Beethoven?" *Allgemeine Musik-Zeitung* 44 (2 March 1917); and Hans Mersmann, "Zu viel Beethoven?" *Allgemeine Musik-Zeitung* 44 (9 March 1917).

124. See Geoffrey G. Field, *Evangelist of Race: The Germanic Vision of Houston Stewart Chamberlain* (New York: Columbia University Press, 1981), 352–395, for discussion of Chamberlain's efforts at wartime propaganda.

125. Houston Stewart Chamberlain, "Deutschland" (21 October 1914) in *Kriegsaufsätze* (Munich: F. Bruckner, 1914), 88–90.

126. Leopold Hirschberg, "Wie Beethoven Krieg und Sieg Besang," *Berliner Tageblatt,* 24 August 1914.

127. Ibid. See also Hirschberg on Beethoven in *Die Kriegsmusik der deutschen Klassiker und Romantiker: Aufsätze zur vaterländischen Musikgeschichte* (Berlin: Vieweg, 1919), a compilation of Hirschberg's wartime essays about patriotic music published just after the fighting stopped.

128. For full discussion of the enthusiasm with which Germany's "young generation" went to war, see Robert Wohl, *The Generation of 1914,* 3rd ed. (Cambridge, Mass.: Harvard University Press, 1981), 42 ff.

129. "Ein musikalischer Französenfeind," *Der Reichsbote* (Berlin), 17 September 1914.

130. Otto Urbach, "Ludwig van Beethoven," *Zeitung der 10. Armee* (Wilna), 1916 (full date not included on copy in the Beethovenhaus Archive).

131. Pfaender, "Beethoven-Feiern in Kriegszeiten."

132. *Signale* (September 1914), reproduced in Muck, *Berliner Philharmonisches Orchester,* 1:433.

133. Lists compiled by the author from concert records in Muck, *Berliner Philharmonisches Orchester,* 3:158–184.

134. Schrade, *Beethoven in France,* 94–107, 203–204, 211, 242.

135. "Beethoven, der Typus des französischen Genies," *Neue Preußische Kreuz-Zeitung*, 8 November 1914.

136. "Der Schrei nach Beethoven," *Berliner Börsen-Zeitung*, 13 November 1915.

137. "Kunst Strategie," *Signale* 73 (May 1915), reproduced in Muck, *Berliner Philharmonisches Orchester*, 1:436.

138. Raymond-Raoul Lambert, cited in Schrade, *Beethoven in France*, 167. Schrade explained this ironic reading of the work by the pacifistic Rolland as follows: "Lambert was a soldier of the World War. He went to the front, as Péguy did, as Rolland refused to do. Now he calls to remembrance his days in the trenches and writes: 'In our dirty bread bag, right between the copy book and the flashlight, with veneration we kept the *Life of Beethoven*.' Is there need for further explanation? This modest passage tells the whole story, which greater eloquence could not make more vivid. '*We* kept.' . . . Around him was the old community of one and the same faith, a 'congregation.' What they kept and venerated, in the hour of trial when endurance was to prove itself indeed in the souls of these Frenchmen, was their sacred scripture. 'Romain Rolland,' says Lambert, 'gave us the idea of the Rhenish Beethoven; Romain Rolland taught us the creed that can redeem, that is stronger than life and stronger than death.' In 1903 [when Rolland's *Beethoven* was first published] the call to restore energy, will, and moral forces went out, and Péguy was exultant with joy when he saw that a whole generation of Frenchmen followed the call. Lambert is only one of them. If Rolland wrote his Beethoven for the purpose of regeneration through will, he did not write in vain. These French intellectuals proved their energy at the time when there was greatest need for it. They never forgave Rolland for failing to do the same . . . , though with respect, [they] sadly disapproved of [Rolland's] attitude above the battle" (167). The last phrase refers to Rolland's pacifistic work, *Above the Battle*, written in response to the Great War.

139. Philipp Witkop, ed., *Kriegsbriefe deutscher Studenten* (Gotha: Friedrich Andreas Perthes, 1916), 14–15, 83.

140. Walther Harich, letter of 4 November 1914, in ibid., 3.

141. "Beethovens C-moll-Sinfonie im Schützengraben," *Deutsche Militär-Musiker-Zeitung* 37 (1915): 4.

142. Hugo Riemann, *Ludwig van Beethovens sämtliche Klaviersonaten: Aesthetische und formal-technische Analyse mit historischen Notizen*, cited in Hans Heinrich Eggebrecht, *Zur Geschichte der Beethoven-Rezeption* (Mainz: Akademie der Wissenschaften und der Literatur, 1972), 71.

143. See George L. Mosse, *Fallen Soldiers: Reshaping the Memory of the World Wars* (New York: Oxford University Press, 1990), 17, 67–68, for discussion of the "legend of the middle-class volunteers," which lent cultural legitimacy to the "Myth of the War Experience" and obscured the reality that members of the lower classes did most of the fighting.

144. "Beethoven an der französischen Front," *Der Reichsbote*, 23 July 1915.

145. "Landsturmmann Beethoven," *Vossische Zeitung* (Berlin), 14 December 1917.

146. Hermann Hesse, "To a Cabinet Minister," August 1917, in *If the War Goes On*, 15–19.

147. This negative assertion is based on a survey of the journals of the major pacifistic organizations in Germany: *Die Waffen nieder!*, *Die Friedens-Blatter*, *Deutsche Friedens-Kongreß*, *Dokumente des Fortschritts*, *Die Eiche*, and *Die neue Zeit*.

148. See Chapter 3.

149. No such invocation was found in a survey of the literature of the Spartakist leaders, including Karl Liebknecht, *Gesammelte Reden und Schriften*, vols. 1–8 (Berlin: Dietz, 1958–60); Rosa Luxemburg, *Politische Schriften*, vols. 1–3 (Frankfurt am Main: Europäische Verlags-Anstalt, 1966–68); and Heinz Gittig, *Karl Liebknecht, Rosa Luxemburg: Eine Auswahlbibliographie der Schriften von und über Karl Liebknecht und Rosa Luxemburg* (Berlin, 1957). See Schrade, *Beethoven in France*, 187, 211, and 248,

for discussion of the development of a French pacifistic interpretation that presented Beethoven as a supranational figure committed to maintaining peace.

150. Ferdinand Scherber, "Beethoven-Kultus," *Signale* 72 (21 November 1914).

151. Artur Nikisch often led orchestras in benefit concerts for workers and prisoners.

152. *Signale* 74 (March 1916), reproduced in Muck, *Berliner Philharmonisches Orchester,* 1:442.

153. For discussion of the gradual disillusionment with the war exhibited by the German "idealistic" community in general, see Roger Chickering, "Pacifism and the Academic Disciplines," in *Imperial Germany and a World without War: The Peace Movement and German Society, 1892–1914* (Princeton: Princeton University Press, 1975), 135–162; and Fritz Ringer's section on "The World War: Harmony and Disharmony" in his *Decline of the Mandarins,* 180–199.

154. Eugen Schmitz, "Eine Kriegserinnerung in Beethovens Missa," *Deutsche Militär-Musiker-Zeitung* 38 (1916): 153.

155. See Erik Levi, *Music in the Third Reich* (New York: St. Martin's, 1994), 1–15; and Michael Meyer, *The Politics of Music in the Third Reich* (New York: Peter Lang, 1991), 1–13, for reviews of the "ideology" of music conservatism and its German purveyors.

156. Cited in Eugen Schmitz, "Zum Verständnis von Beethovens Eroika," *Allgemeine Musik-Zeitung* 44 (1 June 1917). I have used Walter Kaufmann's translation of this passage from Nietzsche's "Tombsong" in *Also sprach Zarathustra* in Kaufmann, ed., *The Portable Nietzsche,* 2nd ed. (New York: Penguin, 1982), 222.

157. Schmitz, "Zum Verständnis von Beethovens Eroika."

158. Sternfeld, "Zu viel Beethoven?"; Klatte, "Zu viel Beethoven?"; and Mersmann, "Zu viel Beethoven?"

159. Klatte, "Zu viel Beethoven?"

160. Ibid.; and Mersmann, "Zu viel Beethoven?"

161. Sternfeld, "Zu viel Beethoven?"

162. Mersmann, "Zu viel Beethoven?"

163. "Die Neunte Sinfonie im Krieg," *Deutsche Militär-Musiker-Zeitung* 37 (1915): 284.

164. "Soll die 'Neunte' für die '9.' werben?" *Deutsche Militär-Musiker-Zeitung* 40 (27 September 1918).

165. *Leipziger neuesten Nachrichten,* 2 January 1919, cited in Lammel, "Beethoven-Rezeption," 158.

3. The Weimar Era

1. A. Mayer, "Was bedeutet uns Beethoven?" *Deutsche Rundschau* (Berlin) 53 (5 March 1927).

2. Ibid.

3. Allan Mitchell, *Revolution in Bavaria, 1918–1919: The Eisner Regime and the Soviet Republic* (Princeton: Princeton University Press, 1965), 113.

4. Sterling Fishman, "Prophets, Poets, and Priests: A Study of the Men and Ideas of the Bavarian Revolution" (Ph.D. diss.: University of Wisconsin at Madison, 1960), 57–59.

5. Ibid. See also Mitchell, *Revolution in Bavaria,* 113; and Lammel, "Beethoven-Rezeption," 158.

6. "Eine Gedächtnisfeier," *Die Rote Fahne* (Berlin), 3 February 1919.

7. Together with the citation that opens this chapter, see confirmation that Germans were aware of the "competition" for Beethoven's legacy during the Weimar era in the following quote from Karl Gerharts, "Wie dachte der junge Beethoven über Politik?" *Allgemeine Musik-Zeitung* 53 (19 March 1926): "What did Beethoven think about politics? Thus far, this question has been answered in many contradictory ways. Some have seen in Beethoven a democrat, even a revolutionary; others seek to brand him

a domineering aristocrat. Particularly during the [First] World War and immediately afterward, the battle over Beethoven's political creed raged."

8. This chapter will treat interpreters of Beethoven who worked within approximately the same ideological paradigms as representative of general groups on the left, center, right, and extreme right of the Weimar political spectrum. The approach will obscure some of the nuances of Beethoven reception within each of these broad associations. For instance, differences in opinion occasionally arose between SPD and KPD interpreters over Beethoven's status as "reformer" or "revolutionary." In-depth analysis of such inconsistencies must be reserved for articles focusing on these differences.

9. See Istvan Deak, *Weimar Germany's Left-Wing Intellectuals: A Political History of the "Weltbühne" and Its Circle* (Berkeley: University of California Press, 1968).

10. Arthur Seehof, "Dem Gedächtnis Ludwig van Beethovens zum 100. Todestag," *Arbeiter-Illustrierte-Zeitung* (Berlin), 4 March 1927.

11. "Beethoven: Zum hundersten Todestag," *Arbeiter-Zeitung* (Vienna), 26 March 1927.

12. Lu Märten, "Ludwig van Beethoven und die Musik," *Die Rote Fahne*, 16 December 1920.

13. "Des Bürgers Beethoven-Ehrung: Der verfälschte Beethoven," *Die Rote Fahne*, 26 March 1927.

14. Hans Heinz Stuckenschmidt, "Nachruhm: Beethoven," *Die Weltbühne* (Berlin) 23 (15 March 1927), 454–457.

15. "Bürgers Beethoven-Ehrung," *Die Rote Fahne.*

16. "Beethoven," *Arbeiter-Zeitung.*

17. "Bürgers Beethoven-Ehrung," *Die Rote Fahne.*

18. Märten, "Ludwig van Beethoven und die Musik."

19. Karl Nef, "Beethovens Beziehung zur Politik," *Zeitschrift für Musik* 5 (May 1925); and "Der Sohn der Revolution," *Vorwärts* (Berlin), 26 March 1927.

20. "Sohn der Revolution," *Vorwärts.*

21. "Beethoven als Republikaner," *Tagespost Graz*, 5 December 1918.

22. "Beethoven: Der Mensch, der Künstler, der Republikaner," *Die Republik* (Berlin) (March 1927).

23. "Beethoven als Republikaner," *Tagespost Graz.*

24. Nef, "Beethovens Beziehung zur Politik."

25. Ibid.

26. Herbert Eulenberg, "Beethoven," *Kulturwille* (1929) [full date not on copy in the Beethovenhaus Archive].

27. Frank Howes, "Beethoven, der Tondichter der Demokratie," *Kulturwille* 4 (1 April 1927).

28. Nef, "Beethovens Beziehung zur Politik."

29. Ibid.

30. Eulenberg, "Beethoven." See also Paul Riesenfeld, "Beethovens Ethik und kosmische Sendung," *Signale* 85 (6 April 1927), 499–503. Eulenberg and Riesenfeld both overlooked Beethoven's strong attachment to his grandfather's portrait.

31. Leopold Hirschberg, "Beethoven als Sänger der Freiheit," *Illustrierte Reichsbanner-Zeitung* (Berlin), 26 March 1927.

32. "Sohn der Revolution," *Vorwärts.*

33. Eulenberg, "Beethoven."

34. Leo Kestenberg, *Beethoven-Feier: Anregungen*, Schriften des Verbandes der deutschen Volksbühnenvereine, 12 (Berlin: Volksbühnen-Verlags und Vertriebs, 1926).

35. "Sohn der Revolution," *Vorwärts.*

36. Immanuel S. Franz, "Beethovens politische Gesinnung," *Die Menschheit* (Wiesbaden), 18 March 1927.

37. Seehof, "Dem Gedächtnis Ludwig van Beethovens."

38. Kurt Singer, "100 Jahre IX. Sinfonie," *Vorwärts*, 7 May 1924.
39. Eulenberg, "Beethoven."
40. "Beethoven," *Arbeiter-Zeitung*.
41. Hugo Zucker, "Beethoven und die Arbeiterklasse," *Die Rote Fahne* (Vienna), 20 March 1927.
42. "Sohn der Revolution," *Vorwärts*; and Nef, "Beethovens Beziehung zur Politik."
43. "Der junge Beethoven," *Kulturwille* 4 (1 April 1927); Leo Kestenberg, "Beethoven," *Die Volksbühne* (Berlin), 15 March 1927; and Nef, "Beethovens Beziehung zur Politik."
44. Nef, "Beethovens Beziehung zur Politik."
45. Ibid.
46. "Bürgers Beethoven-Ehrung," *Die Rote Fahne*.
47. Howes, "Beethoven, der Tondichter der Demokratie."
48. Hirschberg, "Beethoven als Sänger der Freiheit."
49. R. Ling, "Beethoven und Frankreich," *Welt und Leben*, 23 March 1927.
50. See Chapter 1.
51. Franz, "Beethovens politische Gesinnung." See also "Der Mensch, der Künstler, der Republikaner," *Die Republik*; "Beethoven als Republikaner," *Tagespost Graz*; and "Beethoven," *Die Rote Fahne* (Vienna), 27 March 1927.
52. Nef, "Beethovens Beziehung zur Politik."
53. "Beethoven als Republikaner," *Tagespost Graz*.
54. Howes, "Beethoven, der Tondichter der Demokratie"; and Seehof, "Dem Gedächtnis Ludwig van Beethovens."
55. Howes, "Beethoven, der Tondichter der Demokratie."
56. Kurt Weill, "Beethoven und die Jungen," *Sozialistische Monatshefte* 33 (March 1927), 193–194. See also Howes, "Beethoven, der Tondichter der Demokratie."
57. Seehof, "Dem Gedächtnis Ludwig van Beethovens."
58. Much has been written about leftist theories of music and art, especially the theory of "socialist-realism." For further information on how Weimar leftists justified the incoporation of music by long-dead composers into the liturgy of their "modern" proletarian movement, see Märten, "Ludwig van Beethoven und die Musik"; "Arbeiterschaft und Musik," *Kulturwille* 1 (1 October 1924); Seehof, "Dem Gedächtnis Ludwig van Beethovens"; Kestenberg, "Beethoven"; and Zucker, "Beethoven und die Arbeiterklasse."
59. Märten, "Ludwig van Beethoven und die Musik."
60. Seehof, "Dem Gedächtnis Ludwig van Beethovens."
61. Märten, "Ludwig van Beethoven und die Musik."
62. "Bürgers Beethoven-Ehrung," *Die Rote Fahne*; and Nef, "Beethovens Beziehung zur Politik."
63. "Bürgers Beethoven-Ehrung," *Die Rote Fahne*.
64. "Beethoven als Republikaner," *Tagespost Graz*; and Nef, "Beethovens Beziehung zur Politik."
65. Franz, "Beethovens politische Gesinnung."
66. Märten, "Ludwig van Beethoven und die Musik."
67. Singer, "100 Jahre IX. Sinfonie."
68. Seehof, "Dem Gedächtnis Ludwig van Beethovens."
69. Howes, "Beethoven, der Tondichter der Demokratie." This was a reference to the line, "Wollust ward dem Wurm gegeben" in Schiller's and Beethoven's *An die Freude*.
70. Franz, "Beethovens politische Gesinnung."
71. Singer, "100 Jahre IX. Sinfonie."
72. Zucker, "Beethoven und die Arbeiterklasse."

73. Singer, "100 Jahre IX. Sinfonie." The last is a citation from the text of the final movement of the Ninth Symphony.

74. Hanns Eisler, "Ludwig van Beethoven: Zu seinem 100. Todestag am 26. März," *Die Rote Fahne,* Beilage no. 68, *Feuilleton der Rote Fahne,* 22 March 1927. The last is also from the text of the Ninth Symphony.

75. "Fidelio," *Kulturwille* 4 (February 1927).

76. H. Kesser, "Beethoven, der Held," *Vorwärts,* 26 March 1927.

77. Hirschberg, "Beethoven als Sänger der Freiheit."

78. Ibid.

79. Comparison of the various interpretations given the *Missa Solemnis* by political and religious groups in Germany reveals that furious interpretive battles also went on in determining Beethoven's religious beliefs. I have not covered this theme.

80. Weill, "Beethoven und die Jungen."

81. Eisler, "Ludwig van Beethoven."

82. Seehof, "Dem Gedächtnis Ludwig van Beethovens."

83. Märten, "Ludwig van Beethoven und die Musik," and "Der Mensch, der Künstler, der Republikaner," *Die Republik.*

84. Kestenberg, "Beethoven."

85. Zucker, "Beethoven und die Arbeiterklasse"; and Eisler, "Ludwig van Beethoven."

86. For full discussion of the process of the "bourgeoisification" of the DAS, especially after 1920 when at the Third Congress of the Russian Communist Youth Groups, Lenin approved appropriation of "the best cultural achievements of humanity" as a "requirement for the creation of a proletarian culture," see Inge Lammel, "Zur Beethoven-Rezeption in der deutschen Arbeiterbewegung," in H. A. Brockhaus and Konrad Niemann, eds., *Bericht über den Internationalen Beethoven-Kongress in Berlin 10 December 1970* (Berlin: Verlag für Neue Musik, 1971), 160–161; and Werner Kaden, *Die Entwicklung der Arbeitersängerbewegung* (Berlin, 1969), 213, 220–221.

87. Lammel, "Beethoven-Rezeption," 161.

88. Ibid.

89. Inge Lammel, *Arbeitermusikkultur in Deutschland, 1844–1945* (Leipzig: VEB Deutscher Verlag für Musik, 1984), 128.

90. Ibid., 151–153; and Kaden, *Entwicklung der Arbeitersängerbewegung,* 324.

91. Lammel, "Beethoven-Rezeption," 156.

92. Ibid., 157.

93. Lammel, *Arbeitermusikkultur,* 192.

94. Lammel, "Beethoven-Rezeption," 156.

95. Ibid., 157. This tradition was continued in the GDR throughout its existence. See Chapter 5.

96. Lammel, *Arbeitermusikkultur,* 123.

97. *Die Weltrevolution* (1918–1919); and Lammel, *Arbeitermusikkultur,* 128, 161–162.

98. *Deutsche Arbeiter-Sängerzeitung* 27 (1926): 125.

99. Advertisement, *Kunst und Volk: Monatshefte der Breslauer Volksbühne* 4 (March 1927); and Lammel, "Beethoven-Rezeption," 156.

100. Kestenberg, *Beethoven-Feier.*

101. Kestenberg, "Beethoven."

102. Kestenberg, *Beethoven-Feier.*

103. Kestenberg, "Beethoven."

104. Kestenberg, *Beethoven-Feier.*

105. Kurt Rosenhauer, "Beethoven in unserer höheren Schule," *Allgemeine Musik-Zeitung* 47 (10 December 1920).

106. Hans Joachim Moser, "Zu Beethovens hundertfünfzigstem Geburtstag," *Der Tag* (Berlin), 16 December 1920.

107. Advertisement, *Kunst und Volk* 4 (March 1927).

108. Lammel, "Beethoven-Rezeption," 161.

109. Ibid.

110. Ibid.

111. Lammel, *Arbeitermusikkultur*, 138.

112. "Beethovenfeiern im Deutschen Arbeiter-Sängerbund," *Deutsche Arbeiter-Sängerzeitung* 28 (15 May 1927): 81–90. The report included reviews of Beethoven celebrations by the Arbeiter-Kulturkartell Köln, Das Sängerkartell Braunschweig, the Volkssingakademie Mannheim, the Volkschor Pforzheim, the Freier Volkschor Forst-Lausitz, the Freier Volkschor Hannover, the Göttinger Volkschor, the Gemischter Chor Groß-Berlin, the Chemnitzer und Thalheimer Volkschor, the Plauener Volkschor, the Zwickauer Volkschor, the Volkschor Grüna, the Arbeitsgemeinschaft Didamscher Chöre, the Lichtscher Chorverband, the Volkschor "Freiheit" Düsseldorf, the Gesangchor der Freien Volksbühne Altona, the Volkschor "Freie Sänger" Apolda, the Volkschor Heilbronn, the Volkschor Bielefeld, the Volkschor Grimma, the Arbeiterbildungsauschutz Grimma, the Volkschor Zeitz "Konkordia-Waldhorn," the Volkschor Glauchau, the Gruppe Zittau, the Freier Sängerbund Rheydt, the Männergesangverein "Loreley" Besenhorst, the Männerchöre des Bezirks Plauenscher Grund, the Chorgemeinschaft Biblis-Grotz-Rohrheim, the Arbeitergesangverein "Libertas" Hannoversch-Münden, the Volkschor Rötha, the Freier Volkschor "Frohsinn" Geislingen-Altenstadt, the Guedlinburger Arbeitergemeinschaft der Chöre Chorvereinigung, the Volkschor Steele, the Volkschor Gelsenkirchen, the Arbeiter-Bildungsinstitut Markraustädt, the Freier Volkschor Finsterwalde, the Volkschor Pfeddersheim, the Männerchor Friedenau-Steglitz, the Erste Gruppe des 7. Bezirks vom Gau Thüringen, the Volkschor Breslau, the Volkschor Gladdeck, the Gesangverein "Vorwärts" Falkenstein, the Arbeitergesangverein "Vorwärts" Kirn, the Gesangverein "Concordia" Helmstedt, the Arbeitergesangverein Liederkranz Emmendingen, the Volkschor Lüneberg, the Volkschor Eisenberg, the Volkschor Waldfischbach, the Arbeitergesangverein Görnitz und Umgegend und Blumrode, the Gesangverein "Gutenberg" Oldenburg, the Gesangverein "Harmonie" Leipzig-Kleinzschocher, the Gemischter Chor "Freiheit" Bahnhof Kieritzsch, the Arbeitergesangverein "Harmonie" Westerenger, the Gesangverein "Frisch auf" Heidingsfeld, the Männer-, Frauen-, und Gemischter Chor "Freie Sänger" Großdeuben, the Arbeitergesangverein "Deutsche Einheit" Hörde, the vereinigten Männerchöre "Harmonia," "Einigkeit," "Liederbund," und Frauenchor "Freiheit" Wernigerode, the Gesangverein "Typographia" Nürnberg, the "Typographia" Gesangverein Berliner Buchdrucker und Schriftgeißer, the Volkschor Windecken, the Volkschor Streiffeld, the "Freie Sänger" Arnstadt, the Arbeitergesangverein "Liedesfreiheit" Rastatt, the Freie Sport- und Sängervereinigung Wixhausen, the Arbeitergesangverein "Frohsinn" Wyhlen, the Arbeitergesangverein "Sängerlust" Gröningen, the Arbeitergesangverein "Eintracht" Unterweißbach, the Chorvereinigung Leipzig-Ost, the Männerchor "Fichte-Georginia 1879," the Gesangsabteilung des Arbeiter-Zentralvereins Albrechts, and the Arbeitergesangverein "Hoffnung" Coethen.

113. "Beethoven-Konzert der Arbeitersänger," *Vorwärts*, 26 March 1927; "Abgesagte Beethoven-Feier," *Vorwärts*, 27 March 1927; "Herr v. Keudell verhindert eine Beethoven-Feier," *Arbeiter-Zeitung*, 27 March 1927; "Die Beethoven-Feier der Arbeitersänger," *Illustrierte Reichsbanner-Zeitung* (Berlin), 9 April 1927.

114. F. L. Carsten, *The First Austrian Republic, 1918–1938: A Study Based on British and Austrian Documents* (Brookfield, Vt.: Gower, 1986), 97–117.

115. *Festbericht vorgelegt vom Exekutivkomitee der Beethoven-Zentenarfeier Wien 26, bis 31, März 1927* (Vienna: n.p., 1927).

116. "Beethoven-Feier für die Wiener Fortbildungsschüler," *Arbeiter-Zeitung*, 26

March 1927; and "Beethoven-Feier in der Glöckel-Schule," *Arbeiter-Zeitung*, 29 March 1927.

117. "Die Beethoven-Feier in Wien," *Vorwärts*, 27 March 1927.

118. "Aussprachen der Vertreter des Auslandes," *Arbeiter-Zeitung*, 27 March 1927.

119. Carsten, *First Austrian Republic*, 97–117; and Elisabeth Barker, *Austria, 1918–1972* (Coral Gables, Fla.: University of Miami Press, 1973), 39–47.

120. "Die Festversammlung," *Arbeiter-Zeitung*, 27 March 1927.

121. Ibid.

122. "Die Beethoven-Feier und das Radio," *Arbeiter-Zeitung*, 29 March 1927.

123. Daniel Gregory Mason, *The Quartets of Beethoven* (New York: Oxford University Press, 1947). His discussion of the trivial meaning of the "Muß es sein?" theme as Beethoven conceived it in discourse with Karl Holz is reproduced in Thomas K. Scherman and Louis Biancolli, eds., *The Beethoven Companion* (Garden City, N.Y.: Doubleday and Doubleday, 1972), 1004–10.

124. Walther Rathenau, *Gesammelte Reden*, cited by Gordon Craig in *Germany, 1866–1945* (New York: Oxford University Press, 1978), 442.

125. William Carr, *A History of Germany, 1815–1985*, 3rd ed. (London: Edward Arnold, 1987), 253; Peter Gay, *Weimar Culture: The Outsider as Insider* (New York: Harper and Row, 1968), 23–24; and Bärbel Schrader and Jürgen Schebera, *The "Golden" Twenties: Art and Literature in the Weimar Republic* (New Haven: Yale University Press, 1988), 16.

126. The term *Vernunftrepublikaner* is explained by Peter Gay in *Weimar Culture*, 23–24.

127. Arnold Schering, *Beethoven und der deutsche Idealismus* (Leipzig: C. F. Kahnt, 1927), 12.

128. Alexander Berrsche, "Beethoven: Ein Erziehungskapitel," *Der Kunstwart* 40 (March 1927).

129. H. Ruster, "Beethoven als Musikphilosoph," *Deutsche Reichs-Zeitung* (Bonn), 25 March 1927.

130. Felix Weingartner, "Zur Beethoven-Jahrhundertfeier," *Berliner Tageblatt*, 27 March 1927. I have not attended to analysis of Beethoven's religious convictions. It should be noted in passing, however, that they were an integral part of the interpretation of Beethoven suggested by the staunchly Catholic Center Party. *Germania* devoted much space to presenting Beethoven as a convinced Catholic, in contrast to the leftist portrait of him as a secular humanist. See Joseph Lossen-Freytag, "Beethoven," *Germania* (Berlin), 25 March 1927; and Tilly Lindner, "Beethovens Unsterblichkeit," *Germania*, 26 March 1927.

131. Lindner, "Beethovens Unsterblichkeit."

132. Schering, *Idealismus*, 12. This speech was originally given in 1920 on the occasion of Beethoven's one-hundred-fiftieth birthday.

133. Heinrich Luetzeler, "Beethoven: Der Mensch," *Deutsche Reichs-Zeitung*, 25 March 1927.

134. Siegfried Ochs, "Beethoven zur 100. Wiederkehr seines Todestag," *Berliner Illustrirte Zeitung*, 20 March 1927.

135. This negative point is difficult to prove without reviewing the nonpolitical content of all such articles. For a good single example see Michael Grusemann, "Beethoven's inneres and äußeres Gesicht," *Berliner Börsen-Zeitung*, 26 March 1927, a major article that traced the story of Beethoven's life without mentioning the fact that he lived through the French Revolution, the Napoleonic period, and the Metternich era.

136. L. Thurneiser, "Beethoven-Bilanz," *Der Querschnitt*, May 1927. See also Thurneiser, "Der mißbrauchte Beethoven," *Der Deutschen-Spiegel* 4 (25 March 1927), 565–568, where he suggested that none of Beethoven's music be played for a year so that the "party-political propaganda" interpretations could die out.

137. Thurneiser, "Beethoven-Bilanz."

138. Kurt Engelbrecht, "Goethe und Beethoven. Zur Frage: Was ist deutsche Weltanschauung?" *Berliner Börsen-Zeitung,* 8 July 1928.

139. Ochs, "Beethoven zur 100. Wiederkehr seines Todestag."

140. See Maynard Solomon, *Beethoven* (New York: Schirmer, 1977), 132–134, for discussion of how Beethoven's opinion of Napoleon vacillated even after the celebrated incident. Most revealing is the fact that the last addition to the original title page of the Third Symphony is the note, penciled in the composer's hand, "Geschrieben auf Bonaparte."

141. Max Unger, "Beethoven als Kapitalist," *Berliner Börsen-Zeitung,* n.d. See Solomon, *Beethoven,* 290, for information about the London Philharmonic Society's surprise on hearing that Beethoven left behind a substantial financial legacy, after it had sent him funds in the belief that he was destitute.

142. Ludwig Reve, "Beethoven und die Inflation," *Berliner Montagspost,* 14 March 1927.

143. Heinrich Simon, "Das Geheimnis seiner Gestaltung," *Frankfurter Zeitung und Handelsblatt,* 27 March 1927.

144. Ochs, "Beethoven zur 100. Wiederkehr seines Todestag."

145. Leopold Schmidt, "Was ist uns die Beethoven-Feier?" *Berliner Tageblatt,* 26 March 1927.

146. Wilhelm Kleefeld, "Beethovens Lebensbejahung," *Westermanns Monatshefte* 71 (March 1927).

147. Ochs, "Beethoven zur 100. Wiederkehr seines Todestag."

148. Berrsche, "Beethoven: Ein Erziehungskapitel."

149. Paul Hanschke, "Beethovens sinfonische Lebensdeutung," *Deutsche Reichs-Zeitung,* 25 March 1927.

150. For other examples of this recondite style of interpretation see the sources listed above. Otherwise see Karl Holl, "Beethoven und unsere Generation," *Frankfurter Zeitung und Handelsblatt,* 27 March 1927; and Heinrich Simon, "Das Geheimnis seiner Gestaltung," *Frankfurter Zeitung und Handelsblatt,* 27 March 1927. Both are model idealistic interpretations.

151. Ochs, "Beethoven zur 100. Wiederkehr seines Todestag."

152. The Center Party was also involved in organizing the festival in the nation's capital. Many of the themes discussed here also emerge from sources related to the Berlin celebrations. For more on those festivities, see the Berlin Philharmonic Orchestra's program for the event, *Ludwig van Beethoven zum Gedächtnis: 26 März 1927* (Berlin: Magistrat der Stadt Berlin, 1927). To study the Center Party's perspective on the event, see Reich Chancellor Wilhelm Marx's statement concerning the Berlin festivities in "Beethoven der Deutsche," *Vossische Zeitung* (Berlin), 27 March 1927; and "Sein Werk gehört der Menschheit: Die Beethoven-Feier und das deutsche Volk," *Neue Freie Presse* (Vienna), 27 March 1927.

153. See Carl Heinrich Becker, *Kulturpolitische Aufgaben des Reiches* (Leipzig: Quelle & Meyer, n.d.). See also Georg Goetsch, "Nachruf auf Carl Heinrich Becker," in *Besinnung,* vol. 1, *Musische Bildung: Zeugnisse eines Weges* (Wolfenbüttel: Moseler Verlag, 1948); and Walter Laqueur, *Young Germany: A History of the German Youth Movement* (London: Routledge, 1962), 146.

154. Carl Heinrich Becker, speech reproduced in "Die Huldigung der Welt," *Berliner Tageblatt,* 27 March 1927.

155. *Deutsches Beethoven-Fest Bonn vom 21. bis 31. Mai 1927* (Bonn: Hofbuchdruckerei Carthaus, 1927), 15–19.

156. Ibid., 142–143; "Auftakt," *General-Anzeiger* (Bonn), 23 May 1927; and "Frühstück im Königshof," *General-Anzeiger,* 23 May 1927.

157. Carl Heinrich Becker, *Zu Beethovens hundertstem Todestag: Rede, gehalten in Bonn am 22 Mai 1927* (Leipzig: Quelle & Meyer, 1927). The speech also appeared in the *General-Anzeiger*, 23 May 1927. Incidentally, Becker gave a copy of this speech in book form to the conservative historian Friedrich Meinecke for his approval. The inscribed copy, once part of Meinecke's library, is now in the collection of the Universitäts-Bibliothek of the Free University of Berlin.

158. Wilhelm Marx, "Beethoven der Deutsche," *Vossische Zeitung*, 29 March 1927.

159. Thurneiser, "Beethoven-Bilanz."

160. Schmidt, "Was ist uns die Beethoven-Feier?"

161. In the category of "right-wing" publications I have also studied the publications of major religious organizations, especially *Die Christliche Welt* and *Gregoriusbote*, which likewise looked back on the era of monarchical rule with nostalgia. In addition, I have included in this category some articles about Beethoven's political outlook that appeared in the music journals *Zeitschrift für Musik* and *Allgemeine Musik-Zeitung*. Surely these were not political publications; yet they did occasionally allow political issues to seep into their pages, usually in terms preferred by the reactionary segments of German society. Finally, I have also discussed under this rubric essays and speeches of some German music scholars who openly exhibited their affiliation with the political right. (See further discussion below.)

162. Carr, *History of Germany*, 253.

163. A. Stier, "Beethoven und Wir," *Nürnberger Zeitung*, 12 March 1927.

164. G. Ernest, "Beethoven der Zeitlose," *Der Tag*, 26 March 1927.

165. Karl Lotter, "Beethovens Symphonien," *Fränkischer Kurier* (Nuremburg), 26 March 1927.

166. Wilhelm Matthes, "Beethoven und Wir," *Fränkischer Kurier*, 16 December 1920.

167. Arnold Schmitz, *Das Romantische Beethovenbild: Darstellung und Kritik* (Berlin: Ferdinand Dummler, 1927), 71, 176.

168. C. Krebs, "Randglossen zu Beethovens Persönlichkeit," *Der Tag*, 26 March 1927; Ernst Schliepe, "Das Fortschrittliche in Beethovens Symphonien," *Deutsche Allgemeine Zeitung* (Berlin), 25 March 1927; and "Rote Musikwissenschaft," *Wiener Reichspost*, March 1927, republished in *Musica Sacra* 57 (May 1927).

169. Adolf Sandberger, "Das Erbe Beethovens und unsere Zeit: Rede, gehalten bei der am 26. März 1927 vom Verein Beethovenhaus zu Bonn veranstalteten Gedenkfeier des 100. Todestag Ludwig van Beethovens," in *Neues Beethoven-Jahrbuch 1927* (Augsburg: Benno Filser, 1927), 23.

170. Schmitz, *Beethovenbild*, 176.

171. Sandberger, "Erbe," 23.

172. Krebs, "Randglossen zu Beethovens Persönlichkeit."

173. "Sohn der Revolution," *Vorwärts*.

174. Otto Erich Deutsch, "Dichterische Freiheiten in Rollands Beethoven: Ein kritisches Nachwort," *Zeitschrift für Musik* 9 (September 1926).

175. "Beethoven, der Deutsche," *Deutsche Allgemeine Zeitung*, 25 March 1927.

176. "Der 'Österreicher' Beethoven," *Der Tag*, 25 March 1927.

177. Sandberger, "Erbe," 25.

178. Schliepe, "Das Fortschrittliche in Beethovens Symphonien."

179. Krebs, "Randglossen zu Beethovens Persönlichkeit."

180. Hans Joachim Moser, "Zu Beethovens hundertfünfzigstem Geburtstag," *Der Tag*, 16 December 1920.

181. "Der 'Österreicher' Beethoven," *Der Tag*.

182. Wilhelm Matthes, "Zeit und Genius," *Fränkischer Kurier*, 26 March 1927.

183. Friedrich Rießler, "Bismarck und Beethoven," *Tägliche Rundschau* (Berlin), 29 March 1927.

184. Schering, *Idealismus,* 4. One cannot help wondering what victory Schering felt Germany had won in 1914.

185. "Richard Wagner über Beethoven," *Neue Preußische (Kreuz-)Zeitung* (Berlin), 26 March 1927; and *Beethoven-Almanach der Deutschen Musikbücherei aus das Jahr 1928* (Regensburg: Bosse Verlag, 1928).

186. Kurt Kreiser, "Beethoven als Mensch und Künstler," *Neue Preußische (Kreuz-)Zeitung,* 26 March 1927.

187. "Beethoven, der Deutsche," *Deutsche Allgemeine Zeitung.*

188. Wilhelm Furtwängler, "Beethoven der Sieger," *Braunschweiger Neueste Nachrichten,* 20 March 1927. See Fred K. Prieberg, *Kraftprobe: Wilhelm Furtwängler im Dritten Reich* (Wiesbaden: Brockhaus, 1986); and Michael Meyer, *The Politics of Music in the Third Reich* (New York: Peter Lang, 1991), 329–388, for information about Furtwängler's reactionary musical and political opinions.

189. Furtwängler, "Beethoven der Sieger."

190. Moser, "Zu Beethovens hundertfünfzigstem Geburtstag."

191. Ibid.

192. Matthes, "Beethoven und Wir."

193. Sandberger, "Erbe," 23.

194. Krebs, "Randglossen zu Beethovens Persönlichkeit."

195. See Hans Joachim Moser, "Beethoven und der 'Untergang des Abendlandes'," *Allgemeine Musik-Zeitung* 47 (10 December 1920); and "Zu Beethovens hundertstem Todestag: Gedenkrede bei der Feier der Universität Heidelberg am 1. Juni 1927," in *Neues Beethoven-Jahrbuch 1930* (Augsburg: Benno Filser, 1930). See also Lammel, "Beethoven-Rezeption," for discussion of Moser's analysis of Beethoven as a Führer type.

196. Dr. von Graevenitz, "Heldentum und Krieg in Beethovens Musik," *Deutsche Militär-Musiker-Zeitung* 49 (26 March 1927), 108.

197. Schmitz, *Beethovenbild,* 174.

198. Graevenitz, "Heldentum und Krieg in Beethovens Musik," 108.

199. Ibid.

200. Paul Natorp, "Beethoven und Wir: Rede, gehalten zur Beethoven Feier der Universität Marburg, den 16. Dezember 1920" (Marburg: Brühl'sche Universitäts-Buch- und Steindruckerei, 1921), 15.

201. Schmitz, *Beethovenbild,* 174–175.

202. Ibid.

203. Furtwängler, "Beethoven der Sieger."

204. I draw this negative conclusion because I have found no evidence of concerts, rallies, or festivals specifically arranged by members of these parties.

205. C. Krebs, "Beethoven vom Links," *Der Tag,* 3 January 1927.

206. Matthes, "Beethoven und Wir." Emphasis in original.

207. Gordon Craig, *The Germans* (New York: New American Library, 1982), 170–189; and Fritz Ringer, *The Decline of the German Mandarins: The German Academic Community, 1890–1933* (Cambridge, Mass.: Harvard University Press, 1968), 249–252.

208. It was also in their essays, articles, and lectures that the seeds of the worst aspects of Beethoven reception, based on race theory, grew during the Weimar era. The fact that many of these scholars later contributed so willingly to the cultural politics of the Third Reich therefore becomes comprehensible.

209. Sandberger, "Erbe," 18–31. The association of the Beethovenhaus Society with right-wing ideology will become obvious with discussion of the activities of its president, Ludwig Schiedermair, during the Weimar era and afterward.

210. Moser, "Zu Beethovens hundertstem Todestag." See also Lammel, "Beethoven-Rezeption," 172, for discussion of Moser's fascist tendencies as they appeared in his analyses of Beethoven. Moser would see his political ideals played out to the fullest when

he served as a leading musicologist for the Reich Music Chamber during the Nazi era.

211. Th. B. Rehmen, "Beethovenjubiläum," *Gregoriusbote* 43 (March 1927).

212. Friedrich Hussong, "Die Huldigung der Nationen," *Der Tag*, 29 March 1927.

213. "Rote Musikwissenschaft," *Wiener Reichspost.*

214. Werner Liebe, *Die Deutschnationale Volkspartei, 1918–1924* (Düsseldorf: Droste, 1956), 89.

215. "Herr von Keudell verhindert eine Beethoven-Feier," *Arbeiter-Zeitung*; and "Abgesagte Beethoven-Feier," *Vorwärts.*

216. Cartoon, *Illustrierte Kronen-Zeitung* (Vienna), 27 March 1927.

217. Wilhelm Zentner, "Zehn Strophen auf Beethoven," *Zeitschrift für Musik* 3 (March 1927): 129.

218. Houston Stewart Chamberlain to King Ferdinand of Bulgaria, 11 December 1919, *Briefe*, 107–108. My thanks to Roger Lustig and Margaret Mikulska of Princeton University for identifying, via electronic mail on 25 August 1993, Chamberlain's citation of *An die Hoffnung.*

219. Karl Grunsky, "Aus dem Schriftum über Beethoven," *Deutsches Volkstum* (March 1927), 186.

220. Ibid.; and Karl Soehle, "Ludwig van Beethovens hundertjähriger Todestag," *Deutsches Volkstum* (March 1927), 177.

221. For background on volkish ideology see Howard Becker, *German Youth: Bond or Free* (London: Kegan Paul, 1946); Fritz Stern, *The Politics of Cultural Despair: A Study in the Rise of the Germanic Ideology* (Berkeley: University of California Press, 1961); and George L. Mosse, *The Crisis of German Ideology: Intellectual Origins of the Third Reich* (New York: Schocken, 1981).

222. "Beethoven als Österreicher," *Hammer: Blätter für deutsche Sinn* 26 (15 April 1927).

223. Heinz Nonveiller, "Kritik der Presse," *Gewissen: Unabhängige Zeitung für Volksbildung* 9 (4 April 1927).

224. Ibid.

225. Friedrich Rießner, "Bismarck und die Müsik," *Der Stahlhelm* (Berlin), 27 March 1927. See also Helmut von den Steinen, "Beethoven-Feier," *Gewissen* 9 (28 March 1927). Interpretations of Beethoven's tendency to use German music terminology instead of the usual Italian as proof of patriotic fervor appeared soon after his lifetime. In 1832 Ignaz von Seyfried wrote, in an addendum to a collection of composition lessons wrongly attributed to the composer, that "Beethoven, in the truest sense of the word, was a real German, body and soul. Entirely at home in the Latin, French, and Italian languages, he used by preference and whenever possible his native tongue. Had he been able to have his own way in the matter, all his works would have appeared in print with German title pages. He even tried to delete the exotic word *pianoforte*, and chose in its stead the expressive term *Hammerklavier* as a suitable and appropriate substitute" (Ignaz von Seyfried, *L. van Beethovens Studien im Generalbasse, Contrapuncte und in der Compositionslehre* [1832], reproduced in O.G. Sonneck, ed., *Beethoven: Impressions by His Contemporaries* [New York: G. Schirmer, 1967], 45–46).

226. Richard Gottschalk, "Beethovens deutsche Kunstausdrücke," *Muttersprache: Zeitschrift zur Pflege und Erforschung der Deutschen Sprache* 42 (March 1927).

227. "Die tragische Schöpfung Beethovens," *Der Stahlhelm*, 27 March 1927.

228. Von den Steinen, "Beethoven-Feier."

229. Ibid.

230. A. Schubart, "Beethoven," *Propylaen* (1921), reproduced in Hans Heinrich Eggebrecht, *Zur Geschichte der Beethoven-Rezeption* (Mainz: Akademie der Wissenschaften und der Literatur, 1972), 39.

231. See Richard Benz, *Die Stunde der deutschen Musik* (Jena: Diederichs, 1923);

Die ewigen Meister: Deutsche Musikgestalten (Jena: Diederichs, 1935); *Das Ethos der Musik* (Offenbach: Geratung, 1936); *Vom Erden: Schicksal ewiger Musik* (Jena: Diederichs, 1936); and *Von den drei Welten der Musik* (Hamburg: Wegner, 1942).

232. "Richard Benz, *Die Stunde der deutschen Musik*," review in *Die Tat* 19 (September 1927).

233. Richard Benz, "Beethovens geistige Weltbotschaft," *Die Musik* 18 (1926): 405; "Beethoven als Maß unserer Zeit," *Bücherwurm* 12 (1927): 161; "Beethoven und die Wende der Kultur," *Völkische Kultur* (1933).

234. "Die tragische Schöpfung Beethovens," *Der Stahlhelm.* See also advertisements in *Die Tat* 19 (May 1927); and "Aus dem Schriftum über Beethoven," review in *Deutsches Volkstum* (March 1927).

235. Richard Benz, "Beethovens geistige Sendung," *Neue Zürcher Zeitung*, 27 March 1927.

236. Ibid.

237. Richard Benz, "Das Erlebnis Beethoven," *Die Tat* 19 (May 1927).

238. Benz, cited in Herbert Birtner, "Zur deutschen Beethovenauffassung," in Arnold Schmitz, ed., *Beethoven und die Gegenwart: Festschrift des Beethovenhauses Bonn* (Berlin: Ferdinand Dummler, 1937), 37.

239. Ibid.

240. Benz, "Das Erlebnis Beethoven."

241. Benz, cited in Birtner, "Zur deutschen Beethovenauffassung," 37.

242. Ibid.

243. Benz, "Beethovens geistige Sendung."

244. Fritz Jöde, "Mozart, Beethoven, Haydn: Ein Vermächtnis," *Sonderdruck aus Der Kreis: Monatsblätter für Musikpflege* 10 (Wolfenbüttel, Berlin: Kallmeyer, 1932–33).

245. Ibid.

246. Fritz Jöde, "Beethoven und Wir," *Erster Jahresbericht der Volksmusikschule der Musikantengilde* (Berlin: Ortsgruppe Berlin e. V., 1925–26).

247. Jöde, "Mozart, Beethoven, Haydn."

248. See a devastating critique of Jöde's "orakel-dunklen . . . Satz und Gedankenlabyrinthe" in Ludwig Misch, "Fritz Jödes Begegnung mit Beethoven," *Allgemeine Musik-Zeitung* 59 (1932): 499–500.

249. Karl Grunsky, "Musik und Bühne: Eine Umschau," *Deutschlands Erneuerung* 10 (July 1927).

250. See Carsten, *First Austrian Republic*, 27–28; and Barker, *Austria*, 20–22, for descriptions of this anti-Semitic party.

251. "Auch Beethoven ist ihnen zu unsittlich," *Arbeiter-Zeitung*, 19 December 1926.

252. Alfred Rosenberg, "Beethoven," *Völkischer Beobachter*, 26 March 1927.

253. My findings indicate that although predominantly anti-Semitic, the other parties of the extreme right did not concentrate on the controversy of Beethoven's race; unlike the Nazis, most of them glossed over the issues discussed below and simply accepted at face value Beethoven's reputation as a German hero.

254. For more complete discussion of the racial-theoretical bases of National Socialist *Musikpolitik* see Chapter 4.

255. See Alessandra Comini, *The Changing Image of Beethoven: A Study in Mythmaking* (New York: Rizzoli, 1987), for detailed discussion of the iconography of Beethoven reception in the visual arts.

256. Günther, author of the infamous racial-scientific work, *Rassenkunde des deutschen Volkes* (Munich: J. F. Lehmann, 1922), categorized Beethoven's music in this way: "Deutlich ist seinem Werk nicht-nordisches beigemischt. . . . In Beethovens Werk treibt . . . eine 'dunkle' Gewalt, die oft zu mächtig ist, als daß sie noch von nordischer Strenge durchdrungen, umspannt werden könnte. . . . [Also] Beethovens Werk steht 'exzentrisch' im Kreise nordischer Kunst" (*Rasse und Stil* [Munich: J. F. Lehmann,

1926], 30). Clauß hesitantly decided that Beethoven "leib—anthropologisch betrachtet . . . vielleicht ziemlich rein ostisch war" (*Rasse und Seele* [Munich: J. F. Lehmann, 1926], 60). See further discussion of these sources in Heribert Schröder, "Beethoven im Dritten Reich: Eine Materialsammlung," in Helmet Loos, ed., *Beethoven und die Nachwelt: Materialien zur Wirkungsgeschichte Beethovens* (Bonn: Beethovenhaus, 1986), 205.

257. "Erbbild," *Völkischer Beobachter*, 26 March 1927.

258. "Erscheinungsbild," *Völkischer Beobachter*, 26 March 1927. Emphasis in original.

259. See Eichenauer's reworking of "Das Niebelungenlied" in *Deutschlands Erneuerung* 10 (October 1927): 470.

260. Albrecht Dümling and Peter Girth, eds., *Entartete Musik: Zur Düsseldorfer Ausstellung von 1938: Eine kommentierte Rekonstruktion* (Düsseldorf: Kleinherne, 1988). This congress was held in Düsseldorf in conjunction with the infamous exhibit of "Degenerate Music."

261. Richard Eichenauer, *Musik und Rasse*, 2nd ed. (Munich: J. F. Lehmann, 1937), 226–232.

262. Ludwig Schiedermair, "Beethoven und die Politik," *Völkischer Beobachter*, 26 March 1927.

263. "Der Patriot," *Völkischer Beobachter*, 26 March 1927.

264. Richard Wagner, "Der Große Bahnbrecher" (a selection from Wagner, *Beethoven* [1870]), *Völkischer Beobachter*, 26 March 1927.

265. "Wörter Beethovens," *Völkischer Beobachter*, 26 March 1927.

266. Brunnhilde Wastl, "Ludwig van Beethoven: Zu seinem hundertsten Todestag," *Deutsche Arbeiterpresse: Nationalsozialistisches Wochenblatt* (Vienna), 26 March 1927. Emphasis in original.

267. See Hans Büchner, "Zu Beethovens 100. Todestag," *Illustrierte Beobachter*, 15 March 1927, and "Goethe und Bismarck über Beethoven," *Völkischer Beobachter*, 26 March 1927.

268. Josef Stolzing-Cerny, "Landsturmmann Beethoven: Eine Kriegserinnerung," *Volkischer Beobachter*, 26 March 1927. See discussion of the original form of this anecdote in Chapter 2.

269. Wastl, "Ludwig van Beethoven." Emphasis in original.

270. Franz Gottinger, "Eine deutsche Beethoven-Feier," *Deutsche Arbeiterpresse*, 26 March 1927.

271. Eichenauer, *Musik und Rasse*, 228.

272. Schiedermair, "Beethoven und die Politik."

273. Eichenauer, *Musik und Rasse*, 231.

274. Ibid., 229.

275. Rosenberg, "Beethoven."

276. Ludwig Schiedermair, "Die Gestaltung weltanschaulicher Ideen in der Volksmusik Beethovens" (Leipzig: Quelle & Meyer, 1934), and "Beethovens Eltern," *Völkischer Beobachter*, April 1935.

277. See Chapter 4.

278. Schiedermair was elected president of the Deutsche Gesellschaft für Musikwissenschaft in 1937 and chairman of the music section of the Deutsche Akademie in 1940 (Stanley Sadie, ed., *The New Grove Dictionary of Music and Musicians* [London: Macmillan, 1980] 16:641).

279. See Wastl, "Ludwig van Beethoven," which described the "technical" celebrations of most 1927 events as "superficial." See also Rosenberg, "Beethoven," wherein he said that he read of the various celebrations of 1927 while "grinding his teeth." See also Nitsche, "Jonny neben Beethoven," for a scathing attack on the 1927 celebrations in Leipzig, written in retrospect ten years later.

280. Peter Raabe, "Ausbau oder Einschränkung der Beethovenpflege?" *Allgemeine Musik-Zeitung* 47 (10 December 1920). Emphasis in original.

281. Ibid.

4. The Third Reich

1. Julius Nitsche, "Jonny neben Beethoven: Errinerung an eine Jahrhundertfeier in wirrer Zeit," *Völkischer Beobachter* (Berlin), 26 March 1937. See Susan Cook, *Opera for a New Republic: The Zeitopern of Krenek, Weill and Hindemith* (Ann Arbor, Mich.: UMI Research, 1988), 85–105 and 206–210, for a synopsis and discussion of Krenek's operetta.

2. Nitsche, "Jonny neben Beethoven."

3. Ibid.

4. Peter Raabe, *Die Musik im Dritten Reich* (Regensburg: Bosse, 1936), 9.

5. Erik Levi, *Music in the Third Reich* (New York: St. Martin's, 1994), 228–240.

6. A number of scholars have dedicated themselves to the history of National Socialist Musikpolitik. See Joseph Wulf, *Musik im Dritten Reich: Eine Dokumentation*, 2nd ed. (Frankfurt am Main: Ullstein, 1983); Fred K. Prieberg, *Musik im NS-Staat* (Frankfurt am Main: Fischer Taschenbuch, 1982); idem, *Kraftprobe: Wilhelm Furtwängler im Dritten Reich* (Wiesbaden: F. A. Brockhaus, 1986); Hanns-Werner Heister and Hans-Günter Klein, eds., *Musik und Musikpolitik im faschistischen Deutschland* (Frankfurt am Main: Fischer Taschenbuch, 1984); Albrecht Dümling and Peter Girth, eds., *Entartete Musik: Zur Düsseldorfer Ausstellung von 1938: Eine kommentierte Rekonstruktion* (Düsseldorf: Kleinherne, 1988); Michael Meyer, *The Politics of Music in the Third Reich* (New York: Peter Lang, 1991); and Levi, *Music in the Third Reich*.

7. Sometimes at a loss for new ideas about how the life and music of Beethoven could be correlated with Hitler's regime, many Nazi music propagandists merely reproduced interpretations formulated by earlier "comrades." During the National Socialist era the essays and books of Richard Benz were constantly republished, along with new versions of his interpretation; Richard Eichenauer's racial analysis was also frequently cited. Likewise, sycophantic party members were prone to repeat and extol the interpretations of their leaders. For instance, A. Kruell's "Ludwig van Beethoven und unsere Zeit," *Westdeutscher Beobachter* (Bonn), 23 June 1935, was nothing more than a salute to Alfred Rosenberg's 1927 article. Kruell considered Rosenberg's the most "worthy" and "penetrating" study of Beethoven produced during the "years of decay."

8. D. Felix Huch, "Monsieur Herriot: Der Menschenfreund und Beethovenforscher," *Völkischer Beobachter*, 7 March 1933. Written soon after the seizure of power, this article still harped on the interpretation Herriot had made years earlier, deriding it as an "internationalist" product of a "compulsory overseer" of Germany; in the "New Germany" of Adolf Hitler, Huch concluded, publication of Herriot's book and other works like it would be impossible. For a list of Nazi-era articles on the "nationality problem," see Heribert Schröder, "Beethoven im Dritten Reich: Eine Materialsammlung," in Helmut Loos, ed., *Beethoven und die Nachwelt: Materialien zur Wirkungsgeschichte Beethovens* (Bonn: Beethovenhaus, 1986), 203n87. Schröder also compiled a lengthy list of statements about Beethoven's "Deutschtum": in his view, "no word was so popular in the Beethoven literature of the Nazi era as the term 'German'; the 'Germanness' of Beethoven was confirmed over and over again; therefore, his music also had to be German" (ibid., 201).

9. Ludwig Schiedermair, "Der große Sohn der Stadt Bonn, Ludwig van Beethoven," *Ewiges Deutschland: Monatsschrift für den deutschen Volksgenossen* 4 (September 1939). See also Schiedermair's "Beethovens Eltern," *Völkischer Beobachter*, April 1935; "Ludwig van Beethoven und sein Werk," *Westdeutscher Beobachter*, 26 May 1941;

and "Beethoven und die rheinische Landschaft," *Kölnische Volkszeitung*, 15 November 1940, among many others in which he repeated this theme.

10. Hans Joachim Moser, "Ludwig van Beethoven," *Hamburger Fremdenblatt*, 7 May 1941.

11. Walther Vetter, "Eine politische Beethoven-Betrachtung," in Helmut Osthoff, Walter Serauky, and Adam Ario, eds., *Festschrift Arnold Schering zum sechzigsten Geburtstag* (Berlin: A. Gas, 1937), 249.

12. Schröder also perceived this aspect of NS Beethoven reception: "A further 'problem' within the family van Beethoven was the character of the father . . . . 'Gray misery tainted the house daily,' because he 'drank excessively, spent the small amount of household money, and beat the children indiscriminately' " ("Beethoven im Dritten Reich," 203).

13. Hans Pfeiffer, "Die Wahrheit über den Vater Beethovens," *Die Musik* 28 (1935): 13–19.

14. Schiedermair, "Beethovens Eltern." See variations on these arguments in the other Schiedermair sources listed in note 9.

15. Heinrich Zerkaulen, "Beethovens Reise nach Amsterdam," *Völkischer Beobachter*, 7 August 1940. A trip of Beethoven and his mother up the Rhine to Amsterdam is presented here as an escape from the father and his constant exploitation of the son. On the way, Magdalena cooks for the boat crew and dries Beethoven's tears.

16. See Chapter 3 for discussion of Richard Eichenauer's treatment of Beethoven in *Musik und Rasse*, republished and highlighted as essential reading within the Third Reich.

17. Walther Rauschenberger, "Rassenmerkmale Beethovens und seiner nächsten Verwandten," *Volk und Rasse: Organ des Reichsausschußes für Volksgesundheitsdienst und der Deutschen Gesellschaft für Rassenhygiene* 9 (1934). Rauschenberger reprinted this article later in *Familie, Sippe, Volk: Monatsschrift für Sippenkunde und Sippenpflege* (Berlin: Amt für Sippenforschung der NSDAP) 5 (August 1939): 114–119, under the title, "Beethovens Abstammung und Rassenmerkmale."

18. *Unseren Jungen: Ein Buch zur Unterhaltung, Belehrung, und Beschäftigung* (Stuttgart: Loewes Verlag Ferdinand Karl, 1937), 205. As proof, such sources customarily reviewed the stories of Beethoven's rededication of the Third Symphony and his flight from Grätz Castle.

19. Hans Joachim Moser, "Beethovens rheinische Sendung zur Wiener Klassik," *Bonner Geschichtsblätter* 2 (1938), 139.

20. Moser, "Ludwig van Beethoven," *Hamburger Fremdenblatt*.

21. Kruell, "Ludwig van Beethoven und unsere Zeit."

22. Hanns-Werner Heister and Jochem Wolff also identified this tendency on the part of Nazi *Musikpolitiker:* "In Beethoven's and Wagner's music the Nazis perceived powerful representations of German spiritual leadership, which would naturally extend worldwide. [To this music they attributed] in particular the 'spirit' of the age, the 'awakening' of the 'German Volk,' that would go forth in the form of the 'German race' to achieve cultural dominance" ("Macht und Schicksal: Klassik, Fanfaren, höhere Durchhaltemusik," in Heister and Klein, *Musik und Musikpolitik*, 116–117).

23. Vetter, "Eine politische Beethoven-Betrachtung," 249.

24. Ibid., 247.

25. Ludwig Schiedermair, "Zu Beethovens Schicksalsidee," in *Von Deutscher Tonkunst: Festschrift zu Peter Raabes 70. Geburtstag* (Leipzig: C. F. Peters, 1942), 76.

26. Vetter, "Eine politische Beethoven-Betrachtung."

27. Eugen Hadamovsky, *Dein Rundfunk: Das Rundfunkbuch für alle Volksgenossen* (Munich: Zentralverein der NSDAP, 1934), 78.

28. Arnold Schering, "Zur Sinndeutung der 4. und 5. Symphonie von Beethoven," *Zeitschrift für Musikwissenschaft* 16 (1934): 83.

29. Walter Jacobs, "Beethoven im Rundfunk: Musik- und Staatspolitik," *Kölnische Zeitung*, 16 December 1934.

30. Schröder, "Beethoven im Dritten Reich," 196.

31. Jacobs, "Beethoven im Rundfunk."

32. "Beethovens Neunte Symphonie: Das zweite Konzert des Münchener Festsommers," *Völkischer Beobachter*, 23 June 1935.

33. Jacobs, "Beethoven im Rundfunk."

34. "Beethovens Neunte Symphonie," *Völkischer Beobachter*.

35. Schröder, "Beethoven im Dritten Reich," 196.

36. Hans Joachim Moser, "Ludwig van Beethoven," *Stuttgarter Neues Tageblatt*, 26 January 1941.

37. Nazi music policy was grounded in basic notions of music conservatism developed long before 1933. Against the "threatening" music of composers who practiced atonal and serial methods, they posited works composed according to "Germanic" music structures. These included: the "nonproblematic" sonata form—supposedly free of the contradictions introduced by "progressive dialecticians"; traditional folk melodies, accessible to the German masses and capable of instilling pride in their peasant background; and traditional harmonic structures in the major mode, representing the orderly nature of reality and the hierarchical structure of society. Beethoven's music, if "correctly" understood, supposedly contained all these elements. For more on how Nazi *Musikpolitiker* worked to counter the tendencies of musical "modernism," a subject that lies just outside the topic of political interpretations, see Meyer, *Politics of Music in the Third Reich*, 256–288, and Levi, *Music in the Third Reich*, 82–123.

38. Friedrich Blume, "Musik und Rasse: Grundfragen einer musikalischen Rassenforschung," *Die Musik* 30 (August 1938): 736. See other examples of this view listed in Schröder, "Beethoven im Dritten Reich," 190–91, 211. This invocation of a sense of being "at home" was a powerful aspect of National Socialist propaganda. As George L. Mosse put it: "What is often condemned as the politicization of all aspects of life is in reality a deep stream of history, which has always condemned pluralism, the division of politics from other aspects of life. When representative government, which symbolizes this division, threatens to break down, men again wish for a fully furnished home where what is beautiful and gives pleasure should not be separated from the useful and the necessary" (*The Nationalization of the Masses: Political Symbolism and Mass Movements in Germany from the Napoleonic Wars through the Third Reich* [New York: Howard Fertig, 1975], 215).

39. Implicit in all the above examples, the notion that even the least prosperous and educated Germans could sense the significance of Beethoven's music and other high-cultural symbols was frequently discussed in Nazi literature. Certainly it constituted the theoretical background for organizing concerts, exhibitions, and other artistic events for factory workers and soldiers. A curious example of how the Nazis popularized this theme was Zerkaulen's "Beethovens Reise nach Amsterdam," which purported that the boatman who transported the boy composer up the Rhine appreciated his music more deeply than jaded concertgoers ever could.

40. Apart from politicizing Beethoven's and other music in articles such as those discussed here, Moser served the regime in many other ways. A student of Schiedermair, he published in 1935 his infamous *Musiklexikon*, a handbook of music classification by race. From 1940 to 1945 he led the Reichstelle für Musikbearbeitung in Goebbels' propaganda ministry. This organization was devoted, among other goals, to rewriting the texts of liturgical works for use in political rituals and eliminating signs that Jewish artists had anything to do with the composition of "German classics" (as in the case of Lorenzo da Ponte, for instance). See Dümling and Girth, *Entartete Musik*, 87–91, and Prieberg, *Musik im NS-Staat*, 335, for more on Moser.

41. Having outlined the preferred historical approach to Beethoven's biography for

National Socialist musicologists in his "Eine politische Beethoven-Betrachtung," Vetter would after the war become an important purveyor of Musikpolitik for the East German government.

42. A scholar in the "positive" tradition of musicology (see Chapter 5, note 61), one who produced manuscript catalogues and studies of Beethoven's handwriting, Unger became a frequent contributer, along with Moser, to the Nazi wartime music journal *Musik im Kriege.* For this publication he applied his talents to popularizing "Beethovens Militärmärsche" (Heft 7/8 [October 1943]) and "Beethovens vaterländische Musik" (Heft 9/10 [December 1943–44]).

43. Highly criticized during the Third Reich for his free "poetic" interpretations, which lay firmly in the idealistic tradition of Beethoven reception (see reviews of his *Beethoven in neuer Deutung* [Leipzig: Kahnt, 1934] in *Deutsche Musikkultur* 2 [June 1937], 77–99), Schering may have felt more compulsion than enthusiasm when alluding to the Führer in his studies of the symphonies. However, Schering was in strong agreement with Nazi views in 1936 when he dedicated his next book, *Beethoven und die Dichtung* (Berlin: Junker und Dünhaupt, 1936), to "the young Germany" and said in its prologue, "If a brutal, racially foreign music has long threatened the indivisible relationship between high music and high poetry, it will now be Beethoven who will reestablish this ideal bond."

44. Schiedermair's "braune Vergangenheit," as the present head of the Beethovenhaus put it to me, is clear. However, a note on the status of the Beethovenhaus during the Third Reich may be appropriate. In the Nazi state, Reichminister Rust became its official "protector" (*Schirmherr*). On its fiftieth anniversary in 1938, Hitler, Hess, Göring, and Ribbentrop all sent telegrams of celebration (Schröder, "Beethoven im Dritten Reich," 191). Schiedermair served as head of the Beethovenhaus until he retired in 1945. He considered the museum and the archive as "places of pious remembrance of the great genius . . . but also places of serious scientific work for the registration and preservation of German art for the German Volk" (Schiedermair, "Der große Sohn der Stadt," *Ewiges Deutschland*).

45. See Prieberg, *Musik im NS Staat,* and *Kraftprobe;* Dümling and Girth, *Entartete Musik;* and Schröder, "Beethoven im Dritten Reich."

46. *Unseren Jungen,* 210–216.

47. Erich Wintermeier, "Die junge Generation hat das Wort: Beethoven? Ja, Beethoven!" *Deutsche Musikkultur* 2 (June 1937): 73–77.

48. Willi Kahl, "Zur neueren Beethovenliteratur"; and K. Klinck, "Beethovens und Bruckners 5. Symphonie: Zwei nordische Schicksalsbilder"; both in *Der Westfälische Erzieher: Gauamtliche Halbmonatsschrift des N[ational] S[ozialistisches] L[ehrer] B[und] Gau Westfalen-Nord* 5 (1937).

49. Jacobs, "Beethoven im Rundfunk."

50. Ida Deeke, "Beethoven," *Zeitschrift für Musik* 107 (1940): 779.

51. See Obergebietsführer Karl Cerff, "Beethovenfest der HJ: Musikerziehung und Hitlerjugend," *Zeitschrift für Musik* 7 (July 1938): 728–732, for further information on this program.

52. Erich Valentin, "Beethovenfest der Hitlerjugend: Bad Wildbad (Schwarzwald) 20. bis 22. Mai 1938," *Zeitschrift für Musik* 7 (July 1938): 735.

53. "Geleitsätze zum Beethovenfest der Hitler-Jugend," *Zeitschrift für Musik* 7 (July 1938): 732.

54. Ibid.

55. Artur (sic) Haelßig, "Ein Beethoven-Orchester der Hitler-Jugend als Folgerung aus dem Beethovenfest der Hitler-Jugend in Bad Wildbad Mai 1938," *Zeitschrift für Musik* 7 (October 1938): 1095. Haelßig was so excited about his accomplishment that he wanted to found a permanent "Beethoven Orchestra of the Hitler Youth" that would travel throughout Germany "like a giant sperm which goes out to plant smaller sperms"

(*vergleichbar einem Riesen-Sämann, der ausgeht, seinen Samen zu legen*). "It is intoxicating to think," he wrote, of what could happen "if this Beethoven orchestra were to go through all German regions . . . . All of Germany, every German boy, every BDM girl, would have a chance in their lives to come close to this titan. What a community of music listeners would be cultivated for German music! What a source of power would be developed for the German people!" I have not seen evidence that Haelßig was given control of such a cultural-political juggernaut.

56. Johann Georg Bachmann, "Der Rundfunk: 'Beethoven für alle?'" *Deutsche Musikkultur* 2 (June-July 1937): 115.

57. Ibid., 118.

58. *Der Deutsche Rundfunk* 12, no. 4 (19 January 1934): 11.

59. I have not found statistics on National Socialist radio programming arranged by composer. Most literature on this subject refers to the frequent playing of Beethoven's music during the Third Reich as a well-known phenomenon. For information about the quantity of classical music played over the Nazi radio, see Nanny Drechsler, *Die Funktion der Musik im deutschen Rundfunk, 1933–45* (Pfaffenweiler: Centaurus-Verlagsgesellschaft, 1988); and Rita von der Grün, "Funktionen und Formen von Musiksendungen im Rundfunk," in Heister and Klein, *Musik und Musikpolitik*, 98–106.

60. Peter Adams, writer and producer, "Art in the Third Reich," a television program of the BBC, with ALLCOM Film GmBh, 1989.

61. Drechsler, *Funktion der Musik*, 58.

62. Bachmann, "Der Rundfunk," 115.

63. *Mitteilungen der Reichsrundfunkgesellschaft, 11. Januar 1934*, cited in Drechsler, *Funktion der Musik*, 36.

64. Hadamovsky, *Dein Rundfunk*, 77.

65. Bachmann, "Der Rundfunk," 117.

66. Reproduced as part of Adams, "Art in the Third Reich."

67. Dr. Peter Wapnewski, conversation with author, Berlin, January 1989.

68. Berthold Hinz, *Art in the Third Reich*, trans. Robert Kimber and Rita Kimber (New York: Pantheon, 1979), xi.

69. *Schlußakkord* (Berlin: Ufa, 1936). See also F. Herzfeld, "Musik im Film," *Allgemeine Musik-Zeitung* 63 (1936): 670.

70. *Wunschkonzert* (Berlin: Ufa, 1940).

71. Gregory Vitiello, ed., *Eisenstaedt: Germany* (Washington, D.C.: Smithsonian Institution Press, 1980), 27.

72. Nazification was also committed against the memorial marking Mozart's approximate burial place in Vienna. During the 1941 observances of the one hundred fiftieth anniversary of Mozart's death, Baldur von Schirach, the head of the Hitler Youth, laid a wreath at this marker in a highly politicized ceremony. See newsreel reproduced in Adams, "Art in the Third Reich."

73. Rainer Cadenbach, ed., *Mythos Beethoven: Ausstellungskatalog* (Bonn: Laaber, 1986), 157, #234. The designer of this ill-fated sculpture was Peter Breuer.

74. Werner Lasarzewski-Meienreis, "Eine Beethoven Ehrung in Bonn am Rhein," *Der Kämpfer* 6 (February 1939). Dedicated in 1938, the sculpture stood overlooking the Rhine in the park of the old *Zollamt* near the university in Bonn. After the war it was moved to the Bonner Rheingau, where it serves children as a jungle gym (Schröder, "Beethoven im Dritten Reich," 192).

75. I have not compiled statistics on the frequency of Beethoven performances in the Third Reich. (For information on the year 1942–43 alone, see n107.) However, a 1937 article in *Deutsche Musikkultur* discussing the prominence of Beethoven compositions in the repertoire of German orchestras suggests that his music was performed more often than that of any other composer. (Willy Siebert, "Beethoven im Musikleben der Gegenwart: Beethoven im Konzertsaal," *Deutsche Musikkultur* 2 [June-July 1937]

114–115). Again, comparison of concert-hall performances of Beethoven's work and of Wagner's is not altogether valid, since Wagner wrote mainly operas. Certainly, Wagner's music, the personal favorite of Hitler, was an important part of the music world and the political culture of the Third Reich. This fact does not, however, diminish the importance of Beethoven's music in German concert life at this time.

76. "Jüdischer Kulturbund: Geschlossene Gesellschaft," *Der Spiegel* 19, no. 33 (1965): 73.

77. Heister and Wolff, "Macht und Schicksal," 117.

78. "Program zur feierlichen Eröffnung der Reichskulturkammer 15. November 1933," Berlin Philharmonic Orchestra program, Staatliches Institut für Musikforschung, Preußischer Kulturbesitz, Berlin.

79. Prieberg, *Kraftprobe,* 244–245. See this work and Sam H. Shirakawa, *The Devil's Music Master: The Controversial Life and Career of Wilhelm Furtwängler* (New York: Oxford University Press, 1992), for information on Furtwängler's behavior during the Nazi era.

80. Dümling and Girth, *Entartete Musik,* 109.

81. Heister and Wolff, "Macht und Schicksal," 117.

82. "Olympische Dorf-Musik: Eine Militärkapelle, die 50 Nationalhymnen einstudieren muß," *Berliner Tageblatt,* 13 November 1935.

83. *Der Angriff* (Berlin), 22 April 1937, cited in Prieberg, *Kraftprobe,* 276.

84. Incidentally, Karajan had succeeded Peter Raabe as conductor of the Aachen orchestra when the latter took over the Reich Music Chamber in 1935 (Prieberg, *Musik im NS Staat,* 208).

85. Prieberg, *Kraftprobe,* 301.

86. William Shirer, *Berlin Diary* (New York: Alfred A. Knopf, 1941), 18–19.

87. David B. Hinton, *The Films of Leni Riefenstahl* (London: Scarecrow, 1978), 58.

88. "Semaine Artistique Allemand à Paris: 3–12 Septembre 1937," Berlin Philharmonic Orchestra program, Staatliches Institut für Musikforschung, Preußischer Kulturbesitz, Berlin.

89. Herbert A. Frenzel, "Beethovens 'Neunte' unter Furtwängler: Völkerverbindende Macht der Musik," *Völkischer Beobachter,* 9 September 1937.

90. L. Mather, "Grenzland und Grenzvolk in Beethovens *Fidelio,*" *Kölnische Volkszeitung,* 17 July 1938.

91. Prieberg, *Kraftprobe,* 298.

92. Kurt von Schuschnigg, *Ein Requiem in Rot-Weiss-Rot,* cited in William Shirer, *The Rise and Fall of the Third Reich: A History of Nazi Germany* (New York: Simon and Schuster, 1960), 326.

93. F. Bayer, "Generalfeldmarschall Göring in der Staatsoper: *Fidelio,* künstlerisches Symbol der Befreiung," *Völkischer Beobachter* (Ausgabe Wien), 28 March 1938.

94. H. Engels, "Beethoven im Sudetenland," *Deutsche Militär-Musiker-Zeitung* 60 (10 December 1938).

95. Prieberg, *Kraftprobe,* 362.

96. Schröder, "Beethoven im Dritten Reich," 215.

97. E. Wurm, "Beethoven als Schicksalskünder," *Allgemeine Musik-Zeitung* 66 (1939): 643.

98. Erich Schenk, "Beethoven zwischen den Zeiten," lecture given at the University of Bonn as part of a series of War Lectures published in *Neues Wiener Tageblatt,* 3 July 1943.

99. Walther Vetter, "Beethoven und die militärisch-politischen Ereignisse seiner Zeit," lecture given in the series on Science and War at the University at Posen during the summer semester of 1942 (Posen: Kluge and Ströhm, 1943), 27.

100. Schiedermair, "Zu Beethovens Schicksalsidee," 77. See also Ludwig Schiedermair, "Beethoven und die rheinische Landschaft," lecture given at the University of

Cologne on 13 November 1940, in *Kölnische Volkszeitung*, 15 November 1940; and Schiedermair, "Ludwig van Beethoven und sein Werk," lecture given at the University of Bonn, in *Westdeutscher Beobachter*, 26 May 1941.

101. Schiedermair, "Zu Beethovens Schicksalsidee," 74–76.

102. "Die Rede des Führers im Bürgerbräukeller: Der Kampf für Leben und Sicherheit des Deutschen Volkes," *Rheinisch-Westfälische Zeitung* (Essen), 9 November 1939.

103. K. v. Mühlen, "Wem gehört Beethoven? Die Kulturlosen kämpfen für geistige Enteignung," *Deutsche Zeitung in Norwegen* (Oslo), 6 October 1943.

104. "Beethoven-Schriftum von 1939 bis 1952," *Beethoven-Jahrbuch* 1 (1953–54): 131, 201.

105. G. Redl, "Das Bild des Engländers in Richard Wagners 'Eine Pilgerfahrt zu Beethoven,'" *Die deutsche Hauptschule* 3 (1943): 138; and O. Deppermann, "Brite und Deutscher in R. Wagners 'Pilgerfahrt zu Beethoven,'" *Die deutsche höhere Schule* 10 (1943): 169.

106. Many of these articles were penned by the musicologist Max Unger. See "Der Yorcksche Marsch: Schicksal einer volkstümlichen Melodie," *Kölnische Zeitung*, 22 September 1941; "Beethovens Militärmärsche," *Musik im Kriege* (Heft 7/8 October–November 1943); and "Beethovens vaterländische Musik," *Musik im Kriege* (Heft 9/10 December 1943–January 1944), all by Unger. See also Heister and Wolff, "Macht und Schicksal," 117.

107. Based on W. Altmann, "Statistischer Überblick über die im Winter 1942/43 stattfindenden Reihenkonzerte (Orchester und Chorwerke mit Orchester)," *Zeitschrift für Musik* 110 (1943): 59–68. During the 1942–43 season, "among the overtures, Beethoven's *Coriolan* was in second place (ten performances); among piano concertos, his Concerto No. 4 (sixteen performances) and Concerto No. 3 (fifteen performances) took second and third places; the Violin Concerto lay, with twenty-four performances just behind that of Brahms. Nevertheless, the symphonies enjoyed particular popularity. Here the Fifth (twenty-nine performances), the Third (twenty-five performances), and the Ninth (twenty-five performances) all led the way. Even the Seventh ranked in fifth place with twenty-one performances" (Schröder, "Beethoven im Dritten Reich," 218).

108. Uwe Saas, "Berliner Philharmoniker spielen für die Soldaten: Zwei eindrucksvolle Konzerte unter Eugen Jochum in der Liller Oper," *Feldzeitung der Armee an Schelde, Somme, und Seine* 51 (20 September 1940), reproduced in Peter Muck, ed., *Einhundert Jahre Berliner Philharmonisches Orchester*, 3 vols. (Tützing: Hans Schneider, 1982), 2:153–155.

109. "Das Berliner Philharmonische Orchester spielt für die Wehrmacht," Berlin Philharmonic Orchestra program, 1940, Staatliches Institut für Musikforschung, Preußischer Kulturbesitz, Berlin.

110. Prieberg, *Musik im NS-Staat*, 408. In order to maintain relations with Polish leaders whom he considered necessary in the battle against communism, the German governor-general of the Polish territories, Hans Frank, allowed some to attend concerts of "his" orchestras, including a performance of the Ninth Symphony. Frank was sharply reprimanded by Berlin for this action.

111. "In Dankbarkeit und Treue: Ansprache von Reichsminister Dr. Goebbels in der Feierstunde der NSDAP am Vorabend des Geburtstages Adolf Hitlers," *Völkischer Beobachter*, 20 April 1942.

112. "Wir verteidigen Beethoven: Ein Feldpostbrief gibt Rechenschaft über den Sinn des Krieges," *Musik Woche* 9 (1941): 281–282.

113. See other examples listed in Schröder, "Beethoven im Dritten Reich," 219.

114. Flier, reproduced in Muck, *Berliner Philharmonisches Orchester* 2:104.

115. Flier, reproduced in Muck, *Berliner Philharmonisches Orchester*, 2:125.

116. "BBC: Tam-tam-tam-ta," *Der Spiegel* 24, no. 11 (1970): 81–82.

117. Ibid.

118. "Begegnung mit der Unsterblichkeit," *Musik und Gesellschaft* 20 (1970): 838.

119. Inge Lammel, *Arbeitermusikkultur in Deutschland, 1844–1945* (Leipzig: VEB Deutscher Verlag für Musik, 1984), 204–205.

120. *Geheime Staats-Polizei* document, "Ausschnitt aus dem Informationen des Gestapo von 5.10.[19]38" (Berlin), 12 October 1938, reproduced in Ibid., 205.

121. Inge Lammel, "Zur Beethoven-Rezeption in der deutschen Arbeiterbewegung," in H. A. Brockhaus and Konrad Niemann, eds., *Bericht über den Internationalen Beethoven-Kongreß in Berlin 10 December 1970* (Berlin: Verlag für Neue Musik, 1971), 162.

122. Fania Fénelon, *Sursis pour l'orchestre* (Paris, 1976); German trans. *Das Mädchenorchester in Auschwitz* (Frankfurt am Main: Röderberg, 1981), 111.

123. Prieberg, *Kraftprobe,* 400.

124. Schröder, "Beethoven im Dritten Reich," 210.

125. Muck, *Berliner Philharmonisches Orchester,* 2:183.

126. Walter Flex, excerpt from "Ein Wanderer zwischen beiden Welten"; reproduced in Hans-Jochen Gamm, *Der Braune Kult* (Hamburg: Rutten & Loening, 1962), 155.

127. Gamm, *Der Braune Kult,* 155.

5. Germany Divided, and Reunified

1. "Fall Furtwängler," *National-Zeitung* (Basel), 14 March 1945.

2. Thomas Mann, *Briefe, 1937–1947,* vol. 2, *Briefe,* ed. Erika Mann (Frankfurt am Main: S. Fischer, 1961), 444.

3. Karl Laux, "Beethoven und unsere Zeit," *Tägliche Rundschau* (Berlin), 16 December 1945.

4. Ibid. Emphasis in original.

5. "Den Deutschen zur Lehre?" *Der Spiegel* 22, no. 45 (1968), 169.

6. Werner Rackwitz, "Die Bedeutung Beethovens für die sozialistische Nationalkultur der D[eutschen] D[emokratischen] R[epublik]," in Heinz Alfred Brockhaus and Konrad Niemann, eds., *Bericht über den Internationalen Beethoven-Kongress 10.-12. Dezember 1970 in Berlin* (Berlin: Verlag Neue Musik, 1971), 17. Hereafter cited as *Beethoven-Kongress 1970.*

7. The process by which East German authorities incorporated "classic" German heroes such as Schiller and Goethe into their "national-revolutionary" history was ongoing. Even Friedrich II of Prussia was proclaimed a hero of the socialist nation: the reinstallation of his sculpture on Unter den Linden was viewed by West Berliners with derision.

8. Although, in the practical sense, no system of cultural politics can achieve "total" authority, it is obvious that the National Socialist and Socialist Unity regimes did intend to attain complete control of the German art world. In his speech describing "The Meaning of Beethoven for the Socialist National Culture of the GDR," Werner Rackwitz made this clear: "From our standpoint, all areas of life must be penetrated with the socialist worldview and culture in order to make the rich spiritual, ethical, and emotional values of our society form the socialist personality" (Rackwitz, "Die Bedeutung Beethovens," 12).

9. See references to Engels' view of Beethoven in Rackwitz, "Die Bedeutung Beethovens," and Willi Stoph, "Festansprache," *Beethoven-Kongress 1970,* 1–8. See reprint of Hanns Eisler's 1927 article, "Beethoven," under the title "Beethoven gehört uns," in *Musik und Gesellschaft* 20 (1970): 804, and discussion of this essay as a model for GDR musicology in Paul Michel, "Beethoven in unsere Zeit," *Musik und Gesellschaft* 20 (1970): 11.

10. Stoph, "Festansprache," 3.

11. Ernst Krause, "Beethoven und seine Zeit," *Die Weltbühne* 7 (1952): 389.

12. For instance, West Germans were constantly bemused by the GDR television

and radio newspersons who repeated all of Erich Honecker's titles whenever they mentioned his name.

13. Stoph, "Festansprache," 1.

14. For details of this "Marxist-Leninist" portrait see any of the GDR sources mentioned in this chapter, or almost any writings on Beethoven published by government institutions in East Germany between 1948 and 1989.

15. Willi Stoph, "Größe und Schönheit Beethovenscher Musik," *Musik und Gesellschaft* 20 (1970): 308.

16. Cited in Erwin Ernst, "Arbeiterklasse erfüllt revolutionäre Zukunftsvision Beethovens," *Musik und Gesellschaft* 20 (1970): 314. See also Georg Krausz, "Ludwig van Beethoven—der Lieblingskomponist Lenins," *Neues Deutschland* (Berlin), 27 June 1970.

17. Stoph, "Festansprache," 4; and Michel, "Beethoven in unserer Zeit," 11. Lenin's directive is discussed in Chapter 2.

18. Frank Schneider, "Beethoven-Konferenz des Deutschen Kulturbundes in Potsdam," *Musik und Gesellschaft* 20 (1970): 7.

19. Michel, "Beethoven in unserer Zeit," 9.

20. Oskar Neumann, "Ludwig van Beethoven: Genius der Nation," *Wissen und Tat* 7 (1952): 35.

21. Hansjürgen Schaefer, "Zum zweihundertsten Geburtstag Ludwig van Beethovens," *Musik und Gesellschaft* 20 (1970): 630.

22. Stoph, "Festansprache," 2.

23. See Schaefer's many articles in *Musik und Gesellschaft* and his *Konzertführer Ludwig van Beethovens* (Leipzig: VEB Deutscher Verlag, 1988), which demonstrate his consistent adherence to the Marxist-Leninist line on Beethoven.

24. Hansjürgen Schaefer, "Zum Beethoven-Jahr 1970," *Musik und Gesellschaft* 20 (1970): 2.

25. Schneider, "Beethoven-Konferenz," 4.

26. Stoph, "Festansprache," 2.

27. Cited in H.-P. Müller, "Staatsopernkonzert zur Eröffnung des Beethoven-Jahres," *Musik und Gesellschaft* 20 (1970): 157.

28. *Grundstudium für Kulturfunktionäre: Lehrbrief zum Thema Ludwig van Beethoven Kämpfer und Lehrmeister* (Leipzig: Zentralhaus für Kulturarbeit, 1965).

29. *Seid Umschlungen Millionen* (Berlin: Büro des Präsidiums des Nationalrates der Nationalen Front des Demokratischen Deutschland, 1952), 4.

30. Hansjürgen Schaefer, "Der Klassiker Beethoven," *Musik und Gesellschaft* 20 (1970): 630.

31. Stoph, "Größe und Schönheit Beethovenscher Musik," 303.

32. Hansjürgen Schaefer, "Denkmal eines besseren Europa," *Musik und Gesellschaft* 20 (1970): 631.

33. Schaefer, "Der Klassiker Beethoven," 630.

34. Hansjürgen Schaefer, "Schallplattenmosaik Ludwig van Beethoven: Klaviersonate B-Dur, op. 106," *Musik und Gesellschaft* 20 (1970): 670.

35. Schneider, "Beethoven-Konferenz," 4.

36. Werner Rackwitz, "Vorhaben zur Beethoven-Ehrung 1970 in der D[eutschen] D[emokratischen] R[epublik]," *Musik und Gesellschaft* 20 (1970): 311.

37. Stoph, "Festansprache," 5.

38. Ibid.

39. "Künder von Frieden und Freiheit," *Der freie Bauer* (Berlin) 7 (30 March 1952): 11.

40. Stoph, "Festansprache," 5.

41. *Grundstudium,* 4.

42. Dieter Zechlin, "Beethovens Erbe—Besitz unserer sozialistischen Menschengemeinschaft," *Musik und Gesellschaft* 20 (1970): 320.

43. *Seid Umschlungen Millionen,* 11.

44. Michel, "Beethoven in unserer Zeit," 10.

45. Hansjürgen Schaefer, "Angst vor Beethoven," *Musik und Gesellschaft* 20 (1970): 727.

46. Frank Schneider, "Zur Kritik der spätbürgerlichen Beethoven-Deutung," in *Beethoven-Kongress 1970*, 177.

47. Ibid.; and Rackwitz, "Die Bedeutung Beethovens."

48. Cited in Heinz Alfred Brockhaus and Peter Czerny, "Unter anderem: Beethoven, Internationaler musikwissenschaftlicher Kongreß in Bonn," *Musik und Gesellschaft* 20 (1970): 844. This debate made the pages of the daily press in the FRG. See Wolfgang Nitschke, "Beethoven und die Folgen: Streiflichter vom Internationalen Musikwissenschaftlichen Kongreß Bonn 1970," *Der Tagesspiegel* (Berlin), 15 September 1970, and Carl Dahlhaus, "Zerfall der Beethoven-Biographien: Altes und Neues zur Zweihundertfeier," *Frankfurter Allgemeine Zeitung*, 24 November 1970.

49. Brockhaus and Czerny, "Unter anderem," 842.

50. Schaefer, "Angst vor Beethoven," 725.

51. Rackwitz, "Die Bedeutung Beethovens," 16.

52. Schaefer, "Angst vor Beethoven," 724.

53. Stoph, "Festansprache," 7.

54. "Stellungnahme des Zentralkomitee der SED," *Tägliche Rundschau*, 11 March 1952.

55. *Seid Umschlungen Millionen*, 8–9.

56. "Stellungnahme des Zentralkomitee der SED," *Tägliche Rundschau.*

57. *Seid Umschlungen Millionen*, 10–11.

58. See "Zum 125. Todestag Ludwig van Beethovens am 26. März 1952: Stellungnahme des Zentralkomitees der Sozialistischen Einheitspartei Deutschlands," *Musik und Gesellschaft* 3 (1952/3): 72–4; "Erklärung des Zentralkomitees der Sozialistischen Einheitspartei Deutschlands, des Staatsrates, des Ministerrates, des Nationalrates der Nationalen Front und des FDGB-Bundesvorstandes zum 200. Geburtstag Ludwig van Beethovens," *Beethoven-Ehrung der Deutschen Demokratischen Republik 1970* (Dresden: Verlag Zeit im Bild, 1970), 23–29; "Festansprache des Präsidenten der Deutschen Demokratischen Republik, Wilhelm Pieck," *Musik und Gesellschaft* 4 (1952): 106–110; and, for reference to Grotewohl's remarks, Krause, "Beethoven und seine Zeit," 388–389.

59. Cited in "Nazis und Marxisten stritten um den Komponisten," *Bonner Rundschau*, 27 March 1977.

60. Lothar von Ballusek, *Beethoven: Verdienter Aktivist der Musik. Aus dem Instrumentarium totalitärer Kulturpolitik in der Sowjetzone* (Bonn: Bundesministerium für gesamtdeutsche Fragen, 1952), 4.

61. Joseph Kerman's chapter on "Musicology and Positivism" in *Contemplating Music: Challenges to Musicology* (Cambridge, Mass.: Harvard University Press, 1985) describes "positive" musicology dealing "mainly in the verifiable, the objective, the uncontroversial, and the positive" as "the dominant mode in musicology today." This is the approach that East Germans derided as *Faktenforschung.*

62. Schneider, "Zur Kritik," 178, 179.

63. See "Die SED zu Beethovens Geburtstag," *Ost-Probleme* 4 (1952): 392–394; and "Genosse Ludwig van," *Der Spiegel* 31, no. 14 (1977): 215–216.

64. Ballusek, *Verdienter Aktivist*, 10.

65. Reinhard Oehlschlägel, "Handel mit einem Heros: Den Deutschen ist zu Beethoven nur wenig eingefallen," *Vorwärts* (Bonn), 7 April 1977.

66. "Beethoven: Für alle da," *Der Spiegel* 24, no. 18 (1970): 201.

67. "Vom armen Beethoven," *Der Spiegel* 24, no. 37 (1970): 183.

68. Knut Franke, "Er war der Prophet dreier Welten," *Die Welt* (Essen), 26 March 1977.

69. Ibid.

70. This assertion is based on a review of the regular section entitled "Beethoven-Schriftum," in the *Beethoven-Jahrbuch* (Bonn: Beethovenhaus), including the editions of 1954, 1956, 1959, 1966, 1969, 1975, 1977, and 1983. To date this register covers the Beethoven literature produced until 1975.

71. See, for instance, Carl Dahlhaus, Hans Joachim Marx, Magda Marx-Weber, and Günther Massenkeil, eds., *Bericht über den Internationalen Musikwissenschaftlichen Kongress Bonn 1970* (Kassel: Bärenreiter, 1970).

72. See "Vom armen Beethoven," *Der Spiegel*, a review of Richard Sterba and Editha Sterba, *Beethoven and His Nephew: A Psychoanalytical Study of Their Relationship* (New York: Pantheon, 1937).

73. Ibid. Although written and first published in the United States, the Sterbas' book was read in Germany as a product of German scholarship.

74. For further information about the West German commercialization of classical music in general, and Beethoven's in particular, see Norbert Linke, *Musik zwischen Konsum und Kult* (Wiesbaden: Breitkopf & Härtel, 1972).

75. Ballusek, *Verdienter Aktivist*, 19.

76. "Deutscher Bundestag—1. Sitzung. Bonn, Mittwoch, den 7. September 1949," protocol reproduced in Rodolf Pörner, ed., *Kinderjahre der Bundesrepublik: Von der Trümmerzeit zum Wirtschaftswunder* (Düsseldorf: ECON Verlag, 1989), 109.

77. Cited in Pörner, *Kinderjahre der Bundesrepublik*, 114.

78. "NATO Hymne: Deutsche Töne," *Der Spiegel* 21, no. 45 (1967): 166; and Rainer Cadenbach, ed., *Mythos Beethoven: Ausstellungskatalog* (Bonn: Laaber, 1986), 140. In transforming the *Schlußchor* into the "Europahymne," Herbert von Karajan was very much involved; for this purpose he arranged the piece for brass orchestra.

79. Senator Werner Stein, cited in the *Berliner Morgenpost*, 10 June 1969, reproduced in Peter Muck, ed., *Einhundert Jahre Berliner Philharmonisches Orchester*, 3 vols. (Tützing: Hans Schneider, 1982), 2:382.

80. "Beethoven für alle da," *Der Spiegel*; and Christoph Jackel, "Der große Sohn in Gips, Silber, und Schokolade: Geburtshaus und Geschäfte verkaufen Beethoven-Souvenirs," *Bonner Rundschau*, 26 March 1977.

81. Ballusek, *Verdienter Aktivist*, 15.

82. "Beethoven-Ehrungen in Bonn, Ost-Berlin, Peking," *Süddeutsche-Zeitung* (Munich), 28 March 1977.

83. "Ehrungen für Beethoven: Der 150. Todestag des Komponisten wird in West und Ost gefeiert," *Gießener Allgemeine*, 24 March 1977.

84. *BZ (Berlin Zeitung)*, 11 November 1989.

85. Ursula Escherig, "Die Macht der Phantasie: Eindrücke von den Sonderveranstaltungen in der Philharmonie und der Deutschen Oper," *Der Tagesspiegel*, 14 November 1989.

86. Interviews conducted by the author and tape-recorded at the Berlin Philharmonie, 12 November 1989, available at the Ira F. Brilliant Center for Beethoven Studies, San Jose State University, San Jose, California.

87. Reiner Kunze, "Fidelio, erster Akt," *Die Welt*, 13 November 1989.

88. "Menuhin dirigiert Benefizkonzerte in Ost und West," *Berliner Morgenpost*, 17 December 1989; and "Ein Konzertabend für den Wiederaufbau," *Berliner Morgenpost*, 20 December 1989.

89. Martina Helmig, "Konzert an die Freude mit Beethoven," *Berliner Morgenpost*, 20 December 1989.

90. Klaus Umbach, "Platzkonzert urbi et Gorbi," *Der Spiegel* 43, no. 51 (1989): 192.

91. Leonard Bernstein, statement in "The Berlin Celebration Concerts: 23.12.1989, West-Berlin Philharmonie, 25.12.1989, Berlin/DDR Schauspielhaus," concert program, author's collection.

92. Interviews conducted by the author and tape-recorded on the Breitscheidplatz

under the Gedächtniskirche in Berlin (West), 23 December 1989, available at the Ira F. Brilliant Center for Beethoven Studies, San Jose State University, San Jose, California.

93. Hellmut Kotschenreuther, "Freiheit, schöner Götterfunken: Bernstein mit der Neunten in West- und Ost-Berlin," *Der Tagesspiegel*, 26 December 1989.

94. Interview conducted by the author, tape-recorded on the Gendarmenmarkt in front of the Schauspielhaus in Berlin (East), 25 December 1989, available at the Ira F. Brilliant Center for Beethoven Studies, San Jose State University, San Jose, California.

95. Hansjürgen Schaefer, "Die 'Freudenmelodie' im Konzert der Superlative," *Neues Deutschland*, 27 December 1989.

96. Klaus Adam, "Freiheit schöner Götterfunken: Bernstein dirigiert die Neunte in Ost und West," *Neue Osnabrücker Zeitung*, 27 December 1989. I have discovered only one editorial attack on Bernstein's measure in East German papers. In the *National-Zeitung* (Berlin), 28 December 1989, Wolfgang Pötzsch wrote that this measure "falsified Beethoven's humanistic intentions and degraded the otherwise excellent performance into a seminewsworthy (*pseudoaktuellen*) propaganda vehicle for the American sponsors." For other articles that applauded Bernstein's revision of the *Schlußchor*, see Peter Philipps, "Götterfunke Freiheit," *Die Welt*, 27 December 1989; "Bernstein-Konzert: Freiheitsfeier in Ost-Berlin," *Frankfurter Allgemeine Zeitung*, 27 December 1989; and "Für Bernsteins Festkonzerte—Neunte von Beethoven umgetextet," *Bild* (Berlin), 27 December 1989.

Index

Abercromby, Ralph, 117, 182
Anschluß, 165
Apolitical nature of Beethoven's music, 64, 110, 193
Arbeiter-Bildungs-Institut (ABI), 98
Association des Anciens Combattants Volontaires Juifs, 169
Association of German Working-Class Singers (*Deutsche Arbeiter Sängerbund*, DAS), 98, 100, 101–102, 123, 224n. 112, 223n. 86

Bach, Johann Sebastian, 3, 44, 49, 159
Bachmann, Johann Georg, 157
Barenboim, Daniel, 1, 199
Bavarian Republic, 5, 87–88, 116
Becker, Carl Heinrich, 111, 112, 113
Beethoven, Johann van (father), 146–147, 233n. 12
Beethoven, Karl van (nephew), 28, 194
Beethoven, Ludwig van (grandfather), 134
Beethoven, Ludwig van: as apolitical, 63–65, 107–108, 110, 186; as aristocratic, 28, 108, 116, 117–118, 138; as authoritarian, 138; as bourgeois, 109, 193; as conservative, 27–28, 34, 108, 115, 137–138; as democrat, 91; as Dionysian, 43; as educator (*Erzieher*), 56–57, 87; as European, 45; as Francophile, 44, 74, 178; as Francophobe, 16, 34, 40–41, 69, 74, 117, 120, 126, 136–137; as Führer, 53, 120, 128, 131, 150–151; as German, 13, 40–41, 70, 116–117, 127, 130, 146, 165, 232n. 8; as godlike, 52; as having "nationality problem," 73–74, 116–117, 127, 232n. 8; as having French origins, 73–74, 116–117; as insane, 31, 57, 194; as internationalist, 78, 81, 104, 176, 194, 203; as militarist, 16, 32, 35, 40–41, 45, 50–52, 66–68, 77, 118–119, 125, 127, 137, 149, 166; as national hero, 16, 34–35, 39, 40–41, 119–120, 124, 130, 136, 149; as non-Nordic, 55, 133, 230n. 256; as Nordic, 54, 55, 127, 130, 134–136, 146, 149; as pacifist, 79–82; as prophet, 130; as republican, 91, 193; as revolutionary, 11, 15, 25–27, 44, 59, 90, 92–93, 178–183; as role-model for children, 153–156; as seeking a Führer, 120, 137, 150; as stoic, 106, 109–110, 113, 153; as world conqueror, 125, 128, 149–150, 233n. 22; exposure to revolutionary ideals, 25, 33–34, 91; flight from Grätz Castle, 29, 69, 136, 153, 212n. 98; idea of a "store of arts," 26, 211n. 83; impudence toward nobility, 26, 90; incident at Teplitz, 10, 93, 108, 207n. 30; inconsistency about politics, 23, 31, 193; interest in English politics, 30, 91; "noble pretense" of, 28, 90, 116, 211n. 95; respect for enlightened absolutism, 24–25, 108, 210n. 74; religious views of, 113–114, 225n. 130; treatment of servants, 28, 194, 211n. 94; under Metternich, 30–31, 91, 94, 182, 212n. 105; use of German music terminology, 127, 229n. 225
—Chamber Music
Piano Sonata in C-sharp Minor, op. 27, no. 2, ("Moonlight"), 76
Piano Sonata in C Major, op. 53 (*Waldstein*), 37
Piano Sonata in F Minor, op. 57 (*Appassionata*), 34, 36, 37, 137, 178–179
Piano Sonata in B-flat Major, op. 106 (*Hammerklavier*), 183
Piano Sonata in A-flat Major, op. 110: 37
String Quartet in B-flat Major, op. 130: 114

Beethoven, Ludwig van (*continued*)
String Quartet in F Major, op. 135: 106
—Concertos
Piano Concerto no. 1, op. 15: 1, 199
Piano Concerto no. 5, op. 73: 71, 74
Violin Concerto, op. 61: 20, 71, 155, 168–169, 173
—Symphonies
Symphony no. 2, op. 36: 158, 168
Symphony no. 3, op. 55 (*Eroica*): dedication of, 23, 27, 29, 45–48, 64, 81, 95, 108–109, 117–118, 182, 211n. 97, 226n. 140; performances of, 38, 41, 71, 88, 167, 174; interpretations of, 11–12, 20, 34, 69, 70, 80, 110, 121, 130,139, 150, 151, 153, 162, 166, 181
Symphony no. 4, op. 60: 200
Symphony no. 5, op. 67: performances of, 74, 104, 162, 167, 173, 196; interpretations of, 9–10, 11–12, 20, 37–38, 41, 64, 75–76, 95–96, 110, 151, 166, 170
Symphony no. 6, op. 68 (*Pastoral*), 34
Symphony no. 7, op. 92: performances of, 1–2, 168, 174, 199; interpretations of, 14, 69, 121, 168, 179
Symphony no. 9, op. 125: dedication of, 23, 96; premiere of, 30–31; performances of, 2, 35, 39, 59–62, 63, 82–85, 98, 100, 101, 102, 116, 162, 164, 167–168, 179, 182, 200–203; interpretations of, 11–12, 14–15, 20, 43–44, 50–51, 58, 59–62, 64–65, 66, 77, 96–97, 110–111, 114, 121, 137, 143, 151–152, 158, 159, 162, 166–167, 168, 176, 177, 184, 190, 195, 197, 198, 199, 238n. 110
Wellingtons Sieg, op. 91: 29, 30, 69, 120
—Overtures
Coriolan Overture, op. 62: 5, 49, 71, 162
Egmont Overture, op. 84: performances of, 5, 35, 71, 88, 116, 162, 163, 200; interpretations of, 20, 29, 97, 121, 150, 169–170, 182, 190
Leonore Overture, no. 2, op. 72: 5, 20, 87, 116
Leonore Overture, no. 3, op. 72: 20, 63, 71
Die Weihe des Hauses, op. 124: 5, 38, 158, 162, 195
—Masses, Cantatas, Oratorios, etc.
Bundeslied, op. 122: 98, 102, 123
Chor auf die verbündeten Fürsten, WoO 95: 29, 69
Choral Fantasy, op. 80: 104
Christus am Oelberge, op. 85: 98
Elegischer Gesang, op. 118: 98
Germania, WoO 94: 29, 33, 212n. 101
Der glorreiche Augenblick, op. 136: 29, 69, 98, 120, 212n. 102
Joseph Cantata, WoO 87: 23, 24–25, 91
Leopold Cantata, WoO 88: 23, 24–25
Mass in C Major, op. 86: 98
Missa Solemnis, op. 123: 80, 97, 98, 104, 113, 143, 190, 223n. 79
Opferlied, op. 121b: 97, 98
—Operas and Incidental Music
Es ist vollbracht!, WoO 97: 29–30, 69, 212n. 103
Fidelio, op. 72: performances of, 34, 63, 104, 157, 162–163, 164, 165, 171; interpretations of, 27, 29, 33, 97, 114, 138, 156, 164, 165, 171, 175, 182, 190, 199–200
Die Ruinen von Athen, op. 113: 33, 71, 98, 167
—Songs
Abschiedsgesang an Wiens Bürger, WoO 121: 28, 167
An die ferne Geliebte, op. 98: 74
An die Hoffnung, op. 94: 125
Die Ehre Gottes aus der Natur, op. 48, no. 4: 98
Der freie Mann, WoO 117: 26, 97, 98
Gesang der Mönche, WoO 104: 98
Das Glück der Freundschaft, op. 88: 171
Kriegslied der Österreicher, WoO 122: 28, 167
—Other
Karussel Märsche, 167
Marsch zur großen Wachparade, 167
Violin Romances, opp. 40 & 50: 20, 155
Yorcksche Marsch, WoO 18: 167
Beethoven, Magdalena van (mother), 147–149, 233n. 15
Beethovenhaus, 38–39, 139, 158, 159, 197
Bekker, Paul, 65, 80, 110, 217n. 115
Benz, Richard, 128–130, 135, 232n. 7
Berlin Celebration Concerts, 2, 200–203
Berlin Philharmonic Orchestra, 1, 38, 45,

49, 50, 65, 67, 71, 79, 144, 158–159, 162, 164, 167–168, 169–170, 173, 195–196, 199
Berlin Staatsoper, 144
Berlin Wall, 1–2, 190–191, 197–198, 199
Bernadotte, Jean Baptiste, 26, 92
Bernstein, Leonard, 2, 200, 202
Bismarck, Johanna von, 36, 37, 38
Bismarck, Otto von, 36–38, 45–48, 53, 56, 64, 118, 127, 137
Blüthner Orchestra, 50, 63, 88, 98
Bock, Hugo, 84
Böhm, Karl, 165
Bonaparte, Napoleon, 5, 13, 23, 27, 29, 52, 64, 68, 69, 81, 92–93, 95, 108–109, 117–118, 119, 120, 126, 136–137, 138, 149, 153, 179, 182, 211n. 97
Brainin, Norbert, 200
Brentano, Bettina, 10–11, 14, 89, 93, 108
Breuning, Leonore von, 34
British Broadcasting Corporation (BBC), 170, 173
Bruckner, Anton, 173
Bülow, Hans von, 14, 39, 45–48
Bund deutscher Mädel. See League of German Girls
Bundesministerium für gesamtdeutsche Fragen. See Federal Ministry for General German Issues

Center Party, 106, 111, 112–114, 225n. 130, 226n. 152
Chamberlain, Houston Stewart, 52–54, 67–68, 125, 129
Christian-Social Party, 132
Clauß, Ludwig Ferdinand, 133, 135, 230n. 256
Commercialization, 187–188, 191, 194, 196
Comité de Défense des Juifs Persecutés en Allemagne, 169
Communist Party of Germany (KPD), 88, 89–90, 99
Concentration camps, 173

d'Arguto, Rosebury, 100
Dahlhaus, Carl, 186
Deeke, Ida, 154
Deutsche Arbeiter Sängerbund (DAS). *See* Association of German Working-Class Singers
Diederichs, Eugen, 128
Dürer, Albrecht, 18, 56

East German Revolution, 1–2, 197–203
Eichenauer, Richard, 135–136, 138, 149, 232n. 7
Eichoff, Johann Peter, 25
Eisenstaedt, Alfred, 159
Eisler, Hanns, 3, 97, 178, 181
Eisner, Kurt, 57–63, 65, 87–88, 89, 90, 93, 99–100, 115–116, 178, 181, 184
Élan terrible of Beethoven's music, 13, 20, 27, 30
Engels, Friedrich, 41–42, 45, 89, 95–96, 178
Eulenberg, Herbert, 91
European Economic Community (EEC), 195

Federal Ministry for General German Issues (*Bundesministerium für gesamtdeutsche Fragen*), 191
Fénelon, Fania, 173
Ferdinand, King of Bulgaria, 125
Fighting Alliance of the German Working Class (*Rote Frontkämpferbund*), 99
Fighting League for German Culture (*Kampfbund für deutsche Kultur*), 144
First World War, 66–85, 218n. 121, 219n. 138
Flex, Walter, 174
Foreign policy use of Beethoven, 74, 132, 158, 164–166, 195–196
Franco-Prussian War, 32–36, 40–41, 70–71
Frantz, Justus, 2, 200
Freie Volksbühne. See *Volksbühne*
French Revolution, 25, 33–34, 44, 92, 115
Friedrich Wilhelm III, King of Prussia, 96
Fritsch, Theodor, 126
Funk, Walther, 164
Furtwängler, Wilhelm, 119, 158, 162, 164, 166

Gerigk, Herbert, 173
German Democratic Party (DDP), 106, 111
German National Peoples' Party (DNVP), 102, 115, 121, 123
German Peoples' Party (DVP), 115, 121
Giotto, 64
Gleichen, Heinrich von, 126

Gluck, Christoph Willibald, 135
Goebbels, Joseph, 144, 145, 156, 157, 162, 163, 168, 173
Göring, Hermann, 163, 165
Goethe, Johann Wolfgang von, 10, 18, 29, 52, 55, 56, 64, 65, 68, 88, 93, 106, 108, 150, 166, 195
Gorki, Maxim, 178
Grétry, André-Ernest-Modeste, 120
Grotewohl, Otto, 190
Günther, Hans F. K., 133, 134, 135, 230n. 256
Gysi, Klaus, 181, 193

Hadamovsky, Eugen, 150–151, 158
Haelßig, Arthur, 156, 235n. 55
Hainisch, Michael, 104
Handel, Georg Friedrich, 49, 88, 135
Harich, Walther, 75
Haydn, Joseph, 3, 19, 50, 131, 135
Hebbel, Friedrich, 65
Heister, Hanns-Werner, 186
Heroic quality of Beethoven's music, 20, 127, 151, 166
Herriot, Edouard, 102, 117, 126, 132, 176, 232n. 8
Hess, Rudolf, 163
Hesse, Hermann, 66, 77–78
Heuss, Theodore, 195
Himmler, Heinrich, 163, 175
Hindenberg, Paul von, 102, 112
Hirschberg, Leopold, 68–69
Hitler Youth (*Hitler Jugend,* HJ), 154–156
Hitler, Adolf: associated with Beethoven, 150–151, 162–163, 168, 174; performances in honor of, 5, 162–163, 168, 174; mentioned, 5, 18, 145, 159, 164, 165, 167, 169
Hoffmann, E. T. A., 9–10, 14, 22, 65, 89
Hugenberg, Alfred, 115, 122
Humperdinck, Engelbert, 84

Interpretations: idealistic, 63–65, 80–81, 86–87, 106–108, 110–111, 112–114, 115; pacifist, 66, 77–78, 82–84; psychoanalytical, 186–187, 191, 193–194; resistance, 169–171, 173; romantic, 9–11, 14, 59, 65, 89–90, 193; universal, 176, 194, 197, 202–203; volkish, 52–57, 67–68, 125–132

Jacobs, Walter, 151
Jacobsohn, Siegfried, 90
Jewish Cultural Organization (*Jüdischer Kulturbund*), 161
Jöde, Fritz, 130–131
Joseph II, Emperor, 24, 30
Jüdischer Kulturbund. See Jewish Cultural Organization
Jugendmusikbewegung. See Youth Music Movement

Kagel, Mauricio, 187
Kampfbund für deutsche Kultur. See Fighting League for German Culture
Kant, Immanuel, 25, 52, 59–60
Karajan, Herbert von, 162, 242n. 78
Karl-Liebknecht-Orchestra, 99
Kestenberg, Leo, 100–101, 111, 121–122
Keudell, Robert von, 36, 37, 38, 118
Keudell, Walther von, 123
Keyserling, Alexander, 36
Kietz, Gustav Adolf, 12
Klemperer, Otto, 144
Klinger, Max, 64
Klöber, Friedrich August, 134
Knepler, Georg, 186
Koffka, Wilhelm, 35, 70
Krenek, Ernst, 142
Kreutzer, Rodolphe, 26

Lamprecht, Karl, 63–65
Langbehn, Julius, 55–57, 129
Lassalle, Ferdinand, 42
Laux, Karl, 176
Lavelaye, Victor de, 170
League in Defense against Anti-Semitism (*Verein zur Abwehr des Antisemitismus*), 55
League of German Girls (*Bund deutscher Mädel,* BDM), 154–156
Lehmann, J. F., 131
Leipzig Gewandhaus Chorus, 82
Leipzig Gewandhaus Orchestra, 98, 144
Lenin, Vladimir Ilich, 178–179
Lenin-Orchestra, 99
Lichnowsky, Prince Karl, 29, 136, 182
Lichtenberger Propaganda Orchestra, 99
Liebknecht, Karl, 78, 88, 100, 198
Ligue internationale contre l'Antisemitisme, 169
London Philharmonic Society, 109
Ludwig, Günther, 200
Ludwig, Otto, 65
Luxemburg, Rosa, 78, 88, 100, 198

Männerchor Berliner Liederfreunde 1879. See Male Choir of Berlin Friends of Song 1879
Mahler, Gustav, 18
Male Choir of Berlin Friends of Song 1879 (*Männerchor Berliner Liederfreunde 1879*), 171
Mann, Thomas, 22–3, 175–176, 177, 197
Marx, Karl, 179
Marx, Wilhelm, 112, 114
Mascagni, Pietro, 102–103
Maximilian Franz, Elector, 24, 33, 91
Meding, Oscar, 38
Méhul, Étienne-Nicolas, 120
Menuhin, Yehudi, 200
Mersmann, Hans, 82
Metternich, Prince Clemens von, 30, 182
Michelangelo, 64
Militaristic quality of Beethoven's music, 29–30, 50–51, 69, 70, 75–76, 120, 121, 125, 153, 162, 166–167, 184, 190
Molo, Walter von, 175
Moser, Hans Joachim, 122, 146, 152, 153, 228n. 210, 234n. 40
Motion pictures, 158–159
Mozart, Wolfgang Amadeus, 19, 44, 46, 49, 50, 67, 75, 99, 131, 218n. 121, 236n. 72
Mozarteum, 80
Münzenberg, Willi, 89
Music scholars, role in politicization, 122, 139, 152–153, 206n. 14
Mussolini, Benito, 104, 120

Napoleonic wars, 28–30, 52, 68–69, 92, 117, 118, 119, 149, 153, 166
National Broadcasting Company (NBC), 158
National Front (East German), 188
National Socialist Culture Community (*NS Kulturgemeinde*), 144, 145
National Socialist German Workers' Party (NSDAP): Beethoven reception, 17, 133–141, 142–169, 173–174, 176, 178, 236n. 75; policy toward music, 18, 143–146, 234n. 37, 239n. 8
National-Socialist Teachers' Union (*National-Sozialistisches Lehrerbund*), 154
National-Sozialistisches Lehrerbund. See National Socialist Teachers' Union
Neefe, Christian, 25
Nef, Karl, 93
New Years' Eve performances, 100, 182
Ney, Elly, 155–156
Nietzsche, Friedrich W., 42–45, 48, 59, 65, 80–81, 106
Nikisch, Arthur, 79, 84–85, 99
Nitsche, Julius, 142–143
Nordic nature of Beethoven's music, 129–130, 138, 149, 155
North Atlantic Treaty Organization (NATO), 195
NS Kulturgemeinde. See National Socialist Culture Community

Ochs, Siegfried, 84
Olympic Games, 162, 177
Orlow, Princess Katharina, 37

Pan-German League, 70, 126
Pedagogical literature, 153–154, 167, 181, 183
Performance of Beethoven's music: excessive, 49, 50, 67, 78–79, 81–82; insufficient, 140
Pfaender, Hermann, 70
Pfordten, Hermann Freiherr von der, 49
Pieck, Wilhelm, 190
Pop-culture, 187, 198
Popular appreciation of, 50, 61–62, 97–98, 183–184, 234n. 39
Popular ignorance about, 54, 100, 111, 114, 121–122
Preczang, Ernst, 98
Puttkamer, Johanna von. *See* Bismarck, Johanna von

Raabe, Peter, 139–141, 143, 144, 162, 165, 187
Rackwitz, Werner, 177, 183
Radek, Karl, 88
Radio broadcasts, 104, 157–158, 162, 168, 174, 183, 236n. 59
Radoux, Leopold, 134
Rathenau, Walther, 105–106, 109
Rauschenberger, Walther, 149
Reception: by soldiers, 75–76, 168–169, 217n. 120; compared to other composers, 209n. 63, 218n. 121, 236n. 75; in Austria, 206n. 15; in France, 9, 73–74, 75, 76–77, 219n. 138, 219n. 149
Reich Culture Chamber (*Reichskulturkammer*), 144, 162, 164

Reich Music Chamber (*Reichsmusikkammer*), 144
Reich Radio Corporation (*Reichsrundfunkgesellschaft*), 157
Reichardt, Johann Friedrich, 26
Reichsbanner (Schwarz-Rot-Gold), 91
Reichskulturkammer. *See* Reich Culture Chamber
Reichsmusikkammer. *See* Reich Music Chamber
Reichsrundfunkgesellschaft. *See* Reich Radio Corporation
Rembrandt van Rijn, 55–57
Revolution of 1848–49, 12
Revolutionary nature of Beethoven's music, 11–13, 15, 30–31, 58, 59–62, 88, 93–94, 95–97, 101, 181–182, 208n. 41, 208n. 42
Riefenstahl, Leni, 164
Riemann, Hugo, 76
Ries, Franz, 25
Rolland, Romain, 75, 116–117, 219n. 138
Rosenberg, Alfred, 133, 134, 138–139, 144, 145, 146, 173, 232n. 7
Rote Frontkämpferbund. *See* Fighting Alliance of the German Working Class
Rousseau, Jean-Jacques, 25, 44
Rubens, Peter Paul, 64

Samarow, Gregor, 38
Sandberger, Adolf, 116, 120, 122
Schaefer, Hansjürgen, 179–181, 182, 184, 186–187, 202, 240n. 24
Scheel, Walter, 196–197
Schenk, Erich, 166
Schering, Arnold, 107, 151, 153, 235n. 43
Schiedermair, Ludwig, 139, 146, 147, 153, 158, 166, 231n. 278, 235n. 44
Schiller, Friedrich, 18, 23, 26, 61, 64, 68, 82, 151, 200–202
Schindler, Anton, 30, 134
Schlußakkord, 158–159
Schmitz, Arnold, 120, 122
Schmitz, Eugen, 80–81
Schneider, Eulogius, 25, 33–34, 92
Schneider, Frank, 181
Schoenberg, Arnold, 3, 97
Schumann, Robert, 5, 13
Schuppanizigh Quartet, 27
Schuschnigg, Kurt von, 165
Schütz, Heinrich, 135
Second World War, 166–174, 238n. 107
Seitz, Karl, 104, 123
Shakespeare, William, 5, 14, 56
Shirer, William, 163–164
Social Democratic Party (SPD), 42, 57–63, 78, 88, 101, 171, 192
Socialist Unity Party (SED), 177–191, 197, 239n. 8
Sonnenfels, Joseph von, 26
Spartakus League, 78, 88
Speer, Albert, 173
Stahlhelm, 127
State funerals, 38
Sterba, Editha, 186
Sterba, Richard, 186
Stockhausen, Karlheinz, 187
Stoph, Willi, 187
Strauss, Richard, 162
Strub, Max, 156
Swieten, Gottfried von, 26

Tat-Kreis, 128, 129
Tchaikovsky, Peter Ilich, 176
Third World War, 188–190
Tolstoy, Leo, 106
Tucholsky, Kurt, 90

Uhlig, Theodore, 12
Ulbricht, Walter, 182, 190, 191
Unger, Max, 153, 235n. 42, 238n. 106

Verein zur Abwehr des Antisemitismus. *See* League in Defense against Anti-Semitism
Vetter, Walther, 146, 150, 153, 166, 234n. 41
Visual arts, depictions in, 8, 19, 50, 64, 134, 158–159, 187, 213n. 5
Vogelweide, Walther von der, 56
Volksbühne, 57–58, 59, 63, 98, 100–101, 121–122
Voltaire (François-Marie Arouet), 25

Wagner, Richard, 12, 14–16, 18, 36, 39–41, 44, 49, 50–51, 52, 66, 67, 78, 119, 136, 167, 173, 208n. 50, 208n. 52, 218n. 121, 238n. 106
Walter, Bruno, 144
Weill, Kurt, 93
Weingartner-Stüder, Carmen, 175
Western imperialism, 188
Wilhelm I, Emperor, 49
Wilhelm II, Emperor, 49, 50, 52, 57

Woltmann, Ludwig, 54–55
Wolzogen, Hans von, 39–41
Workers' choirs, 42, 58, 98, 101–102, 171, 224n. 112
Workers' orchestras, 99
Wunschkonzert, 159

Youth Music Movement (*Jugendmusikbewegung*), 130–131

Zetkin, Clara, 57, 58, 62–63, 89, 178
Zmeskall, Nikolaus von, 27